Girls at Puberty

Biological and Psychosocial Perspectives

Girls at Puberty

Biological and Psychosocial Perspectives

Edited by

JEANNE BROOKS-GUNN

Educational Testing Service
Princeton, New Jersey

and

ANNE C. PETERSEN

Pennsylvania State University
University Park, Pennsylvania

PLENUM PRESS • NEW YORK AND LONDON

Library of Congress Cataloging in Publication Data

Main entry under title:

Girls at puberty.

Includes bibliographical references and index.
1. Puberty. 2. Adolescent girls. I. Brooks-Gunn, Jeanne. II. Petersen, Anne C.
[DNLM: 1. Adolescent psychology. 2. Puberty. WS 450 G525]
QP84.4.G57 1983   612.661   83-2358
ISBN 0-306-41144-X

© 1983 Plenum Press, New York
A Division of Plenum Publishing Corporation
233 Spring Street, New York, N.Y. 10013

Printed in the United States of America

We dedicate this volume to

Beatrix A. Hamburg, M.D.

for drawing scientists to the critical
problems in early adolescence and
for helping define the field.

Contributors

Constance A. Benjamin • Department of Pediatrics and Child Health, College of Medicine, Howard University, Washington, D.C. 20060

Dale A. Blyth • Department of Psychology, Ohio State University, Columbus, Ohio 43210

Andrew M. Boxer • Clinical Research Training Program in Adolescence, Laboratory for the Study of Adolescence, Department of Psychiatry, Michael Reese Hospital and Medical Center and Committee on Human Development, The University of Chicago, Chicago, Illinois 60637

Jeanne Brooks-Gunn • Institute for the Study of Exceptional Children, Educational Testing Service, Princeton, New Jersey 08541; and Department of Pediatrics, College of Physicians and Surgeons, Columbia University, New York, New York 10019

Florence Comite • Developmental Endocrinology Branch, National Institute of Child Health and Human Development, National Institutes of Health, Bethesda, Maryland 20205

William F. Crowley, Jr. • Vincent Research Laboratories, Departments of Internal Medicine and Gynecology, Massachusetts General Hospital, Boston, Massachusetts 02114

Gordon B. Cutler, Jr. • Developmental Endocrinology Branch, National Institute of Child Health and Human Development, National Institutes of Health, Bethesda, Maryland 20205

William A. Daniel, Jr. • Division of Adolescent Medicine, Department of Pediatrics, University of Alabama School of Medicine, Birmingham, Alabama 35294

Margaret S. Faust • Department of Psychology, Scripps College, Claremont, California 91711

Rose E. Frisch • Harvard Center for Population Studies and Department of Population Studies, Harvard University, School of Public Health, Cambridge, Massachusetts 02138

John P. Hill • Department of Psychology, Virginia Commonwealth University, Richmond, Virginia 23284

Renee R. Jenkins • Department of Pediatrics and Child Health, College of Medicine, Howard University, Washington, D.C. 20060

Jerry R. Klein • Department of Pediatrics, Division of Adolescent Medicine, Michael Reese Hospital, University of Chicago Pritzker School of Medicine, Chicago, Illinois 60616

Iris F. Litt • Department of Pediatrics, Stanford University School of Medicine, Stanford, California 94305

D. Lynn Loriaux • Developmental Endocrinology Branch, National Institute of Child Health and Human Development, National Institutes of Health, Bethesda, Maryland 20205

Mary Ellen Lynch • Department of Psychology, Virginia Commonwealth University, Richmond, Virginia 23284

Karen L. McKinney • Department of Sociology, University of Minnesota, Minneapolis, Minnesota 55455

Karen Eriksen Paige • Department of Psychology, University of California, Davis, California 95616

Anne C. Petersen • Department of Individual and Family Studies, College of Human Development, The Pennsylvania State University, University Park, Pennsylvania 16802

Jean Rivier • Peptide Biology Laboratory, Salk Institute, San Diego, California 92138

Diane N. Ruble • Department of Psychology, New York University, New York, New York 10003

Roberta G. Simmons • Department of Sociology, University of Minnesota, Minneapolis, Minnesota 55455

Maryse H. Tobin-Richards • Clinical Research Training Program in Adolescence, Laboratory for the Study of Adolescence, Department of Psychiatry, Michael Reese Hospital and Medical Center; and Committee on Human Development, The University of Chicago, Chicago, Illinois 60637

Wylie W. Vale • Peptide Biology Laboratory, Salk Institute, San Diego, California 92138

Michelle P. Warren • Departments of Medicine, and Obstetrics and Gynecology, College of Physicians and Surgeons, Columbia University; and St. Luke's–Roosevelt Hospital Center, New York, New York 10019

Ouida E. Westney • Department of Human Development, School of Human Ecology, Howard University, Washington, D.C. 20059

Foreword

The publication of this volume at this time appears particularly auspicious. Biological, psychological, and social change is greater during the pubertal years than at any other period since infancy. While the past two decades have witnessed a virtual explosion of productive research on the first years of life, until recently research on adolescence, and particularly on puberty and early adolescence, has lagged substantially behind. This book provides encouraging evidence that things are changing for the better.

Considered separately, the individual chapters in this book include important contributions to our growing knowledge of the biological mechanisms involved in pubertal onset and subsequent changes, as well as of the psychological and social aspects of these changes, both as consequences and determinants. In this regard, the book clearly benefits from the breadth of disciplines represented by the contributors, including developmental endocrinology, adolescent medicine, pediatrics, psychology, and sociology, among others.

Even more importantly, however, the editors and their colleagues stress the need for avoiding simplistic, unidirectional models of development, whether biological, psychological or social. Development across the life span is dependent on the continual *interaction* of biological (including genetic), psychological, and social influences; appreciating this reality becomes particularly important in designing and coordinating research on puberty because of the magnitude and the rapidity of change in all of these influences during the pubertal years. While much remains to be done in exploring these complex interactions, progress is being made, as a number of the contributions to this volume illustrate. The editors themselves provide one useful approach in their model of possible paths between pubertal changes, sociocultural influences, and psychological responses.

Girls at Puberty also makes an important contribution to our understanding of the varied roles, positive and negative, that such uniquely female developmental events as menarche and reproductive maturity can play in the lives of young women, as a result of the kinds of influences—psychological, sociocultural, and biological—which they encounter. This emphasis, too, seems particularly auspicious. Prior to the Women's Movement, and the impact that it has had on developmental psychology—and psychologists—it seems unlikely that such a sensitive, balanced, and clearly focused approach would have been possible. Furthermore, such a sophisticated approach clearly would not have been feasible without the recent advances that have occurred in the broad range of relevant scientific disciplines, from genetics and endocrinology to anthropology, sociology, and psychology.

The contributors to this volume have done an impressive job in conveying much of what we currently know about girls and puberty. And they have helped to highlight what we still need to learn.

John Janeway Conger

Division of Clinical Psychology
University of Colorado School of Medicine
Denver, Colorado 80220

Preface

Our mutual concern about how best to study the young adolescent's expanding and changing world arose from our individual efforts in following longitudinally various samples of young girls. We were aware of all the influences, both internal and external, that make adolescence a time of anticipation as well as apprehension. Our research, while exciting, also was frustrating in that no forum existed in which to discuss common problems and possible conceptual frameworks. In addition, the fact that the study of pubertal development must, by its nature, take a multidisciplinary approach made the lack of discussion even more glaring. Endocrinologists, pediatricians, and adolescent health researchers in the past several years have amassed a great deal of information that was relevant to the developmental scientist embarking on the study of puberty. Developmental psychologists, on the other hand, have begun to develop methods for investigating psychological aspects of puberty that are relevant for the more medically oriented researcher. Finally, neither group was cognizant of the anthropologically oriented research underway.

The need for better and tighter methodologies and models, as well as the excitement about preliminary findings, led us to feel some urgency about holding a conference of a diverse—one might even say disparate—group of researchers who were in the midst of conducting (or had just completed) longitudinal studies focusing specifically on girls at puberty. Personal Products Company, a Johnson and Johnson company, shared our concerns for integrating knowledge about pubertal girls. Their enthusiasm led to support, via a grant, for a conference on girls at puberty.

Although the majority of those involved in longitudinal studies were represented at our conference, we apologize to those we over-looked due to our own lack of awareness. Longitudinal studies that incorporate puberty as only one of many stages of development were not included, although we recognize the important contribution of these studies in answering questions about pubertal development. In particular, we note the longitudinal studies conducted by the Blocks at Berkeley; by Werner and her colleagues in Hawaii; the New York longitudinal study of Thomas, Chess, and Birch and now by the Lerners; and the Fels and Berkeley Growth Studies. Our hope was that a multidisciplinary conference could advance other theory and methodology for research on puberty. Our goal is to foster the inclusion of more multifaceted approaches in our research. We are, therefore, deeply indebted to the Personal Products Company for their help. Without their generous support, the conference and this volume would not have been possible.

We are grateful to Jonas Salk who graciously offered us the use of the Salk Institute in La Jolla, California as the site for the conference. His enthusiasm for the multidisciplinary approach was irresistible and his warm reception, as well as that of his staff, was instrumental to the success of the conference.

Others who deserve credit for the conference and volume include Hilary Evans at Plenum Press for her always constructive criticism, April Lamendola, Rosemary Deibler, Joyce Bonner, and Alice Kass for their assistance in typing and coordinating, and Lorraine Luciano for her help in proofreading and editing. And finally, we thank the many girls who participated in the longitudinal research in Milwaukee, Boston, New York City, New Jersey, Chicago, California, Washington, D.C., Omaha, and Alabama. Hopefully, this volume will provide information to those adults, parents, teachers, and physicians who give support and guidance to pubescent girls.

Jeanne Brooks-Gunn
Anne C. Petersen

Princeton, New Jersey, and University Park, Pennsylvania

Early adolescent development in females is a subject of great interest to Personal Products Company. Throughout history confusion and ignorance surrounding menstruation and female biological and cultural development have led to myths and fallacies about women and their development.

In past decades, scientists and medical researchers have come to

study the biological aspects of menarche, resulting in a clearer understanding of menstruation and its impact on female development.

Although more and more research is being funded to analyze the
effects of the menses on female development and personal attitudes,
most has been of a longitudinal nature.

Personal Products Company, a Johnson and Johnson subsidiary, is
dedicated to supporting such research through its corporate credo "to
encourage . . . better health and education for all." Through the sponsor-
ship of the conference on early female adolescence, we as a company
were pleased to provide a forum for the presentation of interdisciplinary
research.

To unite the social, cognitive, and physiological aspects of puberty
through this forum, findings about cultural, psychological, and physiological development can be integrated for a more cohesive understanding of this sensitive and complex stage in female development.

Susan N. Keithler
Personal Products Company

Contents

Introduction

Puberty: The time of life in which the
two sexes begin first to be
acquainted.
SAMUEL JOHNSON

Despite its long and distinguished history, puberty has emerged only recently as more than a stepchild to adolescence or a stepping stone from childhood to adolescence. The term *puberty*, derived from the Latin *pubescere* (to grow hairy), has had as long a history as the term *adolescence*, which is derived from *adolescere* (to grow up). However, the former typically has been subsumed under the latter in attempts to divide the life cycle into stages. Adolescence has been considered the third of seven stages of man from medieval times through the present time, being linked to the attainment of sexual and social maturity. According to Isidore, the age is called adolescence because "the person is big enough to beget children" (Aries, 1962). Most definitions stress the social facets of the attainment of adulthood, suggesting that adolescence may continue into the late twenties or early thirties. In contrast, the attainment of sexual maturation does not extend past the teen years. Puberty became a separate life phase as the ages at which one is able to beget children, and the ages at which one actually does, began to diverge. Kett (1977) argues that puberty first became salient when society wished to keep the sexes from becoming acquainted during the period of sexual maturity. This occurred in the late 1800s, when economic and social events led the middle class to separate young adolescents from older adolescents, in part to prolong sexual innocence.

While research on puberty still is overshadowed by research on adolescence, the association with biological changes renders the former more salient, perceptually and perhaps socially, than the latter. In a sense, adolescence has been characterized as an idea masquerading as a fact (albeit one with a long history; Demos and Demos, 1969); puberty has not. Puberty is seen as more than a social or economic construction by many. However, the salience of physical changes has resulted in problems with definitions, measurement, and model building, as well as divisions between medical and social science research.

One might view the emergence of puberty as a distinct entity, as more than a physical phenomenon. Basically, elasticity of the boundaries of adolescence, especially the upper one, and the occurrence of multiple and overlapping significant events, make adolescence difficult to study. In addition, most developmental psychologists still are concerned with the first eighteen years of life, so that they do not venture into adulthood or into issues related to the extension of adolescence. For these reasons, adolescence sometimes is differentiated into three phases: early, middle and late adolescence. Typically, these distinctions are based on the social and psychological events that are more likely to occur during one of these three life phases.

Another approach to the problem of boundary elasticity has been to focus upon the physical events that occur during adolescence. This tactic has been employed most profitably by physical anthropologists, pediatricians, and endocrinologists. However, social scientists have had more difficulty embracing this approach, in part due to the difficulty in studying physical changes outside a medical setting, their interest in social and psychological processes rather than physical change, and their reluctance to accept a more biologically oriented model of development. Consequently, two somewhat separate research lines have evolved, each centering on the physical changes of adolescence. It has been somewhat disconcerting to find that both groups have amassed research findings without reference to one another's work. It was our discovery that not only did the medical research group have much to offer the social scientists but that the issues with which the two groups were concerned might not be as disparate as originally thought. In the following discussion, several issues raised in the Conference on Girls at Puberty are discussed. These include definitions of puberty, boundaries of puberty, models for studying pubertal development, the contribution of the study of risk groups to an understanding of puberty, psychological and sociocultural responses to puberty, and the importance of social context in the study of puberty.

DEFINITIONS OF PUBERTY

Not so subtle differences exist in definitions of puberty used by different groups of researchers. From a medical perspective, puberty typically refers to the biological changes that ultimately lead to reproductive maturity. In contrast, social scientists see puberty as the biological, social, and psychological events that co-occur during early adolescence. This definition, with its origins in the life span developmental approach, focuses on events that occur in the same temporal space, rather than perceiving social and psychological events as necessarily being a response to biological events. Implicit in this view is the rejection of biological deterministic models for explaining psychological change.

As we shall see, these different definitions of puberty influence both the boundaries and markers of puberty as well as the models used to describe the process.

BOUNDARIES OF PUBERTY

Even if consensus could be reached upon a definition, subtle differences exist when attempting to mark the boundaries of puberty. The problem of boundary definition is not unique to puberty or even adolescence (Brooks-Gunn and Kirsch, in press; Rossi, 1980; Neugarten, 1979). However, one might expect medical researchers to have an easier time than social scientists, given their focus on biological change. Somewhat surprisingly then, when attempting to pinpoint the precise onset of puberty, endocrinologists, pediatricians, and physical anthropologists all typically use different markers. In terms of endocrinologic changes, the gonodatropin hormone levels begin to rise in both boys and girls around age 7 or 8. This marks the beginning of the end of the hormonal suppression in effect since just after birth; the mechanisms underlying these changes, however, are not yet well understood (Petersen and Taylor, 1980). The end of puberty is marked by a stabilization in hormone levels with the establishment of hormonal cyclicity in females. As with the onset of endocrinologic change, little is known about the mechanism leading to stabilization. In addition, hormonal cyclicity may not be well established until several years after menarche, suggesting that the endocrinological boundaries of puberty may be quite large, from age 7 to age 17.

More typically, puberty is defined in terms of the physical changes that occur. For girls, the growth spurt may begin as early as age 9, as do the early signs of secondary sexual characteristics such as the appearance of breast buds. The achievement of reproductive maturity and the acquisition of secondary sexual characteristics mark the end of puberty at approximately the age of 15 or 16. Thus, puberty for girls in America today begins at age 9 and ends at age 16. Historical and cultural variations in the physical boundaries of puberty exist, due to nutrition, health, and weight gain patterns (Frisch, this volume). It is believed by many that puberty has reached its lowest age of onset in middle-class Western populations given the high level of nutrition and rapid weight gain seen during childhood.

Social scientists, like pediatricians and physical anthropologists, tend to focus on physical changes in defining the boundaries of puberty. Thus, the onset of the growth spurt, breast buds, and pubic hair all would be relevant onset markers. Offset also is bounded by the end of secondary sexual characteristic development. The important difference between medical and social science definitions has to do with the focus on not only the physical changes, but the fact that these physical changes are observed by the child. Not only is the child observing these changes in herself, but she is observing these changes in her peers. Therefore, while a late maturer may not develop breasts until age 12 and may not reach menarche until 15, she is aware of the changes occurring in many of her friends at age 10 in the first case and 12 in the second case. Given the inevitable social comparisons between girls, it is not surprising that girls themselves may mark puberty in terms of the age span that covers their peer group's development rather than their own. In fact, perceptions of pubertal timing may be more important for psychological functioning than actual pubertal status (Tobin-Richards, Boxer, and Petersen, this volume).

Social scientists also use other boundaries to define puberty. These include school grade (Muuss, 1975), the last two years of childhood and the first two years of adolescence (Hurlock, 1973), and the period in which sexual drive develops (Blos, 1971). Surprisingly, chronological age typically is not used as a boundary, probably in deference to the inter-individual variability in the development of secondary sexual characteristics (Sommer, 1978).

In brief, the age boundaries for the development of secondary sexual characteristics are large, especially when considering individual variation; physical changes may occur over an eight or nine year period. Given the perspective of the entire life cycle, it may seem that maturation occurs within a relatively short time frame. However, given the perspective of the developing child and her parents, the time frame is much longer, comprising one-third of the infant, childhood, and adolescent years.

MODELS OF PUBERTAL CHANGE

Puberty is one of the life events in which rapid physical and reproductive changes occur. For women, there are several such changes during the life cycle: puberty, menarche and menstruation, pregnancy, and menopause. For all of these life events, the fact of biological change may overshadow social and psychological change. That changes in the social life cycle tend to co-occur with changes in reproductive biology (Rossi, 1980) does not imply a causal relationship between the two. However, for all of these events, biological deterministic models have been more popular than more interactive models. This is true historically as well as today (Kett, 1977). However, even in the 1800s, some students of puberty stressed the importance of social context, societal expectations, and family influences upon the development of the pubertal child. For example, one psychiatrist implicated educational pressures, parental indulgence, and errors in diet as causes of disease and insanity in the young adolescent (Kett, 1977).

The difficulty in using co-occurring rather than causal models is highlighted by beliefs about the relationships of hormones to behavior, particularly with reference to hormonal change; specifically, fluctuations during the menstrual cycle, declines for menopause, increases for puberty, and both increases and decreases for pregnancy. While the idea of such a link is seductive, primarily in its simplicity, research has not, by and large, linked behavioral changes to hormonal fluctuations or changes (for exceptions, see research on aggression, activity level, and sexual behavior; Beach, 1974; Money and Highman, 1979; Persky et al., 1976). Another reason that more interactive models have not been embraced may be the perceptual–cognitive salience of physical changes. Research on information processing suggests that individuals often are unable to ignore cues made salient for whatever reason (Nisbett and Wilson, 1977; Tversky and Kahneman, 1974). The salience of different events influences perceptions of associations among those events, with shifts in causal attribution due to variations in the salience of the stimuli being demonstrated (Pryor and Kriss, 1977; Ruble and Feldman, 1976). When salience of information is increased, it is perceived as more important as a cause or explanation of a behavior. The onset of secondary sexual characteristics is a highly distinctive event. Thus, when another event occurs that requires an explanation, such as argumentative behavior or moodiness, the onset of puberty may be perceived as a likely cause (Ruble and Brooks-Gunn, 1979). As an example from the menstrual literature, negative moods of a hypothetical female student were primarily attributed to being in the premenstrual stage of the cycle, even when the environment was described as unpleasant (Koeske and Koeske, 1975). In addition, differential salience of events often results in the report of an association between two events, which in reality may be unrelated. Chapman (1967) has considered this phenomenon an "illusory correlation."

Another example of information processing biases that may favor a more biologically determined model has to do with methods of analysis used to judge the relationship between events (Tversky and Kahneman, 1974). Biases tend to occur as individuals overlook the informational value of nonoccurrence of events and occurrences of one event but not the other, and tend to overemphasize the informational value of the co-occurrence of events (Ross, 1977; Ruble and Brooks-Gunn, 1979). Thus, the pairing of the onset of breast buds and argumentative behavior would be seen as co-occurrence, while the absence of argumentative behavior during the same temporal time period would go unnoticed as information relevant to the association. As individuals construct realities in ways that emphasize certain events, they also may impute causality to events that co-occur at least some of the time. It comes as no surprise that researchers also do this, especially when confronted with salient biological changes.

One interactive model includes the possible exogenous and endogenous variables that may mediate between physical changes and psychological outcomes (Petersen and Taylor, 1980). Figure 1 presents a schematic of this model. Efforts to explain development by only one of these factors will provide an incomplete picture. Changes in interrelationships among factors need to be explored. Even using this model, scientists may focus upon different aspects of change. For example, a developmental psychologist might focus upon the psychological adaptation outcome measures, examining the effects of social context variables upon these. A pediatrician might elaborate upon the physical change measures, a sociologist upon the social context or environmental demand variables. However, the fact that investigators from different disciplines include a set of exogenous and endogenous variables at all is a vast improvement over earlier attempts to relate physical change to psychological adaptation in a deterministic fashion.

THE STUDY OF AT-RISK POPULATIONS

The use of at-risk populations as a method of understanding normal developmental processes has proved invaluable in the study of puberty. Medical researchers have focused on biological risk samples and social scientists on social or psychological risk samples. From a medical approach, clinical disorders in the onset or attainment of puberty have been studied. At one end of the timing of onset continuum, Cutler and his colleagues at the National Institute of Child Health and Human Development (this volume) have demonstrated that the effects of precocious puberty may be retarded or even reversed. This research also

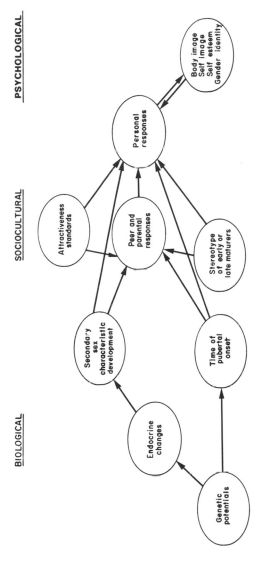

Figure 1. A model for possible paths between pubertal changes, sociocultural influences, and psychological responses. (Reprinted with permission from Petersen and Taylor, 1980.)

underscores the importance of luteinizing-hormone-releasing hormones in the development of normal puberty. Investigations of delayed puberty provide equally important information about biological change (Frisch, this volume; Warren, this volume). Warren, in her study of pubertal ballet dancers, found that girls did not begin to menstruate until they had ceased their extreme exercise because of injury or vacation. Hormonal analyses suggest that activity level may have a modulating effect on the hypothalamic–pituitary set point and, in conjunction with low body weight, may prolong prepubertal status and retard the onset of menstruation. Frisch has examined the contribution of body fat, dieting, and exercise to the retardation of menarche and the onset of amenorrhea. This research allows for the study of factors that are under partial control of the individual. The importance of examining social and psychological aspects of precocious and delayed puberty in girls was underscored at the conference. Since then, the research groups mentioned earlier have begun to collaborate with social scientists in order to investigate psychological adaptation to and concomitants of delayed and precocious puberty.

Social scientists have focused on behavioral problems of adolescence: delinquency, early drug use, early sexuality, and pregnancy. Few of these investigators have focused on pubertal children or related such problems to pubertal change. However, the relationship between pubertal status and sexual behavior is being studied by Westney, Jenkins, and Benjamin (this volume). Others have become intrigued with the apparent rise in vandalism and other antisocial behavior at the time of puberty (Michael, 1981). In a related vein, psychologists have explored risk development in adolescent mental health (Holtzman and Grinker, 1974; Moore, 1981). Again, the focus has not been on the relationship to puberty. Consequently, this volume does not focus on psychological risk development in pubertal girls.

PSYCHOLOGICAL AND SOCIOCULTURAL MEANING OF PUBERTY

Social scientists have been intrigued about young girls' subjective experiences of puberty and whether these experiences affect subsequent behavior or beliefs. Research reported by Brooks-Gunn and Ruble (this volume) and Tobin-Richards, Boxer, and Petersen (this volume) suggests that girls have mixed emotional reactions to menarche and puberty. The importance of peer groups, family openness, information transmission, and social comparisons with others are being explored in order to understand psychological experiences of puberty.

In addition to the individual's response to menarche, sociocultural responses to puberty are discussed by Faust (this volume) and Paige (this volume). Paige has demonstrated the importance of puberty cross-culturally in cultures where daughters' reproductive status is an asset to be protected and to be used in bargaining tactics. Faust focused on a different aspect of a cultural response to puberty, namely the ideal of attractiveness that is embraced by young girls in America today. Finally, the actual demands of the environment upon the pubertal girl are studied by Simmons, Blyth, and McKinney (this volume), Hill and Lynch (this volume), and Westney, Jenkins, and Benjamin (this volume). Hill and Lynch propose that gender identity intensifies at the time of puberty given the salience of gender to the child at this time and the environmental expectations for children to conform to specific roles. Simmons and her colleagues have focused on changes in menstrual status in relation to social achievement, school achievement, social demands, and self-esteem. Westney and Jenkins are concerned with the environmental demands for increased sexuality that occur as a function of maturational status.

PUBERTAL CHANGE AND COGNITION

A growing body of research is examining the role of pubertal hormones — both in terms of their effect on the timing of puberty and potentially disruptive effects of increased hormone levels—in brain functioning and cognitive performance. Petersen (this volume) presents data on cognitive performance and maturational status, placing the relationship in the context of the broader set of influences on young adolescents. Data from her longitudinal study of early adolescence show minimum effects of pubertal status on cognitive performance. Clearly, more collaborative work between endocrinologists, psychologists, and physical anthropologists is needed to address the issue of hormonal change and cognition adequately.

SUMMARY

In spite of the diversity of the views presented, the focus of this volume is what happens to girls at the time of rapid pubertal change. Investigators in this field are examining (1) the effects of physical changes on various aspects of young adolescents' lives, (2) the contribution of exogenous and endogenous variables to physical changes and psychological adaptation, and (3) the factors that contribute to changes in physical growth (Jenkins, this volume). While complex physical changes have been examined in great detail (Daniel, this volume), relationships between physical changes and psychological and social factors are just beginning to be explored.

Furthermore, the volume illustrates the importance of studying reciprocal relationships between behavior and biology. Two examples may be given from the volume. First, there is a greater acceptance of amenorrhea as being multiply determined. The contribution of body fat, exercise, dieting, and stress are now being studied simultaneously (Warren, this volume; Frisch, this volume). Second, the contribution of various biological, psychological, and social factors to menstrual distress is being investigated. Klein and Litt (this volume) have demonstrated the role of prostaglandins in the experience of girls' menstrual pain by showing the effectiveness of antiprostaglandins in the control of pain. Brooks-Gunn and Ruble (this volume) have found that menstrual pain is related to premenarcheal expectations as well as familial openness about menarche. Thus, girls' experience of menstrual pain has both biological and sociocultural concomitants.

Taken together, the chapters in this volume provide a current perspective on what is known about the set of changes stimulated by and happening concurrently with maturation. The data now available on puberty provide clear support for a comprehensive model of biopsychosocial development.

REFERENCES

Aries, P. Centuries of childhood. New York: Knopf, 1962.
Beach, F. Human sexuality and evolution. In W. Montgna and W. Sadler (Eds.), Reproductive behavior. New York: Plenum, 1974.
Blos, P. The child analyst looks at the young adolescent. Daedalus, 1971, 100(4), 961–978.
Brooks-Gunn, J. and Kirsch, B. Life events and the boundaries of midlife for women. In Grace Baurch and Jeanne Brooks-Gunn (Eds.), Neither Young Nor Old. New York: Plenum, in press.
Chapman, L. J. Illusory correlation in observational report. Journal of Verbal Learning and Verbal Behavior, 1967, 6, 151–155.
Demos, J. and Demos, V. Adolescence in historical perspectives. Journal of Marriage and Family, 1961, 31, 632.
Holzman, P. S. and Grinker, Z. Z. Schizophrenia in adolescence. Journal of Youth and Adolescence, 1974, 3, 267–279.
Hurlock, E. Adolescent development. New York: McGraw-Hill, 1973.
Kett, J. F. Rites of passage: Adolescence in America 1790 to the present. New York: Basic Books, 1977.

Koeske, R. K. and Koeske, G. F. An attributional approach to moods and the menstrual cycle. *Journal of Personality and Social Psychology*, 1975, *31*, 474–478.

Michael, R. P. The behavioral changes associated with puberty. In *Second international conference on the control of the onset of puberty*. P. C. Sizonenko (Ed.), Serono Symposia, 1981.

Money, J. and Highman, E. Sexual behavior and endocrinology. In G. Cahill, L. DeGrortz, L. Martini, D. Nelson, W. Odell, J. Potts, E. Steinberger, and A. Winegard (Eds.), *Metabolic basis of endocrinology*. New York: Grune and Stratton, 1979.

Moore, C. D. (ed.), *Adolescence and stress: Report of an NIMH conference*. Washington, D.C.: U.S. Department of Health and Human Services, 1981.

Muuss, R. E. *Theories of adolescence*. New York: Random House, 1975.

Neugarten, B. L. Time, age and life cycle. *American Journal of Psychiatry*, 1979, *136*, 887–894.

Nisbett, R. E. and Wilson, T. D. Telling more than we can know: Verbal reports on mental processes. *Psychological Review*, 1977, *7*, 231–259.

Persky, H., Lief, H., O'Brien, C., Strauss, D., and Miller, W. *Dyadic relationships of personality measures and reproductive hormone levels during the menstrual cycle*. Paper presented at the Second International Congress of Sexology. Montreal, Canada, October, 1976.

Petersen, A. and Taylor, B. The biological approach to adolescence. In J. Adelson (Ed.), *Handbook of Adolescent Psychology*. New York: Wiley-Interscience, 1980, 117–155.

Pryor, J. B. and Kriss, M. The cognitive dynamics of salience in the attribution process. *Journal of Personality and Social Psychology*, 1977, *35*, 49–55.

Ross, L. D. The intuitive psychologist and his shortcomings: Distortions in the attribution process. In L. Berkowitz (Ed.), *Advances in experimental social psychology*, New York: Academic Press, 1977.

Rossi, A. S. Life-span theories in women's lives. *Signs*, 1980, *6*, 4–32.

Ruble, D. N. and Brooks-Gunn, J. Menstrual symptoms: A social cognitive analysis. *Journal of Behavioral Medicine*, 1979, *2*, 171–194.

Ruble, D. N. and Feldman, N. S. Order of consensus, distinctiveness, and consistency information, and causal attributions. *Journal of Personality and Social Psychology*, 1976, *34*, 930–937.

Sommer, B. B. *Puberty and adolescence*. New York: Oxford University Press, 1978.

Tversky, A. and Kahneman, D. Judgment under uncertainty: Heuristics and biases. *Science*, 1974, *185*, 1124–1131.

Biological Aspects of Puberty

Chapter 1

Physical and Biological Aspects of Puberty

Michelle P. Warren

1. Age of Puberty and Menarche

Puberty is a complex biological and maturational event, spans many years, is characterized by marked physical changes which prepare the body for reproduction, and is not well understood in terms of its onset. Menarche (the first menstrual period) occurs fairly late in this maturational process. Since menarche is such a salient event for the pubertal girl, it has been studied with more intensity than the other events of puberty.

For example, the age of menarche has been noted in many cultures and historical times. A number of processes will advance or retard menarche in normal girls, and the progressive decline in the age of menarche in the last 150 years in Western cultures is thought to be due to improvement in socioeconomic conditions, nutrition, and general health (Frisch and Revelle, 1971; Tanner, 1973). The average age of menarche in the United States is 12.8 years (National Center for Health Statistics, 1973). In addition the reproductive system, particularly in the female, is extremely sensitive to alterations in its environment. Crowding, starvation, weight changes, traveling, communal living, exercise, and severe stress of any kind have been shown to be related to altered menstrual cycles. The intricate neuroendocrine mechanisms responsible for the

Michelle P. Warren • Departments of Medicine, and Obstetrics and Gynecology, College of Physicians and Surgeons, Columbia University; and St. Luke's–Roosevelt Hospital Center, New York, New York 10019.

maintenance of this fine homeostatis have fascinated scientists and physicians for several decades (Warren, 1982).

2. THE PHYSICAL CHANGES OF PUBERTY

2.1. *The Fat Spurt*

Extraordinary physical changes occur during the premenarcheal years. Girls experience a rapid gain in fat (an average of 11 kg) and puberty is marked by a "fat spurt," as is illustrated in Figure 1 (Friis-Hanson, 1965; Frisch, Revelle, and Cook, 1973; Pierson and Lin, 1972). Proportional changes in body composition also occur and marked sex differences appear at puberty. Prepubertal boys and girls are similar with respect to lean body mass, skeletal mass, and body fat. By maturity women have twice as much body fat as men, while men have 1.5 times the lean body mass and the skeletal mass of women (Cheek, 1974; Forbes, 1975). In fact the increase in body mass starts at 6 years in females and is the earliest change in body composition at puberty.

Research in the last decade suggests that the initiation of menses depends on the attainment of a critical body weight and composition,

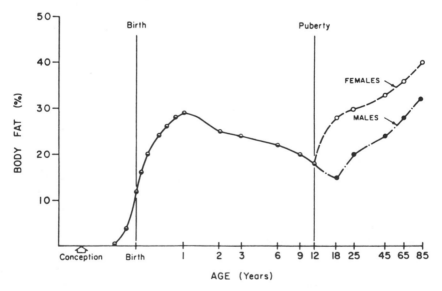

Figure 1. Changing body composition from gestation through adult life. From Bray, G. A. The obese patient. In *Major problems in internal medicine*. Vol. 9. Philadelphia: W. B. Saunders, 1976, p. 23, with permission.

particularly body fat. The progressive decline in the age of puberty is thought to be due to improvement in socioeconomic conditions, so this critical weight or proportion of fat is attained at an earlier age, as the data on age, weight, and onset of menarche over the last 150 years suggest (Figure 2). According to Frisch (1972) the onset of menarche in normal girls is correlated not only to weight but to a calculated amount of body fat of around 16 kg or a percentage of total weight somewhere between 22 and 24% (Frisch and McArthur, 1974; Frisch and Revelle, 1971).

Fat accumulation is often accompanied by the development of a body odor thought to be related to adrenal androgen secretion. A progressive increase in plasma dehydroepiandosterone and dehydroepiandosterone sulphate occurs in both boys and girls by 8 years of age and continues through ages 13–15. These hormones are thought to originate from the adrenal gland and are the earliest hormonal changes seen in puberty (Hopper and Yen, 1975; Reiter, Fuldauer, and Root, 1977). Adrenal androgen secretion precedes that of gonadotropins from the pituitary gland and sex steroids from the gonads.

2.2. *The Growth Spurt*

A growth spurt also occurs prior to menarche and if it is significantly delayed, obesity may result. Females grow a mean of 25 cm with the most rapid growth occurring prior to the first menstrual periods. Growth slows down rapidly after menarche and the growth potential of a postmenarcheal girl is limited (Tanner, Whitehouse, Marubini, and Resele, 1976b). A change in body proportions also occurs at this time. The upper-to-lower (U:L) ratio (defined as length from top of pubic ramus to top of head divided by the distance from the top of pubic ramus to floor) changes in early puberty; this change is due to elongation of the extremities. Later the growth spurt marks a period of equal growth for both torso and lower extremities so that the mean U:L ratio decreases (Styne and Grumbach, 1978; Tanner, Whitehouse, Hughes, and Carter, 1976a). Growth-hormone secretion from the anterior pituitary and gonadal sex hormones appears to be important for regulation of these changes although the initiating factors are still unknown. Adrenal androgens also may play a role, although a less important one.

Bony changes occur during puberty, specifically epiphyseal fusion of different bone centers and osseous maturation, which are evident in X rays. Bone age is a very accurate index of physiologic maturation and correlates closely with pubertal development. It is a valuable tool in the evaluation of children with delayed puberty, and also can be used to predict final height (Styne and Grumbach, 1978).

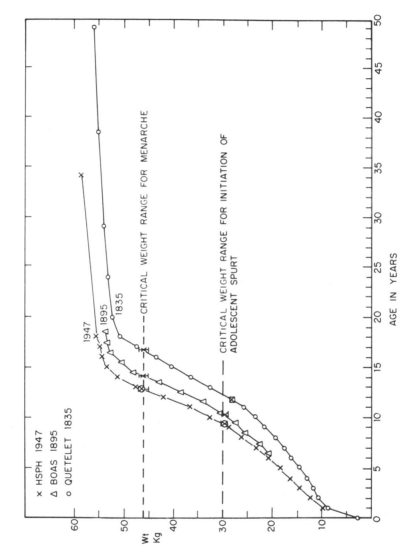

Figure 2. Weight at menarche drawn from three sets of data compiled in 1835, 1895, and 1947. The critical weight range remains the same, but the age decreases. From Frisch, R. E., *Pediatrics,* 1972, *50,* 445, with permission.

2.3. *Adrenarche*

Adrenarche (the development of body hair) and thelarche (breast development) precede menarche by several years. Whether body hair or breasts develop first is still unknown, but either the appearance of downy labial hair or a breast bud may be the first visible sign of puberty (Marshall and Tanner, 1969; Zacharias, Wurtman, and Schatzoff, 1970). Although the initiating components of these two pubertal events are unknown, a large individual variation has been noted among normal girls, suggesting that there may be independent central mechanisms. Adrenarche or pubarche, as it is sometimes known, may be related to androgen secretion and in particular androgen secretion from the adrenal gland. Current data suggest that an unidentified pituitary adrenal-androgen-stimulating hormone may be responsible for adrenarche (Grumbach, Richards, Conte, and Kaplan, 1977). Recent work on the hormones which stimulate the adrenal gland, specifically adrenocorticotropin (ACTH), indicates that they are secreted in association with brain peptides which contain opioidlike properties. These include β-endorphin, β-lipotropin, or fragments of these which may in fact modulate adrenal secretion of androgens, in particular dihydroepiandosterone (DHEA), one of the first hormones to increase in puberty (Givens, Wiedemann, Anderson, and Kitabchi, 1980).

2.4. *Thelarche*

The secretion of estrogen, in particular estradiol from the ovary, determines the onset of thelarche. Other factors may also be important, in particular the secretion of hormones such as prolactin from the anterior pituitary gland. Common indices of estrogen secretion are listed in Table 1. These are clinical indices used to determine if estrogen secretion is present. The presence of a cornified vaginal smear and bone age are particularly valuable in assessing estrogen secretion in the adolescent girl.

Table 1. Indices of Estrogen Secretion

1. Body fat distribution
2. Breast development
3. Bone maturation
4. Vaginal cell cornification
5. Cervical mucous
6. Proliferative endometrium present on biopsy
7. Withdrawal bleeding after the administration of progesterone
8. Plasma estradiol measurement

3. THE PHYSIOLOGY OF PUBERTY

3.1. *The Ovary*

All females are born with ovaries filled with primary follicles that contain eggs (oogonia) in an arrested phase of development. Thus a girl is born with all the follicles she will ever have, a quantity that is estimated at 400,000. However, only a limited number will ever develop; during the entire reproductive years only 400–500 oogonia will be used in the ovulatory process while the majority undergo atresia (involution) after a period of aborted growth (Baker, 1972; Odell, 1979).

3.2. *The Central Nervous System: Hypothalamic–Pituitary–Ovarian Axis*

Luteinizing hormone (LH) and follicle-stimulating hormone (FSH), the pituitary gonadotropins which stimulate ovarian follicular development, also are present in early life and in high concentrations in the serum of the fetus, with levels decreasing as term is reached. Significant levels of LH and FSH are present at birth and in the neonatal period and subsequently drop to barely measurable levels. Later, perhaps beginning as early as age 8 or 9, serum gonadotropins rise with maturation, with FSH increasing earlier than LH (Faiman and Winter, 1971; Winter and Faiman, 1972). As puberty progresses in the female, an interesting phenomenon is noted: there is a change from the constant low-grade secretion of gonadotropins in the prepubertal patterns to a striking sleep-associated rise, particularly of LH (see Cutler et al., Chapter 5). This phenomenon is not present in either the prepubertal child or the adult, as is illustrated in Figure 3 (Boyar, Katz, Finkelstein, Kapen, Weiner, Weitzman, and Hellman, 1974; Swerdloff, 1978). As the child matures fully, the sleep-associated spikes disappear.

Experiments in animals have shown that the prepubertal gonad and its secretions have a restraining influence on the secretion of gonadotropins and in the human this phenomenon is also most likely present. Thus it appears that the gonad has a dampening effect on the hypothalamic–pituitary axis, and with maturation a decreased sensitivity to these effects develops. This decreased sensitivity frees the gonad to secrete increasing amounts of sex steroid, particularly estradiol. A large body of evidence, both experimental and clinical, indicates that the central nervous system, and not the pituitary gland or the gonads, restrains the activation of the hypothalamic–pituitary–gonadal system (Critchlow and Bar-Sela, 1967). This inhibitory effect appears to be mediated via the hypothalmus and its neurosecretory neurons that synthesize and secrete

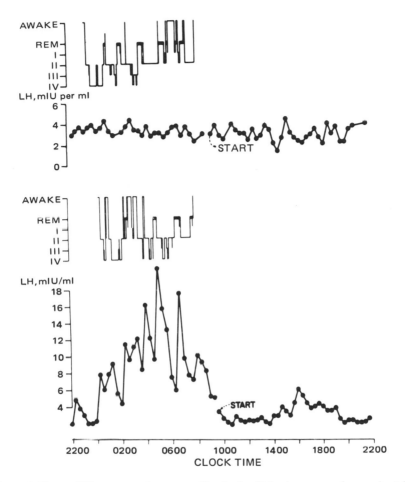

Figure 3. Plasma LH concentration every 20 min for 24 hr in a normal prepubertal girl (upper panel) and an early pubertal girl (lower panel). Adapted from Boyar, R. M. et al., *New England Journal of Medicine,* 1972, *287,* 582–586, with permission.

luteinizing-hormone-releasing hormones (LHRH), which are essential for the release of FSH and LH. The cell bodies of these neurons are mainly in the medial basal hypothalamus in a region called the arcuate nucleus, with axons which end in the median eminence, the central portion of the hypothalamus. It is thought that a chemical transmitter is released from this site into the pituitary–vascular–portal system and thereby brought to the anterior pituitary. Other evidence indicates that extrahypothalamic central nervous system structures may influence gonadotropin secretion and furthermore that biogenic amines such as norepinephrine, dopamines, and serotonin may modify LHRH release. Thus the systems which stimulate or inhibit the hypothalamic–pituitary–gonadal axis are intricate and influenced by complex neural mechanisms which integrate both extrinsic and intrinsic stimuli. The initial events which release the hypothalamic–pituitary–gonadal unit from its inhibitors by sex steroids are still unknown and are the subject of complicated research. Some of this research has shown that in addition to nocturnal spurting of gonadotropins, the pubertal years are marked by an enhanced release of FSH, and later LH, in response to intravenous LHRH and furthermore that episodic LHRH injections can initiate puberty in humans (Grumbach, Roth, Kaplan, and Kelch, 1974; Styne and Grumbach, 1978; Valk, Corley, Kelch, and Marshall, 1980). Episodic release of gonadotropins in an adult pattern and eventual normal menstrual cyclicity occurs when full maturity of the CNS hypothalamic–pituitary–gonad unit develops.

4. NORMAL AND ABNORMAL FACTORS AFFECTING PUBERTAL DEVELOPMENT AND MENSTRUAL CYCLES

4.1. *Anovulatory Bleeding*

One of the most common disorders of young adolescent girls is the absence of regular menses and ovulation which may last as much as two years after menarche. The anovulatory state manifests itself as irregular, occasionally heavy bleeding and rarely a hemorrhage will occur. In this age group, it is not unusual to see prolonged follicular or preovulatory phases of the menstrual cycle. Presumably, in this situation, the immature ovary takes longer than 14 days to produce a mature follicle and initiate an estrogen peak necessary to induce ovulation (Swerdloff, 1978).

4.2. *Constitutional Delay of Puberty*

A common problem presenting with delayed puberty is the so-called constitutional delay of puberty. Generally the history and a growth chart will reveal many indices of delayed puberty. Bone age will be retarded over chronological age. Often treatment is not necessary, and reassurance and continued observation confirm that the onset of puberty and menarche, although delayed, is generally normal. Other factors which may also delay puberty and menarche are outlined in Table 2.

Table 2. Age of Menarche

Advance:
1. Blindness
2. Obesity
3. Urban residence
4. Hypothyroidism
5. Bedridden retarded children
Retard:
1. Food shortage, poor nutrition
2. Altitude
3. Number of children in family
4. Thyrotoxicosis
5. Muscular development
6. Ballet dancing

4.3. *Premature Puberty*

An early puberty and menarche may occur in obese children; puberty is generally not considered premature in North American girls unless its onset is earlier than 8 years (Styne and Grumbach, 1978). Occasionally this is due to premature maturation of the hypothalamic–pituitary–gonadal axis and is called true precocious puberty (see Cutler et al., Chapter 5). A variety of pathologic conditions may also cause premature puberty and menarche, including central nervous system tumors, encephalitis, head trauma, and virilizing conditions.

4.4. *Illness*

Acute and chronic illness can cause pubertal delays generally due to secondary malnutrition. This effect can be seen in uremia, cystic fibrosis, diabetes mellitus, ulcerative colitis, congential heart disease, and regional enteritis. (Sometimes these conditions are not suspected.) The timing of the onset of the illness appears to be important. Recent studies indicate that girls who develop diabetes mellitus or leukemia prepubertally have a fairly normal menarche. If the disease manifests itself in the initial pubertal period, however, menarche is significantly delayed (Schriok, Winter, and Traisman, unpublished). This observation has also been noted in girls with leukemia. Leukemia in most cases is associated with pubertal development at a normal age. Girls with onset of leukemia in late childhood, however, may manifest delayed puberty. This delay may be associated with suppressed serum gonadotropins (Siris, Leventhal, and Vaitukaitis, 1976). This pattern must be differentiated from the elevated circulating gonadotropin levels sometimes found in leukemic patients who have received chemotherapy, particularly busulfan, where ovarian, rather than hypothalamic–pituitary failure, appears to be implicated (Belhorsky, Siracky, Sandor, and Klauber, 1960; Uldall, Kerr, and Tacchi, 1972; Warne, Fairley, Hobbs, and Martin, 1973). The mechanism for drug-induced ovarian failure is not understood, although in one study a leukemic patient had abundant primordial follicles with maturation arrest beyond the primary follicle stage. Follicular resistance to gonadotropin stimulation may occur such as is seen in women with the "resistant ovary syndrome" (Siris et al., 1976).

4.5. Anorexia Nervosa

Recent studies indicate that some adolescent girls are particularly prone to developing eating-related problems during puberty which may lead to obesity and/or undernutrition due to dieting (Coates and Thorensen, 1980; Garell, 1965). Dieting is common in American girls and in extreme cases the syndrome of anorexia nervosa may ensue. Amenorrhea or a delay in puberty and menarche, occurring in the context of weight loss, is now a well-recognized syndrome (Crisp, Palmer, and Kalucy, 1976; Halmi, 1974; Kendell, Hall, Harley, and Babigan, 1973). There is a wide spectrum with this condition from a fairly mild weight loss to the full-blown syndrome of anorexia nervosa. Anorexia nervosa is a syndrome which has fascinated physicians for centuries because of its bizarre manifestations, its seemingly self-imposed food restriction, and its distortion of the subject's mental image of the body. Occasionally there are bizarre food habits (hiding of food, mastication and spitting, vomiting) and hyperactivity (excessive or obsessive running, jogging, or other physical activity). A well-intentioned diet in an overweight individual may precipitate the syndrome. Deep-seated psychological problems also have been implicated as a precipitating factor and are the source of much psychiatric literature (Bruch, 1973, 1977; Crisp, 1974). The multifaceted endocrine manifestations have raised the possibility that this syndrome may be a primary hypothalamic problem rather than psychogenic in nature (Mecklenburg, Loriaux, Thompson, Andersen, and Lipsett, 1974; Vigersky, Loriaux, Andersen, and Lipsett, 1976; Warren and Vande Wiele, 1973). Indeed accumulated evidence, both direct and indirect, indicates that the hypothalamus is malfunctioning. Whether the hypothalamic dysfunction is a primary problem or secondary to the starvation and weight loss is still unclear. The interrelationships between the psychological disturbance, the hypothalamic dysfunction, and the effects of weight loss and starvation are the subject of considerable debate in literature. Unfortunately no data on the early stages of weight loss exist, and prospective studies of anorexia nervosa have not been conducted.

Various criteria have been used to make the diagnosis of anorexia nervosa (Bruch, 1973; Feighner, Robins, Guze, Woodruff, Winokur, and Munoz, 1972), but in general a fairly classic triad of psychiatric disturbance, weight loss, and amenorrhea almost always is observed. The amenorrhea may occur prior to, during, or after the onset of weight loss but can often be pinpointed to the onset of food restriction, even if weight loss has been only slight (Crisp, 1965; Fries, 1977; Warren and Vande Wiele, 1973). Occasionally this condition may occur prior to menarche, and the patient may present with primary amenorrhea and a delay in puberty. With progressive weight loss a familiar syndrome ensues. Some of the most common manifestations are listed in Table 3. As noted in this table, most of these signs and symptoms also have been seen in studies of starvation. Interestingly, despite very significant weight loss, the patient's presenting complaint typically is amenorrhea. Constipation may be extreme (bowel movements once a week) and may be accompanied by abdominal pain. Preoccupation with food may manifest itself as

Table 3. Symptoms and Signs of Anorexia Nervosa[a]

	Total number/ total patients	Total percent	Reported in starvation
Symptoms			
Amenorrhea	22/22[b]	100	Yes
Constipation	26/42	61.9	Yes
Preoccupation with food	19/42	45.2	Yes
Abdominal pain	8/42	19	Yes
Intolerance to cold	8/42	19	Yes
Vomiting	5/42	4.9	No
Signs			
Hypotension	36/42	85.7	Yes
Hypothermia	27/42	64.3	Yes
Dry skin	26/42	61.9	Yes
Lanugo-type hair	22/42	52.4	Yes
Bradycardia	11/42	26.2	Yes
Edema	11/42	26.2	Yes
Systolic murmur	6/42	14.3	No
Petechiae	4/42	9.5	Yes

[a]Adapted from: Warren, M. P., and Vande Wiele, R. L. American Journal of Obstetrics and Gynecology, 1973, 117, 435–449, with permission.
[b]Twenty-two postpubertal girls.

Table 4. Endocrine Changes in Patients with Anorexia Nervosa[a]

Endocrine studies	Total number (total patients)	Total percent	Reported in starvation
Low basal metabolic rate	9 (9)	100	Yes
Atrophic vaginal smear	13 (13)	100	Yes
Low plasma LH (postpubertal)	13 (15)	87	Yes
Low plasma FSH (postpubertal)[b]	7 (15)	47	Yes
Low urinary 17-ketosteroids[b]	13 (34)	38	Yes
Low urinary 17-ketogenic steroids	13 (34)	38	Yes
Low thyroxine	11 (32)	34	Yes
High plasma corticoids	3 (23)	13	Yes
Hyperresponsive adrenocorticotropic hormone test	2 (5)	40	Yes

[a]Adapted from: Warren, M. P., and Vande Wiele, R. L. American Journal of Obstetrics and Gynecology, 1973, 117, 435–449, with permission.
[b]Total urinary.

a fanatic interest in calories, tabulations of intake, and large intakes of lettuce and raw vegetables, diet sodas, and other foods thought to be low in caloric value.

The endocrine changes summarized in Table 4 have fascinated scientists in recent years because they present strong albeit indirect evidence for a hypothalamic dysfunction. Abnormalities of gonadotropin and other hormone secretion patterns include changes in cyclic, sleep–wake, episodic, and stimulated secretion. There is considerable evidence that regulatory mechanisms responsible for these responses are mediated in part by the hypothalamus, particularly the medial central area in the case of LH and FSH. The typical hormone secretory patterns found in anorexia nervosa include a low plasma LH and FSH (Beumont, George, Pimstone, and Vinik, 1976; Warren and VandeWiele, 1973). Luteinizing hormone secretion is particularly affected and may be undetectable. The gonadotropin deficiency is accompanied by a profound estrogen deficiency. The clinical pattern is that of a hypogonadotropic hypogonadism which is at least in part due to the weight loss. The gonadotropin levels return to normal with weight gain although the amenorrhea may persist. The apparent reversible selectively acquired LH and often FSH deficiency seen in this syndrome is fairly unique. The low LH and FSH can be accompanied by low thyroxine and high plasma cortisol; the latter finding differentiates anorexia nervosa from pituitary insufficiency (Warren and Vande Wiele, 1973).

The quantitative abnormalities of gonadotropin secretion also are accompanied by numerous qualitative changes suggestive of a hypothalamic dysfunction. Luteinizing hormone secretion and the response to

LHRH is reduced, a change which is related to the weight loss. In addition the pattern of response in these underweight patients is more akin to the pattern seen in prepubertal children, as the FSH response is greater than the LH response. The return of LH responsiveness is correlated with weight gain (Sherman, Halmi, and Zamudio, 1975; Warren, Jewelewicz, Dyrenfurth, Ans, Khalaf, and Vande Wiele, 1975) or can be induced by repeated injections of LHRH. These findings suggest that the pituitary gonadotropes have become sluggish due to the lack of endogenous stimulation with LHRH (Yoshimoto, Moridera, and Imura, 1975). These patterns have in fact been seen in children as they enter puberty (Job, Garneer, Chaussain, and Milhaud, 1972; Roth, Kelch, Kaplan, and Grumbach, 1972), further suggesting that the CNS–hypothalamic signals revert to a prepubertal or a pubertal state.

If anorectics' gonadotropin levels in the blood are examined over several hours, the episodic secretion is found to be altered (Santen and Bardin, 1973). Over a 24-hour period an immature prepubertal pattern is seen with consistently low levels. As the patient improves and gains weight, sleep-associated episodic LH spikes are noted, a pattern usually seen only in the early pubertal stages of a normal girl (Boyar, Finkelstein, Roffwarg, Kapen, Weitzman, and Hallman, 1972; Boyar, et al., 1974) (Figure 3). With full recovery the 24-hour pattern resumes at a normal adult level without sleep-associated spikes, as is illustrated in Figure 4 (Boyar, et al., 1974). Thus the central mechanism responsible for these patterns regresses to a prepubertal profile in girls with anorexia nervosa. These signals are thought to be mediated via the hypothalamus.

Other responses involving hypothalamic mechanisms are abnormal in this syndrome. Clomiphene, a drug which most likely acts at a hypothalamic level to increase LH, was found to be less effective in patients with anorexia nervosa. The reduced response to clomiphene citrate was significantly correlated with weight loss (Brown, Garfinkel, Jeuniewic, Moldofsky, and Stancer, 1977).

The hypogonadotropic hypogonadism which occurs in this illness is only a partial explanation for the amenorrhea. Indeed the gonadotropin secretory pattern reverts to normal in most patients who gain weight while the amenorrhea persists in almost 30% of the patients (Starkey and Lee, 1969; Warren and Vande Wiele, 1973). Estradiol levels are low due to lack of ovarian stimulation, but in addition the estradiol metabolism is altered. The metabolism of estradiol which normally proceeds with 16 αhydroxylation is decreased with weight loss in favor of hydroxylation in the 2 position and the eventual formation of catecholestrogen 2-methoxyestrone (Fishman, Boyar, and Hellman, 1975). This latter compound has features of an antiestrogen in that it will bind competitively to the

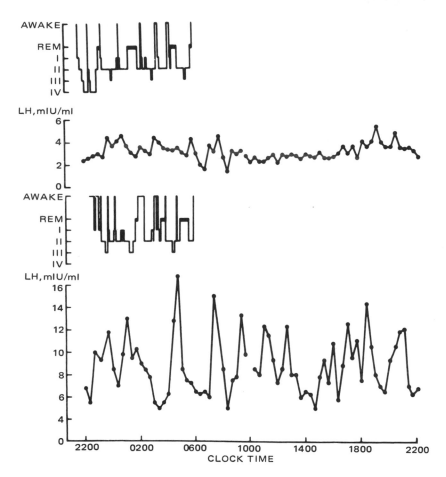

Figure 4. Plasma LH concentration every 20 min for 24 hr during acute exacerbation of anorexia nervosa (upper panel) and after clinical remission with a return of body weight to normal (lower panel). The latter represents a normal adult pattern. From Boyar, R. M., et al., *New England Journal of Medicine*, 1972, *291*, 861–865, with permission.

uterine cytoplasmic estrogen receptor but has no intrinsic biologic activity (Gordon, Cantrall, Leklenick, Albers, Mauer, Stolar, and Bernstein, 1964). Thus the extraordinarily low estrogen levels seen in this syndrome are complicated by the presence of an endogenously produced antiestrogen. The lack of fat tissue also may deny the patient extra ovarian sources of estrogen, as fat tissue is a source of estrone conversion from androstenedione (Schindler, Ebert, and Friedrich, 1972).

Major alteration of other metabolic profiles also have been reported, including altered cortisol metabolism, altered thyroid metabolism, and altered fluid and thermal regulation. Mean levels of cortisol are elevated, and random sampling may suggest an absence or even a reversal in the normal circadian rhythm. Many of these studies suggest a hypothalamic dysfunction.

Girls with anorexia nervosa have a variety of behavioral abnormalities which include an abnormal attitude toward the handling of food. In addition perceptual abnormalities develop, and there is a distortion of body image. These changes are accompanied by the multitude of endocrine changes which are thought to be hypothalamic in origin (Bruch, 1973; Feighner et al., 1972; Garner, 1981; Slade and Russell, 1973; Warren and VandeWiele, 1973).

The early development of amenorrhea and behavioral symptoms also suggests a primary hypothalamic syndrome. Abnormalities thought to be due to a hypothalamic dysfunction include those of gonadotropin release and activity. These abnormalities are associated with the medial central hypothalamus, thermoregulatory control reflecting anterior and posterior hypothalamus interconnections, and water conservation which is controlled by the supraoptic area. The involvement of all these areas in the hypothalamus suggests a lesion too diffuse to be anything but perhaps metabolic. Although anorexia nervosa may be a primary hypothalamic syndrome, it is much more likely that this dysfunction is a result of the diffuse metabolic changes associated with starvation. The high incidence of anorexia nervosa at puberty would suggest that the young adolescent is particularly prone to this illness for reasons which remain unexplained (Warren and VandeWiele, 1973).

The association of psychological and neuroendocrine changes in patients with anorexia nervosa has led investigators to speculate that abnormalities of neurotransmission may be involved in the pathogenesis of the syndrome. Excessive dopamine and norepinephrine in particular have well-documented effects on behavior and appetite (Barry and Klawans, 1976).

In view of strong evidence depicting anorexia nervosa as a hypothalamic syndrome, some of the recently discovered neuropeptides, such as β-endorphin, may have some role in mediating some of the abnormalities seen. These peptides have been isolated from different areas besides the brain, including the gut, and it is not unreasonable to consider that the messages mediated by these neuropeptides may play a role in the alterations seen in anorexia nervosa (Lord, Waterfield, Hughes, and Kosterlitz, 1977; Margules, Lewis, Shibuya, and Pert, 1978).

4.6. *Weight Loss*

Weight loss of a more moderate degree may also be associated with amenorrhea (Fries, Nillus, and Pettersson, 1974; Jacobs, Hall, Murray, and Franks, 1975). Many of the psychological and endocrine changes are also present in these individuals with the degree of abnormality being related more to the amount of illness (weight loss and malnutrition) than any other factor. There appears to be a functional, acquired gonadotropin deficiency which reverses with weight loss, with LH secretion being more profoundly affected than FSH. The amenorrhea is usually secondary, although if the disorder comes before puberty, primary amenorrhea and a delay in sexual maturation may occur. The amenorrhea often occurs early in the onset of weight loss (Crisp, 1965; Warren and VandeWiele, 1973). Generally patients who develop this syndrome may be only slightly obese when the dieting starts, if at all, and the weight often falls to 80–90% of ideal weight (Hall, Murray, Franks, and Jacobs, 1976; Jacobs et al., 1975). Given the individual variability seen, body weight may be only one variable in determining the amenorrhea threshold. Diet-related amenorrhea may be more common in girls who pursue activities where there is emphasis on body image (e.g., ballet, gymnastics, modeling, athletics) and some work shows that ballet dancers appear to be a unique at-risk group for the development of anorexia nervosa. A recent survey of professional dance companies has put the incidence at 5% (Garner and Garfinkel, 1978; Garfinkel, 1981). The frequency of weight-loss-"diet"-related amenorrhea among young women suggests that amenorrhea in this setting may represent a very mild form of the severe hypothalamic disorder seen in anorexia nervosa (Jacobs, et al., 1975; Knuth, Hull, and Jacobs, 1977). On the other end of the scale, a "thin–fat syndrome" has been used to describe individuals whose psychological orientation is similar to patients with anorexia nervosa, but who have little if any weight loss (Crisp, 1977).

The clinical syndrome which develops with weight loss and amenorrhea in general shows no particular abnormality, except that estrogen secretion may be low while gonadotropin secretion is generally in the normal range (McArthur, O'Laughlin, Bertus, Johnson, Hourihan, and Alonso, 1976). With further testing of hypothalamic function, abnormalities of thermoregulation fluid regulation and stimulated gonadotropin response are uncovered, and the findings are qualitatively similar to results seen in patients with anorexia nervosa (*vide supra*) but to a lesser degree (Vigersky, Andersen, Thompson, and Loriaux, 1977).

The presence of a multifaceted endocrine syndrome which appears to develop in anorexia nervosa also has been seen in nonvoluntary starvation, although this entity has not been studied as extensively. In general, the changes reported in starvation reveal an adaptive response of the pituitary–hypothalamic axis similar to that seen in anorexia nervosa.

4.7. Seasonal Changes in Nutrition

The study of primitive foraging populations (desert-dwelling hunter–gatherers) in South Africa suggests that body weight and nutrition are important for normal cyclical gonadal function. The San or Bushmen inhabit the Kalahari Desert in South Africa and are entirely dependent on their natural environment for their food and survival. Studies of these people have revealed that their weights fluctuate within a yearly period in a manner that approximates the availability of food—Bushman eat considerably less than Western people and weigh only 80% of the standard for their heights (Traswell and Hansen, 1968). A decrease in available food and body weight (approximately 6%) occurs during the dry season. Endocrine studies suggest that the San are anovulatory during the dry months (Vander Walt, Wilmsen, and Jenkins, 1978). Their birth rates indicate that the birth peak occurs nine months after the San's maximum weight. Thus a seasonal suppression of ovulation appears to occur in these women, which, in contrast to severe starvation, is readily reversible and may act as a mechanism of natural fertility control. This pattern is similar to variations seen in cases of strenuous exercise, where reversal of amenorrhea occurs fairly quickly following discontinuation of the energy drain (vide infra). The hormonal pattern in the San is similar in that gonadotropins are low to normal and estrogen secretion is suppressed.

4.8. Athletic Training and Exercise

Athletic training and exercise, in combination with low body weight, can delay breast development and menarche and prevent menstrual cyclicity (Warren, 1980). Girls who engage in intensive physical activity in early adolescence have a significant delay in puberty and menarche and a high incidence of amenorrhea as seen in Figure 5. This delay cannot be explained by weight change alone (Malina, Harper, Avent, and Campbell, 1973; Warren, 1980). This phenomenon has been observed in young Olympic athletes as well as the ballet dancers portrayed in Figure 5. Women engaging in long distance running have a high incidence of secondary amenorrhea which is directly related to the energy drain as measured by weekly mileage rates (Feicht, Johnson, Martin, Sparkes, and Wagner, 1978).

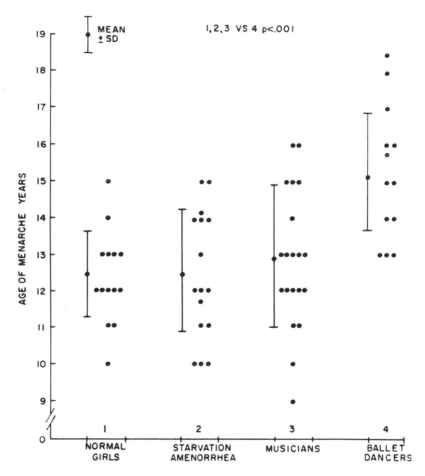

Figure 5. Ages of menarche in ballet dancers compared to those in three other age groups. From Warren, M. P., *Journal of Clinical Endocrinology and Metabolism*, 1980, *51*, 1150–1157, with permission.

Endocrine profiles of the ballet dancers show low gonadotropin secretion and a delay in bone age, suggesting that the prepubertal state is prolonged (Warren, 1980). The gonadotropin pattern in those patients who develop amenorrhea shows a reversion to the premenarcheal pattern except that when gonadotropin suppression occurs, the suppression of LH is more marked than that of FSH. This pattern also is typical of girls who become amenorrheic in the setting of weight loss and in severe nutritional deprivation such as anorexia nervosa (McArthur et al., 1976; Vigersky et al., 1977; Warren et al., 1975). The dancers in fact maintain body weights which are 10–15% below the norm for their age. The retardation of puberty and menarche and the occurrence of secondary amenorrhea is more prominent in children with lower weights and body fat. Thus an energy drain such as exercise has an effect on body weight, and these two variables work together in affecting hypothalamic–pituitary function (Warren, 1980). The occurrence of lower weights and body fats in runners with amenorrhea also has been noted (Dale, Gerlach, and Wilhite, 1979).

Dancers had a dichotomy in breast and pubic hair development. They exhibit a fairly normal pubarche and a remarkable delay in thelarche. This suggests that the mechanism for pubic hair development is not affected or is possibly enhanced by the large energy drain, while the mechanism affecting both breast development and menarche is suppressed (Warren, 1980). That pubarche may be related to androgen secretion and higher testosterone levels has been reported in runners. The source of the testosterone may be adrenal, ovarian, or due to a decrease in aromatization of androstenedione to estrone as a result of a decrease in adipose tissue, where this conversion takes place (Schindler et al., 1972).

Another interesting observation is that the delay in menarche may influence long-bone growth. Dancers have a decreased U:L body ratio and a significantly increased arm span when compared to the female members of their family, although their final heights do not differ (Warren, 1980). Nutritional deprivation may delay epiphyseal closure (Dreizen, Spirakis, and Stone, 1967), but on the other hand, the ballet may be attracting girls with these physical characteristics. Other authors have suggested that the physical characteristics associated with later maturation in females are more suitable for successful athletic performance. For example, in a sample of runners, those with later menarche were more successful athletes (Espenschade, 1940; Feicht et al., 1978; Malina, Spirduso, Tate, and Baylor, 1978).

At the present time, little data is available on the role of varying metabolic requirements and physical exercise on the reproductive system. The fact that the dancers have a delay in menarche and achieve reproductive maturity at a weight and a body fat which is higher than most normal children suggests that the triggering mechanism responsible for the onset of puberty, menarche, and normal cyclical reproductive function may be modified by the large energy drain (Warren, 1980). As can be seen in Figure 6, the body weight and a proportional amount of body fat adequate for menarche is seen at least 4 months prior to the onset of normal menstrual periods. Recent studies do suggest that a curbing of physical activity may advance menarche. Inactive, retarded,

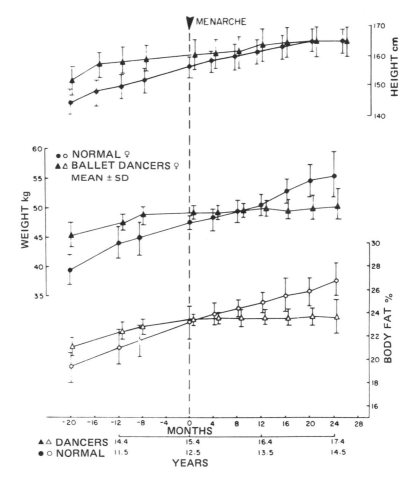

Figure 6. Comparison of heights, weights, and body fat values in ballet dancers and normal controls, with menarche as a point of reference. Weights and body fat values are significantly higher for dancers before menarche ($p < 0.01$). Weight is slightly higher for dancers at menarche ($p < 0.05$), but body fat does not differ. From Warren, M. P., *Journal of Clinical Endocrinology and Metabolism*, 1980, *51*, 1150–1157, with permission.

bedridden children reach menarche at an earlier age and at a lower body fat than their active, retarded counterparts (Osler and Crawford, 1973). In addition children who do not participate in interscholastic sports have an earlier menarche than their athletic classmates or when compared to the general population (Malina et al., 1973). The younger age of menarche in blind children (Zacharias and Wurtman, 1964) may be due in part to their confined activity. Further investigations will be needed before these mechanisms are understood.

In summary altered nutritional states caused by starvation, either self-induced or accidental, appear to cause suppression of the hypothalamic–pituitary–ovarian axis and abnormalities of its central regulating mechanism. As shown in studies on anorexia nervosa, abnormalities are manifested by suppression of gonadotropin secretion, absence of episodic secretion, and a reversion in severe cases to prepubertal 24-hour patterns (Boyar et al., 1974).

A unique feature of the effects of altered nutritional states and illness on the reproductive system is that reversibility of effects occurs with recovery from illness and weight gain. Studies done on patients with anorexia nervosa reveal that gonadotropin levels return to normal and the blunted response to LHRH refers to a normal pattern (Warren et al., 1975). Response recovery can be directly related to weight gain. If the weight loss has been very severe, 24-hour studies reveal that patients progress from completely suppressed gonadotropin secretion to a normal nocturnal episodic pattern and finally to normal fluctuating levels (Boyar et al., 1974). Unfortunately, completely normal cyclicity with estrogen secretion and a menstrual pattern may not return even with weight gain in as many as 30% of the patients (Warren et al., 1975). The central regulation of gonadotropic function, which is undoubtedly altered in these conditions, may not recover completely although the patterns of secretion may approach normal.

Mild forms of the starvation syndrome include self-induced weight loss of a mild degree, strenuous exercise, or a combination of food restriction and strenuous exercise. These forms appear to be more easily reversible, but the neuroendocrine mechanisms for these changes have yet to be elucidated. Studies of reproductive disorders which occur in this setting may provide further understanding of the mechanisms governing puberty.

REFERENCES

Baker, T. G. Oogenesis and ovulation. In C. R. Austin and R. V. Short (Eds.), *Germ cells and fertilization: Reproduction in mammals I.* Cambridge, England: Cambridge University Press, 1972, 14–45.

Barry, V. C., and Klawans, H. L. On the role of dopamine in the pathophysiology of anorexia nervosa. *Journal of Neural Transmission,* 1976, *38,* 107–122.

Beumont, P. J. V., George, G. C. W., Pimstone, B. L., and Vinik, A. I. Body weight and pituitary response to hypothalamic releasing hormones in patients with anorexia nervosa. *Journal of Clinical Endocrinology and Metabolism,* 1976, *43,* 487–496.

Belhorsky, B., Siracky, J., Sandor, L., and Klauber, E. Comments on the development of amenorrhea caused by myleran in cases of chronic myelosis. *Neoplasma,* 1960, *7,* 397–403.

Boyar, R. M., Finkelstein, J., Roffwarg, H., Kapen, S., Weitzman, E., and Hellman, L. Synchronization of augmented luteinizing hormone secretion with sleep during puberty. *New England Journal of Medicine*, 1972, *287*, 582–586.

Boyar, R. M., Katz, J., Finkelstein, J. W., Kapen, S., Weiner, H., Weitzman, E. D., and Hellman, L. Anorexia nervosa: Immaturity of the 24-hour luteinizing hormone secretory pattern. *New England Journal of Medicine*, 1974, *291*, 861–865.

Brown, G. M., Garfinkel, P. E., Jeuniewic, N., Moldofsky, H., and Stancer, H. L. Endocrine profiles in anorexia nervosa. In R. Vigersky (Ed.), *Anorexia nervosa*, New York: Raven Press, 1977, 123–135.

Bruch, H. *Eating disorders, obesity, anorexia nervosa and the person within.* New York: Basic Books, 1973.

Bruch, H. Psychological antecedents of anorexia nervosa. In R. Vigersky (Ed.), *Anorexia nervosa.* New York: Raven Press, 1977, 1–10.

Cheek, D. B. Body composition hormones, nutrition and adolescent growth. In M. M. Grumbach, G. D. Grave, and F. E. Mayer (Eds.), *Control of the onset of puberty.* New York: John Wiley and Sons, 1974, 424–447.

Coates, T. J., and Thorensen, C. E. Obesity among children and adolescents. In B. Takey and A. E. Kazden (Eds.), *Advances in clinical child psychology.* Vol. 3. New York: Plenum, 1980.

Crisp, A. H. Clinical and therapeutic aspects of anorexia nervosa. A study of 30 cases. *Journal of Psychosomatic Research*, 1965, *9*, 67–78.

Crisp, A. H. Primary anorexia nervosa or adolescent weight phobia. *Practitioner*, 1974, *212*, 525–535.

Crisp, A. H. Some psychological aspects of adolescent growth and their relevance for the fat/thin syndrome (anorexia nervosa). *International Journal of Obesity*, 1977, *1*, 231–238.

Crisp, A. H., Palmer, R. L., and Kalucy, R. S. How common is anorexia nervosa? A prevalence study. *British Journal of Psychiatry*, 1976, *128*, 549–554.

Critchlow, V., and Bar-Sela, M. E. Control of the onset of puberty. In L. Martini and W. F. Ganong (Eds.), *Neuroendocrinology.* Vol. II. New York: Academic Press, 1967, 101–162.

Dale, E., Gerlach, D. H., and Wilhite, A. L. Menstrual dysfunction in distance runners. *Obstetrics and Gynecology*, 1979, *54*, 47–53.

Dreizen, S., Spirakis, C. N., and Stone, R. F. A comparison of skeletal growth and maturation in undernourished and well-nourished girls before and after menarche. *Journal of Pediatrics*, 1967, *70*, 256–263.

Espenschade, A. Motor performance in adolescence. *Monographs of the Society for Research in Child Development*, 1940, *5*, 1–126.

Faiman, C., and Winter, J. S. D. Sex differences in gonadotropin concentrations in infancy. *Nature*, 1971, *232*, 130–131.

Feicht, C. B., Johnson, T. S., Martin, B. J., Sparkes, K. E., and Wagner, W. W. Secondary amenorrhea in athletes. *Lancet*, 1978, *2*, 1145–1146.

Feighner, J. P., Robins, E., Guze, S. B., Woodruff, R. A., Winokur, G., and Munoz, R. Diagnostic criteria for use in psychiatric research. *Archives of General Psychiatry*, 1972, *26*, 57–63.

Fishman, J., Boyar, R. M., and Hellman, L. Influence of body weight on estradiol metabolism in young women. *Journal of Clinical Endocrinology and Metabolism*, 1975, *41*, 989–991.

Forbes, G. B. Puberty: Body composition. In S. R. Berenberg (Ed.), *Puberty, biological and psycho-social components.* Leiden: Stenfert Kroese, 1975, 132–145.

Fries, H. Studies on secondary amenorrhea, anorectic behavior and body image perception: Importance for the early recognition of anorexia nervosa. In R. Vigersky (Ed.), *Anorexia nervosa*. New York: Raven Press, 1977, 163–176.

Fries, H., Nillus, S. J., and Pettersson, F. Epidemiology of secondary amenorrhea. A retrospective evaluation of etiology with special regard to psychogenic factors and weight loss. *American Journal of Obstetrics and Gynecology*, 1974, *118*, 473–479.

Friis-Hanson, B. In J. Brozek (Ed.), *Human body composition: Approaches and applications*. (Symposia of the Society for the Study of Human Biology, 7) Oxford: Pergamon Press, 1965, 191–209.

Frisch, R. E. Weight at menarche: similarity for well-nourished and undernourished girls at differing ages, and evidence for historical constancy. *Pediatrics*, 1972, *50*, 445–450.

Frisch, R. E., and McArthur, J. W., Menstrual cycles: fatness as a determinant of minimum weight for height necessary for their maintenance or onset. *Science*, 1974, *185*, 949–951.

Frisch, R. E., and Revelle, R. Height and weight at menarche and a hypothesis of menarche. *Archives of Disease in Childhood*, 1971, *46*, 695.

Frisch, R. E., Revelle, R., and Cook, S. Components of weight at menarche and the imitation of the adolescent growth spurt in girls: estimated total water, lean body weight and fat. *Human Biology*, 1973, *45*, 469–483.

Garell, D. C. Adolescent medicine: A survey in the United States and Canada. *American Journal of Diseases of Children*, 1965, *109*, 314–317.

Garfinkel, P. E. Some recent observations on the pathogenesis of anorexia nervosa. *Canadian Journal of Psychiatry*, 1981, *26*, 218–223.

Garner, D. M. Body image in anorexia nervosa. *Canadian Journal of Psychiatry*, 1981, *26*, 224–227.

Garner, D. M. and Garfinkel, P. E. Sociocultural factors in anorexia nervosa. *Lancet*, 1978, *2*, 674.

Givens, J. R., Wiedemann, E., Anderson, R. N., and Kitabchi, A. E. β-endorphin and β-lipotropin plasma levels in hirsute women: correlation with body weight. *Journal of Clinical Endocrinology and Metabolism*, 1980, *50*, 975–976.

Gordon, S., Cantrall, E. W., Leklenick, W. P., Albers, H. J., Mauer, S., Stolar, S. M., and Bernstein, S. Steroid and lipid metabolism, the hypocholesteremic effect of estrogen metabolites. *Steroids*, 1964, *4*, 267–271.

Grumbach, M. M., Roth, J. C., Kaplan, S. L., and Kelch, R. P. Hypothalamic pituitary regulation of puberty in man: Evidence and concepts derived from clinical research. In M. M. Grumbach, D. Grave, and F. F. Mayer (Eds.), *Control of the onset of puberty*. New York: John Wiley and Sons, 1974, 115–166.

Grumbach, M. M., Richards, H. E., Conte, F. A., and Kaplan, S. A. Clinical disorders of adrenal function and puberty: an assessment of the role of the adrenal cortex in normal and abnormal puberty in man and evidence for an ACTH-like pituitary adrenal androgen stimulating hormone. In M. Serio (Ed.), *The endocrine function of the human adrenal cortex, serono symposium*. New York: Academic Press, 1977, 583–612.

Hall, M. G. R., Murray, M. A. F., Franks, S., and Jacobs, H. S. Endocrinopathy of weight recovered anorexia nervosa in women presenting with secondary amenorrhea. *Journal of Endocrinology*, 1976, *66*, 43–44.

Halmi, K. A. Anorexia nervosa: demographic and clinical features in 94 cases. *Psychosomatic medicine*, 1974, *36*, 18–26.

Hopper, B. R., and Yen, S. S. C. Circulating concentrations of dehydroepiandrosterone and dehydroepiandrosterone sulfate during puberty. *Journal of Clinical Endocrinology and Metabolism*, 1975, *40*, 458–461.

Jacobs, H. S., Hall, M. G. R., Murray, M. A. F., and Franks, S. Therapy-oriented diagnosis of secondary amenorrhea. *Hormone Research (Basel)*, 1975, *6*, 268–287.

Job, J. C., Garneer, P. E., Chaussain, J. L., and Milhaud, G. Elevation of serum gonadotropins (LH and FSH) after releasing hormone (LH-RH). Infections in normal children and in patients with disorders of normal puberty. *Journal of Clinical Endocrinology and Metabolism*, 1972, *35*, 473–476.

Kendell, R. E., Hall, D. J., Harley, A., and Babigan, H. M. The epidemiology of anorexia nervosa. *Psychological Medicine*, 1973, *3*, 200–203.

Knuth, U. A., Hull, M. G. R., and Jacobs, H. S. Amenorrhea and loss of weight. *British Journal of Obstetrics and Gynaecology*, 1977, *84*, 801–807.

Lord, J. A., Waterfield, A. A., Hughes, J., and Kosterlitz, H. W. Endogenous opioid peptides: multiple agonists and receptors. *Nature*, 1977, *267*, 495–499.

McArthur, J. W., O'Laughlin, K. M., Bertus, I. Z., Johnson, L., Hourihan, J., and Alonso, C. Endocrine studies during the refeeding of young women with nutritional amenorrhea and infertility. *Mayo Clinic Proceedings*, 1976, *51*, 607–616.

Malina, R. M., Harper, A. B., Avent, H. H., and Campbell, D. E. Age at menarche in athletes and nonathletes. *Medicine and Science in Sports*, 1973, *5*, 11–13.

Malina, R. M., Spirduso, W. W., Tate, C., and Baylor, A. M. Age at menarche and selected menstrual characteristics in athletes at different competitive levels and in different sports. *Medicine and Science in Sports*, 1978, *10*, 218–222.

Margules, D. L., Lewis, M. J., Shibuya, H., and Pert, C. B. β-endorphin is associated with overeating in genetically obese mice (ob/ob) and rats (fa/fa). *Science*, 1978, *202*, 988–991.

Marshall, W. A., and Tanner, J. M. Variations in pattern of pubertal changes in girls. *Archives of Disease in Childhood*, 1969, *44*, 291–303.

Mecklenburg, R. S., Loriaux, D. L., Thompson, R. H., Andersen, A. E., and Lipsett, M. B. Hypothalamic dysfunction in patients with anorexia nervosa. *Medicine*, 1974, *53*, 147–159.

National Center for Health Statistics: Age at menarche. United States, *Vital and health statistics*, series II. No. 133, 1973.

Odell, W. D. The physiology of puberty: Disorders of the pubertal process. In L. J. DeGroot (Ed.), *Endocrinology*. Vol. 3. New York: Grune and Stratton, 1979, 1163–1379.

Osler, D. C., and Crawford, J. D. Examination of the hypothesis of a critical weight at menarche in ambulatory and bedridden mentally retarded girls. *Pediatrics*, 1973, *51*, 675–679.

Pierson, R. N., Jr., and Lin, D. H. Measurements of body compartments in children: Whole-body counting and other methods. *Seminars in Nuclear Medicine*, 1972, *2*, 373–382.

Reiter, E. O., Fuldauer, V. G., and Root, A. W. Secretion of the adrenal androgen, dehydroepiandrosterone sulfate, during normal infancy, children with endocrinologic abnormalities. *Journal of Pediatrics*, 1977, *90*, 766–770.

Roth, J. C., Kelch, R. P., Kaplan, S. L., and Grumbach, M. M. FSH and LH response to luteinizing hormone-releasing factor in prepubertal and pubertal children, adult males and patients with hypogonadotropic and hypergonadotropic hypogonadism. *Journal of Clinical Endocrinology and Metabolism*, 1972, *35*, 926–930.

Santen, R. J., and Bardin, C. W. Episodic luteinizing hormone secretion in man. Pulse analysis, clinical interpretation, physiologic mechanisms. *Journal of Clinical Investigation*, 1973, *52*, 2617–2628.

Schindler, A. E., Ebert, A., and Friedrich, E. Conversion of androstenedione to estrone by human fat tissue. *Journal of Clinical Endocrinology and Metabolism*, 1972, *35*, 627–630.

Sherman, B. M., Halmi, K. A., and Zamudio, R. LH and FSH response to gonadotropin-releasing hormone in anorexia nervosa: Effect of nutritional rehabilitation. *Journal of Clinical Endocrinology and Metabolism*, 1975, *41*, 135–142.

Siris, E. S., Leventhal, B. G., and Vaitukaitis, J. L. Effects of childhood leukemia and chemotherapy on puberty and reproductive function in girls. *New England Journal of Medicine*, 1976, *294*, 1143–1146.

Slade, P. D., and Russell, G. F. M., Awareness of body dimensions in anorexia nervosa: cross sectional and longitudinal studies. *Psychological Medicine*, 1973, *3*, 188–199.

Starkey, T. A., and Lee, R. A. Menstruation and fertility in anorexia nervosa. *American Journal of Obstetrics and Gynecology*, 1969, *105*, 374–379.

Styne, D. M., and Grumbach, M. M. Puberty in the male and female: Its physiology and disorders. In S. S. C. Yen and R. B. Jaffe (Eds.), *Reproductive endocrinology, physiology, pathophysiology and clinical management*. Philadelphia: B. Saunders, 1978, 193.

Swerdloff, R. S. Physiological control of puberty. *Medical Clinics of North America*, 1978, *62*, 351–366.

Tanner, J. M. Trend towards earlier menarche in London, Oslo, Copenhagen, The Netherlands and Hungary. *Nature*, 1973, *243*, 95–96.

Tanner, J. M., Whitehouse, R. H., Hughes, P. C. R., and Carter, B. S. Relative importance of growth hormone and sex steroids for the growth at puberty of trunk length, limb length, and muscle width in growth hormone deficient children. *Journal of Pediatrics*, 1976a, *89*, 1000–1008.

Tanner, J. M., Whitehouse, R. H., Marubini, E., and Resele, L. F. The adolescent growth spurt of boys and girls of the Harpenden Growth Study. *Annals of Human Biology*, 1976b, *3*, 109–126.

Traswell, A. S., and Hansen, J. D. L. Medical and nutritional studies of !Kung Bushmen in northwest Botswana: A preliminary report. *South African Medical Journal*, 1968, *42*, 1338–1339.

Uldall, P. R., Kerr, D. N. S., and Tachhi, D. Sterility and cyclophosphamide. *Lancet*, 1972, *1*, 693–694.

Valk, T. W., Corley, K. P., Kelch, R. P., and Marshall, J. C. Hypogonadotropic hypogonadism: Hormonal response to low dose pulsatele administration of gonadotropin-releasing hormone. *Journal of Clinical Endocrinology and Metabolism*, 1980, *51*, 730–738.

Vander Walt, L. A., Wilmsen, E. N., and Jenkins, T. Unusual sex hormone patterns among desert-dwelling hunter-gatherers. *Journal of Clinical Endocrinology and Metabolism*, 1978, *46*, 658–663.

Vigersky, R. A., Loriaux, D. L., Andersen, A. E., and Lipsett, M. B. Anorexia nervosa: Behavioral and hypothalamic aspects. *Clinics in Endocrinology and Metabolism*, 1976, *5*, 517–535.

Vigersky, R. A., Andersen, A. E., Thompson, R. H., Loriaux, D. L. Hypothalamic dysfunction in secondary amenorrhea associated with simple weight loss. *New England Journal of Medicine*, 1977, *297*, 1141–1145.

Warne, G. L., Fairley, K. F., Hobbs, J. B., and Martin, F. I. R. Cycle phosphamide-induced ovarian failure. *New England Journal of Medicine*, 1973, *289*, 1159–1162.

Warren, M. P. The effects of exercise on pubertal progression and reproductive function in girls. *Journal of Clinical Endocrinology and Metabolism*, 1980, *51(5)*, 1150–1157.

Warren, M. P. The effects of altered nutritional states, stress, and systemic illness on reproduction in women. In J. Vaitukaitus (Ed.), *Clinical reproductive neuroendocrinology*. New York, Elsevier-North Holland, 1982, 177–201.

Warren, M. P., and VandeWiele, R. L. Clinical and metabolic features of anorexia nervosa. *American Journal of Obstetrics and Gynecology*, 1973, *117*, 435–449.

Warren, M. P., Jewelewicz, R., Dyrenfurth, I., Ans, R., Khalaf, S., and VandeWiele, R. L. The significance of weight loss in the evaluation of pituitary response to LHRH in women with secondary amenorrhea. *Journal of Clinical Endocrinology and Metabolism*, 1975, *40*, 601–611.

Winter, J. S. D., and Faiman, C. Pituitary-gonadal relations in male children and adolescents. *Pediatric Research*, 1972, *6*, 126–135.

Yoshimoto, Y., Moridera, K., and Imura, H. Restoration of normal pituitary gonadotropin reserve by administration of luteinizing hormone releasing hormone in patients with hypogonadotropic hypogonadism. *New England Journal of Medicine*, 1975, *292*, 242–245.

Zacharias, L., and Wurtman, R. J. Blindness: Its relation to age of menarche. *Science*, 1964, *29*, 1154–1155.

Zacharias, L., Wurtman, R. J., and Schatzoff, M. Sexual maturation in contemporary American girls. *American Journal of Obstetrics and Gynecology*, 1970, *108*, 833–846.

Chapter 2

Fatness, Puberty, and Fertility
The Effects of Nutrition and Physical
Training on Menarche and Ovulation

Rose E. Frisch

1. Too Little Fat or Too Much Fat

It is a common sense observation that girls and boys first must "grow up"
before becoming capable of reproduction. But on what scale is the "grow-
ing-up" best measured: age, height, weight, skeletal age, or some other
measure of the body? And how is the synchronization of the "grown-
upness" and reproductive ability brought about (Kennedy and Mitra,
1963)? In this chapter, the relationship of measures of maturation and
reproductive ability in the adolescent female will be explored.

Undernutrition delays sexual development in girls and boys (Frisch,
1972; Frisch and McArthur, 1974), as in other mammals (Hammond,
1955). Therefore, some factor other than chronological age controls maturation. Undernutrition, chronic or acute, also causes the cessation of
established reproductive ability in the human female (Frisch and
McArthur, 1974) and the human male (Keys, Brozek, Henschel, and
Mickelsen, 1950), as in other mammals.

Frisch and McArthur (1974) found that the onset and maintenance
of regular menstrual function in women are each dependent on the
maintenance of a minimum weight for height, apparently representing
a critical fat storage. Data from both nonanorectic and anorectic female
patients showed that a loss of body weight in the range of 10–15% of

Rose E. Frisch • Harvard Center for Population Studies and Department of Population
Studies, Harvard University, School of Public Health, Cambridge, Massachusetts 02138.

normal weight for height, which represents a loss of about one-third of body fat, results in amenorrhea. Weight gain following refeeding restored cycles after varying intervals of time (McArthur, O'Loughlin, Beitins, Johnson, Hourihan, and Alonso, 1976). These findings imply that a particular proportion of fat to lean or fat to body weight may be an important determinant of menarche and of mature reproductive ability. Both the absolute and relative amounts of fat are important, since the lean mass and the fat must be in a particular absolute range, as well as a relative range; i.e., the individual must be big enough to reproduce successfully (Frisch, 1977).

Data of obese women (30% or more of average weight in nonathletic women; Sargent, 1963) show that excessive fatness also is associated with amenorrhea (Hartz, Barboriak, Wong, Katayama, and Rimm, 1979; Nodate, 1969). Therefore, too much fat or too little fat are both associated with disruption of sexual function in the human female (Frisch, 1977).

The recent findings that aromatization of androgens to estrogen takes place in adipose tissue, in female breast fat and abdominal fat (Nimrod and Ryan, 1975), in the omentum (Perel and Killinger, 1979), and in the fatty marrow of the long bones (Frisch, Canick, and Tulchinsky, 1980) suggest that adipose tissue may be a significant extragonadal source of estrogen. Body weight, hence fatness, also influences the direction of estrogen metabolism to the most potent or least potent forms (Fishman, Boyar, and Hellman, 1975). The high percentage of fat, about 24% at menarche and about 26–28% (Frisch, 1976) in the average (165 cm, 57 kg) United States woman at the completion of her growth, thus may influence reproductive ability directly.

2. ATHLETES, BALLET DANCERS, AND MENSTRUAL PERIODICITY

The importance of a critical level of fat in relation to the lean body mass for successful reproduction suggested that high energy outputs, in addition to low nutritional intake, would affect female menstrual periodicity. Ballet dancers (Frisch, Wyshak, and Vincent 1980; Warren, 1980) and athletes who train seriously in fact have a high incidence of irregular cycles and amenorrhea, and girls who begin their training at young ages before menarche have a delayed age of menarche (Frisch, V. Gotz-Welbergen, McArthur, Albright, Witschi, Bullen, Birnholz, Reed, and Hermann, 1981a,b), as will be discussed in detail in a subsequent section of this chapter.

3. Weight at Puberty

The hypothesis that relative fatness is important for female reproductive ability followed from our first findings that the events of the adolescent growth spurt, particularly menarche in girls, were each closely related to an average critical body weight (Frisch and Revelle, 1971). The mean weight at menarche for United States girls was 47.8 ± 0.5 kg, at the mean height of 158.5 ± 0.5 cm at the mean age of 12.9 ± 0.1 years. This mean age included girls from Denver, who had a slightly later age of menarche than the rest of the population due to the slowing effect of altitude on growth rate (Frisch and Revelle, 1971).

Since individual girls have menarche at all different weights and heights, the notion of an average critical weight of 47 kg for early- and late-maturing girls at menarche was analyzed in terms of the components of body weight at menarche (Frisch, Revelle, and Cook, 1973). Body composition was investigated because total body water (TW) and lean body weight (LBW) (TW/0.72) are more closely correlated with metabolic rate than is body weight, since they represent the metabolic mass as a first approximation. Metabolic rate was considered important since a food intake–lipostat metabolic signal was hypothesized to explain Kennedy's elegant findings on weight and puberty in the rat (Kennedy, 1969; Kennedy and Mitra, 1963).

The greatest change in estimated body composition of both early- and late-maturing girls during the adolescent growth spurt was a large increase in body fat, from about 5 to 11 kg, a 120% increase compared to a 44% increase in lean body weight. There was thus a change in ratio of LBW to fat from 5:1 at initiation of the spurt to 3:1 at menarche (Frisch, 1976; Frisch, Revelle, and Cook, 1973) (Table 1).

4. Earlier Menarche: The Secular Trend

Even before analyzing the meaning of the critical weight for an individual girl, the idea that menarche is associated with a critical weight for a population explained simply many observations associated with early or late menarche. Observations of earlier menarche are associated with attaining the critical weight more quickly. The most important example is the secular trend to an earlier menarche of about 3 or 4 months per decade in Europe in the last 100 years. Our explanation, supported by historical data, was that children now are bigger sooner. Therefore, girls

Table 1. Mean and (Standard Deviation) of Height, Weight, Lean Body Weight, Fat,
and Total Water as Percent of Body Weight for Girls of BGS, CRC, HSPS Growth
Studies from Initiation of the Adolescent Growth Spurt to Age 18 Years[a]

Adolescent event and/or age-years	No.	Ht. (cm)	Wt. (kg)	LBW (kg)	Fat (kg)	TW/BWt%
Weight spurt initiation Age 9.5[b] SD 1.2	184	136.3 (10.6)	30.6 (4.1)	25.6 (2.4)	5.1 (2.3)	60.4 (3.8)
Peak weight velocity Age 12.1[c] SD 1.2	173	151.0 (7.8)	39.3 (6.0)	31.7 (3.4)	7.6 (3.1)	58.5 (3.7)
Menarche[d] Age 12.9 SD 1.2	181	158.5 (6.8)	47.8 (6.9)	36.3 (3.3)	11.5 (3.9)	55.1 (3.6)
Age 14	181	162.2 (6.7)	52.4 (8.4)	38.7 (4.0)	13.7 (4.7)	53.7 (3.7)
Age 15[e]	180	164.1 (6.4)	55.2 (8.1)	40.1 (3.8)	15.1 (4.6)	52.7 (3.3)
Age 16	181	165.0 (6.5)	56.3 (8.0)	40.7 (3.7)	15.7 (4.6)	52.4 (3.2)
Age 18	181	165.6 (6.6)	57.1 (7.8)	41.0 (3.7)	16.0 (4.4)	52.1 (3.0)

[a](SD) standard deviation; (Ht.) height; (Wt.) weight; (LBW) lean body weight; (TW/BWt%) total water as percent of body weight.
[b]Height is at weight initiation (Frisch and Revelle, 1971).
[c]Height is at weight peak velocity (Frisch and Revelle, 1969).
[d]Frisch et al. (1973); BGS (Berkeley Guidance Study), CRC (Child Research Council), HSPH (Harvard School of Public Health).
[e]No data available for one HSPH girl.

on the average reach 46–47 kg, the mean weight at menarche of United States and many European populations, more quickly (Figure 1). According to our hypothesis also, the secular trend should end when the weight of children of successive cohorts remains the same because of the attainment of maximum nutrition and child care. There are indications that this may have happened now (Frisch, 1972; Wyshak and Frisch, 1982).

Conversely, a late menarche is associated with body weight growth that is slower prenatally, postnatally, or both, so that the average critical weight is reached at a later age. For example, malnutrition and undernutrition delay menarche (Frisch, 1972, 1978; Tanner, 1962), twins (who weigh less at birth than singletons) have later menarche than singletons of the same population (Tisserand-Perrier, 1953), and high altitude delays menarche (Frisch and Revelle, 1971).

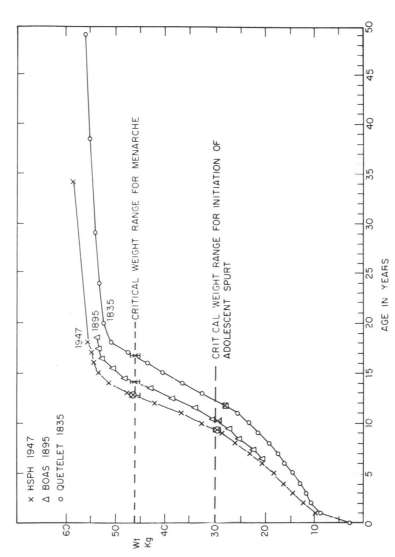

Figure 1. Weight growth with age of Belgian girls in 1835 and United States girls in 1895 and 1947 showing age of attainment of critical weight range at initiation of the adolescent spurt, and menarche. Reprinted from Frisch (1972) with permission from *Pediatrics.*

In the case of undernourishment, the mean weight at menarche of control girls and undernourished Alabama girls did not differ, although the mean age of menarche of the underfed girls was 2 years later, and at a significantly taller height than that of the controls (Frisch, 1972).

For the effects of altitude, well-nourished upper-middle-class girls of the Child Research Council Denver (altitude 5280 feet) Study attained menarche at the same mean weight as the comparable California Berkeley Guidance Study sea-level subjects, but at a later age. The birth weights of the Denver girls were significantly lighter than that of the California girls, and the Denver girls grew more slowly up to the time of initiation of the adolescent spurt (Frisch and Revelle, 1971).

5. Total Body Water as Percent of Body Weight (TW/BWt%): An Indicator of Fatness

Total body water as percent of body weight (TW/BWt%) is a more important index than the absolute amount of total water because it is an index of fatness (Friis-Hansen, 1956; as shown in Table 2). Percentiles of total body water/body weight percent, which are percentiles of fatness, were made at menarche and, for the same girls, at age 18 years, the age

Table 2. Total Water/Body Weight Percent[a] as an Index of Fatness: Comparison of Girl Age 18 and Boy Age 15 Years of Same Height and Weight

	Girl—age 18	Boy—age 15
Height (cm)	165.0	165.0
Weight (kg)	57.0	57.0
Total body water (TW) (liters)	29.5	36.0
Lean body weight (kg) (TW/0.72)	41.0	50.0
Fat (kg)	16.0	7.0
$\dfrac{\text{Fat}^{b}}{\text{Body weight}}$ %	28.0%	12.0%
$\dfrac{\text{Total body water}}{\text{Body weight}}$ %	51.8%	63.0%

[a]Estimated by equations of Mellits and Cheek, 1970; see reference in Frisch, Revelle, and Cook, 1973: Girl (height $\geq$ 110.8 cm): TW = $-10.313 + 0.252$ Wt (kg) $+$ 0.154 Ht. (cm). Boy (height $\geq$ 132.7 cm): TW = $-21.993 + 0.406$ Wt. (kg) $+$ 0.209 Ht. (cm).
[b]Fat/body weight % = $100 - (TW/BWt\%)/0.72$.

ody composition was stabilized (Frisch, 1976). From clinical
und that 56.1% of total water/body weight, the 10th percentile
8 years, which is equivalent to about 22% fat of body weight,
ed a minimal weight for height necessary for the restoration and
intenance of menstrual cycles. For example, a 20-year-old woman
whose height is 160 cm (63 in.) should weigh at least 46.3 kg (102 lb)
before menstrual cycles would be expected to resume (Figure 2).

The weights at which menstrual cycles ceased or resumed in postmenarcheal patients ages 16 and older were about 10% heavier than the
minimal weights for the same height observed at menarche (Figure 2).

In accord with this finding, the data on body composition shows that
both early- and late-maturing girls gain an average of 4.5 kg of fat from
menarche to age 18 years. Almost all of this gain is achieved by age 16
years, when mean fat is 15.7 $\pm$ 0.3 kg, 27% of body weight. At age 18
years mean fat is 16.0 $\pm$ 0.3 kg, 28% of the mean body weight of 57.1 $\pm$
0.6 kg. Reflecting this increase in fatness, the total water/body weight
percent decreases from 55.1 $\pm$ 0.2% at menarche (12.9 $\pm$ 0.1 years in our
sample) to 52.1 $\pm$ 0.2% (S.D. = 3.0) at age 18 years (Frisch, 1976; see Table
1).

Because girls are less fat at menarche than when they achieve stable
reproductive ability, the minimal weight for onset of menstrual cycles in
cases of primary amenorrhea due to undernutrition is indicated by the
10th percentile of fractional body water at menarche, 59.8%, which is
equivalent to about 17% of body weight as fat. For example, a 15-year-old
girl whose completed height is 160 cm (63 in.) should weigh at least 41.4
kg (91 lb) before menstrual cycles can be expected to begin (Figure 3).

The minimum weights indicated in Figure 3 would be used also to
predict the minimum weights for girls who become amenorrheic as a
result of weight loss shortly after menarche, as is often found among
cases of anorexia nervosa in adolescent girls (Crisp, 1970).

The absolute and relative increase in fatness from menarche to ages
16–18 years coincides with the period of adolescent subfecundity (Montagu, 1979). During this time, there is still rapid growth of the uterus, the
ovaries, and the oviducts (Scammon, 1930).

Other factors, such as emotional stress, affect the maintenance or
onset of menstrual cycles. Therefore, menstrual cycles may cease without
weight loss and may not resume in some subjects even though the minimum weight for height has been achieved. Our standards apply as yet
only to Caucasian United States females and European females. Different
races may have different critical weights at menarche, and it is not yet
known whether the different critical weights represent the same critical
body composition of fatness (Frisch and McArthur, 1974).

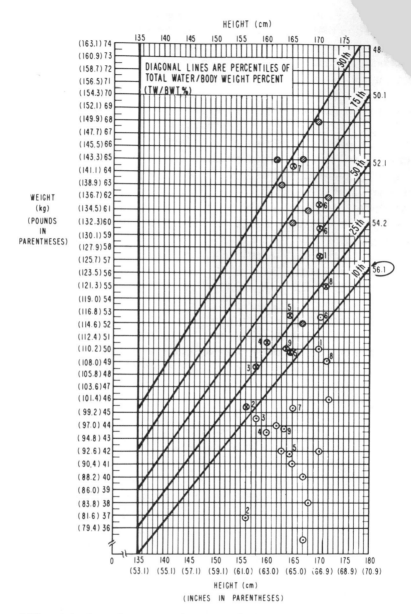

HEIGHT (cm)

WEIGHT
(kg)

(POUNDS
IN
PARENTHESES)

DIAGONAL LINES ARE PERCENTILES OF
TOTAL WATER/BODY WEIGHT PERCENT
(TW/BWT%)

HEIGHT (cm)
(INCHES IN PARENTHESES)

Figure 2. The minimal weight necessary for a particular height for restoration of menstrual cycles is indicated on the weight scale by the 10th percentile diagonal line of total water/ body weight percent, 56.1%, as it crosses the vertical height line. For example, a 20-year-old woman whose height is 160 cm should weigh at least 46.3 kg (102 lb) before menstrual cycles would be expected to resume. Reprinted from Frisch and McArthur (1974) with permission from *Science.*

6. FATNESS AND REPRODUCTIVE EFFICIENCY

The weight changes associated with the cessation and restoration of menstrual cycles are in the range of 10–15% of body weight. Weight loss or weight gain of this magnitude is mainly loss or gain of fat (Kleiber, 1961). This suggests that a minimum level of stored, easily mobilized energy is necessary for ovulation and menstrual cycles in the human female (Frisch, 1975; Frisch and McArthur, 1974).

The main function of the 16 kg of fat stored on average by early- and late-maturing girls by age 18 years may be to provide easily mobilized energy for a pregnancy and for lactation; the 140,000 calories would be sufficient to carry a fetus to term and 3 months lactation as an infant. A pregnancy requires about 50,000 calories over and above normal metabolic needs. Lactation requires about 1000 calories a day above normal needs (Frisch, 1975).

Irrespective of any causal relationship, the weight dependency of menarche in human beings, as in animals (Kennedy, 1969), operates as a "compensatory mechanism" for both environmental and genetic variation. The result is a reduction in the variability of body size at sexual maturity, and therefore, a reduction in the variability of adult body size. As in many other animals, human body size at sexual maturity is close to adult size; weight and height at menarche are 85% and 96% of adult weight and height, respectively (Frisch and Revelle, 1971).

Since infant survival is correlated with birth weight, and birth weight is correlated with the prepregnancy weight of the mother, the regulation of female body size and body composition at menarche has obvious selective advantages for the species. In prehistoric times, when food supplies were scarce or fluctuated seasonally, and lactation was a necessity, stored fat would have been important for successful reproduction (Frisch, 1972, 1975).

7. BODY WEIGHT CHANGES AND GONADOTROPIN SECRETION

Endocrine studies of undernourished, nonanorectic subjects being refed showed that the mean initial serum follicle-stimulating hormone (FSH) concentration was within the limits of normal for young women of reproductive age, but the serum luteinizing hormone (LH) concentration and the vaginal maturation score were low. As weight was regained, serum LH concentration increased and the vaginal maturation score rose. After weight gain to levels close to the normal range, spontaneous menses occurred, but were anovulatory in 70% of the cases. Regular ovulatory cycles began with continued weight gain (McArthur et al., 1976).

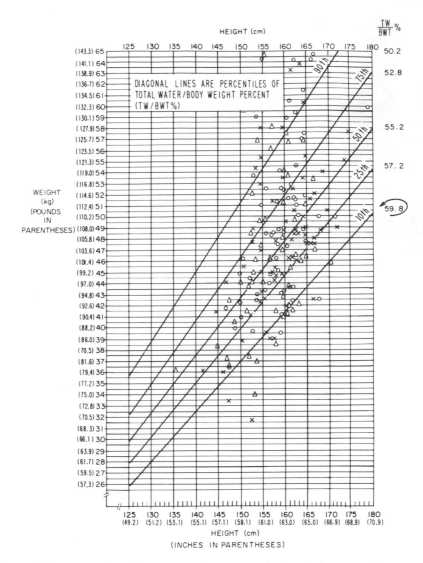

Figure 3. The minimal weight necessary for a particular height for onset of menstrual cycles is indicated on the weight scale by the 10th percentile diagonal line of total water/ body weight percent, 59.8%, as it crosses the vertical height lines. *Height growth of girls must be completed, or approaching completion.* For example, a 15-year-old girl whose completed height is 160 cm (63 in) should weigh at least 41.4 kg (91 lb) before menstrual cycles can be expected to start. Reprinted from Frisch and McArthur (1974) with permission from *Science.*

The type of LH secretory pattern, prepubertal or pubertal, was found to be closely correlated with the extent of loss or gain of body weight (Boyar, Katz, Finkelstein, Kapen, Weiner, Weitzman, and Hellman, 1974). Comparison of total water/body weight percent (TW/BWt%) with the normal values found at adolescence, menarche, and age 18 years showed that a prepubertal body composition was correlated with a prepubertal LH secretory pattern, and a pubertal body composition was correlated with a pubertal LH secretion (Frisch, 1977).

It was concluded from hormonal data and temperature regulation of nonanorectic women with secondary amenorrhea that hypothalamic dysfunction may be caused by weight loss *per se* (Vigersky, Andersen, Thompson, and Loriaux, 1977). Peak plasma LH hormone level response to LHRH was delayed in these subjects and the delay was correlated with percentage below ideal body weight. Thermoregulation at 10°C and 49°C was abnormal and correlated with the percentage below ideal body weight.

No causal relationship is proven by the close association of the hormonal secretory patterns and changes in the fat:lean ratio and fat/body weight percentages. However, it is economical and, from a teleological and evolutionary view, reasonable to hypothesize that the physical ability to reproduce successfully and the hypothalamic control of reproduction are synchronized by the central nervous system. Past research suggests that the most likely integrating signals are metabolic, relating food intake to core temperature and fat storage (Frisch, 1977). Such signals could supplement a direct role of adipose tissue as outlined above.

8. BODY TEMPERATURE, FOOD INTAKE, OVULATION, AND "FLUSHING"

Wakeling and Russell (1970) observed that basal temperature was reduced and temperature regulation was impaired in anorectic girls. These authors reported that the central body temperature of anorectic patients rose in response to a standard meal, whereas in normal subjects central body temperature remained constant. The importance to the human female of a normal lack of such a response to a meal is suggested by the phenomenon of "flushing" in animals (Frisch, 1977): Flushing is the increase in the rate of twinning in sheep resulting from short-term (e.g., a week) high-caloric feeding before mating to the ram. The well-nourished human female fortunately does not normally superovulate in response to a high-caloric intake, like a large steak dinner, although, interestingly, there is evidence for some residual flushing effect even in human beings. The rate of human dizygotic twinning, but not monozygotic twinning, fell during wartime restrictions of nutrition in Holland

and the rate returned to normal after the return of a normal food supply (Bulmer, 1970).

9. DELAYED MENARCHE AND AMENORRHEA OF DANCERS AND ATHLETES

Ballet dancers and athletes have a delayed age of menarche and a high incidence of irregular cycles and amenorrhea. Some dancers and athletes who began their training at ages 9 or 10 years still had not had menarche at ages 18–20 years (Frisch, Wyshak, and Vincent, 1980; Frisch et al., 1981a,b).

However, one can ask: Does intense exercise cause delayed menarche and amenorrhea of athletes, or do late maturers choose to be athletes? To answer this question, the age of menarche and changes in menstrual periodicity of 21 college swimmers and 17 runners, with a mean age of 19.1 ± 0.2 years were studied in relation to the age of initiating training, physical indices, and stress indices (Frisch et al., 1981a,b). The mean age of menarche of all the athletes, 13.9 ± 0.3 years, was significantly later ($p < 0.001$) than that of the general population, 12.8 ± 0.05 years, in accord with other reports (Malina, Spirduso, Tate, and Baylor, 1978). However, the mean menarcheal age of the 18 athletes whose training began *before* menarche was 15.1 ± 0.5 years, whereas the mean menarcheal age of the 20 athletes whose training began *after* their menarche was 12.8 ± 0.2 years ($p < 0.001$). The latter mean age was similar to that of the college controls, 12.7 ± 0.4 years, and the general population (Figure 4). Each year of premenarche training delayed menarche by 5 months. Of the premenarche-trained athletes, only 17% had regular cycles; 61% were irregular and 22% were amenorrheic. In contrast, 60% of the postmenarcheal-trained athletes were regular, 40% were irregular, and none were amenorrheic. During intense training, the incidence of irregular cycles and amenorrhea increased in both groups. Therefore the training directly affected the regularity of the menstrual cycles. These athletes had increased muscularity and decreased adiposity, as determined by physical measurements including ultrasound measurement of subcutaneous fat thickness. The explanation of their menstrual disturbances may therefore be the same as for dieting nonathletic women and dancers: too little fat in relation to the lean mass (Frisch and McArthur, 1974; Frisch, Wyshak, and Vincent, 1980). Some of the swimmers and track and field athletes were above average weight for their height. A raised lean : fat ratio may nevertheless have caused their menstrual problems because their body weight undoubtedly represented a greater amount of muscle and less adipose tissue than the same weight for a nonathletic woman (Sinning, 1978). Behnke, Feen, and Welham (1942) found over three decades ago that physically fit male football players, who had been misclassified as overweight, in fact had little adipose tissue and a great deal of muscle. Pařízková (1965) describes the change to increased muscularity in women athletes and also the reversion, with inactivity, to less muscularity and an increase of adiposity. Also, a high proportion of athletes reported weight changes of more than 10% of their weight in the year preceding the study. Weight loss in this range (Frisch and McArthur, 1974; Vigersky et al., 1977) and rapid fluctuations in weight (Nodate, 1969) were associated with menstrual disturbances.

10. Nutrition and Male Reproduction

Undernutrition delays the onset of sexual maturation in boys, similar to the delaying effect of undernutrition on menarche (Frisch and Revelle, 1969; Tanner, 1962). Undernutrition and weight loss in men also affects their reproductive ability. The sequence of effects, however, is different from that of the female. In men, loss of libido is the first effect of a decrease in caloric intake and subsequent weight loss. Continued caloric reduction and weight loss results in a loss of prostate fluid, and a decrease of sperm motility and sperm longevity, in that order. Sperm production ceases when weight loss is in the range of 25% of normal body weight. Refeeding results in a restoration of function in the reverse order of loss (Bishop, 1970; Keyes et al., 1950).

11. Experimental Evidence: Early First Estrus of Rats on a High-Fat Diet

When rats were fed a high-fat (HF) diet, the fat being substituted isocalorically for carbohydrate, the HF-diet rats had estrus significantly ($p < 0.001$) earlier than did the low-fat (LF) diet rats (Frisch, Hegsted, and Yoshinaga, 1975). Confirming and extending Kennedy and Mitra's (1963) findings, the caloric intake per 100 g body weight of the HF- and LF-diet rats did not differ at vaginal opening or at first estrus, whereas the two groups differed significantly at both events in age, absolute food intake, relative food intake, and absolute caloric intake.

Carcass analysis at first estrus showed that the HF- and LF-diet rats had similar body compositions, although their ages and body weights differed significantly (Frisch, Hegsted, and Yoshinaga, 1977).

12. Nutrition, Disease and Fertility

The findings on minimal weights for heights necessary for the onset and maintenance of menstrual cycles (Frisch and McArthur, 1974) suggests that environmental factors such as nutrition and disease could affect the time of attainment and level of function of each reproductive event in the female, thus affecting the length of the reproductive span and reproductive efficiency. For example, undernourished girls would be expected to have later menarche, a longer period of adolescent sterility, a higher incidence of irregular and anovulatory cycles than normal, amenorrhea when weight loss is in the range of 10–15% of body weight, higher pregnancy wastage, longer lactational amenorrhea (Lunn, Austin, Prentice, and Whitehead, 1980) and therefore, longer birth intervals, and a shorter time to menopause (Frisch, 1975, 1978, as shown in Figures 5 and 6).

British historical data from the 19th century on nutrition, growth,

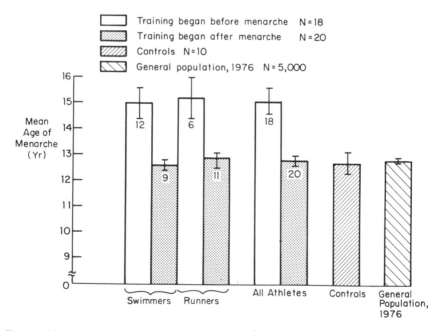

Figure 4. Mean (± SEM) ages of menarche of swimmers, runners, and all athletes according to whether training began before or after menarche, compared to the mean menarcheal age of the controls and the general population, 1976. Reprinted with permission from Frisch et al. (1981), *Journal of the American Medical Association.*

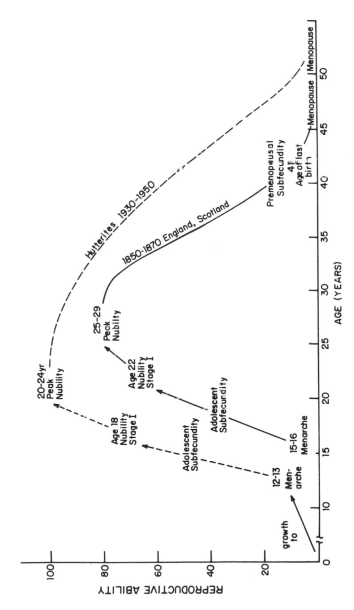

Figure 5. The mid-nineteenth century curve of female reproductive ability (variation of the rate of childbearing with age) compared to that of the well-nourished, noncontracepting modern Hutterites. (Maximum fertility rate is 100.) The Hutterite fertility curve results in an average of 10–12 children; the 1850–1870 fertility curve in about 6–8 children. Reprinted with permission from Frisch (1978) in *Science.*

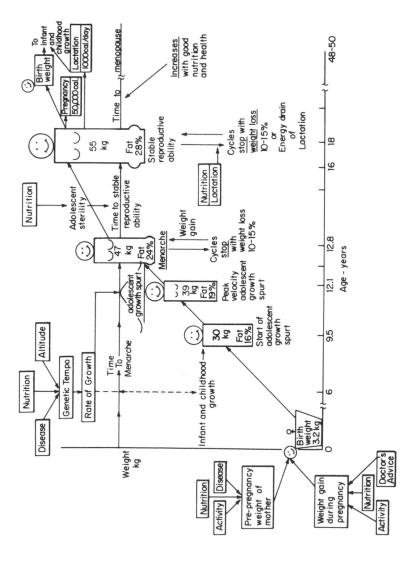

Figure 6. The biological determinants of female reproductive ability. Each reproductive milestone can be affected by environmental factors, as shown. The maintenance of regular ovulatory cycles is related to a critical fatness level and is thus directly affected by undernutrition and energy-draining activities, such as lactation and physical work. Reprinted from Frisch (1975) with permission from *Social Biology.*

age-specific fertility, and the ages of reproductive events show that slow growth to maturity of women and men due to undernutrition, hard work, and disease, is actually correlated with a reproductive span which is shorter and less efficient than that of a well-nourished population. The submaximally nourished females and males are identifiable by a later average age of completion of growth, 20–21 years and 23–25 years, respectively, compared to that of contemporary, well-nourished females and males who complete their growth by ages 16–18 years and 20–21 years, respectively (Frisch, 1978, 1980).

13. HISTORICAL DATA ON AGE OF MENARCHE AND AMENORRHEA

The average age of menarche in mid-nineteenth century Britain was 15.5 to 16.5 years; menarcheal age also differed by social class, upper-class women having menarche 0.5–1 year earlier on average than working-class women. Undernutrition and hard living were the explanations given for the class differences and for the great variability in age of menarche, which ranged from 10 to 26 years in the working class. A girl who did not have menarche by age 17 or 18 years was considered in a weak state of health. Girls who had menarche at 11.5 or 12.5 years were considered to be cases of precocious puberty (Frisch, 1978). The *average* age of menarche in the United States is now about 12.6–12.8 years (Zacharias, Rand, and Wurtman, 1976).

About half of all married women between the ages of 20 and 45 years were reported to have "diseases of the uterus," which included amenorrhea. The main causes given for amenorrhea were those which "impair the constitutional tone and impoverish the blood": poor diet; disease, particularly tuberculosis and chlorosis (anemia); unsuitable employment; and exposure to cold and damp. Doctors noted that working class women were underweight and amenorrheic because of poverty, upper class women because of their desire to be fashionably thin. Stress ("violent fits of passion") was also noted as a cause of amenorrhea.

The greater risks of pregnancy for an undernourished woman were also understood historically. A century ago, when undernourishment was widespread, Dr. J. M. Duncan told the Royal College of Physicians that although sterility of women was often curable, "a good argument may be made out for not curing it, in many cases at least," because an undernourished mother puts herself and her fetus at risk (Frisch, 1978). Of course, as today, it was assumed that pathologic causes of sterility were excluded.

14. SUMMARY AND CONCLUSIONS

The nutrition and fertility data raise some fundamental biological questions. The fact that undernourished human beings and animals are less fecund than well-nourished populations can be regarded as an ecological adaptation to reduced food supplies of the environment and is of obvious advantage to the population. It is a less wasteful mechanism than the regulation of overpopulation by mortality. But by what mechanism is a slower rate of growth of females and males within a population related to a subsequent shorter and less efficient reproductive span (see Figure 6)? Why is a late menarche in a population usually associated with an earlier menopause, with long lactation intervals, and with higher pregnancy wastage? Are there exceptions in some environments to these associated events? How much is reversible after growth is completed?

We still do not know the long- or short-range determinants of menarche. We have proposed that adipose tissue itself may be a determinant of menarche and mature reproductive ability through the following mechanisms: (1) The conversion of androgens to estrogen—a critical amount of estrogen may be necessary to prime the ovary (McArthur et al., 1976). (2) Body weight, hence fatness, influences the direction of estrogen metabolism to the most potent or least potent forms—extreme leanness may be related to the production of antiestrogens, the catechol estrogens (Fishman et al., 1975). (3) Changes in body fat composition are correlated with changes in sex-hormone-binding globulin thus regulating the availability of estradiol to the brain and other target tissues (Nisker, Hammond, and Siiteri, 1980).

Clinically, the minimal weight for height findings have been found useful in cases of nutritional amenorrhea. Knuth, Hill, and Jacobs (1977) point out that "dietary treatment of patients with amenorrhea and loss of weight may replace gonadotropin therapy for induction of ovulation in a significant proportion of patients with anovulatory infertility."

With the ever-increasing number of serious women athletes and dancers, clinicians must also add to the long list of possible causes of delayed menarche and amenorrhea regular, intense exercise (Frisch et al., 1981a,b; Warren, 1980), which may be accompanied by bizarre food intake patterns. These effects of undernutrition and exercise on menarche and the menstrual cycle are apparently reversible. In some subjects a 1- or 2-kg weight change will turn cycles on and off (Frisch et al., 1981a,b). However, nothing is known as yet about the mechanisms involved or about the long-term effects on fertility.

The interest in age of menarche is centuries old, and the suggested modulating influences range from nutrition and stress to artificial light, pheromones, and sweet music. The latter influence was tested in an admirably direct experiment, recounted by Dr. M. A. Raciborski, lauréat of the Royal Academy of Medicine in Paris in 1844. An orchestra was brought to the elephant cage in the Jardin des Plantes, and there the distinguished musicians played sweet music, including the Dance in B minor from Glück's "Iphigénie en Tauride." The emotional reaction of the two elephants, Hanz and Parkie, to each musical selection was carefully noted: "O ma tendre musette," played solo on the bassoon, moved Parkie to "les transports les plus passionnés"; Hanz, indifferent to bassoons, was finally overcome by an overture to Nina, played solo on the clarinet. The elephants matured in 16–17 years, instead of the normal 25 years. An alternative explanation is that elephants in zoos are probably better fed and move around less than those in the wild (Frisch, 1973).

The routine recording of age of menarche, when height and weight are being followed for girls with abnormally slow or rapid growth as well as for normal girls, and the recording of the height and weight at menarche, when possible, would provide useful data for investigation of the mechanisms controlling sexual maturation in girls.

ACKNOWLEDGMENTS. The research on athletes reported in this paper is supported by the Advanced Medical Research Foundation, Boston. I thank Matt Witten for typing the manuscript.

REFERENCES

Behnke, A. R., Feen, G. B., and Welham, W. C. The specific gravity of healthy men. Body weight: Volume as an index of obesity. *Journal of The American Medical Association*, 1942, *118*, 495–498.
Bishop, W. H. M. Aging and reproduction in the male. *Journal of Reproduction and Fertility*, 1970, *12*, 65–87.
Boyar, R. M., Katz, J., Finkelstein, J. W., Kapen, S., Weiner, H., Weitzman, E. D., and Hellman, L. Anorexia Nervosa: Immaturity of the 24-hour luteinizing hormone secretory pattern. *New England Journal of Medicine*, 1974, *291*, 861–865.
Bulmer, M. G. *The biology of twinning in man*. Oxford, England: Oxford University Press, 1970.
Crisp, A. H. Anorexia nervosa: 'Feeding disorder,' 'nervous malnutrition,' or 'weight phobia'? *World Review of Nutrition and Dietetics*, 1970, *12*, 452–504.
Fishman, J., Boyar, R. M., and Hellman, L. Influence of body weight on estradiol metabolism in young women. *Journal of Clinical Endocrinology and Metabolism*, 1975, *41*, 989–991.
Friis-Hansen, B. J. Changes in body water compartments during growth. *Acta Paediatrica* (Stockholm), Supplement 110, 1956, 1–67.

Frisch, R. E. Weight at menarche: Similarity for well nourished and undernourished girls at differing ages, and evidence for historical constancy. *Pediatrics*, 1972, *50(3)*, 445–450.

Frisch, R. E. Influences on age of menarche. *Lancet*, 1973, *1*, 1007.

Frisch, R. E. Demographic implications of the biological determinants of female fecundity. *Social Biology*, 1975, *22*, 17–22.

Frisch, R. E. Fatness of girls from menarche to age 18 years, with a nomogram. *Human Biology*, 1976, *48*, 353–359.

Frisch, R. E. Food intake, fatness and reproductive ability. In R. Vigersky (Ed.), *Anorexia nervosa*. New York: Raven Press, 1977, 149–161.

Frisch, R. E. Population, food intake and fertility. *Science*, 1978, *199*, 22–30.

Frisch, R. E. Pubertal adipose tissue: is it necessary for normal sexual maturation? Evidence from the rat and human female. *Federation Proceedings*, 1980, *39*, 2395–2400.

Frisch, R. E., and McArthur, J. Menstrual cycles: Fatness as a determinant of minimum weight for height necessary for their maintenance or onset. *Science*, 1974, *185*, 949–951.

Frisch, R. E., and Revelle, R. Variation in body weights and the age of the adolescent growth spurt among Latin American and Asian populations, in relation to calorie supplies. *Human Biology*, 1969, *41*, 185–212.

Frisch, R. E., and Revelle, R. Height and weight at menarche and a hypothesis of menarche. *Archives of Disease in Childhood*, 1971, *46*, 695–701.

Frisch, R. E., Revelle, R., and Cook S. Components of weight at menarche and the initiation of the adolescent growth spurt in girls: estimated total water, lean body weight and fat. *Human Biology*, 1973, *45*, 469–483.

Frisch, R. E., Hegsted, D. M., and Yoshinaga, K. Body weight and food intake at early estrus of rats on a high fat diet. *Proceedings of The National Academy of Science* (U.S.A.), 1975, *72*, 4172–4176.

Frisch, R. E., Hegsted, D. M., and Yoshinaga, K. Carcass components at first estrus of rats on high fat and low fat diets: Body water, protein and fat. *Proceedings of The National Academy of Science* (U.S.A.), 1977, *74*, 379–383.

Frisch, R. E., Canick, J. A., and Tulchinsky, D. Human fatty marrow aromatizes androgen to estrogen. *Journal of Clinical Endocrinology and Metabolism*, 1980, *51*, 394–396.

Frisch, R. E., Wyshak, G., and Vincent, L. Delayed menarche and amenorrhea of ballet dancers. *New England Journal of Medicine*, 1980, *303*, 17–19.

Frisch, R. E., v. Gotz-Welbergen, A., McArthur, J. W., Albright, T., Witschi, J., Bullen, B., Birnholz, J., Reed, R. B., and Hermann, H. Delayed menarche and amenorrhea of college athletes in relation to age of onset of training. *Journal of the American Medical Association*, 1981a, *246*, 1559–1563.

Frisch, R. E., v. Gotz-Welbergen, A., McArthur, J. W., Albright, T., Witschi, J., Bullen, B., Birnholz, J., Reed, R. B., and Hermann, H. Abstract No. 147, *Program, Annual Meeting of the Endocrine Society*, Cincinnati, Ohio, June, 1981, 1981b, 119.

Hammond, J. (Ed.). *Progress in the physiology of farm animals* (Vol. 2). London: Butterworths, 1955.

Hartz, A. J., Barboriak, P. N., Wong, A., Katayama, K. P., and Rimm, A. A. The association of obesity with infertility and related menstrual abnormalities in women. *International Journal of Obesity*, 1979, *3*, 57–73.

Kennedy, G. C. Interactions between feeding behavior and hormones during growth. *Annals of the New York Academy of Science*, 1969, *157*, 1049–1061.

Kennedy, G. C., and Mitra, J. Body weight and food intake as initiation factors for puberty in the rat. *Journal of Physiology* (London), 1963, *166*, 408–418.

Keys, A., Brozek, J., Henschel, A., and Mickelsen, O. *The biology of human starvation.* Vol. 1. Minneapolis: University of Minnesota Press, 1950.

Kleiber, M. *The fire of life.* New York: Wiley, 1961.

Knuth, U. A., Hill, M. G. R., and Jacobs, H. S. Amenorrhea and loss of weight. *British Journal of Obstetrics and Gynaecology,* 1977, *84,* 801–807.

Lunn, P. G., Austin, S., Prentice, A. M., and Whitehead, R. G. Influence of maternal diet on plasma-prolactin levels during lactation. *Lancet,* 1980, *i,* 623–625.

Malina, R. M., Spirduso, W. W., Tate, C., and Baylor, A. M. Age at menarche and selected menstrual characteristics in athletes at different competitive levels and in different sports. *Medicine and Science in Sports,* 1978, *10,* 218–222.

McArthur, J. W., O'Loughlin, K. M., Beitins, I. Z., Johnson, L., Hourihan, J., and Alonso, C. Endocrine studies during the refeeding of young women with nutritional amenorrhea and infertility. *Mayo Clinic Proceedings,* 1976, *51,* 607–615.

Montagu, A. *The reproductive development of the female: A study in the comparative physiology of the adolescent organism.* Littleton, MA.: PSG, 1979.

Nimrod, A., and Ryan, K. J. Aromatization of androgens by human abdominal and breast fat tissue. *Journal of Clinical Endocrinology and Metabolism,* 1975, *40,* 367–372.

Nisker, J. A., Hammond, G. L., and Siiteri, P. K. More on fatness and reproduction. *New England Journal of Medicine,* 1980, *303,* 1124.

Nodate, Y. Estrogen metabolism. *Sanfujinka No Jissai* (Tokyo), 1969, *18,* 219–229.

Pařízková, J. Physical activity and body composition. In J. Brozek (Ed.), *Human body composition: Approaches and applications.* Vol. 7. Oxford, England: Pergamon Press, 1965, 161–176.

Perel, E., and Killinger, D. W. The interconversion and aromatization of androgens by human adipose tissue. *Journal of Steroid Biochemistry,* 1979, *10,* 623–626.

Sargent, D. W. Weight–height relationship of young men and women. *American Journal of Clinical Nutrition,* 1963, *13,* 318–325.

Scammon, R. E. The measurement of the body in childhood. In J. A. Harris, C. M. Jackson, D. G. Paterson, R. E. Scammon (Eds.), *The measurement of man.* Minneapolis: University of Minnesota Press, 1930, 174–215.

Sinning, W. E. Anthropometric estimation of body density, fat, and lean body weight. *Medicine and Science in Sports,* 1978, *10,* 243–249.

Tanner, J. W. *Growth at adolescence.* 2nd ed. Oxford, England: Blackwell Press, 1962.

Tisserand-Perrier, M. Étude comparative de certains processus de croissance chez les jumeaux. *Journal de Génétique Humaine,* 1953, *2,* 87–102.

Vigersky, R. A., Andersen, A. E., Thompson, R. H., and Loriaux, D. L. Hypothalamic dysfunction in secondary amenorrhea associated with simple weight loss. *New England Journal of Medicine,* 1977, *297,* 1141–1145.

Wakeling, A., and Russell, G. F. M. Disturbances in the regulation of body temperature in anorexia nervosa. *Psychological Medicine,* 1970, *1,* 30–39.

Warren, M. P. The effects of exercise on pubertal progression and reproductive function in girls. *Journal of Clinical Endocrinology and Metabolism,* 1980, *51,* 1150–1157.

Wyshak, G., and Frisch, R. E. Evidence for a secular trend in age of menarche. *New England Journal of Medicine,* 1982, *306,* 1033–1035.

Zacharias, L., Rand, W. M., and Wurtman, R. J. A prospective study of sexual development and growth in American girls: the statistics of menarche. *Obstetrics and Gynecology Survey,* 1976, *31,* 325–337.

Chapter 3

Pubertal Changes in Adolescence

WILLIAM A. DANIEL, JR.

1. INTRODUCTION

Research in the physical, cognitive, and psychosocial growth of adolescents is increasing. This is particularly gratifying because the quantity and quality of research has been less directed toward adolescents in the past than to any other age group. High death rates of infants, significant mortality and morbidity during childhood from infectious disease, and concerns related to prematurity were the highest priorities in child health research. Now contagious diseases of children have decreased and in general are preventable, and remarkable methods of caring for premature infants have been developed, particularly during the last two decades. The decade of the 1960s, with its disruption of values, experimentation with drugs, increased sexual freedom, rising pregnancy in adolescents, and greater violence and criminal action by juveniles, brought attention to the fact that adolescents exist, that they are a significant population group, and that they do have problems. Thus adults have become interested in the psychosocial aspects of adolescence and adolescents. Secular changes of physical growth have brought more rapid maturing of adolescents and earlier pubertal changes which in general have not been accompanied by earlier attainment of adult cognitive functioning. Another reason adolescent research is needed is the fact that more handicapped children are living to become adolescents and adults, and this in itself has pointed out deficits in our knowledge related to puberty as affected by handicapping conditions or the cognitive and/or psychosocial growth of an individual experiencing a handicapped adolescence.

WILLIAM A. DANIEL, JR. • Division of Adolescent Medicine, Department of Pediatrics, University of Alabama School of Medicine, Birmingham, Alabama 35294.

The interrelationship of physical, cognitive, and psychosocial growth at adolescence has not been studied to the degree it deserves. Pieces of each area have been investigated, but tying them together has rarely been done. More research involving healthy, nonpregnant adolescent girls should be pursued since much of the basic research in adolescent growth relates to boys. Physical growth at adolescence has been studied extensively and much is known about bones, organ size, blood, height, weight, and other physical attributes. Various aspects of cognitive growth and psychologic and social changes during adolescence have been investigated, but most of these have been age-related studies rather than studies considering the biologic maturity of the individuals comprising the subject sample. There is a fertile field for research, particularly research concerning the pubertal changes of girls.

2. PHYSICAL GROWTH

2.1. *Sex Maturity Ratings*

The most useful means of judging the progress of physical growth in an adolescent is the sex maturity rating system developed by Tanner (1962). Although the most accurate estimate of the stage of physical growth and evidence of increasing change is skeletal age, X-ray determination is often unavailable, can be expensive, and probably is contraindicated as a frequent procedure. It has been shown that concordance is high between sex maturity ratings and skeletal age (Harlan, Harlan, and Grillo, 1980). Therefore the use of these ratings provide accurate, easily obtained evidence of the stage of growth during adolescence, and ratings determined over time give evidence of progress toward biologic maturity.

Sex maturity ratings are based on a 1–5 scale with 1 representing prepubertal appearance of secondary sex characteristics and 5 being those of an adult. These are illustrated in Table 1.

The first sign of puberty in a girl is the development of a breast bud, a small mass beneath the nonprojecting nipple; the breast bud occurs in sex maturity rating (SMR) 2. With further enlargement, the areola, the pink portion of the breast surrounding the future nipple, becomes slightly darker and the breast is much larger; the SMR is 3. Further breast development, SMR 4, is characterized by a secondary mound made up of the areola and the future nipple. This change is not always present in development but is frequently present and characteristic. With adult development, SMR 5, the enlargement just described has receded and the nipple projects.

Table 1. Sex Maturity Ratings[a]

	Boys				Girls	
Stage	Pubic hair	Penis	Testes	Stage	Pubic hair	Breasts
1	None	Preadolescent	Preadolescent	1	Preadolescent	Preadolescent
2	Scanty, long, slightly pigmented	Slight enlargement	Enlarged scrotum, pink, texture altered	2	Sparse, lightly pigmented, straight, medial border of labia	Breast and papilla elevated as small mound; areolar diameter increased
3	Darker, starts to curl, small amount	Penis longer	Larger	3	Darker, beginning to curl, increased amount	Breast and areola enlarged, no contour separation
4	Resembles adult type, but less in quantity; coarse, curly	Larger; glans and breadth increase in size	Larger, scrotum dark	4	Coarse, curly, abundant, but amount less than in adult	Areola and papilla form secondary mound
5	Adult distribution, spread to medial surface of thighs	Adult	Adult	5	Adult feminine triangle, spread to medial surface of thighs	Mature; nipple projects, areola part of general breast contour

[a]Adapted from: Tanner, J. M.: Growth at Adolescence, 2nd ed. Oxford, England, Blackwell Scientific Publications, 1962.

Pubic hair is also rated in the Tanner system. The first change, SMR 2, is characterized by the appearance of fine pubic hair along the inner borders of the labia. A few months later hair appears on the pubis above the upper union of the labia and begins to form the classic feminine triangle. As the quantity of hair becomes more dense, it also spreads laterally and becomes more curly and at SMR 4, there is a typical triangle of pubic hair although it is less in quantity than in an adult. In SMR 5, adult development for practical purposes, the triangle is dense and hair also is present along the inner borders of the thighs.

Ratings of the breasts and of the pubic hair may have different ordinal rankings. Clinically many persons use a mean rating; for example, the breast rating may be 4, the pubic hair rating 3, and the mean rating 3.5. In research and perhaps some clinical conditions, it is found that various changes have higher concordance with breast ratings or pubic hair ratings than with a mean rating. For example, the peak height velocity in girls occurs most often after pubic hair rating 2 or breast rating 3. Thus in data analysis, differences in relationships with sex maturity ratings should be kept in mind.

Sex maturity ratings are extremely useful for physicians and other health care providers in the diagnosis of possible disease. For example, scoliosis occurs most often in girls between SMRs 2 and 3 because this is the most rapid period of vertebral growth. Sexually transmitted diseases are most common at ratings 4 and 5 because these stages typify sufficient biologic maturity to engage in sexual activity regardless of age.

There are many findings in which stages of biologic maturity have greater statistical concordance with sex maturity ratings than with chronologic age. Clinically there is always the need to know whether an adolescent is anemic. Rapid increase in size and the onset of menstruation increase the need for iron. To establish iron standards, we have studied the relationship of hemoglobin and hemotocrits (the packed cellular volume of red blood cells) with sex maturity ratings and with chronologic age in adolescent girls and boys. Greater statistical concordance was found with sex maturity ratings than with chronological age, as is seen in Figures 1 and 2. Adolescent females exhibit little change of hematocrit percentages after the growth spurt. In boys, there is a direct association of higher sex maturity ratings with larger hematocrit percentages ($p <$ 0.0001). The increased hematocrit percentages in boys are attributed to the production of increasing quantities of testosterone which stimulate production of erythrocytes by the bone marrow. It should be pointed out that the value of prepubertal girls at SMR 1 in Figure 1 is probably too high and reflects changes for pubescence, although in our sample population of 1000 adolescent girls these pubertal changes were not physically visible to the examiner. Also, values for black and white subjects

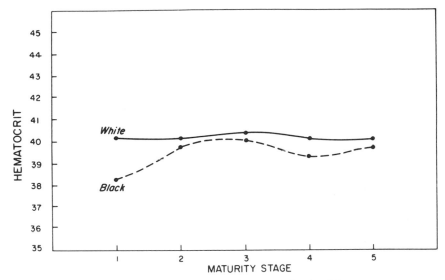

Figure 1. Hematocrit–maturity correlation in girls.

differ; values differ from about 4 months after birth throughout the lifetime of blacks and are thought to represent a genetic racial difference (Garn, Smith, and Clark, 1975). We recommend evaluating hematocrit percentages in adolescents according to sex, race, and sex maturity ratings, as in Table 2.

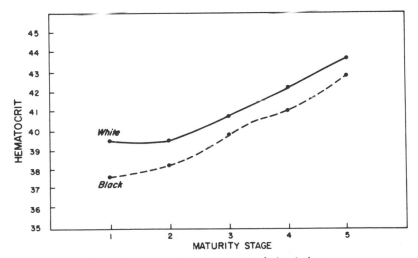

Figure 2. Hematocrit–maturity correlation in boys.

Table 2. Fifteenth Percentiles of Hematocrits

SMR	1	2	3	4	5
Males					
White	35.6	36.9	38.2	39.6	40.9
Black	34.9	36.0	37.1	38.2	39.3
Females					
White	35.8	36.6	37.0	36.7	35.9
Black	34.0	35.3	36.0	36.2	35.8

Iron intake, as shown in Figure 3 for both races combined, approximates the same curve for boys and girls as do the respective curves for hematocrit percentages. It may be that adolescent girls have lower iron intakes because their hematocrits are lower than those of boys. However, cultural patterns of fashion, such as the desire to be thin, may affect dietary intake more than any physiologic relationship.

Another example of the association of sex maturity ratings and blood concentrations is presented in Figures 4 and 5. Folic acid is a necessary part of the diet for the manufacture of purines and pyrimides used in DNA production. The data obtained by multiple regression show higher dietary intakes of folic acid for adolescent boys than for girls. The reverse is shown in plasma values of folate in which there is a decrease with greater maturity and a greater decrease for boys than girls. This seemingly paradoxical finding, that is, higher intake but lower plasma values for boys, is explained by the fact that boys manufacture more cells, particularly red blood cells and muscle cells, than do girls and therefore

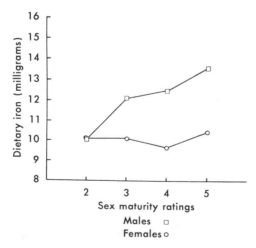

Figure 3. Mean dietary iron intakes of both sexes, according to sex maturity stages.

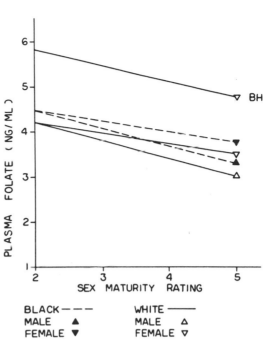

Figure 4. Plasma folate correlated with sex maturity ratings.

BLACK — — — WHITE ———
MALE ▲ MALE △
FEMALE ▼ FEMALE ▽

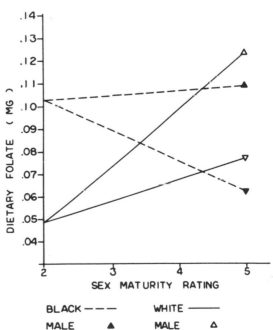

Figure 5. Dietary intake of folic acid correlated with sex maturity ratings.

BLACK — — — WHITE ———
MALE ▲ MALE △
FEMALE ▼ FEMALE ▽

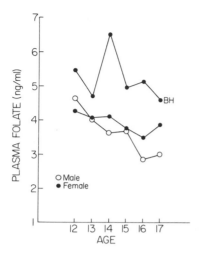

Figure 6. Plasma folate correlated with age. BH: girls from high income families taking supplemental vitamins, including folate.

folate in the plasma is lower because the nutrient has been taken up by the cells. Again, much higher concordance is present using sex maturity ratings than chronologic age, as seen in Figure 6.

When there is rapid increase in height, there must be greater metabolic activity in the skeletal system to produce it. Serum alkaline phosphatase is a biochemical in the blood which is related to bone growth. Figure 7 shows that there are significant increases during adolescent growth (normal values for an adult are about 35 IU), that peak mean values occur at sex maturity ratings associated with peak height velocity in each sex, and with increasing maturity there is a deceleration of growth

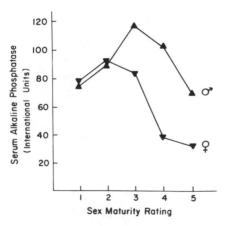

Figure 7. Serum alkaline phosphatase correlated with sex maturity ratings.

and an associated decrease in serum alkaline phosphatase. Such measurements are applicable to assessing delayed puberty, growth affected by chronic illness, and the effect of hormones administered to promote growth.

2.2. Sex Maturity Ratings and Psychologic Research

At this stage of the art, the use of sex maturity ratings in psychological research is extremely limited, presumably because of difficulty in determining the sex maturity ratings of the subjects. Adolescents can assign ratings for themselves using self-examination and illustrations of changes in secondary sex characteristics (Duke, Litt, and Gross, 1980). Figures 8, 9, and 10, which we have developed, illustrate the sex maturity ratings and can be used by subjects for self-ratings. It is necessary to remember that separate ratings of pubic hair and of genitalia should be made for boys as well as breast and pubic hair ratings for girls. Figure 10 shows typical findings for boys at each maturity rating although the two ratings can differ by one or two ordinal ranks; in the illustration, the ratings are the same rank to save space in publication. It should be possible for psychologists and others to use illustrations in an attempt to

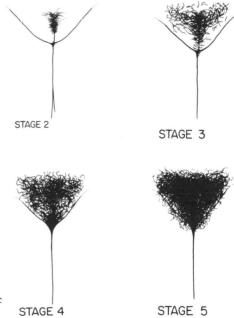

STAGE 2

STAGE 3

STAGE 4

STAGE 5

Figure 8. Sex maturity ratings of pubic hair growth.

explore relationships between biologic and psychologic changes during adolescence. Studies using these self-report ratings might answer questions as to different stages of physical maturity being associated with psychologic differences within a chronologic age group.

Many questions remain in terms of psychologic changes in adolescence at different stages of maturity. A simple example is the obvious expectation that an adolescent boy at SMR 4 would be more sexually interested and perhaps active than another at the same chronologic age who was at SMR 2. In this example, maturity rather than age makes a great difference, but when we begin to evaluate psychologic characteristics, changes, or growth in other areas age has been the chief factor related to maturity, and the association or effects of physical maturity remain untested. It is hoped that in the future Tanner's (1962) ratings will find wider application in cognitive and psychological research.

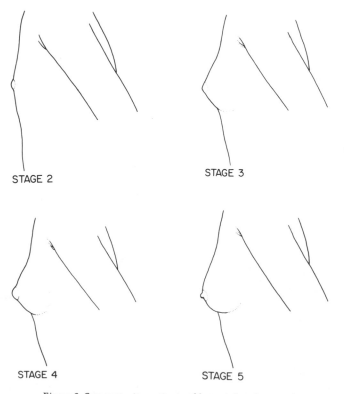

Figure 9. Sex maturity ratings of breast development.

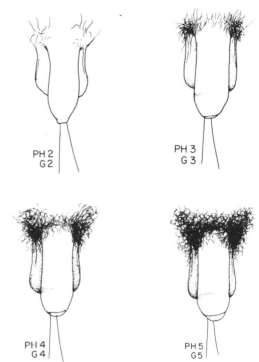

Figure 10. Sex maturity ratings of genitalia for boys.

3. Cognitive and Moral Growth

This chapter is written from the viewpoint of a physician providing care for adolescents, but many of the statements are applicable to other health professionals. Physicians in adolescent medicine quickly learn that cognitive, moral, and psychosocial growth are integral parts of comprehensive health care for adolescents. These physicians attempt to evaluate adolescents and direct therapy in a manner consistent with the particular adolescent and do not limit their concern to the disease state or disability. It is of value to determine where a young patient is along the maturational path of thinking, of moral development, and of social–psychological growth.

3.1. Cognitive Development

We know early adolescents still think in concrete terms and cannot integrate along several lines of thought or compare and contrast them to arrive at a logical conclusion. Formal operational development originates during adolescence but often is not completed, if ever, until young adulthood. The developmental progress of an individual adolescent can be determined by cognitive psychological testing, but this is usually unavailable in a physician's office or in a typical adolescent clinic. It also takes time, money, and a qualified professional to obtain and interpret the results. From the physician's perspective, there is great need for a reasonably accurate, simple, screening instrument to assess stages of cognitive growth.

Cognition also may be important in treating the pregnant teenager. Again, from the practical standpoint, pregnancy occurring in an early adolescent girl must be considered in a different manner than that in a much older adolescent, assuming both have normal intelligence. The early adolescent cannot appreciate the future, often cannot believe she is pregnant or understand the need for prenatal care and continuing medication, and is unable to conceptualize or anticipate the needs of the baby after delivery. Early adolescents idealize, have low compliance, and are extremely dependent when stressful situations occur. It is generally recognized that individual differences in cognitive thought exist and only a few young adolescents seem to have progressed far into formal operational thinking. A physician's approach to such adolescents, whether related to treatment of an illness or in counseling, must take into account cognitive ability.

If the physician provides continuing comprehensive care of adolescents, he/she must be able to assess change in thinking and have some standard by which progress can be measured and used. Actions and reactions of adolescent patients are not the same in a relatively short time span and neither are they consistent in states of wellness or illness. There is need for simple, useful tools, and research efforts in this area would be valuable.

3.2. *Moral Development*

There are many exceptions, but in general physicians pay little attention to the progress of moral development in adolescents unless actions by the patient lead to medical problems or conflict with ethical and moral views of the physician or parents. Little attention is directed toward moral developmental functioning of adolescents but this too is an important concern in treating and caring for the adolescent as a patient. Again, it is difficult in an office or clinic where time is limited to be able to determine quickly and accurately if the adolescent is making progress in moral growth. Physicians can be familiar with the levels and stages of Kohlberg (1973) and in conversation with the adolescent obtain a rough idea of moral growth, but more substantive methods of estimating status and change are needed.

4. PSYCHOSOCIAL GROWTH

4.1. *Separation from the Family and Autonomy*

Physical and emotional separation from the family traditionally has been considered a major task of adolescence. Becoming an individual responsible for oneself and one's actions is a gradual process related not only to biologic growth but to cognitive, moral, and psychosocial development. The interrelationships among these domains can support or disrupt these areas of growth. The effects of cultural and societal changes impinge on adolescents and their families and affect separation and autonomy development. A current concern is the increased incidence of suicide and suicidal attempts in adolescents, particularly adolescent girls. Another area attracting attention is depression in adolescents, and this in itself often has been related to the process of separation from the family in our complex society. Much is being written in academic and lay journals about depressive equivalents in adolescents, how the signs and symptoms differ from those of adults, and what can be done to prevent or cure the condition. Data are now beginning to appear suggesting there are genetically determined instances of unipolar as well as dipolar depression in children and adolescents. Manic-depressive states are typical dipolar conditions for which treatment with a specific chemical, lithium, has had excellent results. Unipolar depression, that is, depression without the manic swing, can also be treated with drugs but usually requires psychiatric therapy. There is then a suggestion that some depression in children and adolescents has an organic basis, but data are still fragmentary and diagnostic criteria are far from being definitive.

Undoubtedly most depression in adolescents is temporary, can be serious or only mildly incapacitating, and often is suggested by behavior considered to be atypical in adults. We do not know how to accurately diagnose this type of depression in adolescents. As with many other psychological areas, experience and intuition seem to be the most useful tools. Various instruments exist to diagnose depression or suicide proneness but the majority of these were developed for adults. Even those specifically related to adolescents often did not consider gender, economic, ethnic, and other cultural factors that seem to be significant. One of the most widely used instruments is Beck's Depression Scale (Beck and Beamesderfer, 1974). This test is valid, at least for adults, and although it included some subjects 15–21 years of age, the number was small. The author and his co-workers gave the Depression Scale and the Suicide Proneness Scale of Beck et al. to 1000 adolescents coming to an adolescent clinic. These subjects were from low-income families and approximately 65% were black. The scales were related to sex maturity ratings as indicators of physical developmental maturity. Although results are not completely analyzed, preliminary data show that Beck's instruments did not significantly help in diagnosing depression or suicide proneness nor was there significant relationship with sex maturity ratings. It is our conclusion that one's clinical acumen and experience are still the best diagnostic means at the present time.

Suicide is considered to be the third leading cause of death in adolescents. Accidents and homicide are the first two causes of death, and since 1974 suicide has replaced malignancies as the third most common cause. About 14 teenagers kill themselves each day, an annual total of approximately 5000. Estimates as to the number of unsuccessful attempts vary from 50 to 200 times that of successful suicides. Many adolescents take pills in anger or to punish a parent or boyfriend and have no wish to die (but may die). Fewer boys attempt suicide, but when they do they are more likely to succeed than adolescent girls. Statistics on suicide are admittedly inaccurate because many deaths, such as one-car accidents, are not considered suicides; also, many adolescent suicides are not reported to the authorities.

There is usually an attempt to link depression with suicide, a relationship which may or may not exist. Depression may or may not be a precursor of suicide, but in general, it is only one aspect of a long-standing difficulty in coping with life because of a multiplicity of causes and social experiences. Depression undoubtedly occurs more frequently than is recognized. However, its association with taking one's life has not been measured, although some professionals may believe all suicides include a depressive factor.

Another interesting observation related to emotional and physical separation from the family is the increased length of dependency by middle- and upper-class adolescents and even by a few young adults of low-income families. It is more difficult for adolescents and young adults to obtain jobs, to secure training for a future vocation, and to cut the ties to parents. Financial dependency, while always present historically, seems to persist for a longer period in our present society. This suggests many areas of interest and possible research. What are the expectancies of adolescents regarding life as self-supporting adults? Are their expectations related to themselves and "self-fulfillment," independence, fluid relationships with others, and so forth? Does depression occur more frequently in older adolescents, or in more mature young adolescents, and if so, why? If separation and depression are associated, detection and means of coping are important to health care providers, teachers, parents, and the adolescents themselves. There is also a pragmatic need for diagnosis and evaluation of treatment methodologies.

4.2. Sexuality

Rapid physical growth is associated with maturing of sexual organs, new and often strange desires and thoughts, and a curious uncertainty about sexual functions and functioning. As separation from the family begins, adolescents are thrust into new situations for which they have had no previous basis for action or decision and many of these situations have a sexual connotation. Much research has been directed toward adolescent sexuality (see Westney, Jenkins, and Benjamin, Chapter 12), and we perhaps know more about the formation of moral values, coping with sexual desires and feelings, and fitting in with the accepted mores of maleness and femaleness than any other task. However, little is known about the interrelationships with other tasks of adolescence. (See Jenkins, Chapter 14.)

It is well known that sexual maturation occurs much earlier than it did during the last century. Menarche occurs at roughly 12 years 3 months in the United States. There are almost no data about changes in the time of first ejaculation or production of sperm in adolescent boys, but it is likely that earlier maturity also has occurred in boys and is comparable to that of girls. It is known that larger numbers of adolescents of both sexes are sexually active at earlier ages than before.

We assume cognitive and moral developmental changes have not kept pace with earlier biologic maturity and that this differential growth has contributed greatly to present problems, such as teenage pregnancy. There is a need to study the interrelationship of early maturers with cognitive and moral stages of growth and to compare these with late maturers. Some work is being done in this area of adolescent growth, but it does not relate to other developmental aspects of adolescents (see Petersen, Chapter 9).

5. Teenage Pregnancy

Available data from surveys and categorical investigations show there is growing awareness that teenage sexual activity and pregnancy are not limited to any one economic, ethnic, or social group. Nor is there any significant geographical difference related to these problems, for all regions of the country, cities and farms alike, report similar rates. Families of all socioeconomic levels, racial groups, and religious denominations are affected, and there is greater concern by adults and society than in previous years.

The latest data concerning sexual activity and pregnancy in adolescents and young adults comes from a recent Guttmacher report (*Teenage pregnancy: The problem that hasn't gone away*, 1981). The following figures are from that report. It is estimated that there are 29 million young people between 13 and 19 years of age, and 12 million of these have had sexual intercourse. Of this group, an estimated 18% of 13- 14-year-olds have had intercourse and the number rises sharply with almost half of 15- to 17-year-old males and one-third of the females being sexually active. Sexual activity of unmarried women aged 15–19 living in cities rose by two-thirds during the 1970s. It is also interesting that during the start of that decade, race, socioeconomic status, residence, and religious affiliation were significant factors affecting the age of onset of sexual activity, but many of these differences no longer exist as more adolescents have become sexually active. Also, fewer teenagers are marrying now than during the early 1970s. There are also data showing decreased use of the most effective contraceptive measures, the pill and the intrauterine contraceptive device (IUD). Many teenagers do not use any contraceptive measures at all or only begin using contraception after having been sexually active for a considerable period of time. Teenagers are, in fact, the least likely users of contraceptive pills to have adverse effects, and complications are far less than those encountered in pregnancy for this age group. It is estimated that the use of contraceptives prevented 680,000 teenage pregnancies in 1 year.

Currently there is a movement to ban use of any contraceptive measures for teenagers, and perhaps even for married adults, and to promote chastity. While abstinence is the surest means of preventing pregnancy, it has never been endorsed by adolescents and young adults. In 1978, there were 1.1 million teenage pregnancies, and half of these occurred within 6 months of first intercourse, an event usually unaccompanied by use of contraceptive methods. Although contraceptives were and are available, 15% of girls having an out-of-wedlock baby became pregnant a second time within a year. It is interesting that babies of teenage mothers are rarely given up for adoption even though the infant was not wanted. Almost all black teenagers and 90% of white teenagers keep their babies.

Risks of pregnancy and fetal complications are higher in teenage mothers than adult females. The infant death risk is twice as high, girls 15 and younger have twice the risk of having low-birth-weight babies, and other risks during gestation also exceed those for women in their 20s. Risk decreases with early and comprehensive prenatal care, but is still higher than average if the mothers are younger than 16 years of age. Although there are physiologic risks, the disruption of education and the eventual socioeconomic damage is also great. The Guttmacher report states that matched samples of young people, using race, socioeconomic status, academic aptitude and achievement, and educational expectations at age 15, showed no difference in school attendance and graduation from high school. The effect of pregnancy is much less for teenage fathers. Pregnancy during the early teen years can be devastating for young women, who end up with low-status, low-paying jobs and few skills. Because of these facts, aid to dependent children (welfare) was 4.7 billion dollars in 1975 when correlated with infants of teenage mothers. This cost to society is even greater as young teenage mothers have 50% more children during their lives than mothers who are older at the time of birth of the first child, and as these children are likely to be supported by the welfare system.

Almost all parents are in favor of sex education for teenagers. At the present time, various fundamentalist groups oppose sex education, and several bills have been introduced in Congress and state legislatures to ban such teaching. Again, surveys of parents show that 8 in 10 Americans favor sex education and 7 in 10 approve the provision of education related to prevention of pregnancy. But organized, vocal groups disregard these views of the majority and promote their own beliefs. There is also divergence of views regarding consent and confidentiality, or notification of parents if contraceptive services are sought by a teenager even though 50% of teenage girls eventually tell their parents about visits to a physician or clinic. We are apparently at a crossroads: while sexual activity is increasing among teenagers, effective contraceptive methods to prevent pregnancy are not being used. At the same time, we are being urged not to provide sex education or contraceptives, to notify parents, and to leave all sex education to parents. There is a great need for our country to decide what it wants.

Cognitive growth during adolescence has not kept pace with more rapid physical maturity. In addition, Western civilization has become more complex and technological, perhaps making it more difficult for some adolescents to fit into society. There are surveys and studies about these factors and how they affect adolescents, but as yet no generally accepted explanation has been produced to explain earlier sexual activity and the increased number of teenage pregnancies. In addition, there are no solutions to this problem which involves biologic and psychosocial aspects of pubertal growth. Research is needed.

5.1. *Vocation*

A third major task of adolescence is to recognize the need to eventually become self-supporting and to prepare for this adult necessity. Most teenagers of both sexes wish to work in order to have money for personal material possessions. Currently much is made of the fact that unemployed adolescents, particularly those belonging to minority groups, are about three times the number of unemployed adults. However, the majority of these adolescents are poorly educated and have few marketable skills. School dropouts constitute a high percentage of unemployed adolescents, and there are data to show that expectations of these adolescents are unrealistic when applied to job possibilities and skill requirements. Data are needed to estimate the intellectual capacity of these adolescents and also how they think; what, for example, is their stage of cognitive thought?

Several hundred thousand youth are in juvenile detention facilities at any one time. Data suggest many of these adolescents, most often boys, are significantly behind expected educational grade levels, and psychological testing shows a high incidence of less than average intelligence. Data also describe the majority of institutionalized youth as being in level 1 of Kohlberg's scale (1973), preconventional moral reasoning, where moral development is still based on power. Rehabilitation efforts have, with a few exceptions, done much less than desired to habilitate these youthful offenders. Recent research also shows a relationship between learning disorders and juvenile delinquency but this association has not attracted as much attention as it probably deserves. These points illustrate the need to consider physical, cognitive, moral, and psychological development as a "package" if we are to better understand adolescents.

5.2. *Ego Identity*

In working with adolescents, there are always trends and instances which seem significant but are not subjects of research. Empirical data or observations are interesting and often useful, but they do lack statistical objectivity. One of these personal observations is what may be called "the need to be special."

Frequently during the last decade, adolescents of both sexes have exhibited a confusion of purpose and lack of commitment because of what can be interpreted as a need to be special. This differs from fear of failure. They are not afraid of failing a course, but are upset if a grade is not high enough to "be special." Most of these young adults have come from upper-middle-class families, apparently are still very narcissistic, expect immediate gratification, have been denied little, and presumably have developed the need to be special. Upper-middle-class parents seem to expect their children to be special, and this need has been internalized from early childhood by these young adults. For example, a "B" or a "C" may be obtained early in a college course, and the course is dropped because a final grade will not be among the highest in the course. The verbalized reason is often the teacher's fault, poor scheduling, lack of interest, or that the course was not required and can always be taken later if desired. This need to be special extends into other areas of living such as personal relationships and social functioning: there is conflict between the need to be special and independent and the continuing dependency upon the parents. Lack of commitment is often seen and expressed as the following: "I'd like to be a doctor, but it takes too long and isn't worth that many years out of my life," or "I could be a concert pianist, but to get to the top requires too much unessential conformity and subjection to what others think you should do. Without going through the system, you can't make it." For many of these young people, there comes a time when they feel purposeless, wandering, and question who they are and what they should be doing. At this point, it is not unusual to have need of services from a clinical psychologist or a psychiatrist. The majority of such young adults we have seen are bright, have developed abstract thought, may be at the stage of moral development in which they reject morality, and yet they are less capable and well-adjusted for adult living than their lesser-endowed counterparts. Psychologically we must ask, "Why?"

6. HANDICAPPED ADOLESCENTS

Current theories and evidence of adolescent growth are based on sequential changes. These may occur at varying ages, the velocity of change may differ greatly, and the time of completion of growth may encompass a relatively long time span. In general, early research was carried out with Caucasian, able-bodied, middle-class boys. Girls were usually not considered. Investigations of handicapped adolescents' growth has been limited in many areas.

If an adolescent is to make sense of the surrounding world, it will be based on the interactions of cognitive ability and individual societal experiences. Handicapped adolescents may or may not have below-average cognitive development, but it is likely that the world and how it functions will be seen differently when compared to that perceived by normal adolescents. Thus the interactions and sequential progress may not be comparable to concepts we use as accepted normal developmental doctrine. For example, repeated hospitalizations, surgical procedures, association with only handicapped children and adolescents, being behind in school, and being viewed as different by peers and adults are some of the factors affecting how handicapped adolescents react to their conditions and the world around them. This leads to several questions: Do handicapped or disabled adolescents progress in the same developmental sequences as their able-bodied age-mates? Are there developmental differences associated with different handicaps or disabilities? Do these adolescents develop according to a logic of their own? Research in these areas would provide guidance to professionals caring for handicapped children and adolescents. At present, experience and intuition are again the best guides related to physical and psychological growth of handicapped adolescents.

Problems with body image and onset of menstruation are commonly encountered in many handicapped adolescent girls. Sickle cell disease is generally associated with late onset of menstruation, scanty menstrual periods, and difficulty becoming pregnant or carrying a baby to term. Ulcerative colitis may be associated with delayed puberty and growth retardation. Cystic fibrosis patients are living longer and more of them are reaching adolescence and young adulthood; these patients, of both sexes, frequently have difficulty accepting their body images. Boys with cystic fibrosis are usually sterile and girls with the disease often have delayed onset of menstruation, perhaps because of nutritional problems. Many other disorders are associated with delayed or distorted adolescent growth and acceptance; for example, females with myelomeningocele may have no sensation in the genital area and lower extremities, as can their male counterparts, and thus not experience sensations associated with sexual arousal and function. Handicapped adolescents, in particular, need understanding and wise counseling as they attempt to accomplish the tasks of adolescence and their responses need to be studied.

7. SUMMARY

Adolescent growth combines significant, rapid changes in physical, cognitive, and psychosocial areas. Research is now being directed to the processes of change in adolescence although compared to other age groups little research has been conducted in the past. Pubertal physical growth always has fascinated observers and great progress has been made in the biologic area, particularly endocrinology, skeletal growth, and other aspects of body composition. The putting together of early studies of maturation with the mixed-longitudinal studies of Tanner (1962) brought about the use of sex maturity ratings as a simple, easily determined method of estimating growth at adolescence. This system of classification is now universally accepted in studies involving adolescent physical maturation.

Piaget's (1950) classic studies are still the basis of viewing change in thought processes in adolescence. This sequential development is sometimes criticized because the observations were made primarily with white, middle-class boys and currently there is much discussion about sexual differences of brain development and intellectual–psychological functioning. Research is needed in these areas, and more pragmatically, a simple instrument to determine stages of change from concrete to formal operational thought would be extremely useful.

Psychosocial growth of adolescence is an almost infinite area for study. Research in separation, sexuality, vocation, moral development, and other facets should be developed, particularly related to females. Physicians and other health workers need simple instruments to determine stages of psychosocial growth and assess progress toward maturity.

Another requisite for understanding adolescence is publication of research findings in disciplines other than those primarily related to our particular fields of interest. Physicians need greater exposure and access to work of psychologists, anthropologists, social workers, nutritionists, and other professionals working with adolescents. The reverse is also needed, for progress in one discipline is frequently unknown in another and real progress can only be made by such cross-fertilization.

REFERENCES

Beck, A. T., and Beamesderfer, A. Assessment of depression: The depression inventory. *Pharmacopsychiatry* (Karger, Basel), 1974, 7, 151–169.

Beck, A. T., Schuyler, D., and Herman, I. Development of suicidal intent scales. In A. T. Beck, H. L. P. Resnik, and D. Lettieri (Eds.), *The prediction of suicide.* Bower, Md.: Charels Press, 1974.

Duke, P. M., Litt, I. F., and Gross, R. T. Adolescents' self-assessment of sexual maturation. *Pediatrics,* 1980, 66(6), 918–920.

Garn, S. M., Smith, N. J., and Clark, D. C. Lifelong differences in hemoglobin levels between blacks and whites. *Journal of the National Medical Association,* 1975, 67, 91–96.

Harlan, W. R., Harlan, E. A., and Grillo, G. P. Secondary sex characteristics of girls 12 to 16 years of age: The U.S. health examination survey. *Journal of Pediatrics,* 1980, 96(9), 1074–1078.

Kohlberg, L. Continuities in childhood and adult moral development revisited. In P. B. Baltes and K. W. Schaie (Eds.), *Life-span developmental psychology: Personality and socialization.* New York: Academic Press, 1973.

Piaget, J. *The psychology of intelligence.* London: Routledge and Kegan Paul, 1950.

Tanner, J. M. *Growth at adolescence.* 2nd ed. Oxford, England: Blackwell Scientific, 1962.

Teenage pregnancy: The problem that hasn't gone away. New York: The Alan Guttmacher Institute, 1981.

Chapter 4

Menarche and Dysmenorrhea

JERRY R. KLEIN AND IRIS F. LITT

1. INTRODUCTION

Menarche is one of the more dramatic signs of female puberty. It occurs late in puberty; for example, menarche occurs during Tanner Stage 4 in two-thirds of females, and in another stage for the other one-third. Tanner staging or classification of sex maturity rating is the clinical determination of secondary sex characteristics for ascertaining developmental age (see Daniel, Chapter 3). Staging of secondary sex characteristics is a relatively convenient and practical method for determining developmental age. Developmental age is superior to chronological age as a predictor for many hormonal, biochemical, and behavioral characteristics during adolescence (Gross and Duke, 1980; Rauh, 1976).

Menarche is regarded as a "rite of passage" for adolescent females in many cultures. It may be anticipated and celebrated, or severely dreaded. The Roman naturalist Pliny said of menstruation,

> But nothing could easily be found that is more remarkable than the monthly flux of women. Contact with it turns new wine sour, crops touched by it become barren, grafts die, seeds in gardens are dried up, the fruit of trees falls off, the bright surface of mirrors in which it is merely reflected is dimmed, the edge of steel and the gleam of ivory are dulled, hives of bees die, even bronze and iron are at once seized by rust, and a horrible smell fills the air; to taste it drives dogs mad and infects their bites with an incurable poison (cited in Novell, 1965, p. 222).

JERRY R. KLEIN • Department of Pediatrics, Division of Adolescent Medicine, Michael Reese Hospital, University of Chicago Pritzker School of Medicine, Chicago, Illinois 60616.   IRIS F. LITT • Department of Pediatrics, Stanford University School of Medicine, Stanford, California 94305.

Menarche has both physiological and psychological significance. With such a historical background, it is not surprising that menarche was often feared and that dysmenorrhea (painful cramps) was anticipated. Dysmenorrhea is a syndrome characterized by recurrent, crampy lower-abdominal pain in association with the menses, often accompanied by nausea, vomiting, increased frequency of defecation, headaches, and muscular cramps (Halbert, Demers, and Jones, 1976). This chapter addresses the epidemiology of adolescent dysmenorrhea, the evidence suggesting its mediation by biologic processes, and future research considerations.

2. Epidemiology of Dysmenorrhea

Dysmenorrhea is the leading cause of recurrent short-term school absenteeism among adolescent females (Ylikorkala and Dawood, 1978). An estimated 140 million hours are lost annually from school or work because of dysmenorrhea. In 1958, Golub, Lang, and Menduke (1958) reported that one-third of Philadelphia public high school females had frequent dysmenorrhea, one-third had occasional dysmenorrhea, and one-third had no dysmenorrhea. This study also suggested the possibility of a higher incidence among blacks. Widholm (1979) described an increase in frequency of dysmenorrhea from 36% to 56% in a large sample of Finnish adolescents between 13 and 20 years of age. Dysmenorrhea was associated with an overall school absence rate of 23.4%.

The epidemiology of dysmenorrhea has not been studied previously in a large representative sample of American adolescents. Accordingly, data for 2699 menarcheal adolescents were drawn from the National Health Examination Survey by the National Center for Health Statistics, (1969), Cycle III, 1966–1970, and analyzed by us for possible correlates of dysmenorrhea (Klein and Litt, 1981). The 7000 adolescents of Cycle III are from a cross-sectional national probability sample of 22 million adolescents of ages 12–17. The Survey is selected to be representative of the United States' noninstitutionalized population with regard to age, race, sex, and geographic region. In the survey, race was recorded as white, black, or "other." The subjects of "other" racial background, which comprise only 0.5% of the sample, have not been included in the present analysis.

For many years, controversy has surrounded the role of psychologic and biologic variables in the pathogenesis of dysmenorrhea (Gough, 1975; Brooks-Gunn and Ruble, 1979; Ruble, 1977; Starfield, Gross, Wood, Pantell, Allen, Gordon, Moffatt, Drachman, and Katz, 1980). The data available from the National Center for Health Statistics included history obtained from parent and daughter by questionnaire, results of a physical examination performed by a pediatrician and a nurse, laboratory and psychological test data, and interviews with school personnel. The sexual maturity of each subject was assessed by the physician using the reference photographic plates developed by Tanner (1962). After analyzing the data to determine the frequency of dysmenorrhea, we correlated the biologic, psychologic, and demographic independent variables with the dependent variable, dysmenorrhea. Biologic variables included chronological age, stage of sexual maturation, and gynecologic or postmenarcheal age (i.e., the number of years since menarche). A single psychologic variable documented preparation for menarche as determined by response to the question, "Were you told about menstruation before the time when your periods began?" Demographic variables consisted of race and socioeconomic status (SES), using as a proxy measure the education level of the parent who was head of the household. All variables were analyzed as possible correlates of dysmenorrhea by bivariate and multivariate analytic techniques. In addition, morbidity from dysmenorrhea was measured by school absence as determined from interviews with school personnel.

The overall prevalance of dysmenorrhea is striking. Of the 2699 subjects who reported menarche, 1611 (59.7%) reported discomfort or pain in connection with their menstrual period. Of those with pain, 14% described it as severe, 37% as moderate, and 49% as mild.

The prevalence of dysmenorrhea positively correlated with all biologic variables. Dysmenorrhea increased with chronological age from 39% of 12-year-olds to 72% of 17-year-olds (Figure 1). Similarly, it increased with sex maturity rating from 38% of those at Tanner Stage 3 to 66% at Tanner Stage 5 (Figure 2), and from 31% at gynecologic age 1 to 78% at gynecologic age 5 (Figure 3). At any chronological age or any sex maturity rating, dysmenorrhea was more prevalent in adolescents at a gynecologic age of 2 years or greater.

Neither the prevalence of dysmenorrhea nor subsequent school absence could be predicted from reports of preparation for menarche. Unfortunately, no other questions were asked by the National Health Examination Survey that look at psychologic variables such as attitudes and expectations about menarche. However, 16.3% of white females having menarche at or before age 11 were not told about menarche prior to menstruation, as compared to 5.5% over age 11. In addition, 9.9% of all black females were not prepared for menarche, as compared to 6.3% of all white females. Although lack of preparation for menarche was not shown to be related to subsequent dysmenorrhea, a surprising number

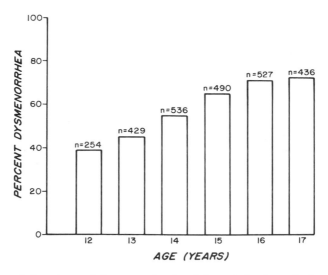

Figure 1. Prevalence of dysmenorrhea in adolescents by chronologic age.

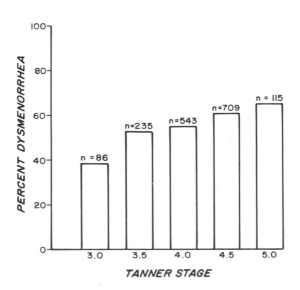

Figure 2. Prevalence of dysmenorrhea in adolescents by sex maturity rating.

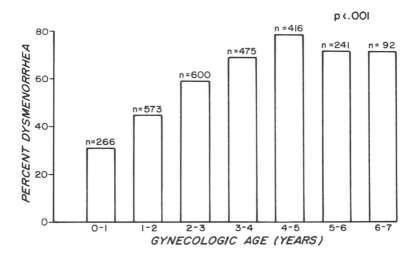

Figure 3. Prevalence of dysmenorrhea in adolescents by gynecologic age.

of adolescents approach their first period without any prior knowledge of menstruation. This is especially true for those girls who begin menstruating early. Although no relationship between dysmenorrhea and preparation for menarche was found, we believe that preparation emphasizing menarche as a sign of maturation will promote positive expectations and attitudes in terms of psychologic development (see Brooks-Gunn and Ruble, Chapter 8).

Social class and its relationship to dysmenorrhea was examined. Although the differences are small, students from a low SES were less likely to report cramps (Figure 4). Unlike the results reported in Golub's earlier study (1958), race was not correlated with dysmenorrhea in our data; 60.6% of white students and 55.7% of black students reported dysmenorrhea. Of the biologic variables, and in fact, of all variables in a graded multiple-regression analysis, gynecologic age predicted the greatest proportion of variation in reported dysmenorrhea. Socioeconomic status, race, and preparation for menarche did not contribute significantly in the regression analysis as predictors of dysmenorrhea.

Morbidity from dysmenorrhea in adolescents is best measured by school absence. In the Survey sample, 14% frequently miss school because of their cramps. Fifty percent with severe dysmenorrhea miss school because of their cramps, while the absenteeism rate was 17% among those with mild cramps. Although black adolescents report no

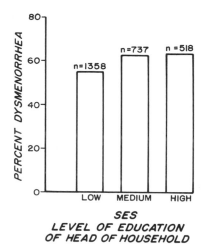

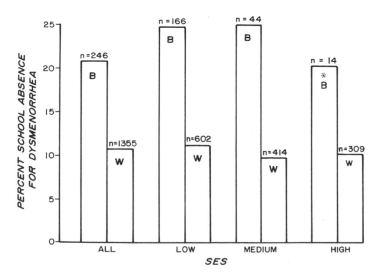

SES
**LEVEL OF EDUCATION
OF HEAD OF HOUSEHOLD**

Figure 4. Prevalence of dysmenorrhea in adolescents by SES ($p < 0.01$).

more dysmenorrhea than white adolescents, they are absent more from school because of their cramps (23.6% vs. 12.3%) even when SES is held constant (Figure 5). Absence for cramps is strongly associated with an "unusual" number of days missed from school. It accounts for 25% of all females with excessive absences from school as determined by teacher reports. Although morbidity is great, only 14.5% of adolescents with dys-

Figure 5. Prevalance of school absence for dysmenorrhea by race and SES ($p < 0.01$). *Indicates insufficient n; B indicates black; W indicates white.

menorrhea have ever sought help for this problem from a physician, including only 29% of those adolescents reporting severe dysmenorrhea. As mentioned earlier, a questionnaire was completed by parents. Unfortunately, the data base does not distinguish mothers from fathers. From this questionnaire, 30% of parents are not aware of their daughter's dysmenorrhea. As a corollary, some parents were not aware that their daughter had had menarche, and other parents reported menarche in their daughters while the daughters did not. Clearly, communication needs to be improved.

These findings from a national probability sample draw attention to both the high prevalence of dysmenorrhea in American adolescents (59.7%) and morbidity related to excessive school absence. Biologic variables, particularly increasing gynecologic age, are strongly correlated with dysmenorrhea. It is distressing to learn that so few adolescents have ever consulted their physician for help with their dysmenorrhea.

3. BIOLOGIC BASIS FOR DYSMENORRHEA

Pickles (1957) described a smooth-muscle stimulant found in menstrual fluid that was later shown to consist of the prostaglandins $F_{2\alpha}$ and E_2. Prostaglandins are derivatives of arachidonic acid, a fatty acid. They are described as locally acting hormones or autacoids. Autacoid is derived from the Greet *autos* (self) and *akos* (medicinal agent) (Douglas, 1980). Prostaglandins have an amazingly broad spectrum of activity, affecting the cardiovascular, respiratory, hematologic, and gastrointestinal organs, as well as the gynecologic organs.

The association of endogenous prostaglandins with primary dysmenorrhea is supported by the following evidence (Halbert, Demers, and Jones, 1976; Yliorkala and Dawood, 1978). First, there is a striking similarity between the symptoms of dysmenorrhea and the effects of administered prostaglandins, as seen in the clinical situations of prostaglandin-induced midtrimester abortions and the induction of labor. It also has been shown experimentally that $PGF_{2\alpha}$ can stimulate an increase in the amplitude and frequency of contractions of human myometrium, the muscular portion of the uterus, with a peak of activity that occurs in the premenstrual period. Menstrual-like cramps and intense uterine contractions occur after intravenous $PGF_{2\alpha}$ is given to nonpregnant women. Second, there are higher levels of prostaglandin in the secretory endometrium (thickened mucous coat of the uterus after ovulation) compared to those in the proliferative endometrium (thin mucous coat of the uterus in the first half of the menstrual cycle). This finding is consistent with the impression that dysmenorrhea occurs in ovulatory cycles, although this association is yet to be proven. It has been shown in one adolescent patient that the amount of prostaglandin recoverable in an anovulatory cycle was only one-fifth that of ovulatory cycles (Pickles, 1967). Third, multiple studies have demonstrated high levels of prostaglandins in the endometrium, or mucous coating of the uterus, and in the menstrual fluid in adult patients with dysmenorrhea. Lundstrom and Green (1978) have shown that on the 1st day of menstrual bleeding the concentration of $PGF_{2\alpha}$ in the endometrium was approximately four times higher in patients with dysmenorrhea than in normal controls. Other studies have shown a great deal of variation between assays, but there has been a suggestion that $F_{2\alpha}$ was considerably higher in some dysmenorrheic patients than normals. Finally, there are now multiple reports on the response of dysmenorrhea to compounds that inhibit prostaglandin synthesis or antagonize the action of prostaglandins (Budoff, 1979; Chan, Dawood, and Fuchs, 1979; Chan and Hill, 1978; Lundstrom, 1978). Uterine pressure can be measured with an intrauterine microballoon both before and after a single dose of a prostaglandin inhibitor. Uterine resting pressure, frequency of contractions, and the active pressure decrease after the prostaglandin inhibitor mefenamic acid is used is coincident with the disappearance of dysmenorrheic pain (Figure 6) (Pulkkinen and Kaihola, 1977). Although the exact action of prostaglandin inhibitors is not known, they probably act by reducing the frequency of spastic contractions, reducing a high resting tone, and reducing high active pressure. The perception of pain of dysmenorrhea may be due to uterine contractions directly or to ischemia, which is a deficiency of blood secondary to uterine contractions.

Although several different prostaglandin synthetase inhibitors have been shown to reduce symptoms of dysmenorrhea in adult women (Budoff, 1979; Chan et al., 1979; Chan and Hill, 1978; Lundstrom, 1978), potential side effects of most of these compounds, such as headache or anemia arising from rapid destruction or inadequate production of red blood cells, make their use in adolescents questionable until further testing demonstrates their safety. Other investigators have previously reported improvement in symptoms of dysmenorrhea in adults taking aspirin (Shangold, Aksel, Schomberg, and Hammond, 1976). During the treatment cycle of their two-cycle study, aspirin was administered according to a fixed and prearranged schedule prior to or at the onset of bleeding. The greatest subjective relief compared to the control cycle was reported by those subjects who began taking aspirin 3 or more days prior to the onset of bleeding. Therefore, we undertook a placebo-controlled double-blind crossover trial with the less toxic prostaglandin synthetase

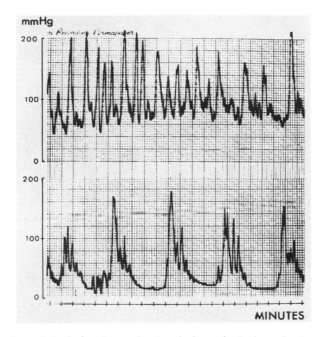

Figure 6. Uterine activity before (upper line) and after a single dose of 750 mg mefenamic acid during first day of menstruation. Original recording. Note the decrease in uterine resting pressure and frequency of contractions, nearly unchanged active pressure (decreasing later on), coincident with the disappearance of dysmenorrheic pain (Pulkkinen and Kaihola, 1977, with permission).

inhibitor, acetyl salicylic acid, or aspirin, for the treatment of primary dysmenorrhea in adolescents (Klein, Litt, Rosenberg, and Udall, 1981).

3.1. *Study Design*

Forty-seven dysmenorrheic females, 21 years of age or younger recruited through the mass media, were selected for study. Prior to acceptance, each patient completed the Moos Menstrual Distress Questionnaire (MDQ) (Moos, 1977), a standardized 47-item questionnaire for assessing menstrual cycle symptomatology. These items have been previously clustered into eight symptom groups: pain, behavior change, autonomic reactions, water retention, negative affect, concentration, arousal, and control. Each symptom is rated on a 6-point scale ranging from "no reaction" to "acute or disabling." Criteria for admission into the study consisted of a base score in the pain subscale of the MDQ greater than Moos's standardized group mean for the menstrual period immediately preceding this study and less than the group mean for the corresponding intramenstrual period. The mean pain subscale for Moos's initial group of 839 adult women is 12.5. The mean baseline subscale for our sample is greater than 21. These criteria were selected in order to choose those patients with moderate or severe dysmenorrhea who were pain-free between menstrual periods. Exclusion criteria included: evidence on physical examination of gynecologic pathology such as endometriosis, pelvic inflammatory disease, or uterine anomalies; the use of an intrauterine contraceptive device (IUD); medical contraindications to salicylate, including allergy, asthma, peptic ulcer disease, a bleeding susceptibility, or scheduled elective surgery during the study; or chronic disease such as kidney disease potentially worsened by prostaglandin inhibitors. Informed consent was obtained that described the medication to be studied as a "prostaglandin inhibitor" without mentioning the specific name of the drug until the completion of the study.

The design was that of a double-blind placebo-controlled crossover study with the dependent variable being the degree of dysmenorrhea. During the four months of study after the baseline month, patients alternated monthly with either 600 mg of aspirin or an identical placebo tablet, four times a day. Medication for the initial month was assigned randomly. The medication was initiated 3 days prior to the expected menstrual period for those who reported regular menses, or 11 days following a sustained rise in basal body temperature for those with irregular menses. Each patient thus served as her own control in the ongoing assessment of the therapeutic effect of aspirin. The MDQ and a separate self-report of pain (on a 5-point scale for each month, and on a 3-point scale compared to the previous month) were assessed monthly. Responses were scored as $1+$ if improvement was noted, $1-$ if the period was worse than the previous one, or 0 if there was no change. Amount of school absence and presence of side effects were also assessed monthly. Data were analyzed using t-tests and paired t-tests.

A battery of personality tests—including the Piers–Harris Self-concept Scale (Piers and Harris, 1969), Cuskey's modification of the Eysenk Autonomy Scale (Cuskey, 1976), and the personal freedom subscale of the California Test of Personality (Thorpe, Clark, and Tiegs, 1953)—were administered at baseline to assess their relationship to treatment outcome and to compare subjects with dysmenorrhea with our general clinic population.

The mean age of the study group was 17.9 years. The majority came from well-educated families, and 44 of 47 were white. The average age at menarche, 12.2 ± 1.2 years, is comparable with that of the current United States population (National Center for Health Statistics, 1974),

Table 1. Comparison of Study Dropouts with Those Who Completed the Study

	Dropouts (n = 18)	Completers (n = 29)	p (t = test)
Age at menarche (yr)	11.7 ± 1.1[a]	12.5 ± 1.1	<0.01
Baseline pain (MDQ pain subscale)	22.4 ± 4.7	21.5 ± 6.2	n.s.
Self-image (Piers–Harris Scale)	56.8 ± 12.8	66.1 ± 8.5	<0.025
Autonomy (Cuskey Scale)	21.8 ± 3.2	24.3 ± 3.9	<0.025
Less relief	22.7 ± 5.2	18.4 ± 5.2	<0.05
Age (yr)	17.8 ± 2.2	17.9 ± 1.8	n.s.
SES (years of education of head of household)	14.8 ± 2.5	14.6 ± 3.0	n.s.

[a]Mean ± 1 S.D.

and mean gynecologic age was 5.7 years. The results of the personality tests revealed no difference between dysmenorrhea patients and our general clinic population.

Of interest is the report of cramps coincident with the first menstrual period in 20 of our patients, an unexpected finding since ovulatory cycles are usually not anticipated at menarche. Some investigators, however, have reported pain at menarche (Brooks-Gunn and Ruble, Chapter 8; Ruble and Brooks-Gunn, 1982; Widholm, 1979).

Of the 47 subjects initially enrolled, 29 completed at least 2 months of participation in the study. The dropouts from the study (Table 1) had an earlier age of menarche, poorer self-image, were less autonomous, and had less relief from the first month's therapy compared to those patients who remained in the study. Of the 8 dropouts after 1 month, 6 were initially assigned to the placebo group. Age and SES were similar for the dropouts and those patients who remained in the study.

The majority of patients reported either severe (23/47) or incapacitating (17/47) dysmenorrhea with cramps persisting for an average of 2.1 days each month and with 1.4 days being lost from school each month. Thirty-seven days were lost from school during the baseline month for the 29 subjects. Of the group, 12 were sexually active. Contraceptive methods included combination oral contraceptives in 4, the diaphragm in 6, and other methods in 2 patients. The patients on oral contraceptives had not obtained relief from their dysmenorrhea prior to the addition of aspirin.

3.2. Results

The results of the MDQ (Table 2) indicate that pain relief was significantly greater in the aspirin months than the placebo months for the

Table 2. Comparison between Aspirin and Placebo Pairs for Menstrual Distress Questionnaire (MDQ)[a]

MDQ subscale	Aspirin	Placebo	p (t = Test)
1. Pain	16.3 ± 5.3	17.7 ± 6.4	<0.05
2. Behavior change	12.1 ± 5.9	14.5 ± 6.8	<0.025
3. Autonomic reactions	8.2 ± 4.3	9.2 ± 4.7	n.s.
4. Water retention	9.9 ± 2.9	10.7 ± 3.7	n.s.
5. Negative affect	17.8 ± 6.6	19.0 ± 7.3	n.s.
6. Concentration	13.8 ± 5.7	15.4 ± 7.2	n.s.
7. Arousal	8.3 ± 3.1	8.5 ± 3.6	n.s.
8. Control	8.7 ± 3.7	7.7 ± 5.4	n.s.

[a]n = 29.

24 patients who completed the study. Each group represents the same 29 patients during a 1-month period of observation. There was no difference in the effect of aspirin given before versus after the placebo, eliminating the possibility of contamination associated with the crossover design. There was improvement in the behavior change subscale of the MDQ that measures school performance, bedrest, staying at home, and efficiency. There was no improvement, however, in the autonomic-reaction subscale that measures nausea and vomiting, nor was any difference noted for the water retention or for the control subscale of the MDQ. The effect of aspirin therapy was also monitored by the subject's self-report of presence or absence of improvement for each menstrual period when compared to the previous one. Based on this self-report, there was greater improvement noted with aspirin than with placebo ($p < 0.025$) (Figure 7). Absence from school was compared both with pretreatment baseline and with the placebo months. There was significantly less absence from school during treatment with aspirin (13 days) compared with placebo (18 days) and compared with the baseline value (27 days). Of interest is the decrease in school absence for the placebo months as well as the aspirin months. Side effects of aspirin consisted of tinnitus (ringing in the

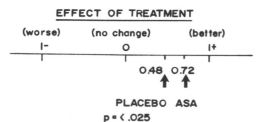

Figure 7. Comparison of aspirin (ASA) and placebo pairs based on subjects' self-report of severity compared with previous month.

ears) present in 3 subjects, and mild gastrointestinal bleeding in 1. Menstrual bleeding was reported as heavier in 6 patients while receiving aspirin, and in 3 patients while receiving placebo. Of 29 adolescents who completed the study, 14 improved on aspirin therapy. There were no differences between responders and nonresponders with regard to demographic or gynecologic variables at baseline.

3.3. *Discussion*

Prostaglandins may be implicated in the pathogenesis of dysmenorrhea by increasing uterine tone, increasing the amplitude and frequency of uterine contractions, or causing uterine ischemia, a deficiency of blood arriving at the uterus. Prostaglandin inhibitors such as aspirin act by inhibiting prostaglandin synthesis (Klein, et al., 1981; Vane, 1971). Other prostaglandin inhibitors such as the fenamates not only inhibit prostaglandin synthesis, but also antagonize prostaglandin action (Budoff, 1979); for example, inhibiting the effect of prostaglandin on uterine tissue. Double-blind crossover studies have previously shown the efficacy of mefenamic acid and naproxen-Na, but widespread use of these drugs should await the result of further testing of toxicity in adolescents. The results of this study suggest that aspirin is effective in relieving dysmenorrhea and reducing school absence in certain adolescents. Although not a panacea, a drug such as aspirin that reduces dysmenorrhea in 50% of patients is clinically significant. The finding of heavier menstrual bleeding of patients on aspirin is contrary to the results of other prostaglandin inhibitors (Anderson, Guillebaud, Haynes, and Turnbull, 1976) and most likely reflects inhibition of platelet aggregation by this agent. Since salicylate works by inhibiting prostasynthetase and not by antagonizing prostaglandin action, it is most effective when started 3 days prior to the menses. Our results indicate that inhibition of prostaglandin synthesis by salicylates, given in advance of the menses, is an effective agent for alleviating incapacitating dysmenorrhea among some adolescents.

4. SUMMARY

In conclusion, we have reviewed the epidemiologic evidence which demonstrates that dysmenorrhea occurs in approximately 60% of American adolescent girls and that it is a major cause of excess school absence. Dysmenorrhea is strongly correlated with a variety of biologic variables, the strongest of these being gynecologic age, or the number of years since menarche. We have reviewed evidence of the role of prostaglandins in the pathogensis of dysmenorrhea and, finally, described the effect of a prostaglandin inhibitor, namely aspirin, on reducing or eliminating dysmenorrhea.

What about future clinical and research considerations? First, as practitioners of preventive medicine and providers of anticipatory guidance in the broadest sense, we must encourage the school, families, and other professionals to assist in the preparation for menarche and to initiate discussions of normal puberty at appropriate developmental ages. It is distressing to learn that so many adolescents still approach their first period without any knowledge of menarche. Recent books such as *Period* by Gardner-Loulan, Lopez, and Quackenbush (1979) and *Changing Bodies, Changing Lives* by Bell (1980) may help those who are unprepared educationally. However, those who are unprepared may have little access to such educational materials because of age, education, or family beliefs. Second, studies to determine the relative relationship of anovulatory and ovulatory cycles to dysmenorrhea in early puberty are needed. Longitudinal prospective studies using serum progesterone as a marker for ovulation would seem to be the best method of looking at this. Third, relatively little is known about endometrial prostaglandin variation in early puberty. As mentioned earlier, one study has reported a fivefold change in prostaglandin levels between anovulatory and subsequent ovulatory cycles. Longitudinal prospective studies that will measure local endometrial prostaglandin levels in adolescents beginning with anovulatory cycles and continuing through the development of regular ovulatory cycles are clearly warranted. The technology to obtain prostaglandins by a noninvasive method of extracting them from menstrual tampons or pads now exists (Chan et al., 1979; Chan and Hill, 1978), allowing analysis by radioimmunoassay. Finally, an interdisciplinary approach to research in dysmenorrhea is clearly needed. In the past, most of the research has either been done by physicians on the one hand or social scientists on the other. If we are ever to truly understand the phenomena of dysmenorrhea, collaborative research by physicians and social scientists that looks at both the psychosocial as well as the medical variables will be necessary.

Prostaglandins have been firmly implicated in the pathogenesis of dysmenorrhea. The ovulation hypothesis is tempting to relate increased levels of prostaglandins to the development of ovulatory cycles. However, the occurrence of dysmenorrhea in some anovulatory adolescents and the failure of oral contraceptives to prevent dysmenorrhea in all adolescents challenge this theory. The nature of the relationship between ovulation, prostaglandins, and sociocultural factors is unknown. The psychoneuroendocrinology of dysmenorrhea remains elusive at this point, waiting to be unraveled.

REFERENCES

Anderson, A. B. M., Guillebaud, J., Haynes, P. J., and Turnbull, A. C. Reduction of menstrual blood loss by prostaglandin synthetase inhibitors. *Lancet*, 1976, *1*, 774.

Bell, R. *Changing bodies, changing lives: A book for teens on sex and relationships*. New York: Random House, 1980.

Brooks-Gunn, J., and Ruble, D. N. Dysmenorrhea in adolescence. Presented to the American Psychologic Association meetings, New York, September, 1979.

Budoff, P. W. Use of mefenamic acid in the treatment of primary dysmenorrhea. *Journal of the American Medical Association*, 1979, *241*, 2713.

Chan, W. Y., and Hill, J. C. Determination of menstrual prostaglandin levels in nondysmenorrheic and dysmenorrheic subjects. *Prostaglandins*, 1978, *15*, 365.

Chan, W. Y., Dawood, M. Y., and Fuchs, F. Relief of dysmenorrhea with prostaglandin synthetase inhibitor ibuprofen: effect on prostaglandin levels in menstrual fluid. *American Journal of Obstetrics and Gynecology*, 1979, *135*, 102.

Cuskey, W. R. A systems approach to the study of drug abuse. National Institute on Drug Abuse, Psychosocial Branch, July, 1976 (RO1-DA00813).

Douglas, W. W. Autacoids. In A. G. Gilman, L. S. Goodman, and A. Gilman (Eds.), *The Pharmacological Basis of Therapeutics*. 6th ed. New York: Macmillan, 1980, 608.

Gardner-Loulan, J., Lopez, B., and Quackenbush, M. *Period*. California: New Glide, 1979.

Golub, L. J., Lang, W. R., and Menduke, H. The incidence of dysmenorrhea in high school girls. *Postgraduate Medical Journal*, 1958, *23*, 38.

Gough, H. G. Personality factors related to reported severity of menstrual distress. *Journal of Abnormal Psychology*, 1975, *84*, 59.

Gross, R. T., and Duke, P. M. The effect of early versus late physical maturation on adolescent behavior. *Pediatric Clinics of North America: Adolescent Medicine*, 1980, *27*, 71–78.

Halbert, D. R., Demers, L. M., and Jones, D. E. Dysmenorrhea and prostaglandins. *Obstetrics and Gynecology*, 1976, *31*, 77.

Klein, J. R., and Litt, I. F. Epidemiology of adolescent dysmenorrhea. *Pediatrics*, 1981, *68*, 66.

Klein, J. R., Litt, I. F., Rosenberg, A., and Udall, L. The effect of aspirin on dysmenorrhea in adolescents. *Journal of Pediatrics*, 1981, *98*, 987.

Lundstrom, V. Treatment of primary dysmenorrhea with prostaglandin synthetase inhibitors: A promising therapeutic alternative. *Acta Obstetricia et Gynecologica Scandinavica*, 1978, *57*, 421.

Lundstrom, V., and Green, K. Endogenous levels of prostaglandins $F_{2\alpha}$ and its main metabolites in plasma and endometrium of normal and dysmenorrheic women. *American Journal of Obstetrics and Gynecology*, 1978, *130*, 640.

Moos, R. *Menstrual distress questionnaire manual*. Stanford, Ca.: Social Ecology Laboratory, Department of Psychiatry and Behavioral Sciences, Stanford University, 1977.

National Center for Health Statistics. *Plan and operation of a health examination survey of U.S. youths 12–17 years of age*. Public Health Service Pub. No. 1,000, Series 1, No. 8, September 1969.

National Center for Health Statistics. *Age at menarche.* United States, Series 11, No. 233, 1974.

Novell, H. A. Psychological factors in premenstrual tension. *Journal of Clinical Obstetrics and Gynecology*, 1965, *1*, 222.

Pickles, V. R. A plain muscle stimulant in the menstrum. *Nature*, 1957, *180*, 1198.

Pickles, V. R. Prostaglandins in the human endometrium. *International Journal of Fertility*, 1967, *12*, 335.

Piers, E., and Harris, D. *The Piers-Harris children's self-concept scale.* Nashville, Tennessee: Counselor Recording and Tests, 1969.

Pulkkinen, M. O., and Kaihola, H. L. Mefenamic acid in dysmenorrhea. *Acta Obstetricia et Gynecologica Scandinavica*, 1977, *56*, 75.

Rauh, J. L. Maturational age and its clinical applications. In J. R. Gallagher, F. P. Heald, and D. C. Garell (Eds.), *Medical care of the adolescent*, 3d ed. New York: Appleton-Century Crofts, 1976, 25.

Ruble, D. N. Premenstrual symptoms: A reinterpretation. *Science*, 1977, *197(4300)*, 291.

Ruble, D. N., and Brooks-Gunn, J. A developmental analysis of menstrual distress in adolescence. In R. C. Friedman (Ed.), *Behavior and the menstrual cycle.* New York: Marcel-Dekker, 1982, in press.

Shangold, M. M., Aksel, S., Schomberg, D. W., and Hammond, C. B. Plasma prostaglandin $F_{2\alpha}$ levels in dysmenorrheic women. *Fertility and Sterility*, 1976, *27*, 1171.

Starfield, B., Gross, E., Wood, M., Pantell, R., Allen, C., Gordon, B. I., Moffatt, P., Drachman, R., and Katz, H. Psychosocial and psychosomatic diagnoses in primary care of children. *Pediatrics*, 1980, *66*, 159.

Tanner, J. M. *Growth at adolescence.* 2d ed. Oxford, England: Blackwell Scientific, 1962.

Thorpe, L. P., Clark, W. W., and Tiegs, E. Q. *Manual, The California test of personality.* Monterey, Ca.: McGraw-Hill, 1953.

Vane, J. R. Inhibition of prostaglandin synthesis as a mechanism of action for aspirin-like drugs. *Nature (New Biology)*, 1971, *231*, 232.

Widholm, O. Dysmenorrhea during adolescence. *Acta Obstetricia et Gynecologica Scandinavica, Supplement*, 1979, *87*, 61.

Ylikorkala, O., and Dawood, M. W. New concepts in dysmenorrhea. *American Journal of Obstetrics and Gynecology*, 1978, *130*, 833.

Chapter 5

Pituitary Desensitization with a Long-Acting Luteinizing-Hormone-Releasing Hormone Analog
A Potential New Treatment for Idiopathic Precocious Puberty

GORDON B. CUTLER, JR., FLORENCE COMITE, JEAN RIVIER,
WYLIE W. VALE, D. LYNN LORIAUX, AND
WILLIAM F. CROWLEY, JR.

1. INTRODUCTION

Normal puberty appears to be initiated by the pulsatile secretion of luteinizing-hormone-releasing hormone (LHRH) from the hypothalamus at a frequency of about 1 pulse/hr (see Figure 1) (Boyar, Finkelstein, Roffwarg, Kapen, Weitzman, and Hellman, 1972; Knobil, 1980). The pulsatile secretion of LHRH stimulates secretion of the pituitary gonadotropins, luteinizing hormone (LH) and follicle-stimulating hormone (FSH), which in turn stimulate gonadal sex steroid secretion. The rise in the gonadal sex steroids estradiol and testosterone induces the secondary sexual changes at puberty.

GORDON B. CUTLER, JR., FLORENCE COMITE, AND D. LYNN LORIAUX • Developmental Endocrinology Branch, National Institute of Child Health and Human Development, National Institutes of Health, Bethesda, Maryland 20205.   JEAN RIVIER AND WYLIE W. VALE • Peptide Biology Laboratory, Salk Institute, San Diego, California 92138.   WILLIAM F. CROWLEY, JR. • Vincent Research Laboratories, Departments of Internal Medicine and Gynecology, Massachusetts General Hospital, Boston, Massachusetts 02114.

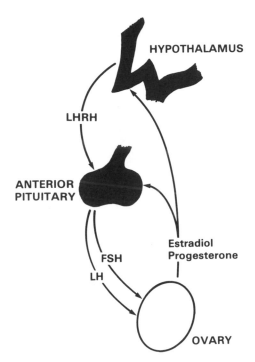

Figure 1. Diagram of the hypothalamic–pituitary–ovarian axis.

When puberty first begins the gonadotropin secretory pulses have greater amplitude during sleep, causing marked sleep–wake differences in plasma gonadotropin levels (Boyar et al., 1972). As puberty progresses a uniform pattern of pulses emerges throughout the day, eliminating sleep–wake differences.

Studies in prepubertal rhesus monkeys have illustrated the pivotal role of LHRH in initiating puberty (Knobil, 1980). Within 7 weeks of beginning a pulsatile LHRH infusion, prepubertal female monkeys develop adult levels of gonadotropins and sex steroids and the onset of menarche. Amenorrheic women with anorexia nervosa, who have gonadotropin levels similar to prepubertal children, also develop an adult pattern of gonadotropin secretion when given a pulsatile LHRH infusion (Marshall and Kelch, 1979). Additionally, Knobil's studies have demonstrated the critical importance of the frequency of LHRH pulsation. Reducing the pulse frequency to once every 3 hr causes a marked fall in plasma LH, while increasing the pulse frequency to 5 pulses/hr or to continuous infusion provokes a striking fall in gonadotropins. This latter phenomenon has been termed a "desensitization response."

The mechanism causing the increased gonadotropin secretion at puberty remains an enigma. Kelch, Kaplan, and Grumbach (1973) observed that the hypothalamic–pituitary–gonadal axis becomes less sensitive to negative-feedback inhibition by estradiol following the onset of puberty. They proposed the "gonadostat" hypothesis that puberty is initiated by the decreasing sensitivity of the hypothalamic–pituitary–gonadal axis to inhibition by estradiol. However, studies of castrated animals and of children with gonadal dysgenesis have shown increased gonadotropin secretion at the normal time of puberty, despite unmeasurably low levels of estradiol (Conte, Grumbach, and Kaplan, 1975; Ryan and Foster, 1980). This suggests a primary central nervous system contribution to the gonadotropin changes at puberty that is independent of steroid feedback. Further information about the mechanisms of normal puberty and its disorders is available in several recent reviews (Knobil, 1980; Ojeda, Andrews, Advis, and White, 1980; Petersen and Taylor, 1980; Sizonenko, 1978a,b; Styne and Grumbach, 1978).

In idiopathic precocious puberty the normal physiologic changes of puberty occur prematurely. For reasons that are unknown this disorder most frequently affects girls. The physical consequences of precocious puberty are accelerated somatic and secondary sexual development during childhood with short stature in adulthood due to early fusion of the bone epiphyses. The psychological consequences of precocious puberty are considerable for both parent and child. Parents are embarrassed by the disorder and find it difficult to discuss with others. Concern about sexuality also interferes with the community support that would be accorded in the case of most other childhood disorders. In the case of one of our patients the neighborhood parents forbade their children to play with our patient, apparently because they did not want to raise questions about breast development and menses in their own children.

The only treatment for precocious puberty available in the United States is medroxyprogesterone acetate, a synthetic progestin. This agent inhibits LH and FSH secretion through negative-feedback action on the hypothalamus or pituitary (Rifkind, Kulin, Cargille, Rayford, and Ross, 1969). It frequently causes cessation of menses and regression of breast enlargement, but it often fails to halt the rapid somatic growth and bone age advancement (Kaplan, Ling, and Irani, 1968; Richman, Underwood, French, and Van Wyk, 1971; Sadeghi-Nejad, Kaplan, and Grumbach, 1971). In addition side effects of adrenal suppression (Kaplan et al. 1968; Mathews, Abrams, and Morishima, 1970; Richman et al. 1971; Sadeghi-Nejad et al. 1971), cushingoid features (e.g., moon-shaped face and weight gain) (Richman et al. 1971), and chromosomal abnormalities (Camacho, Williams, and Montalvo, 1972) have been observed. Thus, we have sought a new treatment for precocious puberty that will have greater efficacy and fewer side effects.

The most logical alternative to medroxyprogesterone treatment, in view of the critical influence of LHRH in initiating puberty, would be an antagonist of LHRH. At the time of our studies, however, there were no LHRH antagonists sufficiently potent for clinical use. We chose, therefore, to take advantage of the observation that intermittent administration of potent agonist analogs of LHRH would "desensitize" the pituitary and inhibit secretion of LH and FSH (Berquist, Nillius, and Wide, 1979; Crowley, Vale, Beitins, Rivier, Rivier, and McArthur, 1979; Dericks-Tan, Hammer, and Tauberg, 1977; Johnson, Gendrich, and White, 1976; Sandow, von Rechenberg, Jerzabek, and Stoll, 1978). This property of LHRH agonist administration suggested that these agents might be useful as a treatment for idiopathic precocious puberty (Crowley, Comite, Vale, Rivier, Loriaux, and Cutler, 1981). This report describes our experience with the short-term treatment of idiopathic precocious puberty with such an LHRH agonist.

2. METHODS

2.1. LHRH Analog

The LHRH analog D-Trp^6-Pro^9-NEt-LHRH (LHRH$_a$) was dissolved in normal saline/10% mannitol to ensure long-term stability (Dermody and Reed, 1976). Once dissolved, the compound was stored at $-20°C$ until prescribed. Each batch underwent bioassay prior to use, and no loss of biologic activity was observed after periods of storage as long as 12 months. The parents were instructed to keep the preparation frozen until use. The LHRH$_a$ was injected subcutaneously by a parent using an insulin syringe. The frequency of administration of the LHRH$_a$ was based on previous studies which demonstrated that daily administration of this analog would suppress gonadotropin secretion (Crowley et al., 1979).

2.2. Patients

The clinical features of the five patients with idiopathic precocious puberty are shown in Table 1. The diagnosis of idiopathic true precocious puberty was made after excluding a brain, adrenal, or ovarian neoplasm, or tumor by computerized tomography of the head and abdomen and ultrasonography of the adrenal and pelvis. Two adrenal hormones, plasma 17-hydroxyprogesterone and 11-deoxycortisol, were measured to exclude the diagnosis of an inherited deficiency of the adrenal enzymes

Table 1. Characteristics of Five Girls with Idiopathic Precocious Puberty

Patient no.	Age (yr)	Height[a] (cm)	Weight[a] (kg)	Stage of puberty[b]			Bone age (yr)	Vaginal maturation index score[c]
				Breast	Pubic hair	Menses		
1	2.3	97 (97)	22 (> 99)	II	II	+	5	78
2	4.9	124 (> 99)	27 (> 99)	III	II	+	10	50
3	7.3	131 (85)	33 (96)	III	IV	0	10	60
4	7.8	136 (93)	40 (> 99)	III	III	+	10	52
5	5.2	123 (99)	20 (50)	III	II	0	9	53

[a]Values in parentheses represent percentile for age.
[b]According to the classification of Tanner (1978, pp. 28–39).
[c]An index of estrogen effect on the vaginal mucosa calculated by adding the percent superficial cells multiplied by 1.0 to the percent intermediate cells multiplied by 0.5 (Meisels, 1967).

21-hydroxylase or 11-hydroxylase. These enzymatic deficiencies can increase the adrenal contribution to plasma testosterone, causing accelerated growth and virilization. Serum human chorionic gonadotropin was measured to rule out a human chorionic gonadotropin-producing tumor.

2.3. Protocol

Patients were admitted to the Clinical Center of the National Institutes of Health or the General Clinical Research Center of the Massachusetts General Hospital. Pretherapy evaluation consisted of basal serum gonadotropin determinations every 20 min for 4 hr during the day (10 AM–2 PM) and night (10 PM–2 AM). This sampling protocol was chosen to allow measurement of the gonadotropin pulses during sleep and wake periods. Four serum estradiol measurements were obtained at the beginning and end of these time periods. On Day 2, an LHRH stimulation test was performed. Serum gonadotropins were measured at -30, -15, 0, 15, 30, 45, 60, 90, 120, and 180 min following intravenous administration of 100 μg LHRH at Time 0. (Patient 3 received 2.5 μg/kg LHRH subcutaneously at time 0 and serum gonadotropin measurements at 0, 30, 60, 90, 120, and 180 min.) On Day 3 a vaginal specimen for cytology was obtained to determine the maturation index. The vaginal smears were evaluated by the cytology laboratory without knowledge of the patient's therapy. Treatment with the LHRH analog was then initiated. Luteinizing-hormone-releasing hormone analog, 4 μg/kg, was given daily by subcutaneous injection for 2 months. During the 8th week of therapy, the patients were reevaluated by the same protocol as before therapy. Luteinizing hormone-releasing hormone analog treatment was then discontinued in Patients 1–3. These three patients returned during the 8th week after stopping therapy for a third inpatient evaluation identical to those prior to and during LHRH$_a$ administration. All patients received biweekly outpatient monitoring during the 2 months of therapy and, in Patients 1–3, during the subsequent 2-month recovery period. These evaluations consisted of inspection of breasts and pubic hair, and measurement of height, weight, vaginal maturation index score, and plasma estradiol (three measurements at 20-min intervals in 4 of the 5 cases; no measurements in Patient 3).

2.4. *Hormone Assays*

Luteinizing hormone, FSH, and estradiol were measured by radioimmunoassay using a modification of previously described methods (Cargille and Rayford, 1970; Odell, Rayford, and Ross, 1967a; Odell, Ross, and Rayford, 1967b; Loriaux, Ruder, and Lipsett, 1971). Delayed addition of trace after 3 days at 4°C reduced the limit of sensitivity for both LH and FSH to 0.5 mIU/ml (2nd International Reference Preparation— Human Menopausal Gonadotropin).

2.5. *Statistical Analysis*

Statistical comparisons between groups were made using paired Student's t-test after logarithmic transformation to achieve uniformity of variance. All data are expressed as mean ± SEM.

3. RESULTS

All the patients had measurable basal gonadotropin levels and a pubertal response to LHRH stimulation prior to therapy (see Figure 2, "pretherapy"). Following 8 weeks of treatment with LHRH$_a$, basal and peak gonadotropins fell significantly compared to pretherapy levels (see Figure 2, "on therapy"). Basal LH fell from 8 ± 3 to 3 ± 1 mIU/ml ($p <$ 0.025) during treatment, while LHRH-stimulated peak LH decreased from 43 ± 10 to 5 ± 1 mIU/ml ($p < 0.01$). Basal and peak FSH declined from 10 ± 2 to 3 ± 1 ($p < 0.01$) and 29 ± 3 to 4 ± 1 mIU/ml ($p < 0.001$), respectively. Basal gonadotropins and the response to the LHRH stimulation test had returned to pretherapy levels 2 months after discontinuing the LHRH analog (see Figure 2, "posttherapy"). Basal and peak LH

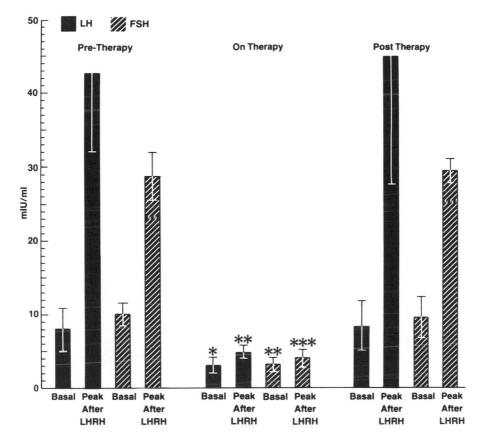

Figure 2. Effect of LHRH analog therapy on basal and LHRH-stimulated gonadotropin levels in five girls with idiopathic precocious puberty. The basal LH and FSH values for each patient were the mean of 26 measurements obtained at 20-min intervals from 10 AM to 2 PM and from 10 PM to 2 AM. The "peak after LHRH" values represent the highest LH and FSH level attained during the standard LHRH stimulation test performed in each patient. The results "on therapy" were obtained during the 8th week of treatment. The "posttherapy" levels were obtained in Patients 1–3 8 weeks after discontinuing LHRH$_a$ treatment. *, $p < 0.025$; **, $p < 0.01$; ***, $p < 0.001$ compared to pretherapy levels.

were 8 ± 4 and 45 ± 17 mIU/ml. Basal FSH was 10 ± 3 and peak FSH was 30 ± 2 mIU/ml. Figure 3 shows the complete LHRH stimulation tests. LHRH$_a$ therapy completely suppressed the LH and FSH response to exogenous LHRH (see Figure 3, "on therapy"). Two months after LHRH$_a$ therapy was discontinued, both the time-course and the magnitude of the response to LHRH were nearly identical to the pubertal pattern observed before therapy.

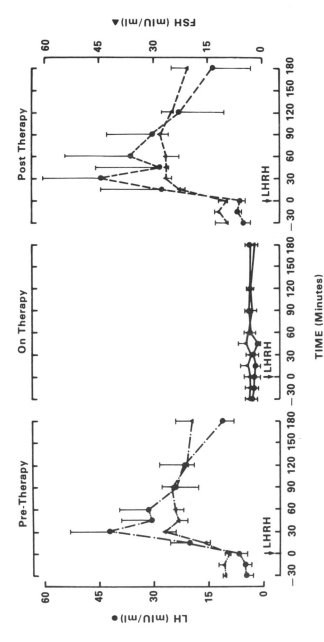

Figure 3. Effect of LHRH analog therapy on gonadotropin response to exogenous LHRH in five girls with idiopathic precocious puberty. As in Figure 1, the posttherapy data are from Patients 1–3.

Plasma estradiol concentrations also fell (28 ± 5 to 16 ± 2 pg/ml) by the 8th week of $LHRH_a$ therapy ($p < 0.05$, see Figure 4). Two weeks following cessation of treatment, plasma estradiol did not differ significantly from the pretreatment level.

The maturation index score decreased 25% following 8 weeks of treatment with $LHRH_a$, a change which did not reach statistical significance ($p = 0.09$, see Figure 5). Two weeks after discontinuing $LHRH_a$ therapy, the maturation index score had returned to the pretreatment value.

4. Discussion

The LHRH analog $D-Trp^6-Pro^9-NEt-LHRH$ possesses greater potency and a longer duration of action than the native decapeptide (Vale, Rivier, Brown, and Rivier, 1977). Continuous administration of native sequence LHRH or intermittent administration of long-acting LHRH analogs elicits "pituitary desensitization" and a resulting decrease in pituitary gonadotropin secretion (Berquist et al., 1979; Crowley et al., 1979, 1981; Dericks-Tan et al., 1977; Johnson et al., 1976; Knobil, 1980; Sandow et al., 1978). The pituitary gonadotrophs apparently require intermittent periods devoid of stimulation by LHRH or its analogs to maintain sustained gonadotropin release. Studies in the rhesus monkey suggest that physiological levels of pituitary gonadotropins are achieved when the LHRH pulse frequency is approximately 1/hr, with no LHRH stimulation for the majority of the interval between pulses (Knobil, 1980).

The daily administration of $LHRH_a$ for 2 months to five girls with idiopathic precocious puberty lowered gonadotropin and estradiol secretion and abolished the gonadotropin response to exogenous LHRH. Reversal of these effects was seen 2 months after cessation of therapy. Although these data provide convincing evidence for pituitary desensitization to LHRH, an additional direct effect of $LHRH_a$ inhibiting steroidogenesis at the gonadal level cannot be excluded. Recent studies in animals have shown that LHRH and its agonist analogs can directly inhibit steroidogenesis by the ovary and testis in addition to their pituitary site of action (Hsueh and Erickson, 1979; Clayton, Harwood, and Catt, 1979; Bourne, Regiani, Payne, and Marshall, 1980).

Both agonist and antagonist analogs of LHRH can inhibit gonadotropin secretion. We chose to use an LHRH agonist rather than an antagonist in this study because only the agonist analogs are sufficiently potent for clinical use. The development of increasingly potent antagonist analogs of LHRH, however, suggests that in the future it may be

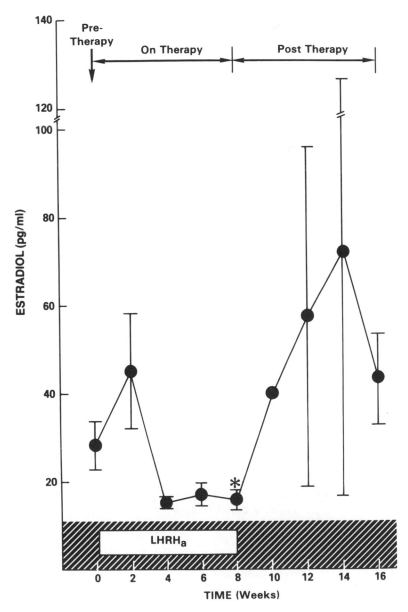

Figure 4. Effect of LHRH analog therapy on plasma estradiol in five girls with idiopathic precocious puberty. The shaded area represents values below the detection limit of the assay. At 4 weeks, only the data from Patients 1, 2, and 4 are available. Posttherapy data are from Patients 1–3. *, $p < 0.05$ compared to pretherapy level.

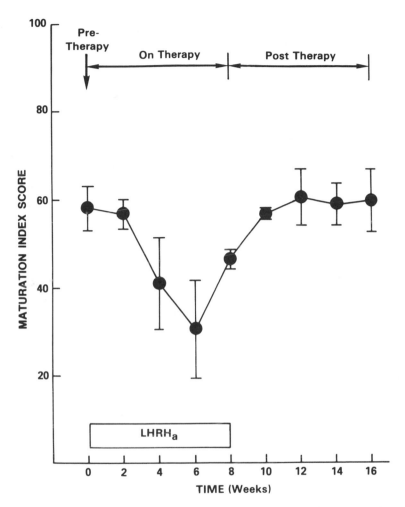

Figure 5. Effect of LHRH analog therapy on vaginal maturation index score in five girls with idiopathic precocious puberty. The legend to Table 1 presents the method of calculating the maturation index score. Posttherapy data are from Patients 1–3.

possible to compare LHRH agonists and antagonists in the therapy of precocious puberty (Rivier, Rivier, and Vale, 1980).

The results of this short-term study of LHRH$_a$ treatment in idiopathic precocious puberty appear promising. No significant adverse affects were seen and full recovery to pretreatment levels of sex steroids was observed in all subjects in whom LHRH$_a$ administration was discontinued. Before the merit of this new therapy can be fully assessed, however, investigation of the effects of long-term treatment on pubertal progression and bone maturation will be necessary.

5. SUMMARY

A fully effective therapy for idiopathic precocious puberty is not available. The pituitary "desensitization" observed in adults during the administration of the luteinizing hormone-releasing hormone analog, D-Trp^{6}Pro^9-NEt-LHRH (LHRH$_a$), suggested that this drug might be useful in treating precocious puberty. We have treated five girls with idiopathic precocious puberty (ages 2–8) with daily subcutaneous injections of LHRH$_a$ for 8 weeks. Prior to treatment the girls had Tanner II–IV pubertal development, advanced bone age, estrogen effect by vaginal smear, measurable basal gonadotropin levels with pulsatile nocturnal secretion, and a pubertal gonadotropin response to LHRH. Irregular vaginal bleeding was present in three patients. Luteinizing hormone-releasing hormone analog therapy significantly decreased basal ($p < 0.025$) and LHRH-stimulated ($p < 0.01$) gonadotropin levels as well as serum estradiol ($p < 0.05$). The vaginal maturation index score, which reflects estrogen effect, fell by 25%. Eight weeks after stopping treatment, all hormonal values and the vaginal maturation index had returned to pretherapy levels. No significant adverse drug reactions were encountered. Luteinizing hormone-releasing hormone analogs merit further study as a potential new treatment for idiopathic precocious puberty.

ACKNOWLEDGMENTS. We greatly appreciate the dedicated expertise of Rebecca Raymond, Penny Colbert, Barbara Filmore, Dolores Schwartz, Carolyn Albers, and Nancy Delaney. We acknowledge the tremendous support of the referring physicians, associates, fellows, and nurses involved in this study.

REFERENCES

Berquist, C., Nillius, S. J., and Wide, L. Intranasal gonadotropin-releasing hormone agonist as a contraceptive agent. *Lancet*, 1979, *2*, 215–216.

Bourne, G. A., Regiani, S., Payne, A. H., and Marshall, J. C. Testicular GnRH receptors— Characterization and localization on interstitial tissues. *Journal of Clinical Endocrinology and Metabolism*, 1980, *51*, 407–409.

Boyar, R., Finkelstein, J., Roffwarg, H., Kapen, S., Weitzman, E., and Hellman, L. Synchronization of augmented luteinizing hormone secretion with sleep during puberty. *New England Journal of Medicine*, 1972, *287*, 582–586.

Camacho, A. M., Williams, D. L., and Montalvo, J. M. Alterations of testicular histology and chromosomes in patients with constitutional sexual precocity treated with medroxyprogesterone acetate. *Journal of Clinical Endocrinology and Metabolism*, 1972, *34*, 279–286.

Cargille, C. M., and Rayford, P. L. Characterization of antisera for human follicle stimulating hormone assay. *Journal of Laboratory and Clinical Medicine*, 1970, *75*, 1030–1040.

Clayton, R. N., Harwood, J. P., and Catt, K. J. Gonadotropin-releasing hormone analogue binds to luteal cells and inhibits progesterone production *Nature*, 1979, *282*, 90–92.

Conte, F. A., Grumbach, M. M. and Kaplan, S. L. A diphasic pattern of gonadotropin secretion in patients with the syndrome of gonadal dysgenesis. *Journal of Clinical Endocrinology and Metabolism*, 1975, *40*, 670–674.

Crowley, W. F., Vale, W., Beitins, I. Z., Rivier, J., Rivier, C. and McArthur, J. Chronic administration of a long-acting LRF agonist (D-Trp[6]-Pro[9]-NET-LRF), in hypogonadotropic hypogonadism: The critical nature of dosage and frequency in enhancement, extinction and restoration of gonadotropin responsiveness. Sixty first Annual Meeting of the Endocrine Society, Los Angeles, June 1979, Abstract no. 16, p. 76.

Crowley, W. F. Jr., Comite, F., Vale, W., Rivier, J., Loriaux, D. L., and Cutler, G. B. Jr. Therapeutic use of pituitary desensitization with a long-acting LHRH agonist: A potential new treatment for idiopathic precocious puberty. *Journal of Clinical Endocrinology and Metabolism*, 1981, *52*, 370–372.

Dericks-Tan, J. S. E., Hammer, E., and Tauberg, H.-D. The effect of D-Ser-(TBU)[6]-LH-RH-EA[10] upon gonadotropin release in normally cyclic women. *Journal of Clinical Endocrinology and Metabolism*, 1977, *45*, 597–600.

Dermody, W. C., and Reed, J. R. Effect of storage on LHRH. *New England Journal of Medicine*, 1976, *295*, 173.

Hsueh, A. T. W., and Erickson, F. G. Extra-pituitary action of gonadotropin-releasing hormone: Direct inhibition of ovarian steroidogenesis. *Science*, 1979, *204*, 854–855.

Johnson, E. S., Gendrich, R. L., and White, W. F. Delay of puberty and inhibition of reproductive processes in the rat by a gonadotropin-releasing hormone agonist analog. *Fertility and Sterility*, 1976, *27*, 853–860.

Kaplan, S. A., Ling, S. M., and Irani, N. G. Idiopathic sexual precocity: Therapy with medroxyprogesterone. *American Journal of Diseases of Children*, 1968, *116*, 591–598.

Kelch, R. P., Kaplan, S. L., and Grumbach, M. M. Suppression of urinary and plasma follicle-stimulating hormone by exogenous estrogens in prepubertal and pubertal children. *Journal of Clinical Investigation*, 1973, *52*, 1122–1128.

Knobil, E. The neuroendocrine control of the menstrual cycle. *Recent Progress in Hormone Research*, 1980, *36*, 53–88.

Loriaux, D. L., Ruder, H. J., and Lipsett, M. B. The measurement of estrone sulfate in plasma. *Steroids*, 1971, *18*, 463–472.

Marshall, J. C., and Kelch, R. P. Low dose pulsatile gonadotropin-releasing hormone in anorexia nervosa: A model of human pubertal development. *Journal of Clinical Endocrinology and Metabolism*, 1979, *49*, 712–718.

Mathews, J. H., Abrams, C. A. L., and Morishima, A. Pituitary-adrenal function in ten patients receiving medroxyprogesterone acetate for true precocious puberty. *Journal of Clinical Endocrinology and Metabolism*, 1970, *30*, 653–658.

Meisels, A. That maturation value. *Acta Cytologica*, 1967, *11*, 249–252.

Odell, W. D., Rayford, P. L., and Ross, G. T. Simple, partially automated method for radioimmunoassay of human thyroid stimulating, growth, luteinizing and follicle stimulating hormone. *Journal of Laboratory and Clinical Medicine*, 1967a, *70*, 973–980.

Odell, W. D., Ross, G. T., and Rayford, P. L. Radioimmunoassay for luteinizing hormone in human plasma or serum: Physiological studies. *Journal of Clinical Investigation,* 1967b, *46,* 248–255.

Ojeda, S. R., Andrews, W. W., Advis, J. P., and White, S. S. Recent advances in the endocrinology of puberty. *Endocrine Reviews,* 1980, *1,* 228–257.

Petersen, A. C., and Taylor, B. The biological approach to adolescence: Biological change and psychological adaptation. In J. Adelson (Ed.), *Handbook of adolescent psychology.* New York: John Wiley and Sons, 1980, 117–155.

Rabin, D., and McNeil, L. W. Pituitary and gonadal desensitization after continuous luteinizing hormone-releasing hormone infusion in normal females. *Journal of Clinical Endocrinology and Metabolism,* 1980, *51,* 873–876.

Richman, R. A., Underwood, L. E., French, F. S., and Van Wyk, J. J. Adverse effects of large doses of medroxyprogesterone (MPA) in idiopathic isosexual precocity. *Journal of Pediatrics,* 1971, *79,* 963–971.

Rifkind, A. B., Kulin, H. E., Cargille, C. M., Rayford, P. L., and Ross, G. T. Suppression of urinary excretion of luteinizing hormone (LH) and follicle-stimulating hormone (FSH) by medroxyprogesterone acetate. *Journal of Clinical Endocrinology and Metabolism,* 1969, *29,* 506–513.

Rivier, C., Rivier, J., and Vale, W. Antireproductive effects of a potent gonadotropin-releasing hormone antagonist in the male rat. *Science,* 1980, *210,* 93–95.

Ryan, K. D., and Foster, D. L. Neuroendocrine mechanisms involved in onset of puberty in the female: Concepts derived from the lamb. *Federation Proceedings,* 1980, *39,* 2372–2377.

Sadeghi-Nejad, A., Kaplan, S. L., and Grumbach, M. M. The effect of medroxyprogesterone acetate on adrenocortical function in children with precocious puberty. *Journal of Pediatrics,* 1971, *78,* 616–624.

Sandow, J., von Rechenberg, W., Jerzabek, G., and Stoll, W. Pituitary gonadotropin inhibition by a highly active analog of luteinizing hormone-releasing hormone. *Fertility and Sterility,* 1978, *30,* 205–209.

Sizonenko, P. C. Endocrinology in preadolescents and adolescents. I. Hormonal changes during normal puberty. *American Journal of Diseases of Children,* 1978a, *132,* 704–712.

Sizonenko, P. C. Preadolescent and adolescent endocrinology: Physiology and physiopathology. II. Hormonal changes during abnormal pubertal development. *American Journal of Diseases of Children,* 1978b, *132,* 797–805.

Styne, D. M., and Grumbach, M. M. Puberty in the male and female: Its physiology and disorders. In S. S. C. Yen, and R. Jaffee (Eds.), *Reproductive endocrinology.* Philadelphia: W. B. Saunders, 1978, 189–240.

Tanner, J. M. *Growth at adolescence.* Oxford, England: Blackwell Scientific, 1978.

Vale, W., Rivier, C., Brown, M., and Rivier, J. Pharmacology of thyrotropin releasing factor (TRF), luteinizing hormone releasing factor (LRH), and somatostatin. *Advances in Experimental Medicine and Biology,* 1977, *87,* 123–156.

Psychological Aspects of Puberty

Chapter 6

Alternative Constructions of Adolescent Growth

MARGARET S. FAUST

1. INTRODUCTION

Textbooks on adolescent development show a remarkable similarity in their descriptions of the physiological, social, and psychological changes that characterize the adolescent period. In addition to providing descriptive information, these textbooks almost uniformly present a discussion of the consequences of the timing of pubertal growth, such as an account of the impact which early or late maturing has upon individuals during the adolescent period and in the young adult years. Yet there seems to be little or no consensus when it comes to explaining how it is that somatic influences affect human behavior and personality development. An important but unanswered question is this: How do the physiological changes of puberty exert an impact upon social and psychological development?

The purpose of this paper is to suggest several ways of conceptualizing the relationship between the somatic changes at puberty and the later development of adolescents, particularly of girls. In case it seems odd that a psychologist would attempt to treat the biological aspects of puberty, I begin with a set of orienting statements by George Kelly, whose presuppositions I find particularly useful for an understanding of adolescence or of anything else that might be thought of as an "event of nature." According to Kelly, meaning is brought to an experience (for example, "puberty") when that event is construed and interpreted by

MARGARET S. FAUST • Department of Psychology, Scripps College, Claremont, California 91711.

someone. "Events don't carry their meanings engraved on their backs for us to discover" (Kelly, 1970, p. 3). Events are meaningful when and only when they are brought within a construction system. "We cannot say that constructs are essences distilled by the mind out of available reality. They are imposed upon events, not abstracted from them" (Kelly, 1970, p. 13). Thus, there are as many meanings as there are construction systems within which any event may be interpreted. As Kelly says,

> Consider . . . specifically the realms of psychology and physiology. Many of the same facts can be construed within either system. Are those facts "psychological facts" or are they "physiological facts"? Where do they really belong? Who gets possession of them, the psychologist or the physiologist? While this may seem like a silly question . . . some individuals get badly worked up over the protection of their exclusive rights to construe particular facts. The answer is, of course, that the events upon which facts are based hold no institutional loyalties . . . The same event may be construed simultaneously and profitably within various disciplinary systems. (Kelly, 1955, p. 10)

What construction systems are useful for viewing the relationships between individual variation in adolescent growth and later psychosocial outcomes? It is not a matter of indifference which system one chooses. One of the most stimulating consequences of meeting with other researchers in the field of adolescent development is that one becomes aware of the fruitfulness and power of different perspectives and construction systems. Each one highlights certain events of adolescence so that they can be perceived and understood more clearly. Depending upon the construction system adopted, one can anticipate and predict certain kinds of outcomes. Different questions may be best answered by different systems. Each system has its central focus with correspondingly appropriate strategies; but each also has its limitations in areas where the system lacks power to define or resolve particular issues.

In this paper, we will look at the phenomena of adolescent growth within the context of four different construction systems:

1. The period of pubertal growth in height, a developmental construction system which is used by some developmental researchers
2. An individual adolescent's construction of the meaning of bodily changes at adolescence
3. The advertising media's construction and portrayal of one dimension of feminine beauty
4. A system of investigating some of the personal constructs that are created and used by individual adolescents

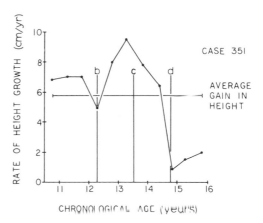

Figure 1. Individual velocity curve depicting period of pubertal growth in height. Onset (b) and end (d) are the first points, on either side of the apex, at which rate in height growth falls below the individual's 5-year average rate of height growth. Midpoint (c) divides the pubertal period into a first and second half.

2. Constructing the Process of Adolescent Growth

2.1. Adolescence as a Developmental Period

The concept of adolescence as a developmental period is commonly presented in discussions about adolescence, but the majority of research studies have not analyzed the phenomena of pubertal growth in relation to an extended or protracted period of development. There are many ways in which this might be accomplished. One method is to use Tanner stages, either as rated by physicians or by adolescent self-ratings (see Daniel, Chapter 3). Another way to identify this period of pubertal development is to use longitudinal measures of height, which can be transformed subsequently into a velocity growth curve. Following Stolz and Stolz (1951) one can define the period of pubertal growth in height as the time interval during which an individual's rate of height growth exceeds his/her own average rate over a specified 5-year period surrounding the individual's peak rate of height growth (see Figure 1). Although there are wide individual differences in the duration of the pubertal period and in the chronological age at which changes in rate of height growth occur, almost all significant pubertal events are encompassed within this developmentally time-framed period.

2.2. When Does Adolescence Begin?

Anyone who is about to embark on a research investigation of adolescent development should be forewarned: The somatic changes of adolescence may begin earlier than you think! To capture the beginning phase of adolescent growth for normally developing girls, one must begin well before they reach the second decade of life. This conclusion was brought home to me in a dramatic way when I undertook an analysis of the growth data for girls who had participated in the California Adolescent Study (now called the Oakland Growth Study). Beginning in fifth and sixth grades, 200 boys and girls were followed longitudinally until they had completed high school. Although Stolz and Stolz (1951) were able to derive complete height growth profiles for most of the male subjects from this sample, it was not possible to do so for most of the female cohort. Using the Stolz definition to identify the period of pubertal growth in height, there was only one case among the 100 girls for whom it was possible to trace the entire period. For the other 99 girls, the acceleration phase in height growth had already begun before the study was launched. The one remaining case was a late developer by anyone's standards. Her menarcheal age was 15.1 years.

The study of Somatic Development of Adolescent Girls (Faust, 1977) was based on a different data set that had been collected previously for the Berkeley Growth Study and the Guidance Study. Some measurements of growth were taken successively beginning during infancy, but assessments of secondary sexual development began at 8 or 9 years of age, depending upon the study. Nevertheless, in 11 of 94 cases the girls were beyond the first stages of breast development when the first assessment was taken; in 51 of 94 cases the first appearance of pubic hair (unpigmented down) could not be recorded because it occurred prior to the first assessment. Obviously, indicators of normal pubertal development of girls appear much earlier than researchers had formerly thought.

Each construction system employed in the study of adolescence brings with it certain advantages as well as limitations. What is problematic or interesting within one construction system may be irrelevant or meaningless within another system. Consider, for example, the relative absence of descriptive information about secondary sexual development of early-developing girls in the aforementioned longitudinal study. The fact that these data were missing would be considered much more unfortunate by some investigators than by others. An investigator who views adolescence as a developmental period of change in rate of height growth, for instance, would find it impossible to describe important concomitants of the early part of the pubertal period for girls who began their height growth period at a relatively young age. On the other hand, for an investigator who conceptualizes adolescence as the "teen years," the lack of longitudinal data on breast development and pubic hair growth of 8- and 9-year-old girls would not be very problematic. The very early appearance of secondary sexual characteristics is interesting and relevant for the first investigator but not for the second, precisely because the issue falls within the construction system of the former but not of the latter.

2.3. *Sequence and Timing of Pubertal Growth*

To describe the extensive physical changes that occur during the pubertal period would take us far afield, but a few examples will be given to illustrate some of the changes in size, proportioning, and appearance that take place during the course of female pubertal development. By using the pubertal period for height growth as a time line against which to view other phenomena of growth, we can learn something about the typical sequence and patterning of pubertal growth. In every dimension of growth, commonalities as well as individual differences in the timing of somatic change are found. For example, although there is always a period of rapid acceleration in rate of height growth followed by a slowing down in rate of growth prior to the attainment of adult stature, there are notable differences among girls in the intensity of growth, the duration of the growth period, the amount of gain in height, and the chronological age at which the pubertal period begins and ends.

The period of pubertal growth in height, which is defined in relation to an individual's own rate of height growth, typically lasts 2.8 years. Yet for some girls it may be as short as 1.5 years and for others it lasts as long as 4 years. Some girls enter the pubertal period as early as 8 years of age while others enter it as much as 5 years later. The average gain in height during this developmental period is considerable; for girls, it averages about 20 cm.

The time of most rapid growth in height, called the "apex," occurs near the midpoint (c) of the period, as shown in Figure 1. The 1½-year period immediately preceding onset (b) of the pubertal period has been designated the *prepubertal period*, and the corresponding period following the end (d) of the pubertal period for height is called the *postpubertal period*. The average velocity of growth in height is always greater during the pubertal period than during either the prepubertal or postpubertal periods. Of the total gain in height from the beginning of the prepubertal period to the end of the postpubertal period, 65% is attained during the pubertal period, 23% occurs during the prepubertal period, and only 12% is gained in the postpubertal period.

The gain in height throughout the prepubertal period and during the first half of the pubertal period is comprised largely of growth in leg length, which typically precedes acceleration in rate of stem length growth. It is this asynchrony in timing of growth in leg and stem length that is reflected in the typical long-legged appearance of adolescents who are at the beginning phase of the pubertal growth period.

Similarly, growth in shoulder width and hip width occurs asynchronously. For girls, the peak rate of growth in shoulder width is likely to precede that of hip width, but hip width actually increases more and at a relatively higher rate during the pubertal period than does shoulder width. Therefore, early in the pubertal period, girls characteristically have rather narrow hips in relation to their shoulder width. Late in the pubertal period and in the postpubertal period, after a time of sustained growth in hip width, girls acquire the shoulder–hip proportioning of adult women. Among girls, the ratio of shoulder width to hip width *decreases* significantly from the beginning of the pubertal period to the end of the postpubertal period, whereas among boys, shoulder/hip width ratio *increases* over this same developmental time period. (A higher ratio indicates that an individual has broad shoulders relative to hip size.)

A further example of somatic change during the pubertal period for height growth is the timing of growth in subcutaneous tissue. The thickness of subcutaneous fat increases for almost all girls, not only during the pubertal period but during the pre- and postpubertal periods as well. By contrast, boys typically show an increase in subcutaneous tissue during the prepubertal and postpubertal periods, but a decrease in thickness of fat during the pubertal growth period.

Some of the earliest indicators of female pubertal development are those of breast development and the growth of pubic hair. The appearance of unpigmented down in the pubic area typically precedes the initial enlargement of breasts (breast bud stage), but as noted above, both may occur among early-developing girls before they reach 8 or 9 years of age. The first appearance of pubic hair corresponds closely to the time of the prepubertal period, while the breast bud stage usually occurs around the beginning of the pubertal period for height growth.

The onset of the first menstrual period (menarche) is an important milestone for girls, but it is a relatively late event compared with the timing of growth in skeletal dimensions and in secondary sexual development. While most girls begin to menstruate between 10 and 16 years of age (the average age is about 12.8 years), menarche normally occurs after the most rapid rate of growth in bodily width and height has taken place. In fact, the rate of height growth decelerates markedly after menarche, and some girls gain only a fraction of an inch in height thereafter. For other girls, the rate in height growth after menarche slows down, but not so precipitously. Some, especially early developers, may continue to grow several inches in height after their first menstruation. Yet, the rate of gain in height is lower after menarche than before it.

The transition from childhood into early adolescence has not been studied as adequately as it warrants, perhaps because researchers have not fully recognized how early some girls begin to show signs of pubertal development. For early-developing girls, the physical status of childhood has been telescoped into a few short years, those of the primary grades in elementary school. Inasmuch as early pubertal development necessarily implies a shorter period of childhood, investigations of the impact of early pubertal onset would be enhanced by examining possible effects of a foreshortened period of childhood.

In Figure 2 it can be seen that early- and late-developing girls are in entirely different phases of pubertal development at the same chronological age. Moreover, early- and late-developing girls differ in ways other than in the age at which the changes occur. Girls who mature early are likely to have higher rates of height growth throughout the pubertal period and to have longer periods of height growth. Girls who are early developers are also shorter in all linear dimensions than are later developers when they reach corresponding developmental points; they are heavier for their height, proportionately shorter-legged, and they make greater gains in all linear dimensions during the pubertal period. Further, as indicated above, the amount of gain in height after menarche is greater for early-developing girls than it is for late developers. Even though these differences in growth rates and body proportions diminish by the end of the postpubertal period (and even more so by 18 years of age), any of these somatic variations may have an impact that lasts well beyond the pubertal transition period. Because early or late maturation is related to different somatic variables, it is not clear which qualities and what asynchronies contribute to later outcomes. Although some significant consequences have been reported (Berzonsky, 1981; Buck and Stavraky, 1967; Eichorn, 1963; Jones and Mussen, 1958; Peskin, 1973), the way in which individual adolescents interpret particular variations in timing warrants much more investigation. Certainly the temporal relations and quality of physical changes during adolescence should be considered in studies on continuity in female development.

Not only do girls differ from each other in the timing of physical change, but sex differences in the average timing of the pubertal changes occur. Figure 3 shows the cumulative percentage of boys and girls who reach the onset, apex, and end of the pubertal period for height growth at successive chronological ages. It can be seen that girls are completing the pubertal period at about the same age that boys are entering it. While the average girl enters the pubertal period for height growth at about 10 years of age, the average boy does so about 2½ years later. Perhaps even more importantly, it should be noted how young some of the girls are when they begin the period of acceleration in height growth. Some girls enter the pubertal period as young as 7½ years of age; the interquartile range of girls' ages at the onset of the pubertal period extends from about 9 years to 10½ years of age. When boys and girls are considered together, the range in age at onset of the pubertal period is very wide indeed; it extends from 7.5 years to 14.75 years!

The variation in levels of maturity in this sample of normal girls and boys around the chronological ages of 11 and 12 years is especially note-

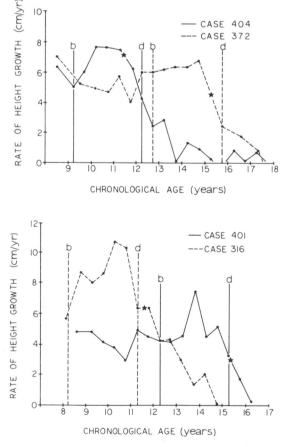

Figure 2. Differences in timing of the pubertal period for height growth for two pairs of early- and late-maturing girls. (Stars indicate onset of menstruation.)

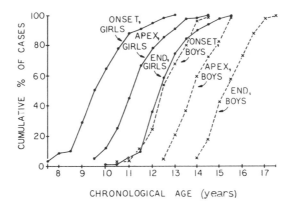

Figure 3. Sex differences in timing of the pubertal growth period in height. Cumulative percentage of girls (*n* = 94) and boys (*n* = 67) who reach onset, apex, and end of the pubertal growth period at each age. (From Faust, 1977. By permission of Society for Research in Child Development.)

worthy. By 11 years of age, the vast majority of girls have entered the pubertal period for height growth, and almost half of them are at or beyond the time of their own apex rate in height growth. By contrast, virtually none of the boys have reached the onset of the pubertal period for height growth by age 11. By 12 years of age, still less than one-fourth of the boys have entered the pubertal period; none has yet attained his apex rate in height growth. From Figure 3, it can be seen clearly that the cumulative percentage of girls at successive ages who are reaching the *end* of the pubertal period for height growth is strikingly similar to the percentage of boys at corresponding ages who are *entering* this period of pubertal development. In summary, sex differences and individual differences in level of physical maturity are illuminated in a developmental construction system that is based on physiological indicators of growth, such as changing rates of height growth.

3. INDIVIDUAL SELF-CONSTRUCTION SYSTEMS

The intense and extensive physical changes at adolescence tend to heighten self-awareness and focus attention on the self. Many of the changes are qualitatively different from those of earlier years; for instance, changes in bodily proportioning and contouring, the growth of pubic and axillary hair, and breast development for girls. When Zachry (1940) suggested that at adolescence the body becomes the symbol of the self, she implied not only that the nature of the changes were significant for self-definition, but that one's evaluation of the changes (whether positive or negative) had direct consequences for one's self-evaluation. The impact of such changes may be attributable to the apparent realism and palpability of physical growth which, unlike changes in the phenomenal self, seem to be experienced quite directly; they are conceptualized as something that can be seen, touched, and felt.

The individual variations in physical form and maturity comprise the backdrop against which adolescents evaluate and interpret their own changing body and growth experience. Not only do adolescents attempt to assimilate these changes into a growing sense of self, but they learn from observing styles of peers who are developmentally ahead of them. The obvious appeal of those already at the next developmental step may be an important factor in constructing what it means to an individual to "grow up." Adolescents begin to figure out not only what to expect of others, but what is expected of them. Moreover, parents, other adults, and peers begin to adapt their expectations to the changing form of an individual whom they had formerly treated as "just a child."

How one's changing body is evaluated and assimilated into a growing sense of self is influenced in part by conceptions of acceptability of bodily appearance that have been derived from past experience, and in part by the present standards of evaluation portrayed by others who are important. Beliefs about what is attractive, sex-appropriate, or "erotic" vary enormously from one culture to another and from one historical epoch to another (Davenport, 1978). By a process that is only vaguely understood, such cultural standards and values become transformed and adapted into the basic structure of individual personality.

In our culture, physical appearance is a significant basis for the impressions that adolescents form and the personal qualities that they attribute to one another (Cavior and Dokecki, 1973; Cavior and Lombardi, 1973; Dion, Berscheid, and Walster, 1972). At adolescence, when acceptability by the peer group is predicated upon conformity to the implicit standards and norms of peers, evaluations and interpretations by peers become incorporated into one's standards for self-evaluation. These, in turn, constitute a frame of reference within which one's own body is evaluated. It may be proposed that variations in the timing of physical changes among age-mates become more important determinants of self-perception and self-evaluation than at preceding periods in life. Appropriate longitudinal studies of this issue are just beginning (see Simmons, Blyth, and McKinney, Chapter 11, and Tobin-Richards, Boxer, and Petersen, Chapter 7).

4. FEMININE BEAUTY, ATTRACTIVENESS, AND ADVERTISING MEDIA

Whether one is an early or late developer, relatively thin or stocky, long- or short-legged, changes in bodily form and contouring will be evaluated—by oneself and by others (Lerner and Korn, 1972; Staffieri, 1972). Both boys and girls enter into this evaluation process, and the physical qualities that are deemed desirable for one sex are not necessarily valued in the same way for the opposite sex. For example, Lerner, Karabenick, and Stuart (1973) found that both men and women subjects (college students) agreed that "shape of legs," "hips," and "thighs" are more important in determining attractiveness of women than of men. Interestingly, for both men and women the degree of positive self-concept was correlated with the degree of satisfaction with one's own bodily characteristics.

Certainly, one's evaluation of physical beauty and attractiveness is made in relation to meanings derived from interactions with people of different sorts, as well as in relation to present cultural standards about what is desirable and attractive. The cultural ideal of physical attractiveness begins to be acquired early in the preschool years (Styczynski and Langlois, 1977), and by the time children are 7 or 8 years of age, their judgments about physical attractiveness are very similar to those made by older adolescents (Cavior and Lombardi, 1973). Research by Cavior and Dokecki (1973) indicates that by the time children are in fifth grade they have adopted society's criteria for evaluating attractiveness and can apply them consistently. Some consensual validation for their judgments about physical attractiveness may be provided by advertisements and by media pronouncements about what is feminine and beautiful.

As one example, the "lean, lithe look" (Figure 4) is a benchmark of feminine beauty today, and it has been so for several decades. This "prepubertal look" is presumably to be emulated by all women, regardless of age, even though it often happens that the models are long-legged 12-year-olds who are coiffured and made up to look chronologically older and more mature than their years. Girls whose proportioning corresponds more closely than others to this "ideal" may be responded to more affirmatively, hold more positive self-evaluations, and gain in self-esteem. For others less fortunately endowed, the consequences may be quite different (Langlois and Stephan, 1981).

It is interesting that fashion-model sketches of the feminine form accentuate the leg length of women and girls, much more so than that of men and boys. This is especially the case in high fashion artistry (see Figure 5). Also, it is easier to find full-length fashion ads of female than

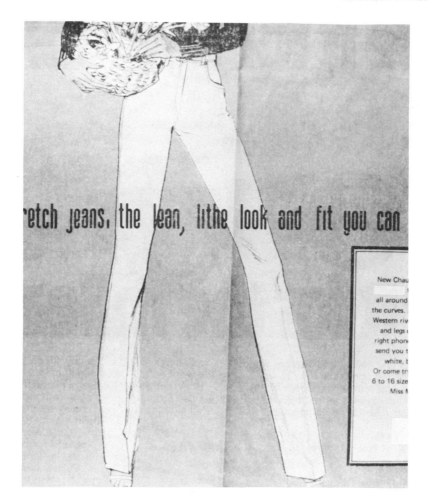

Figure 4. Feminine beauty: the lean, lithe look.

male models. The message may be that leg shape as well as leg length communicates beauty and attractiveness of females but not males. Figures 6 and 7 portray typical differences in fashion sketches of males and females. Although both models are shown in lounge wear and their poses are similar, the woman's legs are proportionately much longer than the man's.

Why should long-leggedness be perceived as "feminine," when all studies of somatic sex differences have found that boys have proportionately longer legs than do girls? As shown in Figure 8, the sex difference in stem length/height ratio is maintained throughout the pubertal period for height, even though the ratio changes slightly for both boys and girls during this period. A low stem length/height ratio indicates long-leggedness in proportion to one's height, and is typical of males; females consistently have higher stem length/height ratios. The decrease in the ratio during the first half of the pubertal period represents, of course, the early growth in leg length; the increase in the second half of

Figure 5. Feminine ideal portrayed in advertising.

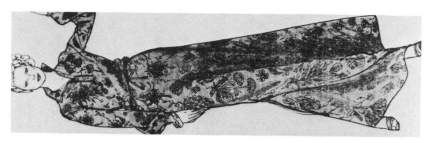

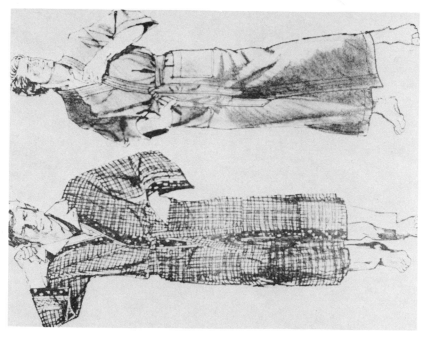

Figures 6 and 7. Male and female proportioning portrayed in advertising.

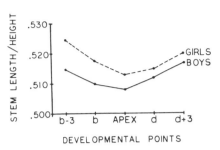

Figure 8. Sex differences in mean stem length/height ratio at developmental points. Points b − 3 and d + 3 mark the beginning of the prepubertal period and the end of the postpubertal period, respectively. (From Faust, 1977. By permission of Society for Research in Child Development.)

the period indicates the later growth in stem length. This developmental change occurs for both boys and girls.

A spot check of women's magazines and the daily newspaper's fashion advertisements over a 2-week period was conducted to find out how male and female figures were portrayed, particularly in height and relative leg length. Using only full-length, standing photographs and sketches, measurements were made from the top of the head to the soles of the feet (excluding heels) and from the waist to the soles of the feet to obtain a proportion of total height which was comprised of leg length. Women were depicted with significantly longer legs than were men. This method can be reproduced reliably; on the average, men's foot-to-waist length comprised only 58% of their total height, whereas for women it comprised 66% of their height. In some sketches of high fashion models, women's leg length was 70% of their total height. Compared with women, stylish men tend to be portrayed as more "low-slung" or mesomorphic in build.

The idealized form of feminine beauty, as illustrated in the preceding figures and represented in the Petty Girls and Varga Girls of the World War II era, is comprised of qualities more typical of adolescent girls who are later developers; that is, who are older when they reach puberty. The idealized feminine form appears to be most similar to the earliest phase of the pubertal period among later-developing girls! Normatively speaking, however, long-leggedness is a "male" quality.

If there is continuity in the psychological impact of somatic variation at puberty, it should be understood in relation to continuities in the individual's concepts, values, and beliefs about what is significant in the world. The acceptability of one's bodily appearance is surely constructed, at the individual level, out of the implicit standards portrayed so redundantly and persuasively in the media. However, it is probably true that not all women place the same degree of value on physical appearance.

The foregoing is not meant to imply that women's beliefs about attractiveness are determined by mere exposure to the media. It is suggested, however, that many women do seem selectively attuned to messages about forms of feminine attractiveness and its value. For advertisers, the young adolescent girl seems to be the prototype of femininity—a model for girls, young and old, to admire and to imitate.

A recent article in the *San Francisco Chronicle* (Schiro, 1981) reports that the toy industry has marketed a new toy—cosmetics for little girls. The make-up kits are targeted for 4- to 9-year-old girls, but the packaging shows a 10-year-old model! Thus, it seems that when a girl is young, she is nudged to "grow up"; when older, she is encouraged to capture or recapture her prepubertal look.

5. PERSONAL CONSTRUCTS AND ADOLESCENT DEVELOPMENT

What makes adolescence a particularly fascinating "event" to interpret and to understand is this: As we are imposing our constructs upon adolescents, they are imposing their own constructs upon themselves and upon others—including peers, parents, and even professional researchers who write about adolescents! Thus, adolescents have the capacity to reflect on what it means to grow, and what it means to grow up. They are in the process of developing implicit theories of personality and personal constructions of adolescent development all on their own. Investigating adolescents' conceptions of themselves and of other people may be a useful way of finding out how adolescents construe the process of growth.

In a pilot study with a small group of high school and college-age subjects, we have been investigating interpersonal perception, specifically the perceptions that adolescents have of each other and the terms in which they cast these perceptions. Among the questions of interest are these: What kinds of differences among peers are important or meaningful to adolescents? On what basis are qualities of personality ascribed to others by adolescents as they engage in the process of describing, comparing, and contrasting certain friends and acquaintances? If early or late maturing does affect behavior and personality at adolescence (and there is plenty of evidence that it does), what personal constructs may describe the differences?

If the timing of pubertal growth is a basis for categorizing friends, it may be because physical changes are very salient for an adolescent or the wide variation among adolescents in maturity makes the existing differences more noticeable or conspicuous (see Tobin-Richards et al., Chapter 7). Perhaps the perception of physical differences is accentuated at adolescence when being "like others" is an important value or norm. If physical development is a significant basis for the impressions that adolescents form of each other, a study of interpersonal perception may shed some light on the process.

In the pilot study, Kelly's Role Construct Repertory Grid Test (Kelly, 1955) was used with 18 college students who were enrolled in a small, private liberal arts college and with 19 high school students from a middle- and upper-middle-class suburban community. Following Kelly, it is proposed that people actively construe their world through their own construction systems; that is, they impose their own constructs upon other people and events. If we want to understand people's conceptions of others, it is important to know not only what they assert in describing others, but what contrasting qualities they implicitly or explicitly reject or exclude. Kelly's method is a useful way to get at the polar-opposite terms in which an individual construes his/her interpersonal world.

What personality terms are used by adolescents to describe their peers? What similarities and differences are attributed by them to early and late developers, and how do these compare with the qualities adolescents attribute to other boys and girls whom they know?

Students were asked to think up the names of friends and acquaintances to fit each of eight roles. The roles included an early- and a late-developing boy and girl and a socially skillful and an academically competent boy and girl. Using an 8 × 8 grid, subjects were asked to consider three designated persons at a time from among those they had named, and to think of an important way in which two of them are alike and the other one was different. The quality on which two of them were alike and the contrasting quality on which the third person differed from the other two, were recorded. Each subject compared 8 triads, and in doing so offered 8 different construct–contrast characteristics. It should be noted here that using Kelly's procedure, the adjective pairs or contrasting descriptive phrases are generated by the subject. This procedure is unlike an adjective checklist in which a standardized list of adjectives is presented to subjects for their consideration.

Some examples of unique pairs of polar constructs that were constructed by college students about early- and late-developing boys are as follows:

Early-Maturing Boys	Late-Maturing Boys
Likes football	Would rather read
Sexy, outgoing	Popular only with own friends
Slow learner	Fast learner
Macho	Unmacho
Acted like typical jock	Didn't goof off or try for attention

Examples of construct–contrast dimensions used by college-age individuals when comparing early- and late-maturing girls are as follows:

Early-Maturing Girls	Late-Maturing Girls
Attracted to opposite sex	Afraid of opposite sex
Egocentric	Unassuming
Absolutely boy crazy	Friends of both boys and girls
Theatrical	Normal behavior

These qualitative respones may be used to examine the question, "When an early and a late developer of the same sex are considered together with one other person, are they seen as being more similar to each other or to the third member of the triad?" For every such comparison of boys' roles, the early-maturing boy and the late-maturing boy were depicted as "opposites" on the subject's construct–contrast dimension; in no case did the early- and late-maturing boy share the same attribute.

In the corresponding comparison between early- and late-developing girls, where the role of the socially skillful girl was the third member of the triad, 66% of the college-age subjects placed the early and the late developer under opposite, contrasting poles. The rest placed them under the same construct. What this suggests is that college students, reconstructing the essential characteristics of their adolescent peers, uniformly find early- and late-maturing boys to be miles apart, conceptually speaking, whereas the differences between early- and late-maturing girls, while evident, are not as pronounced.

Not only can college students describe, classify, categorize, and evaluate the characteristics of their adolescent peers easily, but they delight in doing so, especially women students. The male students in the sample had more difficulty in completing the task.

In the high school sample of 19 tenth graders, contrasts between early- and late-developing girls were much more striking. Early- and late-developing girls were placed at opposite ends of the subject's dimensional construct on 87% of the comparisons; they were perceived as being "alike" on only 13% of them. Qualitatively, the constructs used by the tenth graders in differentiating between early- and late-developing girls were interesting not only because of the aspects of personality selected for mention but because of the uniqueness of the bipolar contrasts, as the following examples illustrate.

Early-Maturing Girls	Late-Maturing Girls
Stuck-up and yecky	Outgoing
Always surrounded by guys	Doesn't have that many friends
Has many friends	Loud-mouthed; blurts things out
Socially involved	More of a homebody
Uncoordinated	Coordinated
Conceited	Nice

Investigation of adolescents' personal constructs seems worthwhile although procedural modifications may be needed for younger students, particularly junior high and elementary school children. Furthermore, measures of physical development would be valuable in order to investigate differences in evaluations of early and late developers as a function of the subjects' maturational levels. In addition, self-ratings and self-evaluations would be worth obtaining, perhaps by including "self" as one of the roles to be considered and compared with the others.

In summary, we need to understand more about the ways in which normal variations in physical development at adolescence are evaluated, and how they affect the experience, self-definition, and choices confronting young adolescents. As better concepts and theories are developed to describe the transition process from childhood to adulthood, we should take into account level of physical maturity of the subjects, both as assessed from outside perspectives and from the adolescent's own frame of reference.

Many questions need to be addressed. How attractive are early-developing third and fourth graders perceived to be, not only by their peers, but by themselves? How do the early indicators of pubertal development affect relationships with peers, parents, and siblings? And, do self-attributions change concomitantly with changes in evaluations by others, or do they precede or follow them? One would expect that younger children might tend to base their evaluations of personality more on concrete, external, descriptive characteristics than would older children (Montemayor and Eisen, 1977; Peevers and Secord, 1973). How such global or superficially based judgments might affect early-developing youngsters is not yet known. Further, one might expect that the affective meanings constructed by both children and adolescents would be different in various school contexts (see Simmons et al., Chapter 11). Beyond the issue of which grade levels are to be included within the elementary, junior high, or high school, does it matter whether schoolroom classes are self-contained or "open," and does it make a difference whether the pupils in each classroom are heterogeneous with respect to chronological age or are age-grouped?

Perhaps one of the reasons why the period of adolescence lags regrettably behind other development periods in research and theory as well as in practical application, is that most of us in the field of adolescent development tend to reject scientific paradigms that emphasize simplicity, surface qualities, and static notions. We are more likely to endorse views that stress complexity, depth, dynamic change, and interactive or transactional notions. Along with Kelly, we appreciate "the creative capacity of living things to represent the environment, not merely to respond to it" (Kelly, 1955, p. 8).

We must try to include in our conceptions about adolescence such notions as adolescents thinking about us, thinking about them, thinking about pubertal development! This is a complicated process to be able to understand. In approaching the task, we should attempt to assess the quality of the adolescent's belief structure rather than uniformly imposing a precoded analysis system upon our subjects. As investigators, we may have to spend time finding out what constructs adolescents use to understand themselves, their friends and parents, and how they construe other "events of nature."

REFERENCES

Berzonsky, M. D. *Adolescent development.* New York: Macmillan, 1981.
Buck, C., and Stavraky, K. The relationship between age at menarche and age at marriage among child-bearing women. *Human Biology,* 1967, *39,* 93–102.
Cavior, N., and Dokecki, P. Physical attractiveness, perceived attitude similarity, and academic achievement as contributors to interpersonal attraction among adolescents. *Developmental Psychology,* 1973, *9,* 44–54.
Cavior, N., and Lombardi, D. A. Developmental aspects of judgment of physical attractiveness in children. *Developmental Psychology,* 1973, *8,* 67–71.
Davenport, W. H. Sex in cross-cultural perspective. In F. A. Beach (Ed.), *Human sexuality in four perspectives.* Baltimore: John Hopkins University Press, 1978.
Dion, K. K., Berscheid, E., and Walster, E. What is beautiful is good. *Journal of Personality and Social Psychology,* 1972, *24,* 285–290.
Eichorn, D. H. Biological correlates of behavior. In H. W. Stevenson (Ed.), *Child psychology.* The sixty-second year-book of the National Society for the Study of Education (pt. 1). Chicago: University of Chicago Press, 1963.
Faust, M. S. Somatic development of adolescent girls. *Monographs of the Society for Research in Child Development,* 1977, *42* (1), serial no. 169.
Jones, M. C., and Mussen, P. H. Self-conceptions, motivations, and interpersonal attitudes of early- and late-maturing girls. *Child Development,* 1958, *29,* 491–501.
Kelly, G. A. *A theory of personality: The psychology of personal constructs.* New York: Norton, 1955.
Kelly, G. A. A brief introduction to personal construct theory. In D. Bannister (Ed.), *Perspectives in personal construct theory.* London: Academic Press, 1970.
Langlois, J. H., and Stephan, C. W. Beauty and the beast: The role of physical attractiveness in the development of peer relations and social behavior. In S. S. Brehm, S. M. Kassin, and F. X. Gibbons (Eds.), *Developmental social psychology.* New York: Oxford University Press, 1981.
Lerner, R. M., and Korn, S. J. The development of body-build stereotypes in males. *Child Development,* 1972, *43,* 908–920.
Lerner, R. M., Karabenick, S. A., and Stuart, J. L. Relations among physical attractiveness, body attitudes, and self-concept in male and female college students. *The Journal of Psychology,* 1973, *85,* 119–129.
Montemayor, R., and Eisen, M. The development of self-conceptions from childhood to adolescence. *Developmental Psychology,* 1977, *13,* 314–319.
Peevers, B. H., and Secord, P. F. Developmental changes in attribution of descriptive concepts to persons. *Journal of Personality and Social Psychology,* 1973, *27,* 120–128.

Peskin, H. Influence of the developmental schedule of puberty on learning and ego functioning. *Journal of Youth and Adolescence*, 1973, *4*, 273–290.

Schiro, A. The newest "toy"—Cosmetics for little girls. *San Francisco Chronicle*, March 17, 1981, p. 15.

Staffieri, J. R. Body build and behavioral expectancies in young females. *Developmental Psychology*, 1972, *6*, 125–127.

Stolz, H. R. and Stolz, L. M. *Somatic development of adolescent boys.* New York: Macmillan, 1951.

Styczynski, L. and Langlois, J. H. The effects of familiarity on behavioral stereotypes associated with physical attractiveness in young children. *Child Development*, 1977, *48*, 1137–1141.

Zachry, C. F. *Emotion and conduct in adolescence.* New York: D. Appleton Century, 1940.

Chapter 7

The Psychological Significance of Pubertal Change
Sex Differences in Perceptions of Self during Early Adolescence

Maryse H. Tobin-Richards, Andrew M. Boxer, and Anne C. Petersen

1. Introduction

Pubertal changes involve a rather dramatic set of events with regard to their rate and magnitude (Petersen and Taylor, 1980), particularly when compared to other biological events through the life cycle. Studies across the life course sensitize us to the fact that when life changes are too rapid or extreme, multiple and simultaneous, or unusually timed, individuals are subjected to varied and extreme challenges of coping with their situations. Such evidence comes to us from studies of adolescence (Coleman, 1980; Simmons, Blyth, Van Cleave, and Bush, 1979), the transition to adulthood (Coleman, et al., 1974; Neugarten and Hagestad, 1976; Hogan, 1978), middle age (Brim, 1976a; Cohler and Boxer, 1983), and old age (Lieberman, 1975; Seltzer, 1976). Individuals need some degree of control and social support to effectively negotiate life changes, and such

Maryse H. Tobin-Richards and Andrew M. Boxer • Clinical Research Training Program in Adolescence, Laboratory for the Study of Adolescence, Department of Psychiatry, Michael Reese Hospital and Medical Center; and Committee on Human Development, The University of Chicago, Chicago, Illinois 60637.   Anne C. Petersen • Department of Individual and Family Studies, College of Human Development, The Pennsylvania State University, University Park, Pennsylvania 16802.

capacities vary according to the events themselves, their transformative qualities (Brim and Ryff, 1980; Hultsch and Plemons, 1979), and individual coping styles and life cycle position. Thus, young adolescents' confrontations with the challenges of pubertal change provide a natural testing ground for understanding (1) the nature of a set of biologically paced life events, (2) the ways in which these are negotiated, and (3) their psychosocial impact upon development.

We are concerned with understanding the markers of pubertal change as adolescents perceive them, as well as the ways in which these changes influence and are related to self-perceptions. In particular, this chapter focuses upon body image, perceived physical attractiveness, and what these young adolescents find most satisfying and troubling about their changing bodies.

1.1. The Self at Puberty

The self can be conceived of as a theory which the individual constructs about himself or herself (Epstein, 1973), what Brim (1976b) has called a "personal epistemology." Cohler's concept of personal narrative (1982), Plath's (1980) concept of cobiography, and Myerhoff's (1982) concept of storytelling provide similar ways of studying human experience. The self theory is a set of ideas, propositions, attitudes, and feelings which an individual holds with regard to the nature of the world, the self, and their interaction (Brim, 1976b). From a developmental perspective, many scholars have underscored the importance of a dynamic, changing concept of the self (Broughton and Riegel, 1977; Cohler, 1981; Epstein, 1973; Erikson, 1959; Gergen, 1977; Haan, 1981; Kohut, 1971; Smith, 1978), which is anchored in historical time, social structure, and life span (Elder, 1980). Every individual comes to develop a set of hypotheses about the kind of person he or she will become in the future (anticipations), as well as who they are and what they have been (retrospections). Most individuals interpret life events in three ways: before they occur, while they are happening, and after they have passed. In addition, individuals assign causal attributions to themselves, to nature, to society, to chance, or to some combination of these. Perceptions of the self can thus be divided into components which correspond to various domains of an individual's life. With young adolescents as the focus of investigation, the "body self" (Epstein, 1973) and its naturally occurring changes during puberty are a central part of our study. The body self or body image (Schilder, 1935; Rosenbaum, 1979) consists of those images of and ideas and feelings about the physical self.

During the rapid physical changes of puberty, perceptions of the body are salient with regard to overall self-perceptions. In an analysis of data collected from the adolescents that we shall discuss, Kavrell and Jarcho (1980) found strong correlations between self-image and body image for both boys and girls (girls, $r = 0.79$; boys, $r = 0.71$; $p < 0.0001$). Research findings from other investigations provide additional evidence supporting the importance of this relationship. In several of the studies conducted by Lerner and his associates, significant relations emerged between self-esteem or self-concept and satisfaction with body characteristics or physical attractiveness, with somewhat stronger relations indicated for females (Lerner and Karabenick, 1974; Lerner, Karabenick, and Stuart, 1973; Padin, Lerner, and Spiro, 1981). The importance of body image to self-image is also confirmed by the greater degree of concern, anxiety, and preoccupation that young adolescents communicate about their changing bodies (Frazier and Lisonbee, 1950; Hamburg, 1974; Jersild, 1952). The importance of this concern may be a response to sociocultural influences since the body builds of adolescents have been found to correlate with peer evaluations, peer relations, and prestige (Clausen, 1975; Lerner, 1969; Staffieri, 1967). Havighurst (1972) has elaborated one of the developmental tasks of adolescents as the acceptance of one's body and adaptation to effective use of it. At its most extreme, body image concerns may result in disorders such as anorexia nervosa and bulimia (Bruch, 1981), or anorexiclike behavior (Thompson, 1979), found particularly among middle- and upper-middle-class females.

Sex differences in both self-image and self-esteem, as well as body image, become apparent during adolescence (Clifford, 1971; Simmons and Rosenberg, 1975; Simmons, Rosenberg, and Rosenberg, 1973). Not only are there differences in average level of self-esteem but also there are differences in patterns of associations with other measures. In their review of the literature, Bar-Tal and Saxe (1976) concluded that attractive individuals relative to less attractive persons are more positively evaluated across a wide range of dimensions; this result was stronger for women than for men. Providing evidence for an internalization of this sex difference, Lerner and Karabenick (1974) found that attractiveness ratings of a larger number of individual body parts were more strongly related to self-concept for females than for males.

1.2. Pubertal Development

The body of an early adolescent is undergoing profound changes in terms of size, shape, and specific secondary sex characteristics. With the appearance of these new physical characteristics, coupled with increased cognitive capacities (Elkind, 1974; Kohlberg and Gilligan, 1971), adolescents must construct, revise, and reinterpret their theories about themselves and their worlds. Young adolescents are developing a set of ideas about their past, present, and future (Erikson, 1968; Sullivan, 1953) which are both personal and social (Erikson, 1959; Faust, 1960 and Chapter 6, this volume; Koff, Rierdan, and Jacobson, 1981). Elkind (1967) has discussed adolescent egocentrism as leading to an increased preoccupation with others' opinions and points of view. Adams (1977) suggests that such thought during early adolescence may result, in particular, with concern about one's appearance. As Haan (1981) stated, adolescents may overexercise their new "cognitive virtuosity," particularly with such changes as the ones arising from their bodies.

Culturally bound (Ford and Beach, 1951: Levine, 1973; Mead, 1958) and socially shared definitions of what is desirable and attractive (Lerner, 1969; Faust, Chapter 6, this volume; Staffieri, 1967; Sorell and Nowak, 1981) play an important part in mediating the psychological experience of puberty (Petersen and Taylor, 1980). This applies both to changing capacities and changing appearances. In Chapter 6 of this volume, Faust provides an example of this with her discussion of the present cultural ideal of feminine looks. She writes that the "benchmark of feminine beauty today" is the prepubertal look of being lean, long-legged, and lithe. Advertising encourages this stereotype by exaggerating the leg length of female models proportionate to male models. Being thin is another important aspect of feminine cultural beauty standards today as evidenced by Brenner and Hinsdale's (1978) findings that an ectomorphic figure was viewed by females as significantly less negative than the endomorphic figure. Thus, it is no surprise that disorders related to body image are more apparent today for females than for males.

Significant others may begin to react differently to young adolescents, stimulating a shift in the socially shared definitions of the self. The visual and apparent changes of puberty affect patterns of family interaction (Hill, 1980; Lynch, 1981; Steinberg and Hill, 1978; Steinberg, 1981) and alter peer relations (Savin-Williams, 1979), particularly with regard to patterns of intimacy (Douvan and Adelson, 1966) and heterosocial behavior (Simmons et al., 1979). Studies in our own laboratory (Wilen and Petersen, 1980) document some of the ways in which adolescents compare their physical development and its timing (onset), to that of their peers (see also Frank and Cohen, 1979; Kestenberg, 1967).

1.3. *Time and Timing in Adolescent Development*

The concept of puberty has been clarified as a set of processes rather than a unitary event (Faust, 1977; Petersen and Taylor, 1980). Girls, on the average, begin and end puberty approximately 2 years before boys. However, while each pubertal change proceeds in an invariant sequence, its timing varies considerably from individual to individual. Therefore, an individual, relative to peers, may vary in his or her overall pubertal timing, as well as the timing of each individual pubertal change relative to the others. Thus, timing may vary within individuals as well as between them. The sequencing of the events produces individual patterns (Faust, 1977; Petersen and Taylor, 1980).

It has been suggested that a psychology of the life cycle is intricately linked to a psychology of time and timing (Neugarten, 1969, 1970). Through their relationship to time, individuals maintain a sense of self-cohesion by their differential use of the past, present, and future, depending upon their position in the life course (Butler, 1963; Cohler, 1981a; Cottle, 1976; Cottle and Klineberg, 1974; Lieberman and Falk, 1971; Neugarten, 1979). For example, it has been stated that the latency age child must forget his or her oedipal past, and the adolescent must create the future (Cohler, 1981b). Individuals also create for themselves an "average expectable life cycle" which contains the sequence of major events to be anticipated as one grows up and grows old (Neugarten, 1970). Adolescents begin to foresee the future in new ways (Lens and Gailly, 1980; Verstraeten, 1980) and must deal with the personal and social meanings of time and time mastery. Thus, as Neugarten (1970) has stated, a sense of the predictable life cycle differentiates the healthy adult personality from the unhealthy one. And indeed also, in younger individuals, Farnham-Diggory (1966) found that normal children (as contrasted with psychotic and brain-damaged children) have a clearly defined image or model of "growing up." These children have a level of self-evaluation and competence which is going forward, parallel to their growth and development.

Therefore, individuals appear to internalize a set of norms (Neugarten, Moore, and Lowe, 1965) not only about what events should occur across the life course, but *when* they should occur. This "social clock" links historical time and life time (chronological age), since age is a meaningless variable without knowledge of the particular social meanings to which a culture attaches given chronological ages or major life periods (Neugarten and Datan, 1973). Our own society is currently coming to be characterized by a multiplicity of timetables with regard to role entry and exit (Neugarten and Hagestad, 1976).

Neugarten (1970) has suggested that when major life events do not occur as they are anticipated, that is, when they are "off-time," a crisis may ensue. Thus, with regard to adolescence, we may say that entry into adolescence is not inevitably crisis-bound, as a number of studies have demonstrated (e.g., Douvan and Adelson, 1966; Offer and Offer, 1975), but that the synchronization of the events within it and the subjective perception of their timing may create such a crisis. To be off-time with regard to a life event means that one will be subject to various sanctions operating in the social system. Psychologically, such deviations may represent a drop in self-esteem and a loss of self-cohesion. A number of studies have attempted to examine the timing of life events in terms of their sequencing and congruence in relation to psychosocial adaptation at adolescence (for example, see Peskin, 1967, 1973; Simmons, et al., 1979) and to other social roles across the life course (for example, see Bacon, 1974; Gubrium, 1976). Most studies of the timing of pubertal change have related timing to an external or objective set of criteria; few studies have assessed the individual's personal sense of time and timing (Wilen, 1980). A sense of being early, late, or on-time in physical development, relative to same-sex peers, may strongly influence perceptions of the self and feelings of adequacy, normality, and the average expectable course of events.

Previous research on puberty has focused primarily on the correlates of early and late maturation. Findings from several longitudinal studies indicate that for boys, during adolescence, early maturation brings social advantages, and late maturation, disadvantages. Early maturers have been found to be more relaxed, less dependent, more self-confident, and more attractive both to adults and peers (Clausen, 1975; Jones, 1965; Jones and Bayley, 1950; Mussen and Jones, 1957). This has been explained by the favorable social response given to the attainment of adult male physical status. A mature male body brings with it the physical advantage of athletic superiority, and the social advantages of greater respect from adults, more attention from girls, and leadership roles among peers.

For girls, the results are rather ambiguous and confusing. The findings indicate that early maturation has psychological and social costs which include lack of popularity, social poise, and greater internal turbulence (Jones and Mussen, 1958; Peskin, 1973; Simmons, Blyth, and McKinney, Chapter 11, this volume; Stolz and Stolz, 1944). Yet, at the same time, early maturation has been found to bring with it greater prestige (Faust, 1960) and self-confidence (Clausen, 1975). Based on these mixed findings, it appears that the unambiguously positive social responses to the physical maturation of boys does not occur for girls. Becoming an adult in this society does not bring with it the same social advantage for a female as it does for a male. Traditionally devoid of several of the social advantages experienced by a similarly maturing boy, such as athletic prowess, leadership roles, and expectations of occupational success (Block, 1978), physical maturation for a girl may carry more explicit sexualized meanings and may generate concomitant social responses. Adolescent sexuality, in general, may elicit fears, envy, and excitement from adults (Anthony, 1969; Seiden, 1976). For an early-maturing girl, on the one hand, lacking the support of a group of peers who are also going through puberty, the experience of physical maturation may be difficult (Petersen, in press). And, on the other hand, retaining a child's body when others are proceeding down the ontogenetic path toward womanhood is equally disconcerting and problematic. Wilen (1980), examining data drawn from our early adolescent sample, found that girls who were on-time in their development, as they subjectively perceived it, tended to experience more positive feelings about their development than those who were either early or late.

Thus, given the past research on puberty, we expect a number of significant differences in early adolescent boys' and girls' psychosocial experience of physical maturation. Results from past research, discussed above, lead us to hypothesize that the models underlying the relationship between pubertal development and the psychosocial meaning of these changes are different for boys and girls. More specifically, we hypothesize that for boys the underlying pattern is a simple linear one, with earlier maturation related to more positive body image and feelings of attractiveness. For girls, the relationship is expected to be more complex, with a curvilinear component which may be reflecting a desire for conformity to the normative status of the group. Additionally, it is hypothesized that girls, more than boys, will be dissatisfied with their weight, perceive themselves as overweight, and that this variable will be more salient to perceptions of themselves. For girls, weight is expected to be an important element in their experience of puberty.

2. METHODS

The theoretical framework for this research employs a biopsychosocial model for development which assumes the occurrence of interactions over time among biological, psychological, and social factors (Petersen, 1980a). Models are being tested which propose specific links between biological change and psychosocial variables (Petersen and Taylor, 1980). The data presented in this chapter are drawn from a larger ongoing longitudinal study of biopsychosocial development at early adolescence, being conducted in the Laboratory for the Study of Adolescence. This investigation utilizes a cohort-sequential design, with a second cohort to replicate the first (Table 1 depicts this design). The respondents were drawn randomly from two middle- to upper-middle-

Table 1. Cohort-Sequential Longitudinal Design
for the Study[a]

	Grade		
Cohort (year of birth)	6	7	8
I (1967)	1979	1980	1981
II (1968)	1980	1981	1982

[a]All entries indicate year of testing.

class, white, suburban school districts. The total number of adolescents in the larger study is approximately 350. The sample size for Cohort I is 188 (103 girls and 85 boys). Information is obtained from the children four times annually, in two individual interviews and two group sessions that take place each fall and spring. The data, to be discussed here, were gathered from an individual interview and group assessment (a time when paper and pencil measures are administered) from the first cohort during their seventh grade school year. Parents are interviewed twice in the study, during their child's sixth and eighth grade school year.

The sample which will be discussed here consists of the 70 girls and 52 boys who completed both the individual interview and group assessment. They do not differ from the larger sample on any variable used here including body and self-image or pubertal status.

Body image is measured by one of nine scales from the Self-Image Questionnaire for Young Adolescents (SIQYA) (Petersen, 1980b), an adaptation of the Offer Self-Image Questionnaire (Offer, Ostrov, and Howard, 1977, 1981). Respondents were asked to indicate how well each of nine items, interspersed among the others, describes them. Examples of the body items include: "I am proud of my body," and "I wish I were in better physical condition." The inter-item reliabilities for this scale are good, with an alpha coefficient of 0.74 for boys and 0.72 for girls. When analyzed by sex, the items were relatively similar in their contribution to the scale. For this particular sample of seventh graders, the first four items which correlated the best with the rest of the scale were the same for boys and girls. The major difference by sex was with the item "I wish I were thinner." For girls, it was correlated modestly with the rest of the scale ($r = 0.33$) while for boys virtually no association occurred ($r = 0.01$).

Pubertal development was measured through a series of questions in the semistructured interview (Petersen, in press). Each adolescent boy was asked whether he had noticed a change on five pubertal dimensions:

body and facial hair, voice and skin change, and growth spurt. Girls were asked about body hair, skin change, menarche, breast development, and growth spurt. Responses to these items were coded on a 4-point scale, with 1 indicating no development and 4 indicating that development was complete. As would be expected, girls tend to be more developmentally advanced in their physical maturation than boys during this chronological age period. The alpha coefficient for the items in these scales indicated high inter-item reliability (boys, $\alpha = 0.68$; girls, $\alpha = 0.78$). These item-total correlations, displayed with the alphas on Table 2, indicate that skin change contributes the least to the scales.

Four other variables with which we are concerned are *perceived physical attractiveness* of self, and *perceived timing of development* relative to same-sex peers, as well as *perception of* and *satisfaction with weight*. In the interview, the adolescents were asked how attractive they felt compared to peers, and whether their physical development was earlier, later, or the same as that of most other boys or girls their age. Additionally, they were asked if they perceived themselves to be underweight, average, or overweight and how satisfied they were with their current weight. The adolescents were also asked what they liked best and least about their bodies. These open-ended responses were coded into a number of categories, based on the frequency of their occurrence. In examining the relationship between the Body Image Scale and the attractiveness variable, it was found that adolescents who perceive themselves to be attractive have higher body image scores, and those who see themselves as less attractive have lower scores ($F = 12.01$, $p < 0.005$ for boys; $F = 3.14$, $p < 0.05$ for girls), thereby providing a measure of validity. It is interesting to note that the relationship is somewhat stronger for boys than for girls.

Table 2. Item-Total Correlation and Alpha Coefficients on the Pubertal Development Scale for Seventh Grade by Sex

	Females	Males
Body hair	0.66	0.58
Facial hair		0.42
Breast development	0.77	
Voice change		0.51
Skin change	0.52	0.26
Menarche	0.33	
Growth spurt	0.64	0.42
Alphas	0.78	0.68

3. RESULTS

3.1. *Body Image*

A multivariate analysis of variance examining sex differences in the body image of early adolescent boys and girls, indicated that boys perceive their bodies significantly more positively than girls in terms of overall body image ($F = 3.25$, $p < 0.005$). Of the individual items which contributed to the significant multivariate F, being proud of their bodies ($F = 7.06$, $p < 0.01$, $d^1 = 0.50$), feeling poorly developed ($F = 4.56$, $p < 0.04$, $d = 0.43$), and wishing they were thinner ($F = 9.94$, $p < 0.005$, $d = 0.60$), were those in which the means for girls were significantly lower relative to the boys. Although the others are not significantly different, all but two of the nine items produce higher means for the boys. The two items, on which boys have lower, though nonsignificant, scores than girls, measure the adolescents' satisfaction with their physical condition and the way their bodies are developing. Figure 1 illustrates these findings for the items of the Body Image Scale, with a bar graph which portrays the magnitude and direction of sex differences.

3.1.1. *The Relations of Pubertal Change to Body Image and Feelings of Attractiveness.* Looking first at the larger picture, we address the question of whether and how the index of pubertal change may relate to body image scores and feelings of attractiveness. Boys who mature earlier tend to perceive themselves more positively than boys who are either on-time or late in their development. They think of themselves as being more attractive ($r = .33$, $p < 0.05$) and have a somewhat higher body image ($r = 0.23$, $p < 0.06$). For girls, no relationships emerge between these variables.

We shall now turn to the relationships between perceptions of the self and specific components of pubertal change; the latter include both the pubertal items and perceptions of the timing of pubertal maturation. These analyses were conducted through individual regressions. Figure 2 displays the models which best represent the patterns in our data, differentially for boys and girls. For boys, a linear trend occurs for 8 out of the 10 relations, with 5 of these producing significant results. The only item which does not follow this pattern is that of skin change. The relationship between skin change and other variables is unusual for both boys and girls. Skin change (pimples) may not be a good measure of pubertal

---

[1] d Represents a standard deviation unit which is the difference between the means of two variables divided by the standard deviation.

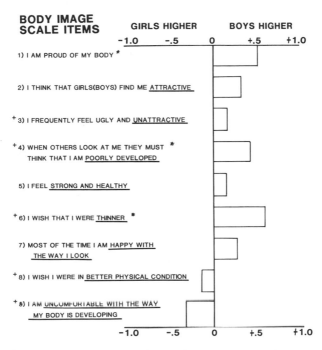

Figure 1. The direction and magnitude of sex differences on items from the Body Image Scale in standard deviation units. Note that * indicates $p < 0.05$ and + indicates these items have been reversed so that a high score indicates high body image.

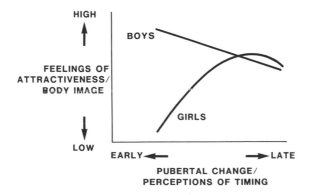

Figure 2. The model describing the relationship of pubertal change to body image and feelings of attractiveness.

change because factors other than pubertal development influence its emergence.

Thus, for boys, greater physical maturity is associated with greater feelings of attractiveness and a more positive body image, both in terms of actual physical changes reported and the adolescent boys' subjective sense of the timing of their development. Those with little physical development, both actual and perceived, tend to feel less attractive and less positive about their bodies. The development of facial hair appears to be the most influential of all the pubertal items with regard to feelings of attractiveness, explaining the highest percentage of variance ($r^2 = 0.19$). Perceptions of the timing of development are related with similar strength to feelings of attractiveness ($r^2 = 0.18$), followed by growth spurt ($r^2 = 0.10$), and body hair ($r^2 = 0.09$). Body image is most affected by voice change ($r^2 = 0.10$), body hair, facial hair, and perceptions of timing producing similar, but nonsignificant, patterns. Thus, for boys, a consistent linear pattern emerges, showing that earlier maturation is perceived more favorably.

With girls, a different and more complex pattern emerges from the relationship between perceptions of the self and components of pubertal change. For most of the variables, there is a significant quadratic component (curvilinear relationship). This pattern requires more than 2 points. One of the puberty items, menarche, therefore could not be considered in this model, because it is dichotomous. For six out of eight relationships, analyses of the three puberty items and perceptions of timing with feelings of attractiveness and body image, quadratic and linear components together, but neither alone, account for significant percentages of the variance. In five out of the six regressions, the quadratic term entered first, indicating that it is the more powerful component, although it cannot explain the relationships without the linear component. The first aspect of the model indicates that those girls who are in mid-development or perceive themselves to be on-time in their physical maturation, feel more attractive and more positive about their bodies than those who are early or late. At the same time, there is a tendency for those who are late, both in the reported physical changes and in the sense of their timing, to feel more positive about themselves in terms of attractiveness and body image than those who are early. The girls' feelings of attractiveness are best explained by the perceptions of the timing of their maturation ($r^2 = 0.14$) and next by breast development ($r^2 = 0.10$). The relation between attractiveness and breast development is different from the others in that it is the only one in which the linear term is more powerful than the quadratic term. In this case, those with more breast development tend to feel more attractive than those with only a little, who feel less attractive.

Thus, for girls, the relations between various perceptions of self and components of pubertal change are more complex. For the girls' body image, timing is the most salient component of pubertal change, although the pubertal items are also described by the interactive quadratic and linear terms.

3.2. *Weight and Satisfaction with Weight*

Based on our review of the literature, we hypothesized that boys more than girls would be satisfied with their weight, might tend to perceive themselves as underweight, and that weight would generally be a less salient variable for them. Girls perceive themselves as heavier than boys ($F = 4.13$, $p < 0.05$), and although girls are somewhat more dissatisfied with their weight than boys, the difference in satisfaction with weight is not significant.

The significant relationship between perceived weight and satisfaction with weight, presented in Figure 3, is linear for girls ($F = 16.19$, $p < 0.005$); perceiving oneself as underweight is associated with the most satisfaction, followed closely by average weight. A large dip in satisfaction occurs with perceptions of being overweight. For boys, a quadratic pattern describes the relationship ($F = 12.10$, $p < 0.005$) with average weight valued most, and perceptions of under- and overweight valued less. As hypothesized, the weight variables are more salient for the girls than the boys. When perceptions of self were analyzed with perception of, and satisfaction with, weight, only for girls did significant relations

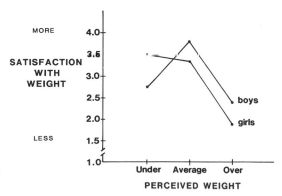

Figure 3. The relationship between satisfaction with weight and perceived weight by sex.

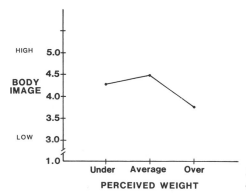

Figure 4. Body image as it relates to perceived weight for girls.

emerge between body image and both weight measures (Figures 4 and 5). A quadratic pattern describes the relation between body image and perception of weight, with average weight associated with the highest body image, followed by underweight and overweight ($F = 6.48$, $p < 0.005$). A simple linear relationship emerges between satisfaction with weight and body image ($F = 3.46$, $p < 0.05$).

Because the weight variables related to body image for the girls, they were entered separately in stepwise regressions with puberty items to predict body image. The weight variables always entered first, with weight explaining 7% of the variance, and satisfaction with weight explaining 16%. When perception of timing entered the equation, the amount of variance explained became 20%. When this is compared to the amount of variance explained by timing alone ($r = 0.10$), it becomes clear that the two variables, weight and timing, explain different components of variance. This is not true with satisfaction with weight and timing,

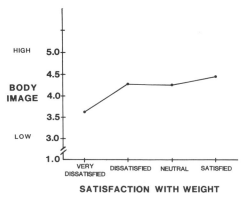

Figure 5. Body image as it relates to satisfaction with weight for girls.

where approximately half of the timing variance is explained by satisfaction with weight. Thus, satisfaction with weight is responsible for half the body image variance originally thought to be explained by timing. Breast development, when entered alone, accounts for 6% of the variance in body image. The two components, linear and quadratic, entered after perceptions of weight, explain approximately 10% and 8% respectively, indicating that breast development explains body image somewhat better once perceived weight has been accounted for. This is more strikingly true when the breast development variables are explained with satisfaction with weight; then the variance explained becomes 17% and 24%, respectively. Therefore, almost a quarter of the body image variance is explained by satisfaction with weight and breast development for girls.

The results from a principal components factor analysis provide more information as to how these variables cluster for boys and girls (Table 3). Three factors emerge for both sexes, explaining about 65% of the variance. Additionally, the amount of variance accounted for by each factor is similar for boys and girls. For both boys and girls, the first factor from the principal components analysis includes the puberty items and timing. The first factor also includes perceptions of the self for the boys and the weight variables for the girls. For girls, the second factor includes the variables missing from the first, plus the weight variables. For boys, satisfaction with weight and voice change join the perceptions of self to create the second factor.

When rotated (varimax procedure), the factors differ somewhat. For boys, the first factor is a measure of puberty, which includes the four puberty items and perceptions of timing. In the second, perceptions of self cluster with facial hair, and in the third, satisfaction with weight and voice change enter. For girls, the first factor also represents a pubertal scale, but excludes perceptions of timing. The second factor includes the weight variables plus timing and all the puberty items except body hair. The third represents perceptions of self plus satisfaction with weight.

These analyses indicate that the puberty items form a scale for both boys and girls and that timing is salient to this scale for the boys. For girls, the weight variables and timing cluster with the puberty items, demonstrating that weight is an important aspect of pubertal change for girls.

3.3. Body Satisfaction

The adolescents were asked what they liked best and least about their bodies. There was substantial variability in the kinds of responses they gave (Table 4). About a third of the boys and girls gave nonsubstan-

Table 3. Results from Factor Analyses

| | Principal components | | | | | | Varimax rotation factors | | | | | |
| | Girls | | | Boys | | | Girls | | | Boys | | |
Variables	1	2	3	1	2	3	1	2	3	1	2	3
Body hair	0.71			0.73			0.87			0.72		
Facial hair[a]			0.49	0.56						0.40	0.42	
Breast development[b]	0.88						0.81	0.41				
Voice change[a]				0.60	0.44					0.67		0.32
Menarche	0.54						0.33	0.48				
Growth	0.77			0.58			0.72	0.34		0.70		
Perceived timing	−0.51			−0.61		−0.46		−0.68		−0.54		
Body image		0.85	0.48	0.48	−0.36				0.91		0.65	
Attractiveness		0.45	−0.33	0.70	−0.62				0.42		0.91	
Satisfaction with weight	−0.51	0.38	−0.36		0.45	0.62		−0.46	0.37			0.78
Perceived weight	0.46	−0.35						0.61				
Percent variance	37	19	13	36	15	13	59	26	16	61	23	16

[a]Girls only.
[b]Boys only.

Table 4. *What Early Adolescents Like Best and Least about Their Bodies*
(Rank Order Percent)

Boys		Girls	
Best			
Athletic strengths/abilities	32	Facial features (and skin, hair)	23
Don't know	24	Don't know	15
Height (tall)	12	Athletic strengths/abilities	14
Nothing	12	Nothing	11
Extraneous body parts	10	Height (tall)	8
Facial features (and skin)	5	Being average	7
Mental abilities	3	Height (short)	6
Body dimensions (thin)	3	Extraneous body parts (and legs)	5
Everything	3	Mental abilities	1
Least			
Nothing	25	Extraneous body parts (and legs, hips)	26
Facial features (and skin, hair)	21	Facial features (and skin, hair)	20
Don't know	17	Nothing	18
Body dimensions (thin)	15	Body dimensions (fat)	16
Extraneous body parts	14	Don't know	13
Body dimensions (fat)	7	Height (short)	8
Height (short)	7	Body dimensions (thin)	5
Lack of athletic abilities	7	Height (tall)	5
Height (tall)	2	Lack of athletic abilities	2

tive responses ("don't know" or "nothing"). Generally, girls mentioned attractiveness dimensions, including facial features, legs, and hips as more important for both positive and negative valuations of their bodies. For boys, the most frequently mentioned body satisfactions derive from athletic-related strengths and abilities. Few boys mentioned dissatisfactions in this area, though some found facial features to be problematic.

4. DISCUSSION

4.1. *Patterns Found for Boys*

Taken together, these data present a consistent pattern of relationships. For boys, perceiving themselves as early in pubertal maturation on several separate indices is related to a more positive body image and greater sense of attractiveness. Perceiving oneself as late on these measures is associated with a more negative body image and decreased sense of attractiveness.

These findings, for boys, are consistent with previous studies. This study, however, has produced an added dimension. By measuring an intermediate stage of pubertal development, we see that it is not early or late maturation alone which differentiates groups. The fact that the group in the middle report a body image that is between the early and late developers indicate that, for boys, it is physical movement toward young adulthood, with all of its advantages, which is generally experienced as positive; it is not just being early which is associated with positive self-perceptions.

By looking at the separate physical changes which occur for boys, we find that facial hair is the pubertal item which most influences positive perceptions of self, explaining twice the variance of other variables. It also combines with perceptions of self to create the second factor from the varimax rotated factor analysis. These two findings indicate that it is the most important pubertal change to be measured for a young adolescent male's feelings about his physical self. In the past, it has been suggested that increased physical size with the concomitant heightened physical prowess might constitute the important element to the positive findings connected with early male puberty (Clausen, 1975). The importance here of facial hair suggests that other dynamics may be more salient. Facial hair is a visually apparent change with powerful symbolic meaning for adult physical status. Thus, the reactions from adults and peers to this physical change may stimulate a change in self-image. In order for this to happen, facial hair must be incorporated into a system of meaning regarding physical maturation.

This finding awaits replication, and it does not stand alone. In general, *all* of the pubertal changes—facial hair, voice change, growth spurt, and body hair—are consistently related to positive self-perceptions of the males. Such changes for boys appear to be linked to positive status attainments and presage the transition to adulthood. Such changes are associated with anticipated life course events.

4.2. *Patterns Found for Girls*

For girls, also, these data maintain consistency in the pattern of relationships, but the picture differs from that seen with boys. A combination of curved and straight lines (quadratic and linear components) describe the relation of pubertal development to perceptions of self. Being in the middle of puberty and perceiving oneself to be on-time are related to a more positive body image and greater feelings of attractiveness. Although perceptions of being early or late, that is, off-time, produce more negative self-perceptions in body image and attractiveness, those who perceive themselves as being late in their pubertal maturation feel better about themselves than those who are earlier.

Perceptions of and satisfaction with weight are important variables for girls. They are more important for a girl's body image than they are for a boy's as evidenced by the sex difference in the item-total correlation coefficient for the Body Image Scale item, "I wish I were thinner." Additionally, only for the girls do significant relationships emerge between the weight questions and body image. A varimax rotation factor analysis indicates that once a puberty scale has been accounted for (Factor 1), three of the four puberty items combine with perceptions of timing as well as perceptions of and satisfaction with weight to form a second factor. Thus, for girls, a second independent scale is one that includes weight. If a girl is further along in puberty and perceives herself as so, she also will tend to perceive herself as heavier and be less satisfied with her weight. Weight somewhat improves the power of the pubertal items to predict body image.

All of these findings indicate that weight, especially satisfaction with weight, must be considered in the relationship between puberty and perceptions of self for girls, but not boys. It appears that being average in weight is most valued and being thin is valued next. These findings are consistent with the research already discussed. Weight is heavily emphasized by this culture as a particularly important aspect of appearance for a female. The prepubertal girl with her svelte body and long legs maintains a cultural ideal in physical shape (see Faust, Chapter 6).

In contrast to this ideal is that of the full-bodied, large-breasted, sexy look representative of the figures displayed in both popular and pornographic media. A more mature body is emphasized with particular focus on large breasts. The one pubertal item where the linear term entered before the quadratic in predicting perceptions of self is breast development. In this case, a girl with breast development tends to feel more positive about her physical self than a girl who is more flat chested.

Interestingly, very little research on breast development exists. Based on exploratory research, Rosenbaum (1979) concluded that because of the relative absence of visibility and mobility of female genitalia, breasts occupy an inordinate amount of psychic space for adolescent girls. Interviews with adolescent girls reveal that all body parts, except breasts, are desired to be small and unobtrusive, and that big breasts are valued for their appeal to boys. Rosenbaum writes. "Thus, breasts were seen as the most consciously sexualized body parts, symbols of the maturing sexuality of the girl." (p. 245). Young adolescent girls, particularly premenarcheal seventh-grade girls, appear to be more preoccupied with breast development than late and postmenarcheal seventh-grade girls, as represented in figure drawings with more explicit breasts (Rierdan and Koff, 1980). Additional support for this finding is the sex difference found on the Body Image Scale item, "When others look at me they must think that I am poorly developed." Girls tend to endorse this item more than boys. Once breasts have developed and there is no more concern as to whether or not this development will ever occur, and a girl becomes accustomed to her "endowment," this preoccupation probably dissipates considerably. There is some evidence, though, that a cultural preoccupation with breasts never allows a woman to become completely unaware of her breast shape and size relative to cultural ideals (Ayalah and Weinstock, 1979).

For girls who are experiencing the events of puberty, the social support of a peer group may serve as an especially important buffer in accommodating to the changes of their bodies. One of the adolescent girls in our study, who perceived herself to be early in her development, responded to the question of how she felt about having gotten her period by saying: "Well, I suppose I felt more grown up. I also felt a little embarrassed." When asked why, she said: "Well, I knew that barely any of my friends had it and it was just kinda embarrassing, even though, you know you can't tell if someone has their period. You feel different inside around your friends, like a little self-conscious."

Past research on females has tended to examine puberty only as if it were a unitary process and dichotomous variable. For example, as with the boys, longitudinal studies have focused on early and late physical maturation. More recent studies have tended to focus on pre- and post-menarcheal status. But by looking at a number of pubertal events, degrees of change within each of them, and subjective perceptions of their timing, we are provided with greater insight into the complexity of pubertal development.

It appears, generally, that physical maturation does not stimulate the same unequivocal social response for girls as it does for boys. Examining the index of pubertal change and body image scores for girls, we found little association between these two measures. This may be due to inconsistencies in expectations across various life domains. For example, the experience of menarche has been found to arouse ambivalent feelings, many of which appear to be culturally determined (Brooks-Gunn and Ruble, 1980; Koff, Rierdan, and Jacobson, 1981). The greater maturity associated with menarche may have a positive personal significance, but the positive impact is reduced by a negative interpersonal significance as girls become increasingly self-conscious, embarrassed, and secretive (Koff et al., 1981). In one study, it was found that messages presented through booklets distributed by sanitary products companies, conveyed conflicting ideas about menstruation. On the one hand, menstruation was portrayed as a normal noninterruptive aspect of life. On the other hand, because of concern with lack of sanitation, it was something to be constantly attended and carefully concealed (Whisnant, Brett, and Zegans, 1975).

Additionally, the family environment may influence the experience of puberty. Recent findings indicate that families with greater acceptance of sexuality and physical maturation may help induce a more positive view of development in their daughters and thereby contribute to a more positive experience of menarche and menstruation (see Brooks-Gunn and Ruble, Chapter 8). However, this does not appear to be a frequent occurrence. Investigators have reported that seventh and eighth grade girls portray menarche as having a primarily negative impact (Bardwick, 1971; Clark and Ruble, 1978). Our results indicate a lower level of body-related esteem for those girls who are most advanced on pubertal markers.

As mentioned in the introduction, physical maturation in girls, not containing the same meaning as for boys, may elicit a more sexualized response from others in the broader social context. This response, perhaps unconscious, may be enacted with restrictions on the pubertal girls' freedoms, with parents becoming concerned with protecting their daughters (Block, 1978; Katz, 1979). It has been suggested that sexual maturity is at this time more a concern than a joy to parents (Brooks-Gunn and Matthews, 1979). When their adolescent daughters were in sixth grade, parents of the girls in our study did not report concern with their daughter's sexuality (Boxer, Solomon, Offer, Petersen, and Halprin, 1983); perhaps this was because pubertal changes were just beginning for these girls. In addition, parents' personal responses to their young adolescent's physical development may be mediated by their life cycle position and experience of aging (Rossi, 1980). As adolescents become more adultlike in appearance, parents may be more likely to identify with their offspring.

The meaning of the lower body image and feelings of attractiveness for postpubertal girls is unclear. It may be that, as postulated earlier, the lack of social support provided by peers experiencing the same events induces this lowered self-esteem for early maturers. Another possibility is that when girls, now in the midst of their puberty, become postpubertal, they too will experience a lowered sense of self-esteem. This prediction is consistent with findings of lower self-image for late adolescent and mature women when compared to men of similar ages (O'Malley and Bachman, 1979; Lerner, Iwawacki, Chihara, and Sorell, 1980; Simmons and Rosenberg, 1975).

4.3. *Patterns Found for Girls and Boys*

We must also consider the fact that boys and girls in our study interact with each other in a sex-integrated peer structure and school environment. Early-developing males are the first of their sex to show physical maturation, but there is a precedent for change; the early-maturing boys begin puberty after the early-maturing girls are well into their pubertal development. It seems inevitable that young adolescents would make cross-sex as well as same-sex comparisons in their developmental status, and this may have a differential impact on their perceptions and experience of pubertal maturation. It may be easier for late-maturing girls to engage in heterosocial interactions with boys of their own age than it is for those who are early in their development. The latest-maturing boys will be at a disadvantage in this regard, at least in relation to girls of the same age. In addition to the ambivalence aroused by menarche and in contrast to other pubertal changes, breast development appears to hold a positive meaning for these seventh grade girls. Thus, while girls who perceive themselves as early maturers tend to hold a more negative set of self-perceptions, breast development is a positive marker for them.

Responses to what adolescents like best and least about their bodies indicate that, for boys, physical capacities as well as attractiveness dimensions provide definitions of the body self. For girls, self-perceptions tend to be focussed on dimensions of attractiveness, both in terms of what is most and least liked about their bodies. With regard to culturally shared definitions of the self, it may be that the latitudes of femininity more than masculinity contract during adolescence (see Hill and Lynch, Chapter 10).

It was also noted that many adolescents could find nothing they liked best or least about their bodies, or simply didn't know how to respond. It is possible that in the midst of puberty, early adolescents were unable to conceptualize or articulate the experience of their bodies. With rapid physical changes and increased cognitive capacities, adolescents become aware of a new state of consciousness. With what Hill and Lynch (Chapter 10) call the "intensification of gender-related role-expectations," adolescents begin to construct self-theories which incorporate new cultural and personal meanings which they themselves are only now beginning to understand. In addition, individuals in their social world respond to them in new ways, differentially for boys and girls

(Block, 1978). Anticipations of young adulthood become more realistic and the future becomes more real and contains more possibilities.

A few caveats about our study are warranted. First, the relations between puberty and self-perceptions, although consistent, are not strong. This may be due to the fact that puberty does not heavily influence the domains on which we have reported: body image and feelings of attractiveness; puberty may be only one among many other determinants. A second explanation for the weak relationship may be methodological. The pubertal variables and attractiveness measure were collected through interviews, while the Body Image Scale, a paper and pencil measure, was administered at a separate time during a group assessment. In addition, because boys and girls systematically vary from each other in the timing of pubertal change, we should be wary when making comparisons of same-aged boys and girls. There may be a confound of sex and pubertal stage, although such an explanation would not hold for the results presented here. In general, however, any sex differences could be the product of pubertal stage differences. With the completion of a full longitudinal panel, we shall be able to control some of these differences in future analyses. Finally, it may be difficult for a young adolescent to describe and discuss his or her development. Bodily changes bring new sexual feelings, increased strength, and a widening array of intellectual and emotional capacities. Young adolescents may be unable to find a set of concepts or language by which to label the experience of their bodies.

No longer a child, but not yet an adult, the young adolescent has a taste of things to come, with new physical characteristics and the emerging variety of social–psychological expectations which accompany them. We hope, in the future, to discover some of the more covert meanings of puberty by using a semistructured technique in which these adolescents are asked to tell stories to a specially designed set of pictures. The study of early adolescence presents the challenge of developing a set of methods and dimensions by which we can understand this unique phase of the life cycle.

ACKNOWLEDGMENTS. The research reported in this study is supported by National Institute of Mental Health Grant MH30252, awarded to Dr. Anne C. Petersen. Portions of the data in this chapter were presented at the Annual Convention of the American Psychological Association, in the Symposium, Puberty: Social and Psychological Significance, August 26, 1981, Los Angeles; and at the Annual Conference on the Psychology of Adolescence, Institute for Psychosomatic and Psychiatric Research and

Training, Michael Reese Hospital and Medical Center, Chicago, June 19, 1981.

REFERENCES

Adams, G. R. Physical attractiveness research: Toward a developmental social psychology of beauty. *Human Development*, 1977, *20*, 217–239.
Anthony, E. J. The reactions of adults to adolescents and their behavior. In G. Caplan and S. Lebovici (Eds.), *Adolescence*. New York: Basic Books, 1969.
Ayalah, D., and Weinstock, I. J. *Breasts: Women speak about their breasts and their lives*. New York: Summit Books, 1979.
Bacon, L. Early motherhood, accelerated role transition, and social pathologies. *Social Forces*, 1974, *52*, 333–341.
Bardwick, J. M. *Psychology of women: A study of bio-cultural conflicts*. New York: Harper and Row, 1971.
Bar-Tal, D., and Saxe, L. Physical attractiveness and its relationship to sex role stereotyping. *Sex Roles*, 1976, *2*, 123–133.
Block, J. H. Another look at sex differentiation in the socialization behaviors of mothers and fathers. In J. Sherman and F. Denmark (Eds.), *Psychology of women: Future directions of research*. New York: Psychological Dimensions, 1978.
Boxer, A., Solomon, B., Offer, D., Petersen, A., and Halprin, F. Parents' perceptions of their young adolescents. In R. Cohen, B. Cohler, and S. Weissman (Eds.), *Parenthood as an adult experience*. New York: Guilford Press, 1983, in press.
Brenner, D., and Hinsdale, G. Body build stereotypes and self identification in three age groups of females. *Adolescence*, 1978, *13*, 551–561.
Brim, O. G., Jr. Theories of the male mid-life crisis. *Counseling Psychologist*, 1976a, *6*, 2–9.
Brim, O. G. Jr. Life-span development of the theory of oneself: Implications for child development. In H. Reese (Ed.), *Advances in child development and behavior*. Vol. II. New York: Academic Press, 1976b.
Brim, O. G., Jr., and Ryff, C. On the properties of life events. In P. Baltes and O. G. Brim, Jr. (Eds.), *Life-span development and behavior*. Vol. III. New York: Academic Press, 1980.
Brooks-Gunn, J., and Matthews, W. S. *He and she: How children develop their sex role identity*. Englewood Cliffs, New Jersey: Prentice Hall, 1979.
Brooks-Gunn, J., and Ruble, D. N. Menarche: The interaction of physiological, cultural and social factors. In A. J. Dan, E. A. Graham, and C. P. Beecher (Eds.), *The menstrual cycle: A synthesis of interdisciplinary research*. New York: Springer, 1980.
Broughton, J. M., and Riegel, K. F. Developmental psychology and the self. *Annals of the New York Academy of Science*, 1977, *291*, 149–167.
Bruch, H. The sleeping beauty: Escape from change. In S. I. Greenspan and G. Pollock (Eds.), *The course of life: Psychoanalytic contributions toward understanding personality development. Volume II: Latency, adolescence, and youth*. Washington, D.C.: U.S. Government Printing Office, DHHS Publication No. (ADM)81–1000, 1981.
Butler, R. The life-review: An interpretation of reminiscence in the aged. *Psychiatry*, 1963, *26*, 65–76.
Clark, A., and Ruble, D. Young adolescents' beliefs concerning menstruation. *Child Development*, 1978, *49*, 231–234.
Clausen, J. A. The social meaning of differential physical and sexual maturation. In S. E. Dragastin and G. H. Elder, Jr. (Eds.), *Adolescence in the life cycle: Psychological change and social context*. Washington, D.C.: Hemisphere, 1975.

Cohler, B. J. Adult developmental psychology and reconstruction in psychoanalysis. In S. I. Greenspan and G. H. Pollock (Eds.), *The course of life: Psychoanalytic contributions towards understanding personality development. Volume III: Adulthood and the aging process.* Washington, D.C.: U.S. Government Printing Office, DHHS Publication No. (ADM)81–1000, 1981.

Cohler, B. J. Personal narrative and life-course. In P. Baltes and O. G. Brim, Jr. (Eds.), *Life-span development and behavior.* Vol. 4. New York: Academic Press, 1982.

Cohler, B. J., and Boxer, A. M. Settling into the world: Person, time, and context in the middle-adult years. In D. Offer and M. Sabshin (Eds.), *Normality and the life cycle.* New York: Basic Books, 1983, in press.

Coleman, J. C. *The nature of adolescence.* London and New York: Methuen and Co., 1980.

Coleman, J. S., Bremner, R. H., Clark, B. R., Davis, J. B., Eichorn, D. H., Griliches, Z., Kett, J. F., Ryder, N. B., Doering, Z. B., and Mays, J. M., *Youth: Transition to adulthood. Report of the panel on youth of the President's Science Advisory Committee.* Chicago: The University of Chicago Press, 1974.

Cottle, T. *Perceiving time: A psychological investigation.* New York: Wiley-Interscience, 1976.

Cottle, T., and Klineberg, S. *The present of things future.* New York: Free Press-Macmillan, 1974.

Douvan, E., and Adelson, J. *The adolescent experience.* New York: Wiley, 1966.

Elder, G. H. Jr., Adolescence in historical perspective. In J. Adelson (Ed.) *Handbook of adolescent psychology.* New York: Wiley-Interscience, 1980.

Elkind, D. Egocentrism in adolescence. *Child Development,* 1967, *38,* 1025–1034.

Elkind, D. *Children and adolescents: Interpretive essays on Jean Piaget.* New York: Oxford University Press, 1974.

Epstein, S. The self-concept revisited: Or a theory of a theory. *American Psychologist,* 1973, *28,* 404–416.

Erikson, E. H. Identity and the life cycle. *Psychological Issues,* 1959, *1.*

Erikson, E. H. *Identity: Youth and crisis.* New York: W. W. Norton, 1968.

Farnham-Diggory, S. Self, future, and time: A developmental study of the concepts of psychotic, brain-damaged, and normal children. *Monographs of the Society For Research in Child Development,* 1966, *31,* 1(Serial No. 103).

Faust, M. S. Developmental maturity as a determinant in prestige of adolescent girls. *Child Development,* 1960, *31,* 173–184.

Faust, M. S. Somatic development of adolescent girls. *Monographs of the Society for Research in Child Development,* 1977, *42,* 1 (Serial No. 169).

Ford, C., and Beach, F. *Patterns of sexual behavior.* New York: Harper-Hoeber, 1951.

Frank, R. A., and Cohen, D. J. Psychosocial concomitants of biological maturation in preadolescence. *American Journal of Psychiatry,* 1979, *136,* 1518–1524.

Frazier, A., and Lisonbee, L. K. Adolescent concerns with physique. *School Review,* 1950, *58,* 379–405.

Gergen, K. J. Stability, change, and chance in understanding human development. In N. Datan and H. W. Reese (Eds.), *Life-span developmental psychology: Dialectical perspectives on experimental research.* New York: Academic Press, 1977.

Gubrium, J. F. (Ed). *Time, roles, and self in old age.* New York: Human Sciences Press, 1976.

Haan, N. Adolescents and young adults as producers of their development. In R. M. Lerner and N. A. Busch-Rossnagel (Eds.), *Individuals as producers of their development.* New York: Academic Press, 1981.

Hamburg, B. Early adolescence: A specific and stressful stage of the life cycle. In G. Coelho, D. A. Hamburg, and J. E. Adams (Eds.), *Coping and adaptation.* New York: Basic Books, 1974.

Havighurst, R. J. *Developmental tasks and education.* New York: D. McKay, 1972.

Hill, J. P. The family. In M. Johnson (Ed.), *Toward adolescence: The middle school years. The seventy-ninth yearbook of the National Society for the Study of Education.* Chicago: The University of Chicago Press, 1980.

Hogan, D. The variable order of events in the life course. *American Sociological Review,* 1978, *43,* 573–586.

Hultsch, D. F., and Plemons, J. K. Life events and life-span development. In P. B. Baltes and O. G. Brim, Jr. (Eds.), *Life-span development and behavior* Vol. 2. New York: Academic Press, 1979.

Jersild, A. I. *In search of self.* New York: Columbia University Press, 1952.

Jones, M. C. Psychological correlates of somatic development. *Child Development,* 1965, *36,* 899–911.

Jones, M. C., and Bayley, N. Physical maturing among boys as related to behavior. *Journal of Educational Psychology,* 1950, *41,* 129–148.

Jones, M. C., and Mussen, P. H. Self-conceptions, motivations, and interpersonal atttitudes of early- and late-maturing girls. *Child Development,* 1958, *29,* 491–501.

Katz, P. The development of female identity. *Sex Roles,* 1979, *5,* 155–178.

Kavrell, S. M., and Jarcho, H. Self-esteem and body image in early adolescence. Paper presented at the Annual meetings of the American Psychological Association, Montreal, Canada, September, 1980.

Kestenberg, J. Phases of adolescence with suggestions for a correlation of psychic and hormonal organizations: Parts I and II. *Journal of the American Academy of Child Psychiatry,* 1967, *6,* 427–463 and 577–614.

Koff, E., Rierdan, J., and Jacobson, S. The personal and interpersonal significance of menarche. *Journal of the American Academy of Child Psychiatry,* 1981, *20,* 148–158.

Kohlberg, L., and Gilligan, C. The adolescent as a philosopher: The discovery of the self in a postconventional world. *Daedalus,* 1971, *100,* 1051–1086.

Kohut, H. *The analysis of the self.* New York: International Universities Press, 1971.

Lens, W., and Gailly, A. Extension of future time perspective in motivational goals of different age groups. *International Journal of Behavioral Development,* 1980, *3,* 1–17.

Lerner, R. M. The development of stereotyped expectancies of body build–behavior relations. *Child Development,* 1969, *40,* 137–141.

Lerner, R. M., and Karabenick, S. A. Physical attractiveness, body attitudes, and self-concept in late adolescents. *Journal of Youth and Adolescence,* 1974, *3,* 7–16.

Lerner, R. M., Karabenick, S. A., and Stuart, J. L. Relations among physical attractiveness, body attitudes, and self-concept in male and female college students. *Journal of Psychology,* 1973, *85,* 119–129.

Lerner, R. M., Iwawaaki, S., Chihara, T., and Sorell, G. T. Self-concept, self-esteem, and body attitudes among Japanese male and female adolescents. *Child Development,* 1980, *51,* 847–855.

Levine, R. *Culture, behavior, and personality.* Chicago: Aldine, 1973.

Lieberman, M. Adaptive processes in late life. In N. Datan and L. Ginsberg (Eds.), *Life-span developmental psychology: Normative life crises.* New York: Academic Press, 1975.

Lieberman, M., and Falk, J. The remembered past as a source of data for research on the life-cycle. *Human Development,* 1971, *14,* 132–141.

Lynch, M. E. Paternal androgyny, daughters' physical maturity level, and achievement socialization in early adolescence. Unpublished doctoral dissertation, Cornell University, 1981.

Mead, M. Adolescence in primitive and modern society. In G. E. Swanson, T. M. Newcomb, and E. K. Hartley (Eds.), *Reading in social psychology.* New York: Holt, 1958.

Mussen, P. H., and Jones, M. C. Self-conceptions, motivations, and interpersonal attitudes of late- and early-maturing boys. *Child Development,* 1957, *28,* 243–256.

Myerhoff, B. Life history among the elderly: Performance, visibility and remembering. In J. Ruby (Ed.), *A crack in the mirror: Reflexive perspectives in anthropology*. Philadelphia: University of Pennsylvania Press, 1982.

Neugarten, B. L. Continuities and discontinuities of psychological issues into adult life. *Human Development*, 1969, *12*, 121–130.

Neugarten, B. L. Dynamics of transition of middle age to old age: Adaptation and the life cycle. *Journal of Geriatric Psychiatry*, 1970, *41*, 71–87.

Neugarten, B. L. Time, age, and the life cycle. *American Journal of Psychiatry*, 1979, *136*, 887–894.

Neugarten, B. L. and Datan, N. Sociological perspectives on the life cycle. In P. Baltes and K. W. Schaie (Eds.), *Life-span developmental psychology: Personality and socialization*. New York: Academic Press, 1973.

Neugarten, B. L., and Hagestad, G. O. Age and the life course. In R. H. Binstock and E. Shanas (Eds.), *Handbook of aging and the social sciences*. New York: Van Nostrand Reinhold, 1976.

Neugarten, B., Moore, J., and Lowe, J. Age norms, age constraints, and adult socialization. *American Journal of Sociology*, 1965, *70*, 710–717.

O'Malley, P. M., and Bachman, J. G. Self-esteem and education: Sex and cohort comparisons among high school seniors. *Journal of Personality and Social Psychology*, 1979, *37*, 1153–59.

Offer, D., and Offer, J. B. *From teenage to young manhood: A psychological study*. New York: Basic Books, 1975.

Offer, D., Ostrov, E., and Howard, K. I. *The offer self-image questionnaire for adolescents: A manual*. Chicago: Michael Reese Hospital, 1977.

Offer, D., Ostrov, E., and Howard, K. I. *The adolescent: A psychological self-portrait*. New York: Basic Books, 1981.

Padin, M. A., Lerner, R. M., and Spiro, A. Stability of body attitudes and self-esteem in late adolescents. *Adolescence*, 1981, *16*, 371–384.

Peskin, H. Pubertal onset and ego functioning: A psychoanalytic approach. *Journal of Abnormal Psychology*, 1967, *72*, 1–15.

Peskin, H. Influence of the developmental schedule of puberty on learning and ego functioning. *Journal of Youth and Adolescence*, 1973, *2*, 273–290.

Petersen, A. C. Biopsychosocial processes in the development of sex-related differences. In J. E. Parsons (Ed.), *The psychobiology of sex differences and sex roles*. Washington, D.C.: Hemisphere, 1980a.

Petersen, A. C. *The Self-Image Questionnaire for Young Adolescents*. Chicago: Laboratory for the Study of Adolescence, Michael Reese Hospital and Medical Center, 1980b.

Petersen, A. C. Menarche: Meaning of measures and measuring meaning. In S. Golub (Ed.), *Menarche*. New York: D. C. Heath, in press.

Petersen, A. C., and Taylor, B. The biological approach to adolescence: Biological change and psychological adaptation. In J. Adelson (Ed.), *Handbook of adolescent psychology*. New York: Wiley-Interscience, 1980.

Plath, D. Contours of consociation: Lessons from a Japanese narrative. In P. Baltes and O. G. Brim, Jr. (Eds.), *Life-span development and behavior*. Vol. 3. New York: Academic Press, 1980.

Rierdan, J., and Koff, E. The psychological impact of menarche: Integrative vs. disruptive changes. *Journal of Youth and Adolescence*, 1980, *9*, 49–58.

Rosenbaum, M. The changing body image of the adolescent girl. In M. Sugar (Ed.), *Female adolescent development*. New York: Bruner/Mazel, 1979.

Rossi, A. Aging and parenthood in the middle years. In P. B. Baltes and O. G. Brim, Jr. (Eds.), *Life-span development and behavior*. Vol. 3. New York: Acadmic Press, 1980.

Savin-Williams, R. Dominance hierarchies in groups of early adolescents. *Child Development*, 1979, *50*, 923–935.

Schilder, P. *The image and appearance of the human body*. London: Kegan, Paul, Trench, Truber, and Company, 1935.

Seiden, A. M. Sex roles, sexuality and the adolescent peer group. *Adolescent Psychiatry*, 1976, *4*, 211–225.

Seltzer, M. Suggestions for the examination of time disordered relationships In J. Gubrium (Ed.), *Time, roles and self in old age*. New York: Human Sciences Press, 1976.

Simmons, R. G., and Rosenberg, F. Sex, sex-roles and self-image. *Journal of Youth and Adolescence*, 1975, *4*, 229–258.

Simmons, R. G., Rosenberg, F., and Rosenberg, M. Disturbance in the self-image at adolescence. *American Sociological Review*, 1973, *38*, 553–568.

Simmons, R. G., Blyth, D., Van Cleave, E. G., and Bush, D. M. Entry into early adolescence: The impact of school structure, puberty, and early dating on self-esteem. *American Sociological Review*, 1979, *44*, 948–967.

Smith, M. B. Perspectives of selfhood. *American Psychologist*, 1978, *33*, 1053–1063.

Sorell, G. T., and Nowak, C. A. The role of physical attractiveness as a contributor to individual development. In R. M. Lerner and N. Busch-Rossnagel (Eds.), *Individuals as producers of their development: A life-span perspective*. New York: Academic Press, 1981.

Staffieri, J. R. A study of social stereotype of body-image in children. *Journal of Personality and Social Psychology*, 1967, *7*, 101–104.

Steinberg, L. D. Transformations in family relations at puberty. *Developmental Psychology*, 1981, *17*, 833–840.

Steinberg, L. D., and Hill, J. Patterns of family interaction as a function of age, the onset of puberty, and formal thinking. *Developmental Psychology*, 1978, *14*, 683–684.

Stolz, H. R., and Stolz, L. M. Adolescent problems related to somatic variation. *Yearbook of the National Society for the Study of Education*, 1944, *43*, Part I, 81–99.

Sullivan, H. S. *The interpersonal theory of psychiatry*. New York: W. W. Norton and Company, 1953.

Thompson, M. Anorexic-like behavior among normal college women. Paper presented at the Conference on the Psychology of Adolescence, Michael Reese Hospital and Medical Center, June, 1979.

Verstraeten, D. Level of realism in adolescent future time perspective. *Human Development*, 1980, *23*, 177–191.

Whisnant, L., Brett, E., and Zegans. L. Implicit messages concerning menstruation in commercial educational materials prepared for young adolescent girls. *American Journal of Psychiatry*, 1975, *132*, 815–820.

Wilen, J. B. The timing of pubertal changes and its psychological correlates. Paper presented at the Annual Conference on the Psychology of Adolescence, Michael Reese Hospital and Medical Center, Chicago, June, 1980.

Wilen, J. B., and Petersen, A. C. Young adolescents' responses to the timing of pubertal changes. Paper presented at the Annual meetings of the American Psychological Association, Montreal, Canada, September, 1980.

Chapter 8

The Experience of Menarche from a Developmental Perspective

JEANNE BROOKS-GUNN AND DIANE N. RUBLE

1. INTRODUCTION

Although just one of a series of physical events that marks the attainment of adult reproductive status, menarche may be the most important pubertal change that a young woman experiences. Being a discontinuous event embedded in a more gradual process may make it even more salient to the young girl. Examining the social, psychological, and physical meaning of menarche is important for several reasons.

First, menarche, as the biological symbol of a shift from child to woman, triggers the exploration of what it means to be a menstruating woman—how the somatic and psychological changes the girl has heard about may translate into personal experiences. The definition of the experience established at this time may be difficult to change in that subsequent experiences are perceived in terms of and may be distorted by this definition. Some cultural beliefs that influence the girl's experience may originate and be maintained by means of biases inherent in processing information about cyclic events (Ruble and Brooks-Gunn, 1979). For example, women and girls may begin to perceive and continue to believe in associations between particular symptoms and cycle phases even in the absence of a true relationship; a particular behavior or feeling may receive a different label (e.g., cramps versus abdominal gas pains or

JEANNE BROOKS-GUNN • Institute for the Study of Exceptional Children, Educational Testing Service, Princeton, New Jersey 08541; and Department of Pediatrics, College of Physicians and Surgeons, Columbia University, New York, New York 10019.   DIANE N. RUBLE • Department of Psychology, New York University, New York, New York 10003.

nausea versus indigestion) depending on the cycle phase during which it is perceived to occur. In terms of the pubertal girl, her perception of the menarcheal experience may have a long-lasting impact upon her definition of menstruation as well as other aspects of psychological functioning, such as self-esteem. If such perceptions are negative, they may have unfortunate consequences for her subsequent menstrual experience.

Second, real and perceived changes occurring at the time of menarche probably affect a girl's more general experience of puberty as well. The importance of puberty in a life span perspective has been suggested but not readily accepted outside the field of adolescence (Brooks-Gunn, 1981). There are several indications that puberty may be a significant developmental period in a person's life. Psychological functioning during puberty may predict later adult functioning better than psychological events during childhood or later adolescence (Haan, 1972; Peskin and Livson, 1972). It even has been proposed that adequate adjustment during puberty is necessary for the oft-mentioned phase of adolescent rebellion to occur and be resolved successfully (Peskin, 1973). In one study of developmental changes in adjustment, Haan (1972) identified six patterns of adjustment from early adolescence to adulthood. Using a Q-sort of psychological adjustment items, she found that 61% of the subjects found late adolescence to be more difficult than puberty or adulthood.

Menarche itself may influence a girl's more general pubertal experience in several ways: for example, the perception of being in phase or out of phase with one's peers vis-à-vis physical status probably is highly related to the onset of menstruation, since it is the most obvious marker of pubertal status. Menarche is used as a benchmark with which to compare oneself with others. Perceptions of one's standing vis-à-vis one's group has been shown to be related to feelings about puberty, acceptance of peers, and popularity with the opposite sex (see Westney and Jenkins, Chapter 12, this volume; Tobin-Richards and Petersen, 1981). The negative impact of being out of phase physically has been suggested in several studies of timing of maturation and psychological adjustment (Clausen, 1975; Faust, 1960). The importance of being on-time cannot be overemphasized. In the study by Tobin-Richards and Petersen (1981), girls were given a picture of an obviously pubertal girl standing in front of a mirror in a bathing suit. (Asking subjects to construct a story from a picture is a projective technique, of which the Thematic Apperception Test is the most common instrument.) A typical story involves embarrassment over development and comparisons with others (often quite negative). The major reason that girls wish to reach menarche is to "be like others," and not be different from one's friends. In response to the question, "If you had your choice, when would you choose to begin to menstruate?" asked in an interview with girls who had just reached menarche, girls are ambivalent: On the one hand, they are relieved to be on-time but, on the other hand, would like to start later in order to put off the hygienic hassles and negative behavioral effects that they associate with menstruation (Ruble and Brooks-Gunn, 1982).

Third, the mystery that seems to surround menarche and puberty also suggests their importance to the young girl. Several studies indicate that girls are reluctant to describe their experiences and that women are likely to have forgotten much of their pubertal experience. Petersen (1980) has termed this interesting phenomenon pubertal amnesia. Girls, when asked about their pubertal experiences, were likely to say that puberty and menarche had little impact upon them, but also recounted vignettes suggesting a profound effect of such experiences. In our research pre- and postmenarcheal girls are eager to fill out our questionnaire and even are willing to talk in informal groups about menarche (often becoming quite animated) but, when interviewed, tend to divulge little information. Although they do not seem to be embarrassed, the girls are reluctant to discuss their feelings about menarche, even with an adult interviewer with whom they have had repeated contact. This is why many investigators are using projective measures, questions about girl friends' attitudes, and distancing techniques (see Westney and Jenkins, Chapter 12, and Tobin-Richards, Boxer, and Petersen, Chapter 7).

Retrospective accounts of puberty have the same puzzling quality. In one study, college students had difficulty remembering events around the time of puberty, but not recounting details prior to and following puberty (Sommer, 1978). Anna Freud's (1958) patients also had less to say and less emotional reaction to pubertal events than to childhood or adolescent events recounted in therapy. The causes of such "amnesia" are unclear but perhaps puberty, as a time of the most rapid (and often bewildering) physical changes that occur after infancy, may result in feelings that are best kept to oneself (or so it seems to the girl and even adult woman). The secretive nature of the pubertal girl with respect to menstruation is illustrated by Anne Frank's oft-quoted diary entry:

Each time I have a period . . . I have the feeling that in spite of all the pain, unpleasantness, hastiness, I have a sweet secret and that is why, although it is nothing but a nuisance to me in a way, I always long for the time that I shall feel the secret upon me again. (1972, p. 117)

In our research, we have found that girls are very reticent to discuss menstruation immediately following menarche. The majority do not discuss the event with anyone except their mothers. After several periods, however, they shed their reluctance, beginning to discuss feelings, symptoms, and practical problems with friends (Brooks-Gunn and Ruble, 1982b,c). It is as if they must integrate the experience before presenting it to others. Thus, secretiveness may be a transient phenomenon.

Because of the intimate link between menstruation, womanhood, and sexuality, menarcheal experiences may have even more general effects, specifically on a girl's identity as a woman and on her self-concept (Brooks-Gunn and Ruble, 1982b,c). Changes in self-identity have been charted from childhood through adolescence, with self-esteem repeatedly being found to be lower during puberty than other stages (Simmons, Rosenberg, and Rosenberg, 1973; Simmons, Brown, Bush, and Blyth, 1978; Simmons and Rosenberg, 1975). Interestingly, this "dip" in self-image is more pronounced in girls than boys. For example, approximately 40% of a sample of girls were self-conscious and had unstable self-images as compared to 30% of a sample of boys (Simmons and Rosenberg, 1975). Although these findings may be related to the fact that girls are more willing to portray negative aspects of themselves (Maccoby and Jacklin, 1974), the reported difference was related to the girls' greater dissatisfaction with their physical appearance and their greater reliance on peer acceptance. Both of these factors stem partially from the pubertal experience. In addition, entrance into junior high school also affected self-esteem. The demands of middle school increase with respect to achievement as well as more puberty-linked concerns—popularity with the opposite sex and acceptance into the peer group (see Simmons, Blyth, and McKinney, Chapter 11).

In this chapter, we shall review data related to four questions. First, what is the developmental course of menstrual distress in early adolescence? Do girls have clear expectations for menstrual distress prior to the onset of puberty and do these expectations change after the onset of menarche? Data from the few cross-sectional adolescent studies as well as from our longitudinal study will be presented. It is anticipated that menstrual symptom expectations exist long before menarche and that severity is anticipated to be more severe than it actually is (based on the finding that women rate symptom severity as greater for other women than themselves; Brooks-Gunn, Ruble, and Clarke, 1977; Ruble and Brooks-Gunn, 1979). Second, what are the sources of information from which girls learn about menarche? It is anticipated that junior high school will result in an increase in information-seeking, due to the increase in number of postmenarcheal peers. Third, what is the relationship of menarcheal experience to perceptions of menstrual distress? Recollections related to being prepared and telling others about menarche have been hypothesized to be related to menstrual distress (Shainess,

1961). Fourth, how does a girl's more general self-esteem relate to menarcheal experience? We anticipate that dips in self-esteem reported by Simmons and her colleagues (1978) may be related to menarcheal status and perceptions of such status and that self-esteem will be related to menstrual distress.

2. METHOD

For the past several years, we have been studying the meaning of menarche and menstruation to young adolescent girls through a series of longitudinal and cross-sectional studies of elementary, junior high school, senior high school, and college women. While data from one study will be presented in this chapter, reference will be made to the other studies. For this reason, both the cross-sectional and longitudinal procedures will be described (even though our focus is on the first and largest cross-sectional study).

2.1. Subjects

Our largest study consists of 795 females ranging from fifth graders to college seniors and from 10 to 23 years of age seen cross-sectionally (Brooks-Gunn and Ruble, 1980a,b). The 639 adolescent girls ranged in age from 10 to 19 years, were public school students, resided in Central New Jersey, and lived with their parents. Ninety-six percent of the sample was Caucasian; the remaining subjects were black or oriental. In terms of religion, 34% of the sample was Catholic, 17% Jewish, and 27% Protestant. Familial socioeconomic status (SES) was quite heterogeneous. Of the one-half of the students who could provide enough parental occupational information to determine SES, 27% were in Hollinghead and Redlich's (1958) Social Class 1, 19% in Class 2, 19% in Class 3, 22% in Class 4, and 7% in Class 5.

The subjects were equally divided among three grade-related groups—Grades 5–6 ($N = 210$; $M = 5.74$), Grades 7–8 ($N = 219$; $M = 7.43$), and Grades 11–12 ($N = 210$; $M = 11.68$). These groups attended elementary, junior, and senior high school, respectively. Thirty-nine percent of the sample was premenarcheal (85% of the fifth and sixth, 33% of the seventh and eighth, and none of the eleventh and twelfth grade girls). Seven of the senior high school girls and none of the younger students reported using oral contraceptives.

In the longitudinal sample, 120 girls were contacted by phone every

6–8 weeks to see if they had begun to menstruate; a subject filled out a second questionnaire immediately following her reported menarche, and a control subject matched on age and school attended who had not begun to menstruate was tested at the same time. Thus, changes due to the effects of menarche as opposed to age could be explored. Additionally, the postmenarcheal sample was interviewed following menarche, and the entire sample is being contacted in the ninth grade. Forty-six pairs of girls (92 subjects) were seen twice: when they were in elementary school and when they were in junior high school. Thus, all of the girls were premenarcheal at the first testing, and one-half were premenarcheal and one-half were postmenarcheal at the second testing. The two samples did not differ in terms of age, school attended, socioeconomic status, religion, or birth order.

2.2. *Procedure*

Each subject filled out a questionnaire which included sections on incidence and severity of menstrual and premventrual symptoms, sources of menstrual-related information, menarcheal experiences, and self-esteem. Girls filled out the questionnaires in gym class or after school. The survey was conducted in 1978–1979.

2.3. *Measures*

2.3.1. *Menstrual Distress.* Each girl rated the severity of 30 symptoms taken from the Moos Menstrual Distress Questionnaire (MDQ) (Moos, 1968) but modified by including more familiar adjectives for the younger girls (i.e., "crabby" as well as "irritable"). Each symptom was rated for severity on a 6-point scale (experience the symptom "not at all" to "a lot") for the menstrual, the premenstrual, and the intermenstrual phases of the cylce. A definition of each of the cycle phases was given prior to filling out the MDQ. For example, the girls were told that "the premenstrual phase are those 1 to 3 days just before the period starts." Then they were asked what they feel or think they will feel (if premenarcheal) *just before your menstrual period.* Eight factors have been generated and replicated for the MDQ (Moos, 1968). These eight are pain (cramps), water retention (swelling), negative affect (crying), arousal (bursts of energy), autonomic reactions (feel dizzy), behavioral change (don't do so well in school), concentration (confused), and control (i.e., blind spots or fuzzy vision, symptoms not believed to be associated with the menstrual cycle). In order to examine menstrual distress, different scores using intermenstrual ratings as a base are used in order to control for response bias or for overall symptom reporting (Ruble and Brooks-Gunn, 1979). In other words, menstrual distress is presented as the difference between menstrual- and intermenstrual-cycle phase scores and premenstrual distress is presented as the difference between premenstrual- and intermenstrual-cycle phase scores.

In addition, girls were asked about whether or not they experienced premenstrual and menstrual cramps (pain), bloating (water retention), and pimples; whether or not they took medication for each of the symptoms; and the frequency of symptom occurrence.

2.3.2. *Sources of Information.* Subjects were asked to rate the amount they have learned about menstruation from each of 15 potential sources on a 4-point scale ("learn nothing" to "learn a lot"). Using a varimax factor analysis, 5 sources were identified: (1) females (girl friends, female adults, sisters, and overheard conversations), (2) males (male friends, male adults, and brothers), (3) media (television, magazines, and books), (4) health (nurses and health education classes), and (5) parents and doctor (mother, father, and doctor).

2.3.3. *The Menarcheal Experience.* Girls have been queried about their first menstrual experience, including whether or not they experienced symptoms, what feelings were associated with the first menstrual experience, who they told about the experience, and how prepared they were for menarche.

Feelings were assessed by asking girls about eight emotions they might have had or had at menarche (happy, proud, excited, embarrassed, angry, scared, upset, and surprise). These feelings were rated on a 4-point scale ("not at all" to "a lot"), and varimax rotation yielded two factors (positive and negative feelings). Girls were asked whether or not they had told their parents and if not, whether or not each of their parents knew they had begun to menstruate. Premenarcheal girls were asked whether or not they would tell their parents.

2.3.4. *Preparation for Menarche.* Girls were asked three questions about preparation: how prepared they were for menarche, how much they knew about menstruation, and how adequate their explanation of menstruation was. Each question was rated on a 4-point scale.

2.3.5. *Self-Esteem.* A 12-item self-image questionnaire based on the research of Simmons and her colleaques (Simmons and Rosenberg, 1975; Simmons, Blyth, and McKinney, Chapter 11, this volume) was completed. Four-point scales were used. The three factors which we have labeled in terms of the negative end of the scale are: (1) Do not like self (e.g., "How happy are you with the kind of person you are?"); (2) Not self-reflective (e.g., "How often do you feel mixed-up about yourself?");

and (3) Not self-conscious (e.g., "If you were to wear the wrong kind of clothes to a party, would that bother you?").

2.4. *Comparisons*

The studies that we are conducting focus on the girl's experience of menstruation as it changes over the adolescent period and the girl's transition from premenarcheal to postmenarcheal status. Consistent with our theoretical orientation, we view the menarcheal experience as reflecting in part cultural beliefs and learned expectations. For example, girls who report pain during menstruation may do so both because of a physically based reality and because of learning that pain is supposed to accompany menstruation (Ruble and Brooks-Gunn, 1979). Therefore, premenarcheal expectations and knowledge are as important as postmenarcheal experiences. In our cross-sectional studies, we have compared premenarcheal and postmenarcheal girls with age-controlled (in which physiological status varies, but presumably sociocultural experiences do not), premenarcheal girls of differing ages (in which physiological status is similar, but sociocultural experiences are not), and postmenarcheal girls of differing ages (in which physiological status of girls who have been menstruating several years may not vary greatly while sociocultural experiences will vary) in order to better understand the contribution of experience, culture, and physiology to menarche. We caution that these comparisons are inferential in nature and presuppose interactions among determinants, making it impossible to assess the separate contribution of physical and psychological variables. Indeed, given a multicausal model, outcomes may be predicted better by interactions rather than by independent effects.

3. RESULTS AND DISCUSSION

3.1. *Menstrual-Related Symptomatology during Adolescence*

A wide range of somatic and psychological fluctuations have been associated with the menstrual cycle. Although such symptoms are assumed to be related to cyclic hormonal changes, self-reports of menstrual-related symptoms may represent, at least in part, a learned set of cultural beliefs (Parlee, 1973, 1974). For example, self-reports of menstrual symptoms have been found to be influenced by experimental manipulations of women's perceptions concerning the nature of the study (Englander-Golden, Whitmore, and Dienstbier, 1978) and by manipulations of women's beliefs concerning whether they are in the premenstrual or intermenstrual phase of the cycle (Ruble, 1977).

If menstrual distress is based partially on sociocultural factors, then it becomes particularly important to examine the development of expectations and perceptions regarding menstrual symptoms during adolescence. We will discuss three types of data related to the development of menstrual symptomatology—early expectations, developmental changes over the adolescent period, and the effect of ovulation.

3.1.1. *Early Expectations.* Do girls have clear expectations regarding menstrual symptoms even before they have actually reached menarche? If they do, then their subsequent experience may be interpreted in terms of expectations already formed and may become, in some sense, a self-fulfilling prophecy. Therefore, we have compared the symptom reports of girls who have recently begun to menstruate with the expectations of girls of the same age who have not yet reached menarche.

Premenarcheal and postmenarcheal girls in our cross-sectional study completed the MDQ (Moos, 1968), in which they rated the incidence on 6-point scales of thirty symptoms during different phases of their cycle. These symptoms have been grouped into several factors indicating several different types of symptoms, such as pain, water retention, lack of concentration, and negative affect (Moos, 1968). Adult women have been found to rate most of these symptoms higher in the menstrual and premenstrual phases of the cycle than at midcycle when they are asked to recount their own symptoms retrospectively (Moos, 1968), when they are asked to respond "as if" they were in one of the phases (Brooks-Gunn, Ruble, and Clarke, 1977), and when they are asked to describe "women in general" (Parlee, 1974).

Like the majority of the adult studies, the premenarcheal girls anticipated experiencing cycle phase differences for menstrual and premenstrual phases (all one-way analyses were significant). Figures 1 and 2 present the MDQ factor scores for the two of the three most common symptoms, pain and water retention, using difference scores (menstrual–intermenstrual and premenstrual–intermenstrual) as a control for response bias and general level of symptoms. As can be seen, both groups of premenarcheal girls expect to experience the three symptoms. When comparing the two premenarcheal groups on all eight factor scales, young girls expected to experience *more* water retention, negative affect, autonomic reactions, and *less* concentration than their junior high-school peers. The elementary school girls may be receiving less specific and more vague (and perhaps more negative) information about menstrual symptoms than their junior high school counterparts.

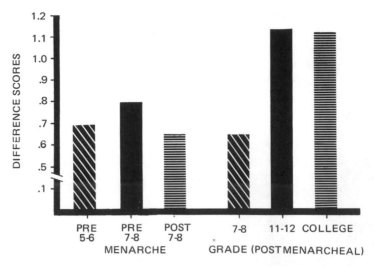

Figure 1. Mean difference scores for MDQ Pain Factor (menstrual–intermenstrual dysmenorrhea) by grade and menarcheal status.

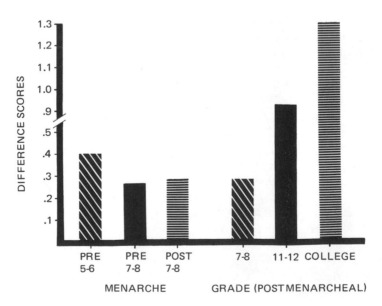

Figure 2. Mean difference scores for MDQ Water Retention Factor by grade and menarcheal status.

    The second comparison involves the premenarcheal and postmen-
archeal junior high school girls; in general, the premenarcheal seventh
through eighth graders expected to experience what their menstuating
peers reported experiencing. The only exception to this "no difference"
finding was that the premenarcheal girls expected to experience *more*
pain than their postmenarcheal counterparts, as is seen in Figure 1. These
findings make it difficult to distinguish between cultural beliefs and
actual physical experience as possible determinants of self-reports of
menstrual symptoms.

    Symptom severity changes also were seen in the longitudinal sam-
ple. Looking at pain and water retention, the premenarcheal comparison
group expected to experience significantly more severe symptoms than
their postmenarcheal peers reported experiencing. Symptom severity
increased for the premenarcheal group (Figures 3 and 4; Brooks-Gunn
and Ruble, 1982b).

    These findings suggest that the initial experience of menstruation
and age both affect to some degree self-reports of menstrual distress.
Changes in symptom reports during the early postmenarcheal years may
occur since girls are likely to receive more and/or different types of
information or because biologic changes may make symptoms more
likely.

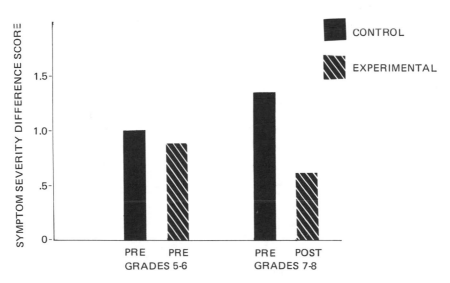

Figure 3. Severity of menstrual pain (difference score) by menstrual status and time tested:
longitudinal study.

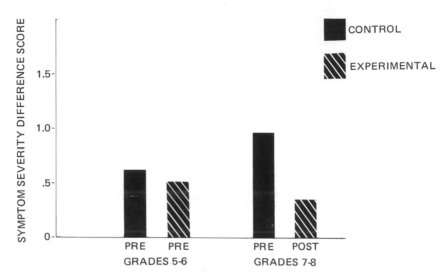

Figure 4. Severity of menstrual water retention (difference score) by menstrual status and time tested: longitudinal study.

3.1.2. *Developmental Change after Menarche.* Grade-related changes were found as symptom severity increased across the three grade levels (see Figures 1 and 2). Eleventh through twelfth graders reported more severe symptoms than seventh through eighth grade postmenarcheal girls. The college women reported similar pain and negative affect as the senior high-school girls, while water retention was rated as more severe by the older than younger girls.

Thus, severity increased with age and years postmenarche. Two other large-scale studies reporting similar results have been conducted. A group of Finnish investigators (Wildholm and Kantero, 1971; Wildholm, 1979) studied several samples of adolescents, the largest of which included 5485 adolescent girls (10–20 years of age) and their mothers. In America, Klein and Litt (1981 and Chapter 4) recently have analyzed the 1969 National Health Survey data on incidence of menstrual symptoms and effects of symptoms upon school and work in adolescent girls. Both studies provide additional normative data on age changes in dysmenorrhea and menstrual symptoms.

These two sets of studies also report age-related increases. In the Finnish studies, the incidence of dysmenorrhea reported (experiencing it occasionally or frequently) rose from 33% to 64% over the adolescent years, with 78% of the mothers reporting experiencing dysmenorrhea (Figure 5).

Similarly, reports of premenstrual edema rose from approximately 5% for the young girls, to 15% for the older adolescents, to 21% for the mothers. Premenstrual tension, or irritability and fatigue, was high across all ages (50–60%) and did not change.

It is important to keep in mind that the incidence data do not indicate how severe the symptom is. Our data suggest that while the majority of women over 16 years of age report dysmenorrhea, they do not rate it as particularly severe (mean MDQ pain scale scores were 2–3, or respondents experience the symptom "somewhat" but not "a lot"). However, the increases are of interest in terms of questions about socialization versus biologic change. Many investigators use the Finnish results to suggest that ovulation indirectly explains the age-related increases. Some of the hormonal changes believed to be responsible for menstrual symptoms do not occur in anovulatory cycles. Early menstrual cycles often are longer, more variable, and anovulatory (Vollman, 1977; Apter and Vilko, 1977; Penny, Parlow, Olambiwonnie, and Frasier 1977). In one study, approximately one-half of all cycles in the 2 years following menarche were anovulatory and only one-fifth were 5 years after menarche (Apter and Vilko, 1977). Hormonal studies suggest that early cycles sometimes are anovulatory and characterized by short luteal phases (Penny et al., 1977; Winter and Faiman, 1973). If the ovulation symptom hypothesis is correct, girls who have just started to menstruate should report fewer symptoms than girls who have been menstruating several years.

We have suggested that the gradual increases and the fairly high

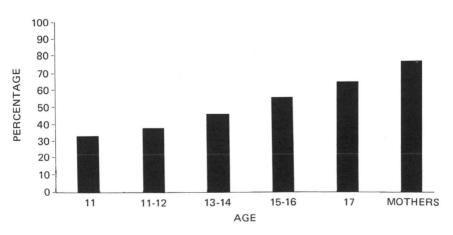

Figure 5. Incidence of dysmenorrhea by chronological age in the Finnish study (Wildholm and Kantero, 1971).

prevalence of symptoms in young girls do not adequately support the ovulation hypothesis as it is currently stated, since changes do not correspond with the fact that regularity of ovulation becomes more or less established 2–3 years following menarche. However, this does not rule out a multicausal model in which socialization and biology facilitate the report of increased severe symptomatology.

3.2. *Acquiring Information Concerning Menstruation*

When menarche occurs, does the young girl actively seek out information and if so, what is she most interested in learning and from which sources? The onset of menarche is an important aspect of becoming a woman. The nature of the information received at this time may have an important impact on a girl's emerging integration of "womanhood" into her self-concept. Additionally, as we have suggested, information received may influence girls' perceptions of menstrual symptoms. Finally, anxieties may accompany menstruation if a girl is inadequately prepared prior to menarche, if she develops extremely negative expectations concerning symptoms, or if she observes negative reactions of significant others.

3.2.1. *Advanced Preparation.* Do some girls begin to menstruate with no knowledge about this event at all? Is there any relationship between prior knowledge and the later experience of menstruation? Interview studies suggest that being unprepared is a terrifying experience (Konopka, 1976). A surprisingly high percentage of girls reach menarche with no advanced preparation at all, although there is great variation within and across cultures. In most of the Western European cultures described by Abel and Joffe (1950), girls were given no advance warning (Germany, Poland, and Ireland). In contrast, adolescents in Italy were likely to have overheard their female relatives and friends discuss menstruation, but were given little specific information. When these cultural groups immigrated to America, girls were more likely to be given information prior to the event, as it was thought to be "old-fashioned" not to do so and it was important to present adolescents with their own group's cultural values.

More recently, up to 50% of all girls queried in the 1950s still had no advance warning (Shainess, 1961). By the 1970s, only 5–10% of girls had no advanced warning (Brooks-Gunn and Ruble, 1980a). Such changes may be due in part to generational shifts toward greater openness in discussing menstruation. Indeed, one study found that girls under 20 reported learning about menstruation from more sources and were less likely to be uninformed at menarche than 20 to 40-year-old women, who in turn were more informed than women over 40 years of age (Larsen, 1961). Additionally, the advent of health education for the pubertal child has made it unlikely that a girl has not heard about menstruation, even if her mother is reluctant to discuss it with her. The girls who had no advance warning may be those who experience a relatively early menarche and have not had health education, or have not been told by the mothers because their mothers did not expect the event to occur when it did, or whose mothers did not wish to discuss menstruation. In any case, being totally unprepared occurs rarely; when a girl is unprepared, its low frequency of occurrence may make it even more salient, traumatic, or embarrassing for the girl.

Findings on the relationship between preparation and symptom reports are mixed (May, 1976; Shainess, 1961). Dunham (1979) found a negative correlation between the age of receiving information and negative attitudes about menstruation at menarche in her study of 198 college women. The older the girls were when they were informed, the more negative they recalled their attitude at menarche as being. In our research (Brooks-Gunn and Ruble, 1978), the simple receipt of knowledge prior to menarche was *not* related to current menstrual distress. The *adequacy* of the explanation, however, was related to current symptoms. Girls who felt that the explanation was inadequate reported more premenstrual symptoms, and girls who felt more prepared at menarche reported less pain. In addition, on a separate measure, feeling "surprised" at menarche was positively correlated with several indications of menstrual distress. It is interesting to note, as an aside, that although 85% of the girls felt the explanation they received was at least "pretty good" and felt they knew at least "pretty much," none of them reported feeling even "somewhat" prepared at menarche. However, when dividing the sample into those who felt unprepared and those who felt prepared, the former were found to report more symptoms, even the older girls who had been menstruating for over three years (Brooks-Gunn and Ruble, 1982b,c). Thus, either the explanations provided do not cover key aspects of the event, or it is the kind of experience that is virtually impossible to feel totally prepared for. However, feeling totally unprepared does effect girls' later experience of menarche.

3.2.2. *Sources of Information.* The particular source of information may be an important determinant of the attitudes and expectations formed during the crucial time around menarche. Within our culture today, almost all girls learn something from their mothers (Brooks-Gunn and Ruble, 1980a; Dunham, 1979; Haft, 1973; Larsen, 1961). Other resource people (e.g., nurses, health classes), however, appear to have an increasingly important role. They are mentioned more frequently in the more recent studies, and in the study comparing different age groups (Larsen, 1961), such sources seemed significant only in the 20 years and younger group.

Peers and older sisters also are an important source of some information. In our own research, approximately two-thirds of the subjects who had older sisters received information from them. Over 75% of our girls learned at least something from female friends (Brooks-Gunn and Ruble, 1980a), and anecdotal comments from interviews suggest that many girls take extremely seriously the information they receive from their friends (Whisnant and Zegans, 1975). Earlier studies report that peers were a much less important source (Larsen, 1961; Dunham, 1979).

Fathers seem to have a minimal role in imparting information about this developmental milestone to their daughters. Fathers were not even mentioned as sources in three studies (Haft, 1973; Henton, 1961) and were sources for only about 20% of the girls in our study. Interestingly, anecdotal evidence suggests that the girls are more wary about discussing menstruation than the fathers are. Over three-quarters of our younger girls say that they will not or did not tell their fathers when they began to menstruate, although a small number of fathers queried said they would not mind talking to their daughters about menstruation.

Changes in amount learned occurred, as senior high school girls learned more from media sources, particularly books and magazines, and less from mothers, doctors, and nurses than did the girls in lower grades (Brooks-Gunn and Ruble, 1982a). It is interesting that female friends and sisters were not a more important source for the older than younger girls, especially since more senior high school girls report learning specific information on menstrual product use from these sources than do younger girls (Brooks-Gunn and Ruble, 1982a).

Few changes occured in early adolescence, either in the premenarcheal elementary and junior high school or in the pre- and postmenarcheal junior high school girls, although the postmenarcheal girls learned more from media sources.

Does it matter from whom or from where a girl receives this information? Although there is little direct data on this question, indirect evidence suggests that the particular source may make a difference. Dunham (1979) reports that the source of information was related both to age of receiving detailed information and to age of menarche. Girls who learned from mothers reported learning earlier. This relationship and the finding that earlier learning was related to fewer symptoms suggest the importance of the interrelationships of timing, source, and menstrual experience.

Taken together, these findings indirectly suggest that different sources convey different kinds of information with varying evaluative overtones. Mothers, particularly when they talk to premenarcheal girls, may be conveying more positive preparatory information, such as representing menarche as a sign of maturity. Information received from peers and general cultural sources seems more likely to result in negative attitudes and expectations, suggesting that possible debilitating and bothersome aspects may be emphasized.

3.3. Menarcheal Experience

3.3.1. *Feelings about Menarche.* The cross-sectional premenarcheal junior high-school girls anticipated being more upset (means, 1.99 vs. 1.66, $p < 0.01$) but less surprised (means, 2.03 vs. 2.45, $p < 0.05$) than their postmenarcheal counterparts actually reported experiencing. Again, even if one is expecting to reach menarche soon, the actual event comes as a surprise, although it is not particularly upsetting.

3.3.2. *Telling Others about Menarche.* The postmenarcheal girls were asked whether or not they told their parents about their first period and whether or not their mothers knew even if they did not tell them about it. Most of the girls told their mothers when they began to menstruate (85%) while only a few told their fathers (16%). The younger girls were more likely to have told their fathers (30% at fifth through sixth grade versus 12% at eleventh through twelfth grade; $p < 0.05$). Of those who did not tell their parents, 48% said their mothers knew anyway, 52% said their fathers knew anyway. The older girls were much more likely to indicate that their father knew anyway (in keeping with the fact that they were less likely to tell their fathers). Interview data suggest that when parents are not told directly by their daughters, fathers are told by their wives, and mothers find out through discovering personal products or are told by their older daughters. Girls who reported that their fathers knew about their first period without their daughters telling them reported less severe pain, negative affect, and water retention symptom scores. Such a relationship was not found for maternal knowledge. Additionally, both parents were perceived as having more positive feelings about their daughter's menarche when the fathers knew about menarche, either directly or indirectly (Brooks-Gunn and Ruble, 1978). Perhaps families in which the father is told about menarche have a more relaxed attitude about menstruation and reproduction, which results in the incorporation of a less negative view about the menstrual experience by the girls.

A large percentage of girls told or were planning to tell their friends or sisters. No girls told their brothers or boyfriends, again indicating the reluctance to talk to the opposite sex and the feeling of menstruation being a "secret" topic, at least in terms of some significant others. The same percentages of premenarcheal girls anticipated telling their sisters and friends as the postmenarcheal girls actually did. However, many girls refrained from telling friends until they had been menstruating for several months.

3.4. *Self-Image*

When mean differences on the factor "likes self" were examined, the elementary school girls were found to like themselves more than their junior high school counterparts (means 1.95 − 2.21). No differences were found between the premenarcheal and postmenarcheal junior high school students. A grade effect was found indicating that the junior high school students disliked themselves more than the younger or older girls. These findings are consistent with those of Simmons et al. (see Chapter 11) in that entrance into middle school, not menarcheal status, was related to a dip in liking oneself.

The correlations between self-esteem and menstrual distress for the premenarcheal and postmenarcheal junior high school students also were examined. Reported menstrual distress was related to self-image for those girls who were menstruating (Figure 6). However, expectations for distress were not related to liking self. Whether or not experience of menstrual distress affected liking oneself or vice versa is not known.

4. CONCLUSION

The findings presented in this chapter provide some insights into the meaning of menarche to the adolescent girl. With regard to symptomatology related to the menstrual cycle, girls expect to experience symptoms as soon as they begin menstruating, having learned about such symptoms as early as fifth grade. (Presumably, even younger girls may have acquired such information; to date, girls under 10 years of age have not been questioned.) Given the strength of the expectations in terms of incidence and severity estimates, it comes as no surprise that the majority of young girls do report experiencing symptoms following menarche.

Some of the variations across menarcheal status and age are quite intriguing, however; and etiology of self-reported menstrual distress seems to be a function of both actual experience and expectations. Premenarcheal girls expect to experience more severe menstrual distress

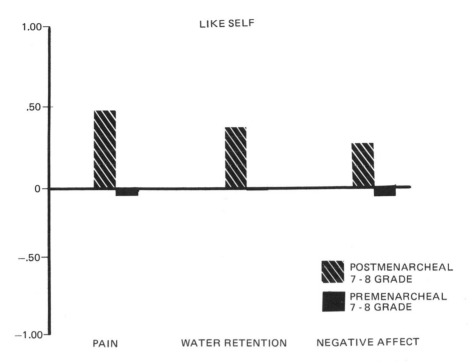

Figure 6. Correlations between MDQ factors and like self factor by menarcheal status.

than immediately postmenarcheal girls actually report experiencing, and still being premenarcheal in junior high school increased anticipated symptom scores as compared to elementary school expectations in the longitudinal study. Interestingly, in the cross-sectional sample, anticipated severity was higher in the elementary school than the junior high school girls. These sample differences may be related to the repeated testing of the longitudinal sample. The stronger pre–post effects in the longitudinal study may have been due in part to the fact that the cross-sectional postmenarcheal Ss had been menstruating over 3 months, the longitudinal Ss less than 3 months. In addition, junior high school heralds a rise in the perception of menstruation as a negative and debilitating event (Brooks-Gunn and Ruble, 1982b,c). We have suggested that the *decrease* in symptom severity after menarche may be a contrast effect: girls who expect debilitating symptoms may underreport them (c.f. Boggiano, 1981).

Thus, social learning processes seem to play a central role in the experience of menarche and menstrual distress. Although it is reasonable to assume that developmental changes in symptoms represent some conbination of physical experience and socialization, at this point information on the physiological contribution is sparse. We have explored socialization processes via information sources, amount of preparedness, family attitudes, and the psychological meaning of the first menstrual experience.

Information sources, the actual information transmitted, and its evaluative tone vary as a function of age and menarcheal status. The main source—the mothers—may provide their premenarcheal girls less specific information than their postmenarcheal girls. Health education, reviewed at different times in various school districts, may emphasize positive aspects of becoming a woman and hygienic matters. What facts peers convey is not well understood: girls report learning from overheard conversations at school as well as from informal discussions, although they have difficulty remembering the substance of such discussions. Peer networks may increase menarcheal discussion in junior high school (even though our girls did not report increases in overall amount learned, the nature of the information may differ). Given that popularity and status are related to menarcheal status in junior high school (Faust, 1960), the network in which premenarcheal and postmenarcheal girls discuss menarche may be somewhat separate. In fact, premenarcheal junior high school girls report having fewer postmenarcheal friends than postmenarcheal girls. In addition, premenarcheal and postmenarcheal girls report that their girl friends have somewhat different menstrual attitudes, suggesting that the information transmitted may differ (Brooks-Gunn and Ruble, 1982b).

Comparisons between the New Jersey and Finnish samples also suggest that cultures socialize differently. From the symptom incidence estimates, we might infer that Finnish girls may not learn about menstrual symptoms except fatigue and irritability until they have been menstruating awhile, while the American girls know a great deal about symptoms from an early age onwards. Given the cross-cultural variation in the extent of advanced preparation and the nature of information transmitted, these differences are not too surprising.

Socialization within the family plays a role in the acquisition of menstrual beliefs and experiences. For example, in families where the father is told about his daughter's menarche (either by his daughter or wife), girls report less severe menstrual symptoms and presumably a less negative view about the menstrual experience is fostered in families with more open attitudes about menstruation.

Our data also suggest that some aspects of the first menstrual experience may affect subsequent experiences. Not being prepared for menarche and feeling surprised at its advent were related to higher symtomatology, as was starting early. The first experience also affected current menstrual distress. These data suggest that an intriguing interplay of individual physiology (e.g., initial pain) and psychology (e.g., preparation) underly the relationship between the initial and later experience.

Given that cultural, socialization, and individual factors contribute to menstrual beliefs and experiences, the relative contribution of each needs to be explicated more precisely. For example, is the first menstrual experience influenced by prior factors and what is the relative contribution of cultural beliefs, socialization, and actual experience to subsequent menstrual experience? Such questions are best answered by the intensive longitudinal examination of the girl's social-psychological experience of physical growth and menarche.

ACKNOWLEDGMENTS. The research reported in this paper was supported by the National Science Foundation (SOC-76 02137 and SOC-76 02129) and by Educational Testing Service. Linda Worcel is to be thanked for her invaluable assistance in all aspects of the project. The contribution of David Freund and Al Rogers in data analysis also is appreciated.

REFERENCES

Abel, T., and Joffe, N. F. Cultural background of female puberty. *American Journal of Psychotherapy*, 1950, 4, 90–93.
Apter, D., and Vilko, R. Serum pregnenolone, progesterone, 17-hydroxyprogesterone, testosterone and 5 alpha dihydrotestosterone during female puberty. *Journal of Clinical Endocrinology and Metabolism*, 1977, 45(5), 1039–1048.
Boggiano, A. K. Self-perception versus the cued expectancy: Analyses of overjustification. Doctoral dissertation, Princeton University, 1981.
Brooks-Gunn, J. Transitions in Gender Role Development in Childhood and Adolescence. Paper presented at a conference on Gender Role Development at NICHD, Bethesda, October 1981.
Brooks-Gunn, J. and Ruble, D. N. Menstrual related symptomatology in adolescents: The effects of attitudes, first menstrual experience, and parental factors. Paper presented at the second annual Conference on Interdisciplinary Research on the Menstrual Cycle, St. Louis, May 1978.
Brooks-Gunn, J., and Ruble, D. N. Menarche: The interaction of physiology, cultural, and social factors. In A. J. Dan, E. A. Graham, and C. P. Beecher (Eds.), *The menstrual cycle: A synthesis of interdisciplinary research.* New York: Springer, 1980a.
Brooks-Gunn, J., and Ruble, D. N. The menstrual attitude questionnaire. *Psychosomatic Medicine*, 1980b, 42(5), 503–512.
Brooks-Gunn, J., and Ruble, D. N. Psychological determinants of menstrual product use in adolescent girls. *Annals of Internal Medicine*, 1982a, 96(6), 962–965.

Brooks-Gunn J., and Ruble, D. N. The development of menstrual-related beliefs and behaviors during early adolescence. *Child Development*, 1982b, *53*, 1567–1577.

Brooks-Gunn, J. and Ruble, D. N. Developmental processes in the experience of menstruation. In A. Baum and J. E. Singer (Eds.), *Handbook of medical psychology*. Vol. 1. Hillsdale, New Jersey: L. Erlbaum, 1982c.

Brooks, J., Ruble, D. N., and Clark, A. College women's attitudes and expectations concerning menstrual-related changes. *Psychosomatic Medicine*, 1977, *39*, 288–298.

Clausen, J. A. The social meaning of differential physical and sexual maturation. In S. E. Dragaster and G. H. Elder, Jr. (Eds.), *Adolescence in the life cycle*. New York: Halstead, 1975.

Dunham, G. Timing and sources of information about and attitudes toward menstruation among college females. *Journal of Genetic Psychology*, 1979, *117*, 205–207.

Englander-Golden, P., Whitmore, M. R., and Dienstbier, R. A. Menstrual cycle as a focus of study and self reports of moods and behaviors. *Motivation and Emotion*, 1978, *2*, 75–86.

Faust, N. S. Developmental maturity as a determinant in prestige of adolescent girls. *Child Development*, 1960, *31*, 173–186.

Frank, A. *The Diary of a young girl*. New York: Pocket Books, 1972.

Freud, A. Adolescence. In R. S. Eissler (Ed.), *Psychoanalytic study of the child*. Vol. 13. New York: International Universities Press, 1958.

Haan, N. Personality development from adolescence to adulthood in the Oakland growth and guidance studies. *Seminars in Psychiatry*, 1972, *4(4)* 399–414.

Haft, M. H. An exploratory study of early adolescent girls: Body image, self acceptance, acceptance of traditional female role, and response to menstruation. Unpublished doctoral thesis, Columbia University, 1973.

Henton, C. L. The effect of socio-economic and emotional factors on the onset of menarche among Negro and white girls. *Journal of Genetic Psychology*, 1961, *98*, 255–268.

Hollingshead, A. B., and Redlich, F. C. *Social class and mental illness: A community study*. New York: Wiley and Sons, 1958.

Klein, J. R., and Litt, I. F. Epidemiology of adolescent dysmenorrhea. *Pediatrics*, 1981, *68*, 66.

Konopka, G. *Young girls: A portrait of adolescence*. Englewood Cliffs, NJ: Prentice-Hall, 1976.

Larsen, U. L. Sources of menstrual information: A comparison of age groups. *Family Life Coordinator*, 1961, *10*, 41–43.

Maccoby, E. E., and Jacklin, C. N. *The psychology of sex differences*. Stanford, Calif: Stanford University Press, 1974.

May, R. R., Mood shifts and the menstrual cycle. *Journal of Psychosomatic Medicine*, 1976, *20*, 125–130.

Moos, R. H. The development of the Menstrual Distress Questionnaire. *Psychosomatic Medicine*, 1968, *30*, 853–867.

Parlee, M. B. The premenstrual syndrome. *Psychological Bulletin*, 1973, *80*, 454–465.

Parlee, M. B. Stereotypic beliefs about menstruation: A methodological note on the Moos Menstrual Distress Questionnaire. *Psychosomatic Medicine*, 1974, *36(3)*, 229–240.

Penny, R., Parlow, A. F., Olambiwonnie, N. O., and Frasier, S. D. Evolution of the menstrual pattern of gonadotropin and sex steroid concentrations in serum. *Acta Endrocinology*, 1977, *84*, 79.

Peskin, H. Influence of the developmental schedule of puberty on learning and ego development. *Journal of Youth and Adolescence*, 1973, *2*, 273–290.

Peskin, H., and Livson, N. Pre and post pubertal personality and adult psychologic functioning. *Seminars in Psychology*, 1972, *4*, 343–355.

Petersen, A. C. Puberty and its psychosocial significance in girls. In A. J. Dan, E. A. Graham, and C. P. Beecher (Eds.), *The menstrual cycle: A synthesis of interdisciplinary research.* New York: Springer, 1980.

Ruble, D. N. Premenstrual symptoms: A reinterpretation. *Science,* 1977, *197,* 291–292.

Ruble, D. N. and Brooks-Gunn, J. Menstrual symptoms: A social cognition analysis. *Journal of Behavioral Medicine,* 1979, *2*(2), 171–194.

Ruble, D. N., and Brooks-Gunn, J. The experience of menarche. *Child Development,* 1982, *53,* 1557–1566.

Shainess, N. A re-evaluation of some aspects of femininity through a study of menstruation: A preliminary report. *Comparative Psychiatry,* 1961, *2,* 20–26.

Simmons, R. G., and Rosenberg, M. Sex, sex-roles and self-image. *Journal of Youth and Adolescence,* 1975, *4,* 229–258.

Simmons, R. G., Rosenberg, F., and Rosenberg, N. Disturbance in the self-image at adolescence. *American Sociological Review,* 1973, *38,* 553–568.

Simmons, R. D., Brown, L., Bush, D. M., and Blyth, D. A. Self-esteem and the achievement of black and white early adolescents. *Social Problems,* 1978, *26,* 86–96.

Sommer, B. *Puberty and adolescence.* New York: Oxford, 1978.

Tobin-Richards, M. H., and Petersen, A. C. Early adolescents' perceptions of their physical development. Paper presented in a Symposium on Puberty: Social and Psychological Significance presented at the American Psychological Association Meetings in Los Angeles, CA, September, 1981.

Vollman, R. F. *The menstrual cycle.* Philadelphia: WB Saunders, 1977.

Whisnant, L. and Zegans, L. A. A study of attitudes toward menarche in white middle-class American girls. *American Journal of Psychiatry,* 1975, *132,* 809–814.

Wildholm. O. Dysmenorrhea during adolescence. *Acta Obstetrica et Gynaecologica Scandinavica,* 1979, *87,* 61–66.

Wildholm, O., and Kantero, R. L. A statistical analysis of the menstrual patterns of 8,000 girls and their mothers. *Acta Obstetrica et Gynaecologica Scandinavica* (Suppl.), 1971, *14.*

Winter, J. S. D., and Faiman, C. The development of cyclic pituitary and gonadal function in adolescent females. *Journal of Clinical Endocrinology and Metabolism,* 1973, *37,* 714.

Chapter 9

Pubertal Change and Cognition

ANNE C. PETERSEN

1. COGNITION IN EARLY ADOLESCENCE

Early adolescence, the stage of life during which puberty takes place, is a time of some very interesting changes in cognition. It is the time for the onset of the final stage in Piaget's (Inhelder and Piaget, 1958) conceptualization of cognitive development, a stage characterized by the development of the capacity for abstract thinking, or formal operational thought. While not all early adolescents, or even adults, manifest such thinking (Elkind, 1974), early adolescence is a time when some young people first manifest abstract thinking.

A second change in cognition at early adolescence is that sex differences emerge at this age. Maccoby and Jacklin (1974) concluded that all three of the cognitive tasks that differentiate boys and girls first show consistent, reliable results in early adolescence. These differences are seen in three areas: mathematics performance, spatial ability, and verbal ability. Differences on the first two favor boys while those on the latter favor girls. While many hypotheses might be proposed for the timing of the emergence of these sex differences (e.g., see Petersen and Wittig, 1979, or Petersen, 1980), biological explanations have received the most attention. One of these biological explanations is pubertal change.

The third and most controversial cognitive change in early adolescence has been proposed by Epstein (1974a,b, 1978). His overall proposal (1978) is controversial with some questionable recommendations, perhaps because of the speculative nature of some of his assertions. At the

---

ANNE C. PETERSEN • Department of Individual and Family Studies, College of Human Development, The Pennsylvania State University, University Park, Pennsylvania 16802.

same time, there are some cogent and compelling aspects to his argument, some now supported by data from other investigators. For this reason, I will describe Epstein's hypothesis in some detail.

2. Epstein's Hypothesis about Brain Growth

Epstein argues that, while brain cell growth is completed by the end of the second year of life, brain growth continues but with a period of particularly slow growth at early adolescence, from ages 13 to 14 years. He posits that additional brain weight added during childhood is due to: (1) more extended and branched axons and dendrites, (2) myelinization (producing the fatty insulation around axons), and (3) an increase in the arterial system. He describes spurts in brain growth based on measures of head circumference, arguing that head circumference is a good measure of brain weight (Epstein and Epstein, 1978) and of intelligence (Epstein, 1978). (The argument linking head circumference with intelligence is particularly weak, since it is based on showing that head circumference increases with occupational status; the possibility that nutrition may mediate this association is not considered.) Epstein argues that these spurts in brain growth are independent of general body growth. Figure 1 presents the data Epstein uses to support his argument regarding developmental changes in brain circumference. These data are based upon thousands of children in twelve countries. They reveal a dramatic spurt in brain circumference for both boys and girls from ages 10 to 12 years followed by an even sharper decline for girls; for boys there is a less sharp decline, with a second peak just past age 15. While Epstein argues that brain circumference is unrelated to other aspects of body growth, this seems unlikely. Surely the head would increase in size along with other parts of the body at puberty. The similar timing of the male and female spurts in head circumference at puberty in his data is somewhat perplexing. The data (Eichorn and Bayley, 1962) on changes in head circumference from the Berkeley Growth Study show the predictable sex difference in timing of the pubertal spurt (Figure 2). The Berkeley data also show no divergence between boys and girls after the pubertal spurt.

While Epstein discusses the role of experience in developing brain functions, he argues that intervention to enhance learning will be effective only during the spurts of growth. He states, "Thus, there would appear to be little or no store of creative intelligence around ages twelve to fourteen years, in good agreement with the brain growth plateau found at that period" (p. 359). He proposes that head circumference mea-

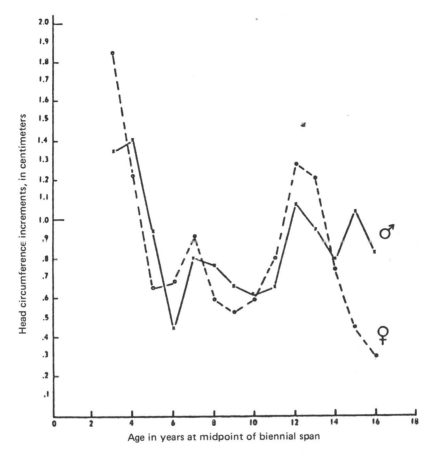

Figure 1. Head circumference increments. Produced from Epstein (1978) with permission. Data are from Nellhaus.

surement be incorporated into the school program and that learning goals at all stages be linked to head growth. His recommendation has been taken up by some educators in the middle school (e.g., Toepfer, 1976, 1980).

Several assumptions and associations in this work are troublesome. The curves are based on group data and may not represent any individual's growth. One would expect as much variability in head growth as seen in height; group data on height at adolescence smooth over the growth spurt so much that the distinctive spurt seen with most adolescents disappears. Eichorn and Bayley (1962), in their analysis of head circumference data, report, "The peak adolescent gain is not large, but it

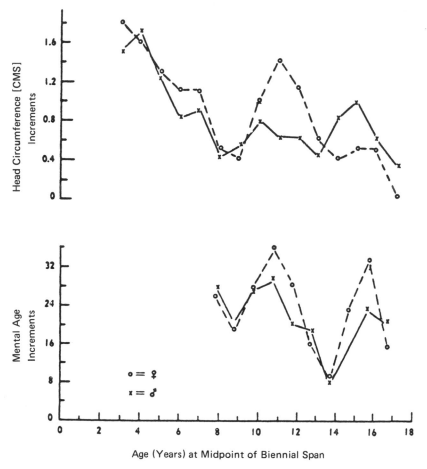

Figure 2. Increases in head circumference and in mental age. Produced from adaptation by Epstein (1978) with permission.

can be noted in almost every individual increment curve in each sex" (p. 265). We might conclude then that there is a spurt in head circumference in early adolescence that parallels the pubertal growth spurt with the appropriate sex differences such that females mature earlier. While Epstein focuses on the period of decreased growth, it seems equally appropriate to consider the spurt in growth.

This raises the issue of interventions. The present chapter is not about interventions so the discussion will be brief. Epstein proposes that learning can occur only during periods of brain growth. If this were the case, the education of adults and, indeed, all postpubertal persons would be ineffective. It is also inappropriate to apply inferences about average growth in a group to individual growth; the curriculum in a single grade would surely be inappropriate for the stage of brain growth of most of the students in the class.

Epstein (1978) links the information on the brain growth spurts to the emergence of the capacity for abstract thinking and the emergence of sex differences in cognition. If we embed brain growth within the broader pubertal growth spurt, as seems appropriate from our understanding of puberty (Petersen and Taylor, 1980), as well as from the data just discussed, these links may well be tenable. The pubertal growth spurt, however, is not simply a biological event. It has great social and psychological significance (Petersen and Spiga, 1982; Petersen and Taylor, 1980). Therefore, the meaning of any cognitive changes observed needs to be embedded within the context of the entire pubertal process, with its biological, psychological, and social aspects.

2.1. The Data Showing Cognitive Changes Related to Puberty

Epstein (1974b, 1978) focused on general intelligence in his discussion of cognitive changes. Table 1 shows his summary of the literature. Carey and Diamond (1980) reviewed a broader literature to identify

Table 1. Age of Peaks or Troughs in Mental Growth[a]

References	2–4	6–8	8–10	10–12	12–14	14–16
Jones and Conrad, 1933				+?	−	+
Freeman and Flory, 1937				+	−?	+
Shuttleworth, 1939		+?		+	−	+
McNemar, 1942						
S.D. IQ	±	+	−	+	−	+
Vocabulary test				+	−	+
Memory test	+?	+		+	−	+
Ebert and Simmons, 1943		+	−?	+	−	+?
Sanford, Adkins, Miller, and Cobb, 1943				+	−	+
Werner and Kaplan, 1950				+		
Bayley, 1949	+	+		+		
Sontag, Baker, and Nelson, 1958		+	−			
Stevenson, Hale, Klein, and Miller, 1968				+	−	
Rosenthal and Jacobson, 1968		+		+		
Kennedy, 1969				+	−	+
Cattell, 1971				+	−	

[a]Reproduced with permission from Epstein (1974).

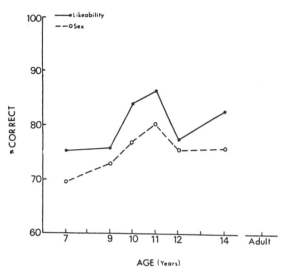

Figure 3. Recognition of faces judged during inspection for likeability or sex, at ages 7, 9, 10, 11, 12, 14, and in young adults. Reproduced from Carey, Diamond, and Woods (1980) with permission.

which cognitive processes might be maturational and might change during early adolescence. One task selected for study was face recognition, which involves the productive ability to encode, together with subsequent recognition capacity.

Carey's results (Carey, Diamond, and Woods, 1980) show cross-sectional changes with age similar to those described earlier by Epstein (see Figure 3). She links these changes to right-hemisphere functioning and proposes that "perhaps hormonal upheavals at puberty might in some way affect right hemisphere involvement in the processing of unfamiliar faces" (p. 266). Since the decrement in face recognition is temporary, Carey sees pubertal change as having a temporary disruptive effect on cognition. Note that this hypothesis would not explain the persistent, not temporary, sex differences seen beginning at early adolescence, unless other factors intervene to cause the temporary effects to continue.

In contrast, Waber (1976, 1977) as well as Wolff (1978) discusses the timing of maturation in terms of permanent effects on cognition. Waber proposed that degree of lateralization of brain function is a developmental process curtailed by puberty. Since girls reach puberty before boys, their brain functioning would be likely to be less lateralized than that in boys. While there is controversy about whether brain lateralization develops with maturation (Kinsbourne and Hiscock, 1977; Waber,

1979), Waber's data comparing early and late maturers supported her hypothesis about laterality, though only among older subjects. Later maturers, both younger and older, as well as both male and female, were better at spatial tasks than earlier maturers. Waber's hypothesis is appealing in that it explains both the sex difference in spatial tasks and the timing of its emergence. This explanation is comparable to that seen in the sex differences in adult height: men are taller than women because women start their adolescent growth spurt about two years earlier, which eventually causes closure of the bony epiphyses and cuts off the linear component of growth as well as the more rapid adolescent growth (Petersen and Taylor, 1980).

In two previous studies examining the association between timing of maturation and spatial performance, we (Herbst and Petersen, 1979; Petersen, 1976) failed to replicate Waber's result. In a recent study, we did find an association between timing of maturation and spatial performance (Figure 4), but no association of either of these variables to brain lateralization (Herbst and Petersen, 1980). Carey and Diamond (1980) replicated Waber's timing result with a pilot sample ($n = 11$) on the Embedded Figures Test, a measure of field independence, a construct related to spatial ability.

In a recent study, Newcombe and colleagues (Newcombe, Bandura, and Taylor, in press) also investigated the Waber hypothesis with pubertal girls. She found that later maturers were better spatial visualizers but, like our recent study, failed to find an association between brain lateralization and either pubertal timing or spatial ability. She did, however, find that later maturers were less feminine and were more likely to engage in spatial activities than were earlier maturers.

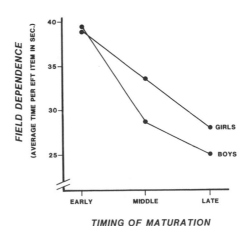

Figure 4. Field independence scores by timing of maturation for a sample of 135 high school seniors. A lower score indicates more field independence.

2.2. *Alternative Models for Explaining Cognition in Pubertal Girls*

The results reviewed suggest some alternative models for cognitive change in early adolescence. Epstein (1978), Carey (1980), and Waber (1976, 1977, 1979) all assume that there are some biological changes in the brain that disrupt cognition. Epstein (1978) sees such disruption as part of the continuing process of growth and plateaus in brain development. Carey and her colleagues (Carey and Diamond, 1980; Carey, Diamond and Woods, 1980) adopt a similar perspective but also raise the possibility that pubertal hormones are in some way involved. In addition, Carey (1981) has suggested that hemispheric laterality of functioning may be a dynamic process rather than a fixed mode as so many researchers have assumed. Both Epstein (1978) and Carey (1980) posit temporary disruptive effects. Such temporary effects would not explain the observed sex differences in these cognitive tasks, unless some other processes intervene in a sexually differential way. Waber's model (1979) does explain sex differences but support for the mechanism she proposes—functional hemispheric specialization (i.e., lateralization)—has not been forthcoming. Newcombe's research (e.g., Newcombe et al., in press) suggests that engaging in spatial activities also is involved, independent of the timing of maturation effect.

There is evidence that the experiences of the individual, by developing skill, influence not only the behavioral outcomes, in this case spatial ability, but that the experiences may influence underlying brain development as well (e.g., Greenough, Volkmar, and Juraska, 1973; Starck, Genesee, Lambert, and Seitz, 1977). Both Warren and Frisch (see Chapters 1 and 2) describe how exercise and nutrition can delay menarche and cause a corresponding change in body shape toward the longer, slimmer limbs characteristic of late maturation (see also Faust, chapter 6). It is possible, then, that the associations between timing of maturation and behavioral outcomes result from the *interaction* of factors, rather than representing the unidirectional effects of biological change on behavior, as is commonly believed.

The recent suggestion of Carey (1981) that laterality may be dynamic rather than fixed raises further possibilities. The previous paragraph discussed maturational change in laterality, with influences from experiences (exercise, if you will) as well as from a biological "script." This further suggestion is that there may be plasticity in hemispheric specialization such that laterality of functioning might shift during development. If this is substantiated with longitudinal data, data currently lacking, then we could posit several mechanisms by which change occurs.

A plausible model for cognitive change at puberty is shown in Figure 5. It proposes that there is a disruptive effect of puberty, due primar-

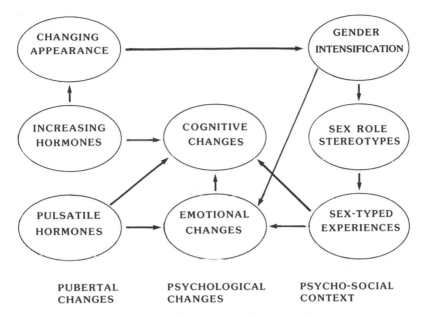

Figure 5. A model for cognitive change at puberty.

ily to the visible changes in appearance which initiate a series of effects which could cause emotional distress leading to disrupted performance on the behavioral level as well as the biochemical and brain level. In addition, there may also be direct effects of pubertal hormones on the brain. The social stimulus of pubertal change is likely to be amplified for girls in a way that channels their behavior in "sex-appropriate" ways. Hill and Lynch (see Chapter 10) have described the phenomenon of gender intensification at puberty. The change in appearance, then, provides a stimulus for gender intensification. For boys, pubertal change and gender intensification propel them along a linear trajectory in which they are pleased to reach puberty and to become a man. (See Tobin-Richards, Boxer, and Petersen, Chapter 7, for a description of the psychological correlates of pubertal change in boys.) For girls, however, the picture is entirely different. Previous research (Simmons, Rosenberg, and Rosenberg, 1973) has shown that girls decline in self-esteem at puberty. Our research (see Tobin-Richards et al., Chapter 7) supports this finding in terms of several psychological constructs in relation to timing of maturation. Girls who are on-time relative to their peers have the best feelings about themselves, but later maturers (among seventh graders) have the next best feelings, with early maturers feeling least positive about themselves. This is an entirely different pattern from the linear one seen in boys, and cannot be an artifact of the earlier puberty among girls since the linear aspect of the pattern for girls goes in the opposite direction of that seen in boys (i.e., earlier maturation is better for boys and later is better for girls). Therefore, the psychological results cannot be explained by any hormonal change alone and require a complex interactive model. It is difficult, then, to justify a simple hormonal or brain lateralization explanation for cognitive changes at puberty. Both cognition and affect are coordinated by the brain, involving both integrating systems: the central nervous system and the endocrine system. Furthermore, puberty is experienced by an individual in the context of social and cultural values about manhood or womanhood, as well as familial, peer group, and individual values about and meanings attached to these same issues. While there surely may be some behavioral specificity in the biological processes involved in, say, spatial ability versus body image, there also similarly would be different meanings attached to these constructs.

Spatial activities are generally considered to be masculine activities in our society (Newcombe, Bandura, and Taylor, in press; Tobin-Richards and Petersen, 1981). With gender intensification at puberty, it seems likely that most girls would choose not to engage in these "masculine" activities. They therefore limit their experiences, especially those relevant to the further development of spatial skill. Measured spatial ability would be reduced accordingly.

To summarize the proposed model focusing on cognitive change at puberty in girls, we suggest that pubertal change, in addition to its direct hormonal stimulation of the brain, may also set off a series of events in response to the change in physical appearance. In girls, the new appearance provides the stimulus for gender intensification which may have (at least) two effects: (1) it may be upsetting and conflictual, causing biochemical imbalances that disrupt cognition and (2) it may channel the behavior of girls in a way that limits their performance of tasks labeled as masculine. This limitation could occur both directly on sex-typed cognitive tasks, as well as by limiting sex-typed activities that might affect brain development which then would affect cognitive performance.

3. A TEST OF THE MODEL

3.1. Design

The data presented here are taken from the Early Adolescence Study, an ongoing longitudinal study of biopsychosocial development over the early adolescent years. The cohort-sequential design is described in Chapter 7, Table 1. It involves two successive cohorts, each followed over

Table 2. Sampling Design for the Study

| Cohort | Community A | | Community B | | Total |
| | Sex | | Sex | | |
	M	F	M	F	
I	50	50	50	50	200
II	50	50	50	50	200

3 years, from sixth grade through eighth grade. We have just completed the third year of testing.

3.2. Sample

Subjects for the study were sampled randomly from two upper-middle-class suburban school districts. The sampling design is shown in Table 2. Both school districts are declining in enrollments, one more than the other, so our actual samples are somewhat smaller than planned. The total n for Cohort I is 188. For the longitudinal analyses in the study, we have identified for Cohort I a sample that has maximal data across time. To be included in this longitudinal sample, a subject can have missed no more than two of six group assessments and no more than one of five interviews. This sample includes 57 boys and 78 girls for a total n of 135. A major source of loss to this sample occurred early in the study when we had to schedule a group testing during the summer; many children were on vacation or at camp on the day of assessments. The data presented here do not differ significantly from those on the complete sample at any age on any test.

3.3. Measures

The adolescents are interviewed twice annually and tested in group sessions at the same intervals. The assessment design is shown in Table 3. We had planned to obtain pubertal stage data by pediatrician ratings of Tanner stages. In one school district, this aspect of the study was refused at the outset. In the other, pubertal ratings were deleted after a year of negotiations. After our initial despair, we began instead to ask the adolescents about their stage of growth on the various indices (menarche, breast development, pubic hair growth, height growth, and skin change for girls). In fact, our scales show the predictable sequence of pubertal events and form scales with the desired psychometric properties

Table 3. Assessments in the Early Adolescence Study

Assessments	Description	Frequency
For adolescents		
Interview	Semi-structured; focuses on school, friends, family, and self	Twice annually
Self-Image Questionnaire for Young Adolescents	Nine scales and total score of adjustment	Annually
Cognitive measures	Formal operations (Linn, Peel); spatial ability (PMA); fluent production (DAT); field independence (Water Level, GEFT)	Annually
Sentence Completion Test (Loevinger)	Measures stage of ego development	Annually
Sex role inventories	Bem Sex Role Inventory; Attitudes toward Women Scale for Adolescents (Petersen)	Annually
Lowman Inventory of Family Feelings	Measures feelings about family members	6th, 8th grades
Teacher ratings	Ratings of classroom behavior	6th, 8th grades
School achievement	Average GPA, standardized test ranking	Obtained once for all three grades
For parents		
Interview	Parallels child interview plus	6th, 8th grades
Self-Image Questionnaire for Young Adolescents (parent form)	Parent report of child's self-image	6th, 8th grades
Lowman Inventory of Family Feelings	Measures feelings about family members	6th, 8th grades

(Petersen, in press.) In the present paper, we have classified pubertal growth as prepubertal (or beginning puberty in no more than 1 of the five indices), pubertal, or late pubertal (postmenarcheal). These stages correspond roughly to Tanner's stages P0–P1, P2–P3, and P4–P5, respectively. The percentages of girls falling into each category at each assessment is shown in Table 4.

The cognitive measures used to test the hypotheses are spatial visualizing ability as measured by the Space Relations subtest of the Primary Mental Abilities Test (form for Grades 6–9) and field independence as measured by the Group Embedded Figures Test (see sample items in Figure 6). Fluent production has been commonly examined in sex difference studies; we measured this with Clerical Speed and Accuracy Subtest from the Differential Aptitude Test. We will use data from this test as a cog-

Table 4. Changes in Pubertal Status over Early Adolescence for Girls in the Longitudinal Sample[a]

		Seventh grade		Eighth grade	
	Sixth grade, spring	Fall	Spring	Fall	Spring
Prepubertal	44	6	5	0	0
Pubertal	39	72	55	36	23
Late pubertal	12	22	40	64	77
Missing[b]	5	0	0	0	0

[a]$N = 78$. All numbers are percentages.
[b]These values could not be interpolated but in all cases would be either prepubertal or pubertal.

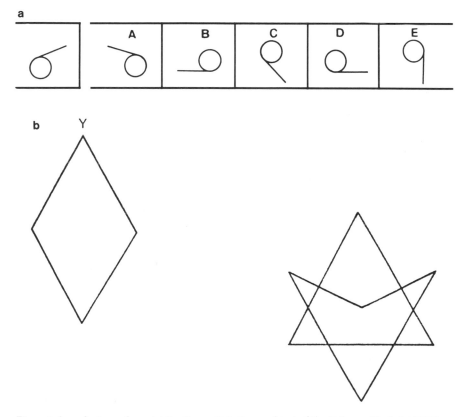

Figure 6. Sample items from (a) the Space Relations subtest of the Primary Verbal Abilities Test and (b) the Group Embedded Figures Test.

cognitive comparison, to test the specificity of any longitudinal or puberty-related change.

3.4. Results

3.4.1. *Cognitive Change.* Table 5 shows the cognitive scores by grade and sex for the longitudinal sample of subjects in Cohort I. Average scores increase steadily across this span of years for both boys and girls for all measures except spatial ability with boys. The scores for boys do not change from sixth grade to eighth grade; we initially wondered if this was a ceiling effect, but few scores even approach the top score of 72 points on this test. All of these scores are much higher than the national norms for these tests, a result to be expected among an upper-middle-class sample such as ours, with an average IQ of 115.

3.4.2. *Puberty and Cognitive Change.* Pubertal status was obtained in each semiannual interview while cognitive performance was obtained once annually. In the results that follow, cognition is examined in relation to the most proximate assessment of pubertal status.

As can be seen in Table 6, there are no significant effects of pubertal status on any of the cognitive measures for girls. Even ignoring significance and simply examining patterns, it is difficult to conclude that there are effects. In sixth grade, spatial ability is linearly related to pubertal status, while the pubertal girls perform *best* in seventh grade; in eighth grade there is little difference between the groups. From looking at individual scores, it appeared that there might be more variability during the peak period of pubertal change, but the group standard deviations suggest that the pubertal group is *least* variable.

Table 5. Means (and Standard Deviations) on Cognitive Measures by Sex and Grade

Measure	Grade	Boys	Girls
PMA Space	6	49.96(15.71)	39.66(20.46)
Relations	7	50.76(17.17)	43.39(10.81)
	8	50.60(14.84)	48.86(16.67)
DAT Clerical	6	43.57(10.79)	45.21(12.24)
Speed and Accuracy	7	49.34(10.46)	54.33(11.48)
	8	54.69(17.50)	61.88(13.47)
GEFT	6	ng[a]	ng
	7	9.85(4.65)	8.34(4.99)
	8	10.54(4.62)	10.04(5.05)

[a]ng: Not gathered.

Table 6. Means (and Standard Deviations) of Cognitive Measures by Grade and Pubertal Status

Measure	Grade	Pubertal status			F
		Prepubertal	Pubertal	Late pubertal	
PMA Space	6	37.88(23.55)	40.44(17.66)	42.33(21.81)	0.12
Relations	7	44.75(22.40)	46.94(16.62)	43.81(17.46)	0.22
	8	—[a]	47.42(17.56)	48.18(17.81)	0.03
GEFT	7	9.00 (5.10)	7.97 (5.09)	8.44 (5.07)	0.12
	8	—[a]	9.74 (5.16)	9.90 (5.17)	0.01
DAT Clerical	6	44.29(10.37)	45.69(15.14)	46.50(10.04)	0.09
Speed and Accuracy	7	64.50 (4.95)	52.66(11.76)	58.73 (9.43)	2.12
	8	—[a]	62.69(14.09)	61.32(13.18)	0.16

[a]No prepubertal subjects at this time.

The pattern of field independence scores is more consistent with the pubertal disruption hypothesis: the pubertal group at each grade scores lower, though not significantly so.

The pattern of scores on fluent production, the "control" measure is inconsistent from grade to grade. The pattern is linear in sixth grade, the pubertal group has the lowest scores in seventh, and the groups are similar in eighth.

The ideal design to test the questions posed here would include longitudinal sampling on both pubertal status and grade (or age), the latter being an important control for cognitive changes due to learning or maturation of cognition unrelated to puberty. Unfortunately, such a design would be difficult since adolescents mature at such variable rates. For example, among the 78 girls discussed here, only 19 (25%) traversed all three pubertal stages. Two of these girls were probably misclassified in the initial interview (where they reported no pubertal changes), since they reported menarche in the next interview and consistently thereafter; while such speedy development is possible, it is highly unlikely. (See Petersen, in press, for a further discussion of such cases.) Most girls (58%) traversed only two stages (18% prepubertal to pubertal and 40% pubertal to late pubertal) but 17% remained in a single stage over the 3 years of the study (5% pubertal and 12% late pubertal.) It is possible that the rate of change itself may be a potent variable; for example, girls who have longer to adjust to changes might do better. Therefore, a design that only sampled on pubertal status would miss any variation due to rate. In addition, given the variability in change of pubertal status, it would be impossible to use a complete design with pubertal status by grade (or age). In any case, the present data do not permit a simultaneous examination of these two factors.

We did fit, within each grade level, linear and quadratic polynomials to the data. As would be expected from the patterns of results presented above, there were no significant trends by pubertal status over time.

4. Discussion

Since the hypothesized decline in cognitive performance was not seen in these data, it does not seem fruitful to explore the model described to explain such a decline. The model was developed because preliminary analyses of a subsample of the present one (Petersen, 1981) did find a significant decline with increasing pubertal status on both spatial ability and field independence.[1] These results were not replicated here with the larger sample of subjects.

The present results may mean that there is no effect of pubertal change on cognition, or methodological problems may have reduced the likelihood of finding an effect if it exists. The cognitive measures are well-standardized and appropriate for this age group, so it is unlikely that they are producing excessive error variance. The pubertal measure, on the other hand, is crude and relies on self-report. Yet the fact that we had five assessments of pubertal changes enabled us to check the sequence and compare it with other data such as date of menarche. We do feel that in the vast majority of cases we have accurately assigned the three-level pubertal status code used here. Future analyses comparing these statuses with the interviewers' ratings and the parents' reports will enable us to further validate the pubertal status assignments.

Another possibility to consider is that because our sample is unusually high in cognitive performance, it may have limited the relationship with pubertal status. Apart from the statistical issue of restricted range (which does not seem applicable here since the variance in the cognitive measures is not restricted, and the method of analysis is analysis of variance rather than correlation), it is unclear how high perfor-

---

[1]The preliminary 34 subjects were those who had all pubertal and cognitive data at every time in the study and with no problems in the data. A major problem causing exclusion at that point was "pubertal regression," a regression in the pubertal status codes from one interview to the next. Since this is impossible (except in disease states), the problem had to be resolved. We have since done this. Much of the problem was due to a methodological artifact (i.e., a change in the way the scale was coded) and was easily resolved. There were a few cases where girls changed their reports (e.g., of date of menarche). We have now been able to resolve these by examining the longitudinal data, and in some cases by referring to the mother's report. We can not think of any way in which the initial problems with these additional 42 subjects should bias the final results.

mance would bias the results since what is hypothesized is a disruption in performance, not low performance. The only logical artifact here could be the possibility that disruption is not uniform across performance levels, with high performers affected least. But there is no evidence for this, in the present data or elsewhere.

We have occasionally found our group testing sessions to be somewhat chaotic, with some students finding it difficult to attend to the tasks. Those who administered the tests reported anecdotally that this sort of disruption seemed worse in seventh grade. The standard deviations in the cognitive measures do not, however, seem to vary in any systematic way. If anything, they are *lowest* across sex, measures, and cohorts in seventh grade. In any case, scores produced in the context of behavioral disruption do not appear to relate systematically to pubertal status.

Carey and colleagues (1980) have found the disruption effect primarily with face recognition, a task quite different from the present ones. She has, however, seen occasional effects with field independence, also used in the present studies. The field Independence measure, GEFT, was the only one even to show the predicted pattern, though not to a significant extent.

If pubertal disruption does exist for some cognitive tasks, it may be a weak effect as has been seen with time of maturation: appearing most predictably when extreme samples are compared (e.g., Herbst and Petersen, 1980; Waber, 1977).

The general model proposed earlier may yet be a useful one, but may be applicable only if an individual "salience" factor is built in. Puberty, in terms of its direct effects as well as effects mediated through the individual's structure of meanings, may be important only to some individuals. Pubertal change *is* important, for example, to early-maturing girls (Petersen, in press). If it is the case that general pubertal effects on cognition are not found, they may yet exist for subgroups of individuals. For example, in the present data, about one-fourth of the girls showed a decline in spatial scores as they moved from a prepubertal to a pubertal state. It would be of interest to explore whether and how these girls differ from those whose scores increased or remained the same over the pubertal transition. Do they show concomitant changes in sex role orientation, or self-image?

We have found no support in this research for plateauing or declining skills, as proposed by Epstein, except perhaps in spatial ability among boys. We have addressed in another paper (Kavrell and Petersen, in press) achievement over these years and there, as well, fail to find support for Epstein's hypothesis. Our longitudinal series is a relatively short one and may miss significant changes in the *rate* of cognitive growth.

But we do not find evidence of a decline in cognitive capacity during early adolescence.

Author's note. Since the preparation of this chapter, two findings have emerged that add importantly to information provided here. First, on page 179 I stated that sex differences in cognition emerge during early adolescence. In a major review and meta-analysis of research on sex differences in spatial ability, Marcia Linn and I have found that for those aspects of spatial ability on which sex differences appear, they exist as early as the constructs can be measured, and clearly prior to early adolescence.

Second, we have now conducted extensive studies of the self-reports of pubertal status. We find substantial agreement between these self-reports and assessments made by the interviewer and parents. More importantly, self-reports of height and weight show very high correlations, never lower than 0.85, with measures obtained by the school nurse in one of the school districts. Using a triple logistic model for growth in height to maturity, we find the predicted associations between three parameters of adolescent growth and the self-reports of pubertal status. All of these results lead us to conclude that young adolescents can accurately report their pubertal status.

ACKNOWLEDGMENTS. The research reported here is supported by NIMH, grant MH30252, to A. Petersen. The assistance of Suzanne Kavrell, Harry Jarcho, and Florence Halprin is gratefully acknowledged.

REFERENCES

Carey, S. Maturational factors in human development. In D. Caplan (Ed.), *Biological studies of mental processes.* Cambridge, Mass.: MIT Press, 1980, 1–7.
Carey, S. Spatial reorganization at adolescence. Presentation at a conference on Gender-Role Development: Conceptual and Methodological Issues sponsored by NICHD in Bethesda, MD, September 30–October 2, 1981.
Carey, S., and Diamond, R. Maturational determination of the developmental course of face encoding. In D. Caplan (Ed.), *Biological studies of mental processes.* Cambridge, Mass.: MIT Press, 1980, 60–73.
Carey, S., Diamond, R., and Woods, B. Development of face recognition—maturational component? *Developmental Psychology,* 1980, *16,* 257–269.
Eichorn, D. H., and Bayley, N. Growth in head circumference from birth through young adulthood. *Child Development,* 1962, *33,* 257–271.
Elkind, D. *Children and adolescents: Interpretive essays on Jean Piaget.* New York: Oxford University Press, 1974.
Epstein, H. T. Phrenoblysis: Special brain and mind growth periods. I. Human brain and skull development. *Developmental Psychobiology,* 1974a, *7,* 207–216.

Epstein, H. T. Phrenoblysis: Special brain and mind growth periods. II. Human mental development. *Developmental Psychobiology*, 1974b, *7*, 217–224.

Epstein, H. T. Growth spurts during brain development: Implications for educational policy and practice. In J. S. Chall and A. F. Mirsky (Eds.), *Education and the brain*. Chicago: Society for the Study of Education, 1978.

Epstein, H. T., and Epstein, E. B. The relationship between brain weight and head circumference from birth to age 18 years. *American Journal of Physical Anthropology*, 1978, *48*, 471–474.

Greenough, W. T., Volkmar, F. R., and Juraska, J. M. Effects of rearing complexity on dendritic branching in frontolateral and temporal cortex of the rat. *Experimental Neurology*, 1973, *41*, 371–378.

Hamburg, B. A. Early adolescence: A specific and stressful stage of the life cycle. In G. V. Coelho, D. A. Hamburg, and J. E. Adams (Eds.), *Coping and adaptation*. New York: Basic Books, 1974.

Herbst, L., and Petersen, A. C. Timing of maturation, brain lateralization and cognitive performance in adolescent females. Paper presented at the meeting of the Fifth Annual Conference on Research on Women and Education, Cleveland, November 1979.

Herbst, L., and Petersen, A. C. Timing of maturation, brain lateralization and cognitive performance. Paper presented at the meeting of the American Psychological Association, Montreal, September 1980.

Inhelder, B., and Piaget, J. *The growth of logical thinking from childhood to adolescence*. New York: Basic Books, 1958.

Kavrell, S. M. and Petersen, A. C. Patterns of achievement in early adolescence In M. L. Maehr and M. W. Steinkamp (Eds.), *Women and science*. Greenwich, Conn.: Jai Press, in press.

Kinsbourne, M. and Hiscock, M. Does cerebral dominance develop? In S. J. Segalowitz and F. A. Gruber (Eds.), *Language development and neurological theory*. New York: Academic Press, 1977.

Kinsbourne, M., and Hiscock, M. Cerebral lateralization and cognitive development. In J. S. Chall and A. F. Mirsky (Eds.), *Education and the brain*. Chicago: National Society for the Study of Education, 1978.

Maccoby, E. E., and Jacklin, C. N. *The psychology of sex differences*. Stanford: Stanford University Press, 1974.

Newcombe, N., Bandura, N. M., and Taylor, D. G. Sex differences in spatial ability and spatial activities. *Sex Roles*, in press.

Petersen, A. C. Physical androgyny and cognitive functioning in adolescence. *Developmental Psychology*, 1976, *12*, 524–533.

Petersen, A. C. Differential cognitive functioning at adolescence. In M. Sugar (Ed.), *Female adolescent development*. New York: Brunner/Mazel, 1979.

Petersen, A. C. Biopsychosocial processes in the development of sex-related differences. In J. E. Parsons (Ed.), *The psychobiology of sex differences and sex roles*. Washington, D.C.: Hemisphere, 1980.

Petersen, A. C. Does pubertal change affect cognition in girls? Invited presentation at a Female Adolescent Development conference sponsored by the Personal Products Company at LaJolla, California, March 1981.

Petersen, A. C. Menarche: Meaning of measures and measuring meaning. In S. Golub (Ed.), *Menarche*. New York: Heath, in press.

Petersen, A. C. and Spiga, R. Adolescence and stress. In L. Goldberger and S. Breznitz (Eds.), *Handbook of stress: Theoretical and clinical aspects*. New York: Free Press, 1982.

Petersen, A. C., and Taylor, B. The biological approach to adolescence. In J. Adelson (Ed.), *Handbook of adolescent psychology.* New York: John Wiley and Sons, 1980.

Petersen, A. C., and Wittig, M. A. Sex-related differences in cognition functioning: An overview. In M. A. Wittig and A. C. Petersen (Eds.), *Sex-related differences in cognitive functioning: Developmental issues.* New York: Academic Press, 1979.

Petersen, A. C., Tobin-Richards, M., and Crockett, L. Sex differences. In H. E. Mitzel (Ed.), *Encyclopedia of Educational Research.* 5th ed. New York: Free Press, 1982.

Simmons, R. G., Rosenberg, F., and Rosenberg, M. Disturbance in the self-image at adolescence. *American Sociological Review,* 1973, *38,* 553–568.

Simmons, R. G., Blyth, D. B., Van Cleave, E. F., and Bush, D. M. Entry into early adolescence: The impact of school structure, puberty, and early dating on self-esteem. *American Sociological Review,* 1979, *44,* 948–967.

Starck, R., Genesee, F., Lambert, W. E., and Sikes, M. Multiple language experience and the development of cerebral dominance. In S. J. Segalowitz and F. A. Gruber (Eds.), *Language development and neurological theory.* New York: Academic Press, 1977.

Tobin-Richards, M., and Petersen, A. C. Spatial and sex-appropriate activities. Presented at the Annual Meeting of the American Psychological Association, Los Angeles, August 1981.

Toepfer, C. F. The process of the middle school. Paper presented at the annual conference of the National Middle School Association in St. Louis, November 1976.

Toepfer, C. F. Brain growth periodization in young adolescents: Some educational implications. Paper presented at the annual meeting of the American Educational Research Association, Boston, April 1980.

Waber, D. P. Sex differences in cognition: A function of maturation rate? *Science,* 1976, *192,* 572–574.

Waber, D. P. Sex differences in mental abilities, hemisphere lateralization, and rate of pysical growth at adolescence. *Developmental Psychology,* 1977, *13,* 29–38.

Waber, D. P. Cognitive abilities and sex-related variations in the maturation of cerebral cortical functions. In M. A. Wittig and A. C. Petersen (Eds.), *Sex-related differences in cognitive functioning: Developmental issues.* New York: Academic Press, 1979.

Wolff, P. H. Measuring maturation: Myelinogenesis and brain function. *Andover Review,* 1978, *5,* 69–79.

Sociocultural Aspects of Puberty

Chapter 10

The Intensification of Gender-Related Role Expectations during Early Adolescence

JOHN P. HILL AND MARY ELLEN LYNCH

1. INTRODUCTION

It has been argued that there is an acceleration of gender-differential socialization during adolescence, perhaps at the onset of puberty or shortly after, and perhaps especially for girls. New domains may become the object of gender-differential socialization pressure and demands for conformity may increase in domains previously subject to such pressure. We shall refer to this argument as the Gender-Intensification Hypothesis. The hypothesis frequently is invoked to explain observed behavioral differences between adolescent boys and girls. Here we shall review information bearing upon the hypothesis and suggest some new points of departure for research related to it and to the study of gender-differential socialization during adolescence in general. We begin by considering some forms in which the hypothesis appears and then turn to our review and to its implications.

2. THE GENDER-INTENSIFICATION HYPOTHESIS

The hypothesis that an intensification in gender-related role expectations occurs during adolescence can be found in many places in the

JOHN P. HILL AND MARY ELLEN LYNCH • Department of Psychology, Virginia Commonwealth University, Richmond, Virginia 23284.

literature. Among illustrative passages are the following. For Stein (1976, pp. 241–242):

> A number of authors have proposed that adolescence represents the first point in development when females receive intense social pressure to be feminine. Before they reach puberty many girls can happily be tomboys, not worry much about how they look or whether they are sweet, attractive, and feminine. Girls who prefer baseball to dolls are tolerated during elementary school. With the onset of adolescence, however, comes a high premium on being socially successful, attractive to boys, and on giving up masculine activities and interests. Some girls exhibit a flight into femininity, perhaps in a long-range effort to attract a husband.

For Brooks-Gunn and Matthews (1979, p. 239):

> Girls find themselves in another predicament during puberty. Not only are they expected to give up sports, but they find their sexual maturity is a concern rather than a joy to their parents. Girls are told to protect themselves, never walk at night alone, always to call. . . .

For Bardwick and Douvan (1971, p. 149):

> Although girls are rewarded for conformity, dependence, passivity and competence, they are not clearly punished for the reverse. Until adolescence the idea of equal capacity, opportunity and lifestyle was held out to them, but sometime in adolescence the message becomes clear that one had better not do too well; that competition is aggressive and unfeminine; that deviation threatens the heterosexual relationship.

There is some consistency in the explanations that have been advanced for a presumed intensification of gender-related role expectations during early adolescence. Several, probably interrelated, factors are held to operate for girls. Given lack of preparation for and the negative cultural context in which menstruation occurs (see Brooks-Gunn and Ruble, Chapter 8) as well as expectations for physical discomfort (Paige, 1973), menarche is believed to be a stressful event and adaptation to regular menstruation stressful as well (Katz, 1979). Changes in physical appearance characteristics may lead to changes in self-views and in the expectations of others. When pubertal change coincides with entry into a new, larger, and less personal school environment and with dating pressure from older boys, stress is held to result (Simmons, Blyth, Van Cleave, and Bush, 1979). This line of thought leads to predictions of (and has led to some findings of) greater anxiety, greater stereotyping of expectations for the behavior of peers, especially in dating relationships (Rosen and Aneshensel, 1976), and to greater self-consciousness and decreases in self-esteem among post- than prepubertal girls (Simmons et al., 1979). The principal emphasis in such arguments is upon socializing effects of relations with opposite-sex peers. Early dating activity also may affect relations with same-sex peers. Girls appear to learn intimacy skills through sharing initial and anxiety-provoking dating and sexual experiences with same-sex peers (Douvan and Adelson, 1966). For males, braggadocio is commonly held to replace sharing of anxiety-provoking dating experiences, although there has been no empirical attention to this claim.

As our quotations from earlier reviews suggest, entry into the dating and rating perplex also may have effects on other behavioral domains, especially on achievement for young women. As Coleman (1961) has commented, girls have grades higher than those of boys, have aspirations equal to theirs, and yet receive fewer social rewards for achievement: "In the normal activities of a high school, the relations between boys and girls tend to increase the importance of physical attractiveness, cars, and clothes, and to decrease the importance of achievement. . . ." (p. 50). It is important to note, once again, that gender-intensification effects are presumed to operate principally through peers. Immersion of girls in dating is inhibitory to the display of competence. Effects of parents as role-definers or models are not emphasized.

Another common theme in explanations advanced for the intensification of gender-related role expectations during adolescence does implicate parents. *Chaperonage* (Newson and Newson, 1968), *vigilance* (Block, 1978), and a *lessening of permissiveness* (Katz, 1979) have been remarked. As reproductive maturity becomes imminent, traditional parents are held to respond in a variety of ways to ensure fittedness for marriage (Stein, 1971). They encourage not only virginity but compliant femininity in their daughters (a set of behaviors labeled the Chameleon Syndrome by Rosen and Aneshensel, 1976). A counterpart syndrome for boys has not been offered for empirical study but could easily be explicated along machismo lines: that is, traditional parents respond to pubertal change in males with increased tolerance for independence and decreased tolerance for emotional display, less protectiveness, and subtle encouragement of sexual conquest.

Despite the many sensible and intriguing notions about the mechanisms underlying differential gender socialization during adolescence, most existing studies focus upon gender differences alone and do not include conceptually relevant explanatory or mediating variables in their designs. This is especially unfortunate when the implicit or explicit hypothesis held to underlie an observed gender difference has to do with the onset of or the imminence of pubertal status or reproductive maturity. The modal girl reaches the peak of pubertal growth in the seventh grade and the modal boy in the ninth grade. Simple comparisons between seventh-grade boys and girls (or sixth, eighth, ninth, or tenth graders for that matter) may be more reflective of the normal 2-year gap in *maturation* rate than of gender-differential *socialization*. Pubertal status itself can and should be employed as an independent or mediating variable. Employing this and other conceptually relevant independent or mediating variables could eliminate or substantiate explanations of the sort sketched above.

3. EMPIRICAL INFORMATION BEARING UPON THE GENDER-INTENSIFICATION HYPOTHESIS[1]

In their extensive review of the literature on gender differences, Maccoby and Jacklin (1974) drew the following overall conclusion about parental differentiation by gender: "Our survey of the research on socialization of the two sexes has revealed surprisingly little differentiation in parental behavior according to the sex of the child. However, there are some areas where differential 'shaping' does appear to occur" (pp. 338–339). These areas are: more parental encouragement of sex-typed activities, more negative physical and nonphysical reinforcement, and more praise and positive reinforcement for boys than girls.

Block (1978) has argued that there are at least five reasons why the Maccoby and Jacklin conclusion of little parental differentiation may be premature. First, investigators have not systematically studied those specific age groups where intraindividual and situational changes might lead one to expect and to conceptualize changes in socialization as well. We believe that early adolescence is one such age group, as it requires adaptation to puberty, to new levels and kinds of information-processing skills, and to entry into larger, less personal and more bureaucratic organizations (e.g., the junior high school). Second, Block notes that gender-related differences in parental socialization in fact have been examined primarily when the children in question were age 6 and under. Extrapolation of conclusions from such studies to the second decade of life ignores the greater immersion of adolescents in the institutions and organizations of community and the broader society, their increasingly greater bodily dimorphism, and their increasing capacities for social reasoning in the manner of adults—all of which may contribute to changes in gender-related role expectations.

[1]This review is not the result of an exhaustive review of the literature for this volume. It is the by-product of several reviews of the literature undertaken for other, closely related purposes (Hill, 1980; Lynch, 1981, for example) over the past few years.

Third, most of the studies rely upon maternal report, whereas existing research suggests that the father may be the more critical parent for sex-typing (see Biller, 1976; Johnson, 1963; and Lamb, 1976, for reviews and discussion). In the studies reviewed by Block, 49% of investigators gathered data from mothers about their behavior; 9% from fathers about their behavior; and 30% had mothers report for both parents. Fathers appear to differentiate more than mothers, on the whole, although Block's (1978) caution that careful examination of interdomain differences may be fruitful is noteworthy here. We would add that during adolescence it is not only parents but peers of the same and opposite gender and other adults who define roles in gender-differential terms. In adolescence, "sex roles" are much, much more than a matter of displaying behaviors transmitted from parents through imitation and direct tuition. One does not learn "dating" from parents nor are universalistic norms of the sort encountered in schools (Dreeban, 1968) typical of family interaction.

Fourth, Block suggests that Maccoby and Jacklin may have grouped the studies they examined under rubrics that are too general. If the specific behaviors studied were considered, more evidence might be found for differentiation. Finally, Block notes that most existing studies have small sample sizes. There is little statistical power, and the null hypothesis is more likely to be accepted than it should be.

Block goes on to present her own review of the literature on parental differentiation by gender. Her review is to be recommended for its attention to these issues and its life-span coverage. Our own review will focus on the second decade of life and especially upon the first half of that decade. To provide some continuity with Block's work and an opportunity for comparison with it, we have organized this review around Block's topics: susceptibility to anxiety, achievement-related behavior, self-concept and self-esteem, social relationships, activity, and aggression. Block reviews gender-differential behavior of parental socializing agents. In addition, we shall consider studies involving gender differences *per se* and socializing agents other than parents. In embarking upon the present review, it is useful to bear in mind that "there is some evidence suggesting that sex differences in socialization emphases appear to increase with the age of the child, reaching a maximum during the high school years" (Block, 1978, p. 73).

3.1. Susceptibility to Anxiety and Coping Strategies

Early adolescent girls seem to experience more anxiety than their male counterparts and are taught to cope with it in gender-differentiated ways. Rosenberg and Simmons (1975) report data from a sample of white and black third through twelfth graders from working-class backgrounds. Dramatic gender differences emerged during early adolescence in self-consciousness. Girls were significantly higher than boys in the 12- to 14-year age group and the gap increased in the older group. Girls in the 12- to 14-year age group also worried significantly more than boys about what other people thought of them and cared more about being well liked; these differences were not significant in the older group although the pattern remained the same.

Girls also may have greater insecurity about social status (Savin-Williams, 1979). Female and male campers 12–14 years of age were asked to estimate their sociometric rankings by other campers. Boys were significantly more likely than girls to be accurate in estimating their own rankings by other campers; girls were likely to underestimate their own rankings.

Girls may cope with anxiety or insecurity by avoiding negative reactions or being compliant. Rosen and Aneshensel (1976) discuss the Chameleon Syndrome, defined as "an essentially accommodative response to an environment perceived as hostile to inappropriate sex role behavior" (p. 605). The components of the Chameleon Syndrome are sex-role stereotyping, perception of the reward structure for sex-role behavior (how members of the opposite sex respond to sex-role appropriate or inappropriate behavior), and reports of compliant, self-abasive, and dependent behavior. Girls in their seventh through twelfth grade sample scored higher than boys on the entire index and on each component. No grade analyses were reported in this study. Data reported by Rosenberg and Simmons (1975) also showed that adolescent girls try to avoid negative reactions from others more than boys do. These behaviors appear to be stronger in the 15 and older group than among the younger groups.

The data suggest that early adolescent girls do experience more anxiety and self-consciousness than boys of the same age. The Rosen and Aneshensel sample did not include students younger than seventh grade nor were analyses by grade completed, so it was not possible to infer when the gender difference in the Chameleon Syndrome emerged.

Rosen and Aneshensel found that perceived parental control and the importance of interpersonal relationships to the adolescent were significantly related to the Chameleon Syndrome. Although interaction with opposite-sex peers was negatively related to the Chameleon Syndrome, the relation was an artifact of age-related changes. When age was controlled by including only eleventh and twelfth graders, girls reporting only one serious relationship received the lowest Chameleon Syndrome scores, while girls reporting several nonserious relationships received the highest scores ($p < 0.005$). Analyses of younger students showed a similar pattern. According to the authors (p. 613),

> Collectively, the data on heterosexual involvement suggest a developmental process during which changes in the nature of the dating relationship ultimately weaken the Chameleon Syndrome by making it less necessary.

The later, more serious, and secure relationships presumably permit older adolescents to act in less stereotyped ways.

In summary, the data suggest that gender differences emerge in early adolescence on self-consciousness, with girls reporting much higher levels than boys. It also appears that adolescent girls are more likely than boys to cope with anxiety-provoking situations by being compliant or by avoiding negative reactions. The gender difference in avoiding negative reactions was stronger in older (15 years or more) than younger groups. There is some suggestion that perceived parental restrictiveness in combination with emphasis on interpersonal relationships is related to occurrence of the Chameleon Syndrome in adolescent girls. The importance of opposite-sex peers in female socialization also was emphasized by the finding that the occurrence of the Chameleon Syndrome was negatively related to serious involvement in dating relationships.

3.2. *Achievement-Related Behaviors*

Several writers have noted gender differences during adolescence in sex-role standards for achievement, achievement performance, risk-taking behavior, and achievement aspirations. While differences do appear to exist in all these areas, changes in early adolescent behavior consonant with the Gender-Intensification Hypothesis do not appear in all areas. In this section, literature on gender differences and changes in these differences during early adolescence will be discussed. Special attention will be paid to work on changes in parental expectations for daughters as a function of pubertal development.

3.2.1. *Sex-Role Standards.* Stein (1971; Stein, Pohly, and Mueller, 1971; Stein and Smithells, 1969) did a series of studies on the definition of sex-role standards for achievement. When Stein and Smithells (1969) asked second, sixth, and twelfth graders to rate items representing six achievement areas as "more girlish" or "more boyish," they found that the areas were ordered from feminine to masculine in the following way: social, artistic, reading, arithmetic, spatial, mechanical. In general, as the age of the subjects increased, the differences between sexes decreased. The authors (p. 256) suggest that:

Younger children—second and sixth graders—agreed closely with older subjects in areas which were considered by twelfth graders as appropriate to their own sex, but the younger subjects' views of areas appropriate to the opposite sex (on the basis of twelfth grade ratings) were deviant and changed only gradually with age.

In a later study of sixth and ninth graders, Stein (1971) reported that sex differences existed in the attainment value of sex-typed achievement areas. These differences were much stonger among ninth than sixth grade students, with girls placing more importance on feminine areas and boys on masculine areas. These data suggest that during adolescence, both boys and girls become more aware of sex-appropriate standards for achievement. In addition, achievements in these domains are viewed as more valuable by members of the appropriate sex; this effect appears stronger in older than younger adolescents.

3.2.2. *Performance.* Maccoby and Jacklin (1974) and Elkind (1968) reviewed gender differences in various domains of achievement, noting that boys tend to excel in spatial areas while girls excel in verbal areas. Both reviewers conclude that these differences emerge in early adolescence. Shaw and McCuen (1960) also suggest that early adolescence may be a critical time for girls' achievement development. They compared academic records for girls classified as achievers or underachievers on the basis of their high school grades. Results showed that the mean grade point average of the achievers did not exceed that of the underachievers until sixth grade. The differences gradually increased until they were significant in grades 9–11.

3.2.3. *Risk-Taking.* Gender differences also have been reported in a study of another achievement-related behavior: risk-taking. Slovic (1966) examined risk-taking behavior in volunteer subjects ranging in age from 6 to 16. Girls were less likely than boys to exhibit risk-taking behavior in a decision-making game at all age levels above 8 years. Differences were significant at ages 11 and 14–16. These data are consistent with the hypothesis, but generalizations from one study of behavior in a game situation only can be tentative.

3.2.4. *Aspirations.* In her recent review of literature on gender differences in aspirations, Marini (1978) concludes that adolescent girls' educational aspirations decrease while those of boys increase during the high school years. She tentatively suggests that a similar pattern exists for changes in occupational aspiration levels, but points out that data of this nature are difficult to interpret given the limited range in which most "female-appropriate" occupations fall. Bush, Simmons, Hutchinson, and Blyth (1977–1978) reported that gender differences in educational aspirations were not consistent in their comparisons of 1968 and 1975 samples of sixth and seventh graders. There were no significant gender differences among white seventh graders in either sample. Among white sixth graders, fewer girls than boys planned to attend college in 1968; the opposite effect appeared in three of the four analyses for black subgroups.

Bush et al. (1977–1978) report no gender difference in the number of early adolescents aspiring to high-level occupations, but note considerable differentiation in aspirations for blue-collar and white-collar, and clerical and sales jobs. Marini (1978) suggests that the degree of stereotyping in occupational aspirations increases during the high school years. However, the differentiation in environmental influences and expectations begins well before adolescence, as noted by Spenner and Featherman (1978) and Marini (1978).

Evidence discussed above suggests that girls' achievement behavior changes during early adolescence, but little research is available on the determinants of this change. Block's (1978) studies suggest that parents perform in ways to encourage achievement in sons more than in daughters. In her six studies, parents were asked to Q-sort statements about their expectations for their child. Block's samples included parents of children ranging in age from 3 to 20. Parents emphasized taking responsibility, being independent, and the importance of competition and achievement for their sons. The data from samples of parents of adolescents were, for the most part, consistent with the overall pattern. Gender differences in expectations or reported parental behavior toward the child were intensified at adolescence only in a few instances (competition items, most notably). Because parents were not asked to focus their Q-sorts on a specific period of development, it is possible that their responses reflect general reactions to and expectations for the child rather than those more specific to adolescence.

Hill (1964) interviewed a sample of middle-class parents of seventh graders about their expectations for their children. Parents' responses to four questions (what they found appealing about their child, what they would like to teach their child, what characteristics "good models" for their child would have, and what they would like their child to be like as an adult) were coded for frequency of sex-typed content categories. He reported that parents of boys gave significantly more responses categorized as achievement-success, individualism, and self-confidence than parents of girls. A dissertation by Lynch (1981) suggests that parents respond to their daughters' pubertal development with more traditional expectations for them. Traditionally masculine and androgynous fathers of early and later pubertal daughters (as defined by menarcheal status) were asked to Q-sort a deck of 40 cards listing instrumental and expressive characteristics and goals. Both parents in these families were asked to "sort these cards as to how important you think each characteristic or goal *should be to your daughter right now in her life.*" Some sample items in the instrumental composite include: "to do the best she can in most situations," "to be independent," and "does not give up easily; persistent." The interaction of paternal androgyny and daughter's pubertal status for this variable ($p = 0.078$) suggests that traditionally masculine and androgynous fathers respond to their daughters' pubertal development in different ways. Traditionally masculine fathers appeared to place less emphasis on instrumental characteristics for later pubertal than early pubertal daughters; androgynous fathers placed slightly more emphasis on these characteristics for later pubertal than early pubertal girls. Mothers also viewed instrumental characteristics as less important for their later pubertal than early pubertal daughters.

Data from the same study on amount of verbal help offered by fathers in two dyadic tasks also conform to the pattern described above. Traditionally masculine fathers offered more help (and allowed less autonomy) to later pubertal than early pubertal daughters; androgynous fathers offered less help (and allowed more autonomy) to later pubertal than early pubertal daughters. These data suggest that traditionally masculine fathers are less likely to behave in ways that will encourage their daughter's achievement with later pubertal than early pubertal daughters. Androgynous fathers may be slightly more likely to encourage achievement in later pubertal than early pubertal daughters.

That peers also are important in the socialization of achievement has been shown by the work of Coleman. Coleman (1961) asked his high school subjects to indicate which of a list of standard attributes (determined through pretesting) were important for popularity with peers of the same and opposite gender. For both boys and girls, popularity with one's own sex was believed to involve good grades and school activities more than was popularity with the opposite sex. For popularity with the opposite sex, attributes prominent in dating—cars for boys and clothes for girls—were more important than good grades and school activities. This study is of less interest for what it says about gender differences than for the implication of the differential importance of the gender of peers as socializing agents.

In summary, available information suggests that, during early adolescence, gender-appropriate standards for achievement (as traditionally defined) become more stringently applied. Girls and boys begin to excel in different areas. Risk-taking behavior in achievement tasks may decrease for girls. Evidence is somewhat conflicted on changes in aspiration levels but data do exist showing that occupational choices are differentiated along traditional lines during adolescence. While traditional gender-related differences in gender-appropriate standards for achievement exist prior to adolescence, they become stronger during this period. Most striking are early-adolescent gender differences in achievement performance and risk-taking behavior where none appeared before. Differences in parental expectations for instrumental behavior among daughters have been linked to daughters' pubertal status, suggesting that environmental responses to physical change may be partially responsible for these behavior changes.

3.3. Self-Concept and Self-Esteem

Results from several studies suggest that girls' self-concepts change during early adolescence in two ways: (1) they experience greater disruption of the self-concept than males and (2) they become more concerned about interpersonal aspects of their lives and physical appearance. Each of these areas will be discussed in this section.

Simmons and Rosenberg (1975) report that in their predominantly working-class sample of third through twelfth graders, white adolescent females showed more disruption (higher self-consciousness, more instability of self-image, lower self-esteem) of self-concept than white males or black females of the same age. Differences between white males and females emerged in the 12- to 14-year age group on self-consciousness and instability of the self-image; the difference between these groups on self-esteem was significant only in the 15 or older category. These data suggest that at least some of these differences may be explained by gender-differential socialization; white adolescent girls had more negative attitudes toward their sex roles than boys had toward theirs. The investigators suggest that this may be due to perceptions of limited future role opportunities as well as present role expectations. Although these data were collected in 1968, results on sixth and seventh graders' self-esteem and perceptions of gender role are very similar to those collected from a sample of sixth and seventh graders interviewed in Milwaukee in 1975. The percentage of girls reporting low self-esteem did not decline between 1968 and 1975. The disparity between boys and girls is even greater in the later sample (Bush et al., 1977–1978).

Some data also suggest that during early adolescence, girls' self-images become more interpersonally oriented. In her longitudinal study, Carlson (1965) examined self-descriptions by males and females in sixth grade and again 6 years later. There were no gender differences in the sixth graders' data, but the girls showed a higher social orientation than the boys did at the second time of data collection. Simmons and Rosenberg (1975) also found that girls were more likely than boys to rank popularity as most important when compared to being independent or competent. Ranking popularity as most important was associated with higher self-consciousness and lower stability of self-image among the adolescents. Rosenberg and Simmons (1975) provide data on analyses for age. Even in the 8- to 11-year group, more girls than boys were most concerned about being well liked. The gender differences increased at early adolescence although greater percentages of both males and females ranked this alternative highest in adolescence than in preadolescence.

When Bush et al. (1977–1978) compared responses of sixth and seventh graders only in this sample and in the 1975 sample, they found a less strong shift toward an interpersonal orientation in 1975 than appeared in 1968. Seventh grade girls from the 1975 sample still valued popularity more than boys, but a smaller proportion chose this alternative. Larger proportions chose the competence and independence alternatives in the later sample. Simmons and Rosenberg (1975) also reported that white girls were more concerned about their appearance, and less satisfied with their looks than white boys. The gender difference in concern about appearance was significant for the overall sample, but not within age groups; the difference in satisfaction emerged in the 12- to 14-year age group and was significant in the older age group as well.

In their recent longitudinal study, Dusek and Flaherty (1981) report similarity between males and females for factor structure of the self-concept in fifth through twelfth grade students. The four factors emerging for both groups were named adjustment, achievement/leadership, congeniality/sociability, and masculinity/femininity. Even though the factor structure was similar, gender differences occurred in factor scores, with males having higher mean scores on achievement/leadership and masculinity/femininity (high score = masculine score), and females having higher mean scores on congeniality/sociability. Sex and grade interaction effects did not occur very consistently across the 3 years of data collection, but such interactions were significant for the congeniality/sociability scale for two of the analyses: Significant gender differences on this scale occurred in Grades 5–10 in 1976 and in Grades 5–9 in 1977.

Taken together, these studies suggest that early adolescent girls experience decreased self-esteem and increased self-consciousness. There is also some support for the idea that early adolescent girls become more invested in interpersonal matters and more dissatisfied with physical appearance, but the mechanisms of these changes have not been explored.

In one of the few studies relating the self-concept changes to structural and personal life events, Simmons et al. (1979) investigated effects of pubertal development, school structure, and participation in dating behavior on adolescent girls' self-esteem. The 240 white girls in the sample (this is the 1975 Milwaukee sample also discussed in Bush et al., 1977–1978) were drawn from two types of school structures: K–8 and K–6, followed by junior high school. Pubertal level was defined by menarcheal status. Girls were interviewed in both sixth and seventh grades. These researchers report that girls who made the transition to junior high school experienced a decline in self-esteem, while girls in the K–8 school environment and boys in both structures experienced an increase in adjusted mean scores. In addition, they report that junior high girls who are pubertal and have started dating have the lowest self-esteem of all girls. Simmons et al. (1979) suggest that these results may be due to the development of a new value system emphasizing popularity and appearance; they report that among these seventh graders, girls do place more value on looks and on popularity than boys do. Another suggested source of influence is increased sexual pressure. More mature junior high girls who are dating may be more susceptible to both these influences.

In summary, the data suggest that, during early adolescence, girls begin to experience heightened self-consciousness, less stability of self-image, and a decrease in self-esteem. Differences between males and females emerge at this point where none existed before. Girls also may become more oriented toward interpersonal goals. Changes in these self-image variables rarely have been linked to changes in environmental responses to pubertal change, although the self-image of the junior high-school girls who are pubescent *and* engaged in dating behavior may be especially vulnerable to downward shifts.

3.4. *Social Relationships*

More data relevant to the Gender-Intensification Hypothesis exist in the area of social relationships than in any of the areas previously discussed. The evidence suggests that adolescent girls maintain qualitatively more sophisticated and intimate friendship relationships than boys do; that girls' behaviors toward infants may change; and that status patterns, friendship patterns, expectations for friendship, and parental expectations for sex-appropriate "expressive" behavior are related to daughters' pubertal level.

Girls' capacities for intimacy appear to change more in adolescence than do those of boys, especially in relation to self-disclosure. Even by the end of high school, boys' friendships are like those reported by preadolescent girls. They involve "doing things" with a congenial companion as opposed to the sharing of feelings and ideas more common to the friendships of older adolescent females (Douvan and Adelson, 1966). Hill, Thiel, and Blyth (1981) asked seventh- to tenth graders to list significant others (both adults and other young people) in their lives. Girls were more likely to provide longer lists of peers who were important to them and, at every grade level, a greater proportion of their significant peers were seen as accepting, understanding, and sharing feelings than was the case for boys. The gender differences did not increase or decrease from the seventh through the tenth grade. More acceptance, understanding, and sharing of feelings were reported at each successive grade level for both boys and girls. However, the proportion of significant-other peers with whom boys report intimacy at the tenth grade level is below that for girls at the seventh grade level.

Most studies of self-disclosure (but not all) have found that girls disclose more to parents than do boys. Disclosure is greater to mothers than to fathers. Disclosure to peers is greater than that to parents and greater to same- than to opposite-sex peers (Balswick and Balkwell, 1977; Douvan and Adelson, 1966; Mulcahy, 1973; Rivenbark, 1971; Sharabany, Gersoni, and Hofman, 1981; West, 1970).

Duck (1975) examined the types of constructs used as bases for friendships among adolescents and found gender differences in middle and later adolescent groups. Girls progressed from use of fact and physical constructs in the youngest group ($\bar{x}$ age = 12) to use of psychological constructs in the middle group ($\bar{x}$ age = 14) and to use of physical and psychological constructs in the oldest group ($\bar{x}$ age = 15½). Boys used fact constructs in the youngest group, interaction constructs in the middle group, and physical constructs in the oldest group.

Other researchers have examined behavior toward infants in preadolescent and early adolescent samples of boys and girls; their results are rather mixed in terms of the Gender-Intensification Hypothesis. Feldman, Nash, and Cutrona (1977) found that there were no sex differences among 8- to 9-year-old subjects in observed responses to a live baby or in their reactions to pictures of babies. A difference did emerge among their 14- to 15 year-old subjects. Analyses of data from several measures showed trends ($p < 0.10$) for girls to be more responsive to babies than boys in the older age group. Girls in this group also were significantly more likely than boys to choose pictures of babies as favorites. Frodi and Lamb (1978) studied behavioral and psychological responses to babies in preadolescent and adolescent groups. They found that girls interacted with babies more than boys, but the increased differentiation predicted with age did not occur. Although girls also ignored babies less than boys, this gender difference was smaller in the older group. There were no sex differences on the psychophysiological measures. While the Feldman et al. (1977) data are consistent with the Gender-Intensification Hypothesis, the Frodi and Lamb (1978) data are not. Frodi and Lamb's finding that differences occurred in behavioral but not psychophysiological measures suggests that gender or developmental differences that do occur are the result of socialization rather than biological changes.

Data discussed above suggest that girls begin to display more gender-appropriate social behavior (as traditionally defined) in early adolescence. Hill and Block have shown such differentiation in parental expectations for adolescent children as well. In his study of parental expectations for seventh graders, Hill (1964) reported parents of girls were more likely to value warmth, instrumental nurturance, courtesy and manners, and "personality" than parents of boys. Block's (1978) survey of Q-sort studies showed that daughters were expected to act in more traditionally defined ways than sons were. Parents discouraged rough-and-tumble play more in girls than in boys; they encouraged control of affect more in boys than in girls. Mothers expected girls to stay clean while playing, and fathers were more likely to discourage fighting in their daughters than sons. The parent–daughter relationship was more warm and involved greater expression of physical affection than parent–son relationships. Parents also reported that it was more difficult to punish daughters than sons. An examination of data for samples with children of varying age levels shows that the only differences that are intensified at adolescence are the degree to which rough games are allowed and the father's attempts to discourage fighting. As mentioned earlier, differences may not appear in these data because parent responses may reflect more general than current expectations.

Several researchers have related changes in expectations of parents and peers to the pubertal status of the adolescent girl. With the same sample of seventh graders and their families discussed earlier, Lynch (1981) examined fathers' and mothers' expectations for their daughters' expressiveness with a Q-sort measure. Sample items in the expressiveness scale included "to be kind," "to be able to talk to others in an interesting and entertaining manner," "to be personally charming," and "to be popular with kids her own age." A marginally significant interaction effect ($p = 0.064$) occurred for paternal androgyny/traditionality and daughter's pubertal status. An examination of the means showed that traditionally masculine fathers of later pubertal daughters placed more importance on expressive characteristics than those of early pubertal daughters; androgynous fathers of later pubertal daughters placed slightly less importance on the expressive items than the androgynous fathers of early pubertal girls. Mothers also placed significantly more emphasis on the expressive characteristics and goals for later pubertal than for early pubertal daughters.

That pubertal level also influences socialization experiences within the peer group has been demonstrated by Savin-Williams (1979) in his study of dominance interactions among campers. Savin-Williams used observations of behavior and sociometric techniques to study the dominance hierarchies that developed during 5-week camp sessions. Four cabins of five girls each were observed for the study. Physical encounters and arguments were more common dominance interactions among boys than girls. Girls were much more likely than boys to engage in behaviors that provide recognition of the dominance of another (e.g., asking advice, imitating, complimenting). Girls in general were less likely to use the overt forms (e.g., verbal challenges, arguments, direct orders, name-calling) of dominance than boys were. Behavioral dominance was correlated with relative ranking of pubertal status for both sexes. Peer popularity was correlated with behavioral dominance only for girls.

The literature discussed in this section suggests that changes take place in the ways girls deal with people during early adolescence. The content and bases for peer friendships appear to become more sophisticated for girls than for boys. It is possible that sex differences also emerge at early adolescence in behaviors displayed toward infants but results to date have not been consistent.

In this domain, more clear links can be drawn between changes in behavior and the responsiveness of parents and peers to the pubertal change in the adolescent. Both mothers and traditionally masculine fathers placed greater emphasis on expressive characteristics and goals for later pubertal than early pubertal daughters. Relative pubertal status also was related to behavioral dominance in peer groups. This rating is based on interaction, so both how the adolescent treats others and how she is treated by others are related to her comparative physical development level.

3.5. *Activity Level*

There are few data available for early adolescent samples on traditional "activity level" variables such as amount of exploratory behavior or display of curiosity. Some studies do suggest that adolescent girls adopt less active, more compliant ways of responding and that they are more cautious in dealing with their environments.

When Walberg (1969) studied senior high school students who participated in Harvard Project Physics, he reported from semantic differential results that girls had more cautious attitudes about science experience than boys. They viewed physics as less "safe," experiments as more "important" but less "simple," and self as a physics student as less "facile" and more a "starting" student than boys did. In his study of risk-taking behavior, Slovic (1966) also showed that from age 9 through 16, boys were more likely to take risks in a decision-making game than girls were. Differences were significant at age 11 and for the 14- to 16-year age group. Other data discussed above suggest that girls tend to adopt compliant modes of dealing with anxiety-provoking situations (Rosen and Aneshensel, 1976; Rosenberg and Simmons, 1975). Data on parental expectations in this area are sparse. Hill (1964) reports that parents of boys more frequently mentioned activity level when describing expectations for and desirable characteristics of sons than parents of daughters.

Several theorists (e.g., Brooks-Gunn and Matthews, 1973; Katz, 1979) have suggested that parents become more protective of their daughters than sons at early adolescence, but little research has been done. Based on her survey of several samples of parents and students' perceptions of parents, Block (1978) reports that mothers more closely supervise their daughters than their sons. An examination of the results for the Q-sort item "kept close track of C" showed that this pattern characterized all samples of mothers, regardless of the age of their children. It was significant only for the sample of mothers of urban high school students. Rosen and Aneshensel (1976) also suggest that parental restrictiveness in conjunction with an emphasis on the importance of interpersonal relationships is related to the occurrence of the Chameleon Syndrome in adolescent girls. No age analyses were provided.

In summary, there are few data available on activity level in adolescent girls. Those that exist suggest that girls are less confident and more cautious about dealing with their environments than boys are; other data suggest that females are more likely than males to adopt compliant ways of dealing with anxiety-producing situations. The one study of risk-taking shows that gender differences emerged at age 9. Other studies discussed in detail in this section did not provide analyses for age or developmental level. There is some support for the notion that parental protectiveness is greater for daughters than for sons and that the difference is stronger for high-school-age adolescents than younger children and for mothers than for fathers.

3.6. Aggression

Most reviewers and researchers agree that males display more aggression than females and that this difference appears early in life (e.g., Block, 1981; Maccoby and Jacklin, 1974). We are aware of little research pertinent to the Gender-Intensification Hypothesis in this area. Kagan and Moss (1962) do report that when correlations across age groups are examined to indicate stability of behavior, some discontinuity appears at adolescence for girls. For the variable behavioral disorganization [defined for school-age subjects as "destructive activity, rages, and failures" displayed when child is frustrated (p. 86)], stability was greater from ages 3–6 to 10–14 and from 6–10 to 10–14 for boys than for girls. Behavioral disorganization in girls 10–14 was not significantly related to their behavior from 3–6 or 6–10. However, correlations across childhood age periods for girls on other aggression variables (e.g., aggression toward mother, indirect aggression toward peers) were significant. Kagan and Moss also reported that "it was difficult to predict adult aggressive behavior or anger arousal for women from their childhood behavior . . . this is because young girls are subjected to more severe socialization of aggression than boys are" (p. 112).

Other evidence (Block, 1978) suggests that parental expectations for aggressive behaviors in male and female children are more differentiated in adolescence. An inspection of the Q-sort data Block presents for several samples of parents suggests that expectations may become more differentiated at adolescence for physically aggressive behaviors and competitive behavior. We are not aware of data explicitly linking parental socialization of aggression to pubertal changes in their daughters.

In summary, there seems to be agreement in the literature that boys display more aggressive behavior than girls do and that this differentiation appears early in life. One study suggests that early adolescent girls experience some discontinuity in expression of aggressive behavior. Parents are likely to discourage aggressive behavior more in girls than in boys, and there is some suggestion that this differentiation by parents increases at early adolescence.

3.7. Summary and Implications of the Review

For virtually all areas covered by Block's earlier review, we have found some information confirming gender differences during the second decade of life. The reported differences are in the directions to be expected on the basis of traditional sex-typing. The presence of such differences in a given age group during adolescence is consonant with the Gender-Intensification Hypothesis but certainly not proof of it. First, gender differences observed during adolescence may well have existed earlier. Second, such differences may be attributable to factors other than differential socialization—changes in information-processing skills or hormonal activity, for example.

In some domains, there are studies that are more relevant to the Gender-Intensification Hypothesis in that two or more age groups are included, permitting the comparison of children and adolescents or early and late adolescents. If gender differences become greater with age, the case for the hypothesis is stronger than in the single age-group studies. The domains where such studies exist follow.

3.7.1. *Susceptibility to Anxiety.* Gender differences in level of self-consciousness appear to emerge in early adolescence.

3.7.2. *Achievement-Related Behavior.* Standards for achievement become more sex-stereotyped with age, and boys begin to demonstrate better spatial skills while girls demonstrate better verbal skills during adolescence.

3.7.3. *Self-Concept and Self-Esteem.* The overall factor structure of the self-concept appears to be similar for the two genders throughout adolescence. However, girls may become more invested in interpersonal areas of competence than boys. Early adolescent girls also appear to experience more disruption of the self-concept than boys, as shown in decreased self-esteem, increased self-consciousness, and instability of the self-concept.

3.7.4. *Social Relationships.* There are data suggesting that girls develop more intimate friendships and use more sophisticated bases for friendship than boys do during adolescence.

3.7.5. *Activity Level.* There are few studies comparing early and late adolescents in this area. The results of one study suggest that girls become less likely than boys to take risks in a game situation during early adolescence.

3.7.6. *Aggression.* Data show that males are more aggressive than females from an early age. Researchers have suggested that discontinuity exists for girls at early adolescence on one measure of aggression.

Since the Gender-Intensification Hypothesis is a hypothesis principally about socialization, studies of (1) gender-differential socialization and (2) age differences in gender-differential socialization are the two subsets of studies that ought receive most attention. The studies of gender-differential socialization in a single age-group are certainly compatible with the hypothesis. Studies of age-differences in socialization are more to the point, but these are quite rare.

There is no direct information bearing upon *changes* in socialization with the exception of Steinberg's (1977) longitudinal data which shows increasing deference on the part of mothers to sons as the child moves through the pubertal cycle. Short-term longitudinal studies examining possible changes in expectations and rearing strategies (and concomitantly, relevant outcomes in the children) are the needed commodity here and their absence the principal barrier to any strong conclusion that the Gender-Intensification Hypothesis is a useful summary of our knowledge to date. Before going on to discuss what some of the other characteristics of such future studies might be, we conclude this section with brief attention to six issues that merit future study. First, it is not clear from the existing literature that either parent exercises greater influence than the other within or across domains. Put another way, we do not know which parent, if either, intensifies expectations more and if so, in what domains. (But the notion that parental influence may be domain-differential appears to be a promising one to build into future research designs.)

Second, we may well explore the same question in relation to same- and opposite-sex peers. (It seems clear, for example, that intimacy skills are strengthened principally—for girls anyway—through interactions with girl friends.)

Third, it would be useful to compare the nature of gender differences, changes in gender differences, and the Gender-Intensification Hypothesis in samples of early and late adolescents. While pubertal events may instigate increased differentiation into train, it may not be until later adolescence that changes in expectations are reflected in stable behavioral differences. (However, see below for an opposite argument.)

Fourth, dating and sexual activity are heavily implicated in almost everyone's version of the whys and wherefores of gender intensification during adolescence yet there is very little study of this topic. (It is the impression of many observers of the adolescent scene that early dating may be the most potent force toward conventionality of sex roles. Often it is suggested that behaving in accord with commonly held stereotypes is a means of coping with anxiety presumed to be associated with early dating.)

Fifth, versions of the Gender-Intensification Hypothesis are more often employed to account for gender differences from the perspective of female than of male development, e.g., as in the Chameleon Syndrome. The Machismo Syndrome would appear to deserve direct study as well. (In her study of college males, Komarovsky (1976) found, for example, that many males whose attitudes were equalitarian had highly conventional behavioral expectations for their future wives' behavior.) It seems likely that the early male experience in dating relationships, athletics, and same-sex cliques could provide some insight into college-age outcomes of this type (and others).

Sixth, it is our impression that conventional gender roles continue to thrive among adolescents in America. The obvious exception would appear to be that of achievement aspirations for girls (which do seem to have shifted, and rather dramatically). In the face of greater consciousness of equalitarian standards over the past decade and new attempts to implement them, the absence of other dramatic changes in adolescents is puzzling to some observers. It is possible that, as we have noted, early adolescence brings with it a rather rigid conventionalization in gender-related behavior (although this need not be the *only* way of coping) that diminishes with greater certainty about relationships with the opposite sex and greater certainty about personal and social competence. Another explanation for the apparent absence of notable changes outside the achievement arena for women is that not many social-action efforts have been directed toward males. There is no concerted effort to improve males' intimacy skills, for example; yet in many ways, this is the reciprocal of stressing assertiveness and aspiration for women. Whatever the explanation (and there are many others) for the conservation of traditional gender roles among adolescents, short-term longitudinal studies designed to track such changes in populations identified as particularly likely to be subject to them would have high pay-off (and especially if they were designed to attend, as well, to the six points made above).

4. Reflections and Recommendations for Future Study

4.1. *Role and Sex in "Sex Roles"*

Heretofore, we have argued that, while the report of significant gender differences or differential change in behavior by gender might be consonant with the Gender-Intensification Hypothesis, it is not proof of it. The basis for our argument has been that relatively few studies have focused upon any presumed social–psychological processes that might bring about such changes. The existing literature provides few clues that would help with the perennial question of fixing causes, particularly as between biological/maturational versus environmental. Now the focus of our argument shifts somewhat. Within the perspective of the social psychology of gender differences, there is good reason to be wary of interpreting adolescent behavioral differences *alone* in terms of the Gender-Intensification Hypothesis.

In research of this sort, it is common to employ the concept of *sex role*. There are sound reasons for examining this concept. We argue that the word *gender* is preferable to the word *sex* in this expression and, more importantly, that the term *role* can stand some examination too. The term *sex role* implies a relation to social structures and social situations that is more profound than the operations in most studies exemplify. Strictly speaking, *role* refers to a pattern of demands, conceptions, or behaviors associated with a given position in a given social system, that is, a formal organization or some other social group. In adolescence, the relevant social settings are schools, families, and work places, and peer friendships, cliques, and crowds. Yet *sex role* is typically used at a far higher level of abstraction to connote sets of demands, conceptions, and behaviors abstracted from and distal from the actual groups in which adolescents live their social lives.

The term *sex role* often is used in such a way as to invite the assumption that consistency of demands, conceptions, and performance across settings is more remarkable than variation. This assumption may be a barrier to framing studies of the extent to which gender-related demands, conceptions, and behaviors in positions located in particular social situations actually vary and the extent to which such variations are processed and eventually become integrated into a self-theory. For example, it may be the case that the intensification of gender-related expectations is far more common in peer than in familial contexts. That is, the demand to be a "manly man" or a "lady" may be greater in peer contexts than in the familial ones.

In his consideration of the effects of early versus late maturing upon social and personality development during adolescence, for example, Clausen (1975) suggests that parents may be less responsive than peers to the rate and course of somatic change. While dramatic in its overall outcomes, somatic change is gradual. School hallways, locker rooms, and gang showers provide opportunities for day-to-day comparisons of overall stature and the shape and size of body parts that are not accessible to parents. On the other hand, there are some data that demonstrate transformations in family interaction patterns as a function of pubertal status (Steinberg, 1977; Steinberg and Hill, 1978) and developmental change in pubertal status. Our point is not to rank-order environments in relation to gender-related role expectations. It is to raise the possibility that not taking settings seriously in relation to gender-differentiated socialization during adolescence may be to miss the boat. Continuing to think only in terms of a "master sex role" interferes with our studying situational variations. Framing research on notions of a unitary sex role at such an abstract level assumes that "sex role" phenomena are at bottom individual characteristics that people carry with them from situation to situation. Research on the relative impacts of peer versus parental influence in general suggests that early adolescence includes, for the first time, comprehension of two social worlds of influence: peer and parent and, in later adolescence, their integration (Berndt, 1979; Devereux, 1970; Emmerich, Goldman, and Shore, 1971; Garbarino and Bronfenbrenner, 1976; Hill, 1980). When we conceptualize "sex roles" independent of particular social settings we are psychologizing events that are social–psychological in nature.

The phenomena encompassed by the term *sex role* have not often been studied as *role* matters at all. It will be useful in future empirical research to take *role* more seriously by examining the gender-relatedness of demands, characteristics, and behaviors of occupants of positions in particular social systems. Adolescents do occupy positions in particular social systems—families, peer groups, schools, and workplaces. These systems do place demands upon individual position occupants. The questions to be asked are: "To what extent are those demands gender related? How does the degree of gender relatedness of those demands differ from setting to setting?" By being more particular about settings than is characteristic of most research, we would be taking the term *role* in *sex role* seriously. The title of our paper is intended to convey this emphasis.

Parenthetically, the word *sex* in *sex roles* might better be rendered as *gender*. The implication of *sex role* for practitioners, policy-makers, and others outside the field, especially when the term is used in reference to adolescents, is that sexual activity is implied. One of the items of adolescent development we know least about is how expectations for, conceptions of, and sexual behaviors themselves are integrated into the positions adolescents occupy in social systems. Insofar as we are aware, only Kagan and Moss (1962) provide data that explicitly link sexual activity in adolescence with childhood sex-typing, for example. It is not at all clear how preferences for sexual objects and specific sexual activities are related to "masculinity" and "femininity."

4.2. *Putting Roles Back into the Study of Gender Differences*

Not taking *role* seriously in *sex role* has important consequences in addition to those for studying variations by setting. There are also problems of assumed consistency *within* roles. The conceptual issues underlying such problems have been best identified and analyzed by Levinson (1959). Levinson's paper is a conceptual *tour de force* on the relations among social structure, the concept of role, and personality. Levinson notes that *role* has been employed in three different ways in the study of organizations and their impact on social–psychological change, development, and adjustment. The first way in which *role* is employed is in terms of demand. What are the norms, the expectations, and the responsibilities that govern or define that role in the social system? Others have focused upon role conceptions, individuals' definitions of what they are supposed to do or think when occupying a given position. The third way in which *role* is used is in the sense of performance; that is, to refer to how people act or fail to act when they occupy a specific position in a concrete social system.

Levinson reviewed studies of effects upon role-incumbents in formal organizations and concluded that there were problems of slippage across the three ways of looking at roles. The assumption of isomorphism among the three elements was more common than not: expectations, conceptions, and performance have been treated as reflections of a single entity—*the role*. Levinson argues that the assumption of isomorphism is unrealistic and theoretically constricting. No social system would survive if there were not some congruence between demands, conception of these demands, and performance. However, the assumption of isomorphism predisposes investigators to ignore how it is that role demands are processed and how conceptions of such demands affect role performance. Levinson's conclusions appear to be important for the study of "sex roles" as well. Isomorphism often is assumed rather than demonstrated, and the result is that we know little about the differential impacts of fathers and mothers, of peers of same and other gender, and the like (*within* or across positions in family and peer systems). This issue is especially important for the study of gender-related role expectations during adolescence when young people come to be able to deal in more cognitively sophisticated ways with inconsistent information from their social worlds (Hill and Palmquist, 1978) and when they begin to occupy positions in more formal organizations such as secondary schools and workplaces. The bottom line is that congruence of role definitions should be studied and not assumed.

Levinson argues that one might profitably examine at least five separate characteristics of role demands: (1) how *explicitly* they are given, (2) how *clear* they are, (3) the degree of *consensus* that there is among various role definers, (4) the extent to which the demands are *coherent* or patterned, and (5) the extent to which there is narrowness or *latitude* in relation to the demands. To the extent that there is a wide range in any role, there is more room for personal choice. To the extent that there is a narrow range backed up by powerful sanctions, there is less room for personal choice. Then the individual's role behavior might be expected to be a better match to the demands.

Levinson points out that in most studies of organizational roles it is assumed that norms are absolute prescriptions. This is also often the case for the study of "sex roles." There is the prescription that boys be aggressive and react actively to frustration, and that girls be dependent and respond passively. Existing research is not sensitive to issues of latitude in relation to gender-related role expectations. The matter of latitude is especially interesting in relation to so-called tomboys and sissies. Prior to puberty, girls may have a good deal more latitude about role in family, peer, and school settings than do boys. Perhaps there is now less tolerance for display of "masculine" behaviors and sanctions for such display may be greater.

In considering role conceptions, we are dealing with personal definitions and rationales of position occupants. The point to be made about role conceptions is that, contrary to the isomorphism notion, diverse conceptions of role are influenced not only by present demands, but by earlier experience, values, other personality characteristics, and formal education. And, most interesting in relation to adolescence, cognitive change surely should modify role conceptions as well. For example, changes in demands from parents at and during adolescence may be less potent than changes in how they are conceived by adolescents. Because of their more sophisticated information-processing equipment, young peoples' conceptions of parents' demands for more or less intense towing the line and being a real boy or a little lady may be what changes most. Adolescents are surely better able than children to process the extent to which there is in fact consensus among role definers in relation to gender-related expectations. There may be an increase in the extent to which they can perceive patterning and coherence. In investigating the Gender-Role Intensification Hypothesis further then, it will be fruitful to look at changes in the nature of role conceptions and the presence or absence of changes in role definers' demands. This is not an alternative one thinks of if locked into the usual isomorphic view of the relations between demand characteristics, conception, and action.

Earlier discussions of role expectations suggest that when we look at role performance in actual settings, we strengthen the focus upon variability as well. We may expect that differential information-processing skills will produce different kinds of role conceptions and, in turn, produce variability in actual role performance among occupants of similar positions.

There is surprisingly little compelling evidence that puberty gives rise to changing expectations on the part of socializing agents and, in turn, to changing role conceptions and role performance in concrete situations. There are very few studies that employ pubertal status as an independent variable and there are even fewer studies that take environmental demands or expectations seriously as opposed to role conceptions or actual role performance. Our analysis calls attention to the promise of considering biological and cognitive change in the same designs. Taking the *role* notion more seriously extends the terrain. It calls attention to the dangers of assuming isomorphism. It invites us to compare potentially differential gender-role intensification in family, peer, school, and work contexts. It invites us to take situational differences seriously as we have in the last decade in virtually every other area of personality development. It invites us to look at role expectations far more seriously than we have before. It suggests studies of changes in various aspects of role expectations; that is, coherence, clarity, latitude, and the like. At the individual level, it invites questions about how self-theories are developed, involving the integration of role demands and conceptions across situations. At the group level, it moves us toward the comparison of social groups as environments which foster, say, more androgynous kinds of development as opposed to traditionally masculine and traditionally feminine outcomes. In short, differentiating the *role* concept or, perhaps better put, applying it more formally and rigorously as a social–psychological construct, could make the study of sex roles a more rich and less stereotypical enterprise than it is at present.

ACKNOWLEDGMENTS. The preparation of this chapter was supported by Father Flanagan's Boys' Home, Inc., through its budgetary allocation to the Boys Town Center for the Study of Youth Development Research Program on Social Relations in Early Adolescence.

REFERENCES

Balswick, J. O., and Balkwell, J. W. Self-disclosure to same- and opposite-sex parents: An empirical test of insights from role theory. *Sociometry*, 1977, *40*, 282–286.
Bardwick, J. M., and Douvan, E. Ambivalence: The socialization of women. In V. Gornick and B. K. Moran (Eds.), *Women in sexist society: Studies in power and powerlessness*. New York: Basic Books, 1971.
Berndt, T. J. Developmental changes in conformity to peers and parents. *Developmental Psychology*, 1979, *15*, 608–616.
Biller, H. B. The father and personality development: Paternal deprivation and sex-role development. In M. E. Lamb (Ed.), *The role of the father in child development*. New York: Wiley, 1976.
Block, J. H. Another look at sex differentiation in the socialization behaviors of mothers and fathers. In J. Sherman and F. Denmark (Eds.), *Psychology of women: Future directions of research*. New York: Psychological Dimensions, 1978.
Block, J. H. *Personality development in males and females: The influence of differential socialization*. Unpublished manuscript, University of California, 1981.
Brooks-Gunn, J., and Matthews, W. S. *He and she: How children develop their sex-role identity*. Englewood Cliffs, N.J.: Prentice-Hall, 1979.
Bush, D. E., Simmons, R., Hutchinson, B., and Blyth, D. Adolescent perceptions of sex roles in 1968 and 1975. *Public Opinion Quarterly*, 1977–1978, *41*, 459–474.
Carlson, R. Stability and change in the adolescent's self-image. *Child Development*, 1965, *36*, 659–666.
Clausen, J. A. The social meaning of differential physical and sexual maturation. In S. E.

Dragastin and G. H. Elder, Jr. (Eds.), *Adolescence in the life cycle: Psychological change and social context.* Washington, D.C.: Hemisphere, 1975.

Coleman, J. S. *The adolescent society.* New York: Free Press of Glencoe, 1961.

Devereux, E. C. The role of peer group experience in moral development. In J. P. Hill (Ed.), *Minnesota symposia on child psychology.* Vol. 4. Minneapolis: University of Minnesota Press, 1970.

Douvan, E., and Adelson, J. *The adolescent experience.* New York: Wiley, 1966.

Dreeban, R. *On what is learned in school.* Reading, MA: Addison-Wesley, 1968.

Duck, S. W. Personality similarity and friendship choices by adolescents. *European Journal of Social Psychology,* 1975, 5, 351–365.

Dusek, J., and Flaherty, J. The development of the self-concept during the adolescent years. *Monographs of the Society for Research on Child Development,* 1981, 46, 1–70.

Elkind, D. Cognitive development in adolescence. In J. F. Adams (Ed.), *Understanding adolescence: Current developments in adolescent psychology.* Boston: Allyn and Bacon, 1968.

Emmerich, W., Goldman, K. S., and Shore, R. E. Differentiation and development of social norms. *Journal of Personality and Social Psychology,* 1971, 18, 323–353.

Feldman, S. S., Nash, S., and Cutrona, C. The influence of age and sex on responsiveness to babies. *Developmental Psychology,* 1977, 13, 675–676.

Frodi, A., and Lamb, M. Sex differences in responsiveness to infants: A developmental study of psychophysiological and behavioral responses. *Child Development,* 1978, 49, 1182–1188.

Garbarino, J., and Bronfenbrenner, U. The socialization of moral judgment and behavior in cross-cultural perspective. In T. Lickona (Ed.), *Morality: A handbook of moral development and behavior.* New York: Holt, Rinehart, and Winston, 1976.

Hill, J. P. Parental determinants of sex-typed behavior. Unpublished doctoral dissertation, Harvard University, 1964.

Hill, J. P. The family. In M. Johnson (Ed.), *Toward adolescence: The middle school years. The seventy-ninth yearbook of the National Society for the Study of Education.* Chicago: University of Chicago Press, 1980.

Hill, J. P., and Palmquist, W. J. Social cognition and social relations in early adolescence. *International Journal of Behavioural Development,* 1978, 1, 1–36.

Hill, J. P., Thiel, K. S., and Blyth, D. A. Grade and gender differences in perceived intimacy with peers among seventh- to tenth-grade boys and girls. Unpublished manuscript, Boys Town Center for the Study of Youth Development, 1981.

Johnson, M. M. Sex role learning in the nuclear family. *Child Development,* 1963, 34, 319–333.

Kagan, J., and Moss, H. A. *From birth to maturity: The Fels study on psychological development.* New York: Wiley, 1962.

Katz, P. The development of female identity. *Sex Roles,* 1979, 5, 155–178.

Komarovsky, M. *Dilemma of masculinity: A study of college youth.* New York: Norton, 1976.

Lamb, M. E. The role of the father: An overview. In M. E. Lamb (Ed.), *The role of the father in child development.* New York: Wiley, 1976.

Levinson, D. J. Role, personality, and social structure in the organizational setting. *Journal of Abnormal and Social Psychology,* 1959, 58, 170–180.

Lynch, M. E. *Paternal androgyny, daughters' physical maturity level, and achievement socialization in early adolescence.* Unpublished doctoral dissertation, Cornell University, 1981.

Maccoby, E. E., and Jacklin, C. N. *The psychology of sex differences.* Stanford: Stanford University Press, 1974.

Marini, M. M. Sex differences in the determinants of adolescent aspirations: A review of the research. *Sex Roles,* 1978, 4, 723.

Mulcahy, G. A. Sex differences in patterns of self-disclosure among adolescence: A developmental perspective. *Journal of Youth and Adolescence*, 1973, 2, 343–356.

Newson, J., and Newson, E. *Four years old in an urban community*. Harmondworth: Pelican Books, 1968.

Paige, K. E. Beyond the raging hormone: Women learn to sing the menstrual blues. *Psychology Today*, 1973, 7, 41–46.

Rivenbark, W. H. Self-disclosure patterns among adolescents. *Psychological Reports*, 1971, 28, 35–42.

Rosen, B. C., and Aneshensel, C. S. The chameleon syndrome: A social psychological dimension of the female sex role. *Journal of Marriage and the Family*, May 1976, 605–617.

Rosenberg, F. R., and Simmons, R. G. Sex differences in the self-concept during adolescence. *Sex Roles*, 1975, 1, 147–160.

Savin-Williams, R. C. Dominance hierarchies in groups of early adolescents. *Child Development*, 1979, 50, 923–935.

Sharabany, R., Gersoni, R., and Hofman, J. E. Age and sex differences in the development of adolescent intimate friendships. *Developmental Psychology*, 1981, 17, 800–808.

Shaw, M. C., and McCuen, J. T. The onset of academic underachievement in bright children. *The Journal of Educational Psychology*, 1960, 51, 103–106.

Simmons, R. G., and Rosenberg, F. Sex, sex roles, and self-image. *Journal of Youth and Adolescence*, 1975, 4, 229–258.

Simmons, R. G., Blyth, D., Van Cleave, E. F., and Bush, D. M. Entry into early adolescence: The impact of school structure, puberty, and early dating on self-esteem. *American Sociological Review*, 1979, 44, 948–967.

Slovic, P. Risk taking in children: Age and sex differences. *Child Development*, 1966, 37, 169–176.

Spenner, K. I., and Featherman, D. C. Achievement ambitions. *Annual Review of Sociology*, 1978, 4, 373–420.

Stein, A. H. The effects of sex-role standards for achievement and sex-role performance on their determinants of achievement motivation. *Developmental Psychology*, 1971, 4, 219–231.

Stein, A. H. Sex role development. In J. F. Adams (Ed.), *Understanding adolescence*. Boston: Allyn and Bacon, 1976, 233–257.

Stein, A. H., and Smithells, J. Age and sex differences in children's sex role standards about achievement. *Developmental Psychology*, 1969, 1, 252–259.

Stein, A. H., Pohly, S. R., and Mueller, E. The influence of masculine, feminine, and neutral tasks on children's achievement behaviors, expectations of success, and attainment values. *Child Development*, 1971, 42, 195–207.

Steinberg, L. D. A longitudinal study of physical growth, intellectual growth, and family interaction in early adolescence. Unpublished doctoral dissertation, Cornell University, 1977.

Steinberg, L. D., and Hill, J. P. Patterns of family interactions as a function of age, the onset of puberty, and formal thinking. *Developmental Psychology*, 1978, 14, 683–684.

Walberg, H. J. Physics, femininity, and creativity. *Development Psychology*, 1969, 1, 47–54.

West, L. W. Sex differences in the exercise of circumspection in self-disclosure among adolescents. *Psychological Reports*, 1970, 26, 226.

Chapter 11

The Social and Psychological Effects of Puberty on White Females

Roberta G. Simmons, Dale A. Blyth, and Karen L. McKinney

1. Introduction

There is general consensus that adolescence is an important stage in the life cycle. It is certainly a period of dramatic physical, emotional, and social changes. However, whether it is also a time of stress and disturbance is an issue of controversy (Douvan and Adelson, 1966; Douvan and Gold, 1966; Bealer, Willits, and Maida, 1969; Offer, 1969; Bandura, 1972). Furthermore, it is unclear what the contribution of the phyical changes of puberty is in exacerbating or alleviating whatever stress occurs at this age (see Eichorn, 1963; Clausen, 1975). The present study focuses on the latter problem, in particular on the impact of pubertal development on a wide variety of social–emotional reactions of the adolescent girl. To be investigated are the effects of pubertal change on the girl's self-concept and on many of her behaviors, values, and attitudes.

The study to be reported here has a long history. In 1968, the first author and Morris Rosenberg undertook a study of 1917 school children from Grades 3–12 in Baltimore in order to determine which ages were most stressful for the self-picture of the child (Simmons, Rosenberg, and Rosenberg, 1973). Although *a priori* it was not hypothesized that the transition into adolescence would be particularly stressful, the findings

Roberta G. Simmons and Karen L. McKinney • Department of Sociology, University of Minnesota, Minneapolis, Minnesota 55455.   Dale A. Blyth • Department of Psychology, Ohio State University, Columbus, Ohio 43210.

revealed that beginning suddenly with the movement into seventh grade, *early adolescence* became a period of disturbance, and girls fared more poorly than boys (Simmons and Rosenberg, 1975; Rosenberg and Simmons, 1975). In seventh grade as compared to earlier years, children demonstrated significantly more discomfort on measures of self-consciousness; they scored less favorably on a scale of stability of the self-image; they scored lower both on a global measure of self-esteem and on a variety of specific self-ratings; and, finally, they were less likely to perceive significant others as rating them highly. On most of these variables, scores continued to worsen throughout the junior high school years and thereafter either leveled off or improved.

This identification of early adolescence as a time of disturbance[1] led to a search for the factors that brought about these changes in early adolescence.

First, one possible determinant of stress could have been *pubertal change.* These are years of rapid endocrinological and external bodily changes culminating in menarche for girls; and it is certainly possible that the internal and external changes of puberty could have been responsible for this disturbance.

Second, the negative effects could have been caused by a change in *school environment.* Between sixth and seventh grade, the children in Baltimore were subjected to a sharp environmental discontinuity (Benedict, 1954). They moved from a small, intimate elementary school, where teachers, peers, and classes remained essentially the same throughout the day, to a large impersonal junior high school in which teachers and peers shifted through the school day. In fact, data from the Baltimore study suggested that change in school environment was a more important determinant of the self-image disturbance than calendar age (an imperfect indicator of puberty). Children age 11 and 12 in sixth grade (elementary school) differed little on the various self-image measures; those age 12 and 13 in seventh grade (junior high school) also differed little; but 12-year-olds in junior high school demonstrated significantly more negative scores than 12-year-olds in elementary school.

Third, in addition to pubertal and environmental change as stressors, Erikson (1968) has pointed to the major decisions that must be made during adolescence, e.g., choice of occupation and opposite-sex partner—decisions that help to establish one's adult identity. However, while such choices are undoubtedly stress inducing, they are choices of late, rather than early, adolescence, and therefore, we feel, are unlikely to be the major sources of disturbance found in seventh grade.

Finally, another possible explanation for this apparent decrease in self-image in early adolescence is purely methodological. Since the Baltimore study was cross-sectional rather than longitudinal, it is possible that what was being observed were simply cohort differences.

In sum, it was hypothesized that the self-image disturbance found in early adolescence in the Baltimore study was due either to pubertal change, to change in school environment, to cohort differences, or to a combination of these factors. However, the Baltimore study itself was limited in the extent to which it allowed tests of these alternate possibilities. There were no adequate measures of puberty in the survey, calendar age being a poor substitute. Furthermore, there was no way of comparing different school environments in seventh grade, since *all* children in Baltimore were supposed to enter junior high at that point. Finally, since each girl was measured only once and could not be compared to herself over time, it was impossible to rule out cohort effects. The only possibility was to compare the cohort then in sixth grade to the cohort then in seventh.

To overcome these limitations and to determine which of these factors—pubertal change, environmental change, cohort differences—was operative, a new study was begun (the "Milwaukee Study"). This new research, while in part a replication, was also an attempt to overcome the limitations of the Baltimore survey. First, a longitudinal design was used and a sample of children was followed from sixth to tenth grade, in order to rule out cohort effects. Second, the level and timing of their pubertal development were carefully monitored from sixth to tenth grade. Third, children in two types of school environments in Milwaukee were studied, those who remained in elementary school from kindergarten to eighth grade (in a K–8 school) and those who resembled the Baltimore children in moving from an elementary school (K–6) to a junior high school in seventh grade. In our earlier publications from this study (Blyth, Simmons, and Bush, 1978; Simmons, Brown, Bush, and Blyth, 1978; Simmons, Blyth, Van Cleave, and Bush, 1979; Bush, Simmons, Hutchinson, and Blyth, 1977–1978; Blyth, Thiel, Bush, and Simmons, 1980; Blyth, Simmons, Bulcroft, Felt, Van Cleave, and Bush 1981) it was reported that *school environment* did have a significant impact on early adolescent self-image. Specifically, we found that (1) in seventh grade, girls who moved into junior high school demonstrated lower self-esteem and more negative changes in self-esteem than girls who remained in a K–8 system; and (2) that girls fared worse than boys in self-esteem (Simmons et al., 1979).

Given these prior findings concerning school environment, this chapter will examine the impact of the other major independent variable, *pubertal development*, on the adolescents' adjustment. We will focus here on the subgroup that has been shown to be more vulnerable—that is, on girls. Unlike prior publications, this chapter will report effects for 4 years of the study and for a wide variety of dependent variables in addition to the self-image.

Why do we expect pubertal development to have an impact? Several alternate conceptualizations and general hypotheses have been proposed concerning the relationship between pubertal changes and social–psychological reactions:

1.1. *Alternate Conceptualizations and General Hypotheses*

1.1.1. *Pubertal Change Will Have Negative Consequences.* The major reason for expecting a negative impact is that change itself is viewed as inherently stressful. In this case, the internal endocrine changes as well as dramatic alterations in physical appearance are seen as major stressors (see Petersen and Taylor, 1980). According to this reasoning, the negative impact of pubertal change should be relatively immediate and short-lived, diminishing as the girl adjusts to her new physiology and self-image. In this view, the period of psychological disturbance should start and end earlier for early-developing girls than for later-developing girls, but both will exhibit signs of distress close to the time of maximum change. No predictions are made about any longer-lasting effects of being an early versus late developer.

1.1.2. *Pubertal Change Will Have Some Positive Consequences.* If change occurs in such a way that the adolescent's looks more closely approximate those of an adult and hence grant her the prestige of adult status, then the change may be advantageous (see Faust, 1960).

1.1.3. *The Timing of Development Is the Critical Factor.* Pubertal development, in and of itself, cannot be labeled as positive or negative. Subsumed under this conceptualization are two distinct lines of thought.

First, being part of a minority and deviant in relationship to peers is stressful, so puberty will have the greatest impact on two deviant groups: the early developers who are changing when few others are doing so, and late developers who lag behind the rest of their peer group (see Gold and Tomlin, 1975; Petersen and Taylor, 1980). According to both Hypothesis 1.1.1 and this hypothesis (1.1.3a), *early developers will exhibit negative effects during and just after pubertal change.* However, the two hypotheses do not yield identical predictions for late developers. According to Hypothesis 1.1.1, the late developers also will show negative effects during and just after greatest pubertal change; according to Hypothesis 1.1.3a, in contrast, *the later developers will demonstrate negative reactions* before *they change when they are in the minority.* Once they experience pubertal change and join the majority, negative effects will no longer be evident.

A second line of thought that emphasizes timing stems from the psychodynamic school. According to this approach, not having enough time in a life stage (i.e., childhood) will have negative consequences which will extend into the next life stage (see Peskin and Livson, 1972; Petersen and Taylor, 1980). Therefore, *early pubertal development will be disadvantageous during adolescence* insofar as it shortens the latency period. The latency period, generally thought of as extending from ages 6–12, is supposed to be a period of ego development. The period is characterized by absence of sexual experience and by the presence of ego dominance, reality organization, and integration. If the latency period with these gains for ego development is prematurely cut short, then the individual will experience adolescence as a time of difficulty. On the other hand, late development will limit the period of adolescence, thereby not allowing the individual enough time to adjust prior to reaching adulthood and *the late developer will show more difficulty during adulthood.* This conception fits with Erikson's notion of an identity crisis (1968), his key idea being that adolescence should be a time of experimentation with new identities; if adolescence is too short, there may be identity foreclosure (i.e., premature affixing of one's self-image).

Since our research extends only to middle adolescence, we are not in a position to test this last hypothesis about adulthood. However, several theorists have noted that what is a short-run disadvantage for the adolescent may turn out to be a long-run advantage for the adult. Because an adolescent crisis is likely to enhance experimentation by the individual, it may have long-term advantages (Peskin and Livson, 1972; Livson and Peskin, 1980).

Our study does focus, however, on the immediate and short-term effects of pubertal development during early and middle adolescence. In terms of adolescence, the above hypotheses are not necessarily mutually exclusive. During the teenage years, it is possible that pubertal development affects various dependent variables differently, and that both negative and positive consequences can be found.

The primary source from which we have extrapolated and derived the above conceptualizations and hypotheses has been the California longitudinal research. The major studies in the past that have investigated the impact of pubertal development on females have been these California longitudinal studies: the Berkeley Growth Study, the Berkeley Guidance Study, and the Oakland Growth Study (e.g., Jones and Mussen, 1958; Jones et al., 1971; MacFarlane, 1971; Peskin and Livson, 1972; Clausen, 1975). In fact, these and other studies have provided some evidence that pubertal change *is* stressful at the time it occurs, particularly when those who are changing thereby become part of a minority in relation to their peers (see Petersen and Taylor, 1980). That is, girls who reach puberty earlier than most of their peers (early developers) *initially* show more negative reactions to their bodies (Stolz and Stolz, 1944), less popularity with same-sex peers (Jones and Mussen, 1958; Faust, 1960[2]; Dwyer and Mayer, 1968–1969), lower degrees of sociability (Peskin and Livson, 1972), less leadership (Jones and Mussen, 1958), and lower levels of general happiness (early developers being described as cheerless and whining by Peskin and Livson, 1972; submissive and listless by Jones and Mussen, 1958; and in a greater degree of undisguised crisis and unrest by Peskin, 1973). Such girls are described as bigger than most of their male and female classmates and as feeling unattractive as a result (Stolz and Stolz, 1944; Dwyer and Mayer, 1968–69). In addition, early-developing girls demonstrate more interest in the opposite sex (Dwyer and Mayer, 1968–1969). On the other hand, there is some evidence that once pubertal changes are far behind and early-developing girls move into adulthood, they actually attain higher levels of well-being than do other girls (Peskin and Livson, 1972; Livson and Peskin, 1980).

The purpose of the present research then is to further investigate whether pubertal development has a patterned impact on the social–psychological status of the girls during adolescence itself. And, if so, in what direction? Is pubertal change stressful as the above findings indicate? Does early development have unfavorable consequences? Aside from the negative–positive dimension, do early developing girls who resemble adult women more than their peers also approximate adult behavior and attitudes more? And are they expected to act older by teachers, peers, and parents? If there are effects of early pubertal development, are they short-lasting or do they persist into middle adolescence even after almost all girls have reached menarche?

Finally, upon which dependent variables is pubertal development likely to have an effect? Table 1 lists the social–psychological areas that we identified as important in adolescence. There are two ways of conceptualizing our dependent variables. First, three commonly used dimensions have been derived from a social–psychological framework: these dimensions involve (1) perceptions of the self (or the self-image), (2) behaviors, and (3) other attitudes and values. Table 1 reflects this framework; under each of the three major rubrics are listed the clusters of dependent variables that have been measured (the exact variables will be presented below). Thus, we are asking which aspects of the self-image, which attitudes and which behaviors will be most affected by the transition into puberty.

The second way of conceptualizing these variables crosscuts the above framework and focuses on the "developmental tasks" of the early and middle adolescent (Aldous, 1978).[3] In Havighurst's words (1953, p.

Table 1. Social–Psychological Reaction: Major Dimensions and Variable-Clusters

Self-concept
  Global self-image
  Perceptions that adults evaluate one highly
  Perceived social image among same- and opposite-sex peers
  Perceived body image
  Perceived self-competence
  Perceptions of sex role
Behavior
  Participation in activities
  Academic performance
  Dating behavior
  Victimization
  Problem behavior
  Independence from parents
Values, attitudes, and related perceptions
  Concern with body image
  Concern with popularity
  Concern about competence and independence
  Perception that others expect one to act older
  Perception of others' expectations about opposite-sex relationships
  Perception that others expect one to make career plans
  Educational, marital, and occupational aspirations
  Perception of parent–peer relationships

2), an individual developmental task is one "which arises at or about a certain period in the life of an individual, successful achievement of which leads to his happiness and to success with later tasks, while failure leads to unhappiness in the individual, disapproval by the society, and difficulty with later tasks."

First, one task of early and middle adolescence is to achieve a new and positive sense of self in response to the many changes that occur at that age (Aldous, 1978). Perhaps most dramatic are the biological changes and the alterations in physical appearance which require a change in the *body image* and in the relevant self-evaluations. At a more global level, the adolescent should develop a new acceptance of the self as a person of worth (Aldous, 1978); that is, a favorable level of self-esteem. In addition, in Erikson's classic conception (1968), adolescence is a time to experiment with possible identities and ultimately to achieve a *stable*, specific picture of the self. Therefore, we shall investigate whether pubertal development affects the accomplishment of the tasks involving these various aspects of the self-picture.

A second, major task of adolescence is to establish strong, intimate relations with peers (Douvan and Adelson, 1966; Douvan and Gold, 1966), and to learn to relate to members of the opposite sex, so that at a later age the individual will be emotionally prepared to leave his or her family of origin and set up a new family of procreation.

Third, the adolescent has the task of developing independence (Douvan and Adelson, 1966; Aldous, 1978). Typically, at the beginning of adolescence, children are physically and emotionally dependent upon their parents, but by the end of adolescence they are capable of leaving their family of orientation and assuming responsibility for self and others.

As a result of new levels of independence and as part of adolescent exploration and rebellion, the teenager has a much greater opportunity than before to engage in deviant behavior. A final task, or more accurately a final problem, results from this situation. The adolescent has to deal, on the one hand, with adult pressure to conform to rules and, on the other hand, with peer and/or internal pressure to violate those rules. He or she may choose to strive for academic success or instead to engage in problematic or delinquent behavior in the school setting. (For a more elaborate discussion of the problem, see Jessor and Jessor, 1977.)

We shall turn to the question of which, if any, of these key tasks and problem areas of adolescence are affected by pubertal development after a description of our methods.

2. Methods

2.1. *Sampling*

The present study was conducted within the Milwaukee Public School System from 1974 to 1979. Eighteen schools were randomly selected from specific strata, and all sixth grade students in these schools were invited to participate. This design gave every student within a given stratum of the sample an equal probability of being included. The sample was stratified according to the type of school the children attended, but these aspects of the design are not relevant for the analysis to be presented here. (See Simmons et al., 1979; Blyth et al., 1981, for more detail about the sample and strata.) Nine hundred and twenty-four school children were interviewed in sixth grade and were followed in each remaining grade through tenth if they remained within the school system. Each of these children had signed parental consent. In total, we obtained signed parental consent from 82% of those from whom we originally sought this permission.[4]

The interviews were conducted privately in Grades 6, 7, 9, and 10 by trained survey interviewers using a structured interview format. In addi-

Table 2. Number of Cases Interviewed, Differential Mortality, and Relationship between Relative Onset of Menses by Grade Level

	Grade				
	6	7	8	9	10
Number interviewed					
Early developers	80	69	—	53	44
Middle developers	69	69	—	49	44
Late developers	88	87	—	67	63
Total	237[a]	225	—	169	151
Percent of sixth grade sample not interviewed					
Early developers	—	14	—	34	45
Middle developers	—	0	—	29	36
Late developers	—	1	—	24	28
Percent of total	—	5	—	29	36
Percent who have menstruated by interview					
Early developers	74	100	100	100	100
Middle developers	0	68	100	100	100
Late developers	0	0	69	92	99
Percent of total	25	54	89	97	100

[a]Eight cases were eliminated from all analyses because they were either too old (7) or too young (1) for their grade level (i.e., they were more than 1.96 standard deviations from the mean age for their grade). For an additional 41 white girls, we were unable to determine when they reached menarche.

tion, a private, registered nurse interviewed and measured each student to establish the level of the child's physical development. These physical measures were obtained in the fall and spring of sixth and seventh grade and in the spring of eighth, ninth, and tenth grades. One set of physical measurements in Grades 6, 7, 9, and 10 were gathered as close to the day of the survey interviews as possible. Finally, a variety of data including achievement test scores and GPAs were obtained from school records.

This analysis will deal only with white girls for whom we were able to obtain puberty measures ($N = 237$) and who in Grade 6 were not "too old" or "too young" for their grades (Table 2). Also, only girls in the correct grade are included in the analysis for that grade (e.g., if a girl "stayed back" before ninth grade, she was omitted from the ninth-grade analysis). Table 2 shows the number of cases interviewed each year by relative time of onset of puberty. We were able to obtain interviews with 64% of these original white girls in the final year of the study (237 vs. 151). The table also gives the differential mortality rates over the 5-year period for early, middle, and late developers. It can readily be observed from Table 2 that the greatest percentage loss of respondents was among the early developers, with 45% lost from the sample by tenth grade, as compared with 36% of the middle developers and 28% of the late developers. The possible effects of this sample loss will be discussed later in the paper. In fact, the primary source of sample mortality was the students leaving the Milwaukee school system, rather than subsequent refusal to participate in the study. Furthermore, in tenth grade, we went to the homes to do interviews with those youngsters who were frequently absent from school. For white children in general, there was greater sample loss in cases of broken families and among the highest socioeconomic group. Since the children are too young to leave school legally and since we attempted to interview those who were frequently absent outside the school setting, much of the sample loss reflects the family's moving (as is more likely to occur in broken families) or the family's removal of the child from the city public school system and their use of suburban, private, or parochial schools instead (as is more likely in the highest socioeconomic-status strata).

The data presented represent the total number of white females available in *each* year. In this way, we approximate the original random sample as closely as possible. This strategy provides more confidence in the generalizability of the results to the public school population from which we drew the sample. Therefore, in sixth grade before any dropout occurs, the data are the most generalizable. In subsequent years, we cannot generalize to children who left the Milwaukee school system, but only to those who remain. In order to make certain that differences in results between early and late years are not due to the fact that some children have dropped out of the study, we have run all analyses reported here for that subset of children present for interviews in all 4 years (Grades 6, 7, 9, and 10). In cases where the results are different, we will report and discuss them. In other cases, it can be assumed that the results are the same.

2.2. *Measurement*

2.2.1. *Girls' Puberty.* Two different but related measures of pubertal development were constructed. The first refers to the presence versus absence of menstruation at the time of any one survey interview. On each occasion at which the girl was interviewed by a nurse (seven times in total), she was asked, "Have you ever had a menstrual period or monthly bleeding, or haven't you had a period yet?" If the response was affirmative, she was then asked to report the month and year of her first period and her age at time of onset.

The second aspect of puberty we shall refer to as the "relative onset of menses" or as "early/middle/late development." It is a longitudinal measure derived from the same questions considered over the seven points in time. Girls were categorized as early, middle, or late developers based on when they reported having had their first period. This trichotomy was designed to split the distribution into equal thirds, but to still relate the time of onset of menses to natural school year breaks. The resulting split is not a perfect trichotomy, but it is as close as is possible. Those girls who reached menarche prior to the beginning of seventh grade were classified as early developers. Of the girls in the sample, 38% are in this category. Girls labeled as middle developers reached menarche during seventh grade or the following summer. Of the girls in our sample, 27% are in this category. Finally, girls who had not reached menarche prior to the beginning of eighth grade were considered to be late developers. Of the girls in our sample, 35% are in this "late-developing" category. By spring of ninth grade, only seven girls had not reached menarche. All but one of these was pubertal by the spring of tenth grade (see Table 2).[5]

While the comparison of early, middle, and late developers is relevant all 4 years, contrasting those who have begun menstruating to those who have not is meaningful only in sixth and seventh grade. In later years, there are simply not enough girls without menstrual periods to make valid comparisons.

These two variables—"presence versus absence of menstruation" and "relative onset of menses"—are slightly different ways of looking at pubertal development. Knowing whether a girl is an early, middle, or late developer in relation to her peers ("relative onset") does not indicate whether the significant event of menarche ("presence of menstruation") had occurred at the time of the interview. This is particularly a problem in sixth and seventh grade, since a random half of the sample was interviewed in the fall and the other random half in the spring. Alternately, classifying a girl as to presence or absence of menstruation at the time of a particular interview often does not in itself establish whether she is an early, middle, or late developer. For example, if we find a girl has begun menstruating by the seventh-grade interview, we still do not know if she is an early or middle developer, since members of both groups are likely to have attained menarche by this interview. If she has not begun menstruating, we cannot tell with this information alone whether she will become a middle or late developer.

Thus, while the two variables (presence of menstruation and early versus late development) are significantly correlated, they are not identical (see Table 2). Both early developers and the girls who have begun menstruation by the time of the interview at issue are more advanced in pubertal development than their respective counterparts. While we expect the two variables to relate in the same direction to most dependent variables, it is possible that they might not do so if (1) the actual presence or absence of a period is highly significant psychologically for the girls; or (2) if there are relevant endocrine differences at work pre- and postmenarche. For example, regardless of whether she is an early, middle, or late developer, it is plausible that, following menarche, a girl's feminine self-image may take a sharp jump upward, either because of her attitude toward the symbol of menstruation or because of a greater likelihood that cyclic endocrine fluctuations are operating.

One more point about the early and late developers needs to be made. Our classification is not intended to isolate extremely deviant children. Instead, for this report, girls are categorized into subgroups sizeable enough for complex statistical analysis. In future reports, more extreme early and late developers will be identified and studied. In their classic work, Jones and Mussen (1958) focus on more extreme early- and late-developing children; this distinction should be taken into account when comparing the studies.

The relationship of early/middle/late development and of presence of menstruation to several other indicators of pubertal development is presented in Table 3 for each grade. In sixth and seventh grade, girls who develop earlier or who have already begun menstruating are objectively taller, heavier, and less lean and have begun to grow more slowly (presumably having attained peak height growth). They are also more likely to report underarm hair, presence of a figure, and an awareness of physical changes. Adult raters are more likely to perceive them as having acne, as being fatter, having a more developed figure, and looking physically more mature. In tenth grade, many of these same relationships hold, but to a lesser degree. However, by tenth grade, it is the late developers who are somewhat taller (while still weighing less and being leaner) and who are more aware of recent physical changes. These intercorrelations are all in the predicted direction and help to validate the two indicators of pubertal development that we will use. These interrelationships also suggest the complexity of what is happening during this period of physical change. The fact that the late developer ends up slightly taller and is always slimmer should be kept in mind for the following analysis.

2.2.2. *Dependent Variables.* The dependent variables used are either multiple-choice items, Guttman scales, or scores derived from combining several multiple-choice items. Many of these measures have been described elsewhere; in particular, the self-image variables and their validation (Simmons et al., 1973, 1979), victimization (Blyth et al., 1978), and satisfaction with body-image (Blyth et al., 1981). Other measures will be described below as relevant.

Table 3A. Correlations of Relative Onset of Menses and Presence of Menstruation with Physical Characteristics and with Self and Stranger Perceptions of Physical Development by Grade for White Females Only

| | Grade Level | | | | | | |
| Characteristic measured or rated | Sixth | | Seventh | | Eighth | Ninth | Tenth |
	Relative onset of menses[a]	Presence vs. absence of menstruation	Relative onset of menses	Presence vs. absence of menstruation	Relative onset of menses	Relative onset of menses	Relative onset of menses
Physical characteristic							
Height (mm)	0.48	0.45	0.37	0.40	0.06	−0.01	−0.11
Weight (lb.)	0.46	0.44	0.41	0.45	0.00	0.26	0.16
Ponderal index (ht./wt.$^{-3}$) (measure of leanness)	−0.24	−0.23	−0.27	−0.32	−0.36	−0.32	−0.22
Rate of ht. growth (mm/yr)	−0.33	−0.32	−0.51	−0.5	−0.70	−0.47	−0.36
Self-perceptions							
Presence of underarm hair	0.22	0.22	0.30	0.29	0.11	0.04	—
Presence of figure	0.26	0.12	0.26	0.20	—	—	—
Degree of physical changes	0.23	0.25	0.04	0.03	−0.05	−0.13	−0.23
Strangers' perceptions[b]							
Presence of acne	.23(0.19)	0.25(0.22)	0.30(0.24)	0.39(0.20)	0.21	0.22(0.07)	0.17(0.11)
Rate child as fatter	.16(0.23)	0.16(0.20)	0.26(0.16)	0.28(0.15)	0.27	0.27(0.15)	0.19(0.18)
Rating of figure development	.48(0.40)	0.38(0.39)	0.49(0.50)	0.54(0.45)	0.46	0.26(0.22)	0.25(0.27)
Rating-relative physical maturity	.42(0.38)	0.29(0.37)	0.44(0.36)	0.49(0.37)	0.40	0.23(0.20)	0.15(0.06)
Average N	236	275	224	249	201	163	145

[a] Early developers and girls with their period are scored with a higher number. A positive sign thus indicates a positive association between greater pubertal development and the characteristic at issue.

[b] Both the nurse and the interviewer rated these children. The interviewer's ratings are in parentheses.

Table 3B. Relative Onset of Menses and Median Weight

| | Median weight in pounds for white females | | |
Grade	Early developers	Middle developers	Late developers
6	113.88	98.62	86.12
7	122.81	108.00	96.50
9	134.50	126.00	116.91
10	132.62	127.06	122.96

Table 3C. Relative Onset of Menses and Median Height

| | Median height in millimeters for white females | | |
Grade	Early developers	Middle developers	Late developers
6	1559.75	1510.00	1476.00
7	1600.12	1573.00	1539.83
9	1636.25	1616.50	1636.50
10	1643.00	1631.00	1650.25

3. FINDINGS

As indicated above, the object of this analysis is to explore the impact of girls' pubertal development upon a wide variety of dependent variables. Table 4 lists these variables utilizing a social–psychological framework and differentiating self-image, behavior, and other values and attitudes. In Table 4, we can see which dependent variables are and are not significantly related to pubertal development over the 4 years. Although the bulk of our discussion will focus on the effects of pubertal development upon the tasks to be accomplished in adolescence, this table indicates those variables which were consistently unaffected by relative onset and presence of menses: e.g., global self-image, girls' view of the opinion teachers and parents hold of them, participation in extracurricular activities, club leadership, and future aspirations.

All statistical analyses to be presented are based on analyses of covariance and multiple classification analysis, using height and weight as the covariates. Thus, if a finding is statistically significant, it means that pubertal development is related to that variable after height and weight have been controlled or held constant.[6] We will present all statistically significant results for those dependent variable-clusters in which there are several findings consistent in direction across similar variables and/or ages.[7]

We will now turn to the issue of how pubertal development affects the girls' accomplishment of the specific tasks of adolescence.

3.1. Self-Image

3.1.1. *Global Measures.* In light of the widespread changes occurring during these years, it has been posited that the adolescent has the task of developing a new stable and positive self-image (see Introduction). Thus, in line with prior literature, one might expect that those girls in sixth and seventh grade who are changing physically earlier than their peers, and becoming bigger and heavier than most age-mates, would demonstrate impaired self-esteem, increased self-consciousness, instability of the self-picture, and greater depressive-affect[8]. (Peskin, 1973, for example, described early developers as "cheerless.") Nevertheless, level and timing of pubertal development appears to have little or no significant effects on these variables in our study. It should be noted that our earlier research shows these same exact variables to be responsive to change *in school environment.* Self-esteem particularly was among those variables affected by school change (Simmons et al., 1973, 1979). While *pubertal development* does not seem to affect these global or overall dimensions of the self-picture, several more specific aspects of the self-picture are influenced by puberty, particularly the body image.

3.1.2. *Body Image.* We suggested earlier that a major task of adolescence is to incorporate the dramatic physical changes of puberty into a favorable body image. Therefore, we asked respondents to report how satisfied they were with their height, weight, and figure; we also asked them how much they cared about each of these dimensions.[9]

Overall, early developers are less likely to be satisfied with their physical characteristics than are late developers, and are more likely to care about these characteristics. In Figures 1–4, we can see the statistically significant relationships of these body-image factors to presence/absence of menstruation as well as to early, middle, and late development.

The bars in the graphs show the adjusted deviations from the grand mean of a variable for a specific year for a particular developmental subgroup, unless otherwise specified. These adjusted deviations are obtained from an analysis of covariance and multiple classification analysis, holding height and weight constant. Only statistically significant relationships are presented. Where bar graphs are not shown for a grade, the results are not significant. In the case of presence versus absence of

Table 4. Pubertal Development and Dependent Variables
(White Girls)

Self-concept

Dependent variable	Significance[a]	Dependent variable	Significance
GLOBAL SELF-IMAGE		Satisfaction with weight	X*
Self-esteem		Satisfaction with figure/muscles	6*, VI*, X**
Self-consciousness	X**	PERCEIVED SELF-COMPETENCE	
Self-stability		Intelligence	
Depression	VI**	Athletic ability	
PERCEPTIONS THAT ADULTS EVALUATE ONE HIGHLY		School work	VII**
Parents		PERCEPTIONS OF SEX ROLE	
Teachers		Positive feelings about being a girl	7**, VII*, IX*
PERCEIVED SOCIAL IMAGE		Care about not acting like a boy	6*
Same-sex popularity	7*	How often acting like a boy	IX**
Opposite-sex popularity	6*, 7*, VII*, IX*		
PERCEIVED BODY IMAGE			
Perceive self as good-looking	X*		
Satisfaction with looks			
Satisfaction with height	7*, VII*, IX*		

Behavior

Dependent variable	Significance	Dependent variable	Significance
PARTICIPATION IN ACTIVITIES		Probations or suspensions[b]	6*
Total in-school clubs		Truancy	7**
Total out-of-school clubs		INDEPENDENCE FROM PARENTS	
Coed clubs		Times/month babysit	6**, 7*
Leadership in clubs		Part-time job	
ACADEMIC PERFORMANCE		Perceive self as independent of parents	
GPA	VII**	Make own decisions (not parents)	6*
Reading achievement score	7*, VII*	Take a bus without adult	6*, VI**
Math achievement score	VI*, 7**	Go places without parents permission	IX**
DATING SCALE	6*, 7*, X**	Parents permission required after dark	
VICTIMIZATION	IX*	Left alone when parents not home	7**, VII
PROBLEM BEHAVIOR			
Problem behavior scale	6**		

Values, attitudes, and related perceptions

Dependent variable	Significance[a]	Dependent variable	Significance	Dependent variable	Significance	Dependent variable	Significance
CONCERN WITH BODY IMAGE		Value opposite-sex popularity more than competence	7**, VII**, IX*	PERCEPTION OF OTHERS' EXPECTATIONS ABOUT OPPOSITE-SEX RELATIONSHIPS		EDUCATION, MARITAL, AND OCCUPATIONAL ASPIRATIONS	
Concern about looks		CONCERN ABOUT COMPETENCE AND INDEPENDENCE		Parents pressure to date		Plan to go to college	VI**
Concern about height	6**VII*, IX*	Concern about Intelligence		Same-sex friends pressure to date	IX**	Want to get married	
Concern about weight	IX*, X*	Athletic ability	X*	Parents expect interest in opposite sex		Want to have children	
Concern about figure/muscle development	6*, VI**, IX*, X*	School work		Same-sex peers expect interest in opposite sex	VI**	SES of ideal job	
CONCERN WITH POPULARITY		Independence from parents	6*, VI*	PERCEPTION THAT OTHERS EXPECT ONE TO MAKE CAREER PLANS		SES of expected job	
Concern about same-sex popularity		PERCEPTION THAT OTHERS EXPECT ONE TO ACT OLDER		Parents		Expect to work regardless of family	VI**
Concern about opposite-sex popularity	VI**	Parents	7**, VII*	Friends		PERCEPTION OF PARENT-PEER RELATIONSHIPS	
Value popularity more than competence or independence	6**	Friends		Teachers	6*, VI**	Parents like close friends	IX**
		Teachers	VI*, X*			Close friends like parents	X*

[a] Numbers in this column indicate that a pubertal development variable has a statistically significant effect on the dependent variable in a particular grade in school. All results are based on an analysis of covariance controlling for height and weight. The table should be interpreted as follows: If there is a significant effect of presence/absence of menstruation, the grade level of that significant effect is indicated by arabic numbers: 6 = sixth grade; 7 = seventh grade; 9 = ninth grade; 0 = tenth grade. If there is a significant effect of early/middle/late development, the grade level of that significant effect is indicated by Roman numerals: VI = sixth grade; VII = seventh grade; IX = ninth grade; X = tenth grade. The significance level is indicated as follows: $*p \le 0.05$; $**p \le 0.10$.

[b] There is some overlap between the problem behavior scale and the probations–suspensions variable, since the probations–suspensions variable is one of four items in the scale.

menstruation, only Grades 6 and 7 are relevant; for early/middle/late development, Grades 6, 7, 9, and 10 are at issue.[10] If the bars rise above the middle line, then the scores for that subgroup as a whole are significantly higher than the mean for the total sample of white girls; similarly, if the bars descend below the center line, that subgroup is scoring significantly below the mean. Thus, in Figures 1–3 the bars that go up represent greater-than-average body satisfaction, while the bars that go down reflect lower-than-average body satisfaction.

Let us look at Figure 1B first. Figure 1B shows the impact of early/middle/late development on girls' satisfaction with their height. In Grades 7 and 9, the bars for the early developers descend below the line while the bars for the late developers rise above, indicating that even after height and weight are controlled, early developers are significantly less satisfied with their height than are late developers. In Figure 1A we find a similar result in Grade 7, when we contrast girls who have begun

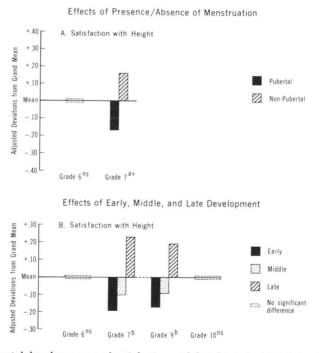

Figure 1. Pubertal development and satisfaction with height. Actual height and weight are controlled. A separate grand mean is used for each year and each variable. Significance of relationship between puberty and variable: (a) $p \leq 0.01$, (b) $p \leq 0.05$, (c) $p \leq 0.10$, (ns) not significant, (+) independent variable–covariate interaction significant, $p \leq 0.05$.

menstruation to those who have not. The bar for girls who have begun menstruating descends below the line indicating lower-than-average satisfaction; the bar for girls who have not begun menstruating rises above the line showing greater than average satisfaction with height. Thus, those who have reached menarche are significantly less satisfied with their height than girls who have not yet attained menarche.[11]

In sum, whichever way we measure pubertal development, girls who have matured earlier are less satisfied with their height than are their peers. Do they also show less satisfaction with their weight? The answer depends on whether or not we control for height and weight. When height and weight are controlled, there are generally no statistically significant differences in satisfaction with weight. When height and weight are not controlled, however, significant differences in satisfaction are found. Since the findings *without* controls have clear substantive meaning, they will be presented. In Figure 2, deviations are shown for the variable "satisfaction with weight," unadjusted for height and weight. The bars in the graph indicate that without controlling for weight and height, early developers are significantly more dissatisfied with their weight than are later developers. In Figure 2B, each year, the bars for early developers descend below the line indicating less than average satisfaction with weight, while the bars for late developers rise above the line indicating greater than average satisfaction with weight. Similarly, in Figure 2A, in both Grades 6 and 7, girls who have begun menstruating show low satisfaction with their weight, and girls who have not attained menarche reveal relatively high satisfaction.

The reason for this set of findings appears clear. As shown in Table 3, early developers are heavier and fatter than late developers. Since fatter girls are more dissatisfied with their weight,[12] early developers will be more likely to be dissatisfied with this aspect of their body than late developers. The fact that the significant difference between early and late developers usually disappears when actual weight is controlled indicates that it is the early-developing girls' greater weight that is the primary culprit in causing dissatisfaction.[13]

In any case, early developers tend to be more dissatisfied with their height and weight than later developers. The level of a girl's satisfaction with her figure shows a more complex pattern, however (see Figure 3). In sixth grade when early developers are probably the only ones to have much of a figure (see Table 3), they show greater-than-average satisfaction with their figure (Figure 3B). Late developers, on the other hand, indicate less-than-average satisfaction. Similarly we find that in Grade 6 when girls who have begun menstruating are contrasted to those who have not (Figure 3A), those who have begun menstruating are more sat-

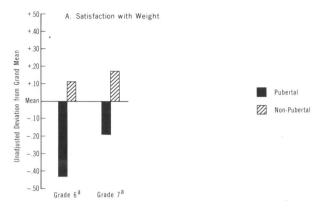

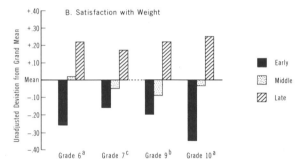

Figure 2. Pubertal development and satisfaction with weight (unadjusted deviations). A separate grand mean is used for each year and each variable. Significance of relationship between puberty and variable: (a) $p \leq 0.01$, (b) $p \leq 0.05$, (c) $p \leq 0.10$, (ns) not significant.

isfied with their figure. However, a test for homogeneity of variance also indicates that there is significantly more variance among girls who have begun menstruating; that is, they show more variability in satisfaction with figure than do girls who have not reached menarche.[14] In short, while the more developed, menstruating girls are generally more satisfied with their figures, they also show a greater range of satisfaction.

However, by ninth and tenth grades, the relationship has reversed. When all girls are developed and all have a figure, it is the late developers who are more satisfied (although the relationship remains significant after the covariates are controlled only in tenth grade). Now it is the late developers who are more satisfied than average (Figure 3B), and early developers who are less satisfied.

Thus, by ninth and/or tenth grade, early developers are less satisfied with their height, weight, and figure than are late developers. These findings agree with literature cited earlier. The fact that the early developers in ninth and tenth grade are shorter and stockier and the late developers are taller and slimmer helps to explain these findings.[15] One could conclude that by ninth and tenth grade the late developer approximates the current American ideal of female beauty better than her early-developing peer—she is tall and slim and now has a figure. The early-developing girl starts out in sixth grade with the advantage of a figure when her peers have none but with the disadvantage of being heavier and bigger than all of her age-mates, boys and girls alike. Then in middle adolescence (Grades 9 and 10) she finds herself somewhat shorter and fatter than the other more recently developed girls in her class.[16]

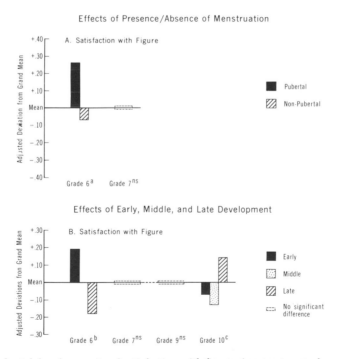

Figure 3. Pubertal development and satisfaction with figure. A separate grand mean is used for each year and each variable. Actual height and weight are controlled. Significance of relationship between puberty and variable: (a) $p \leq 0.01$, (b) $p \leq 0.05$, (c) $p \leq 0.10$, (ns) not significant, (+) independent variable–covariate interaction significant, $p \leq 0.05$.

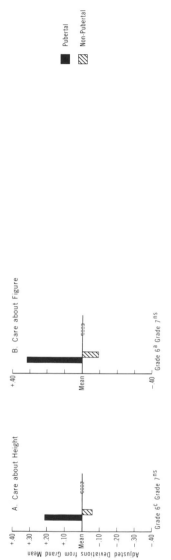

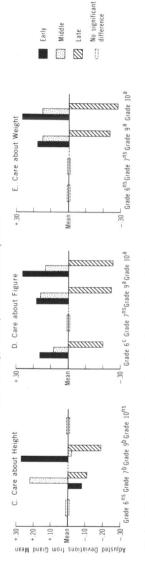

Figure 4. Pubertal development and caring about physical characteristics. A separate grand mean is used for each year and each variable. Actual height and weight are controlled. Significance of relationship between puberty and variable: (a) $p \leq 0.01$, (b) $p \leq 0.05$, (c) $p \leq 0.10$, (ns) not significant, (+) independent variable–covariate interaction significant, $p \leq 0.05$.

Not only are the early-developing girls more dissatisfied with their physical self, but in general they care more about it. (See Figures 4C–E.) With only one exception (Grade 7—caring about height), early developers indicate significantly greater-than-average concern with each body characteristic[17] and late-developing girls show a lower-than-average concern.[18] In general, then, early-developing girls care more about height, weight, and figure than do late-developing girls. Similarly, if we contrast girls who have begun menstruating to girls who have not (Figures 4A, 4B), we find in Grade 6 that the menstruating girls care significantly more about their figure and height than the girls who have not attained menarche.

Rating oneself low or unsatisfactory on a specific characteristic need not be personally distressing unless the characteristic is one about which the individual cares a great deal (James, 1950; Rosenberg, 1967). A person can be an extraordinarily poor bowler, but if he does not care at all about bowling, his poor performance will not be a source of distress. In this case, however, the early developers and the physically more mature girls not only rate themselves as more unsatisfactory on physical characteristics but, as a group, they care a great deal about these very characteristics. Those early developers who suffer from this combination of attitudes (a low self-rating and a high degree of caring) would be expected to experience significant distress.

3.2. Same- and Opposite-Sex Peer Relations

A major task of adolescence is to learn to establish intimate relationships, and to begin to relate to members of the opposite sex. Table 4 shows that neither level nor timing of pubertal development is consistently related to perceived popularity with the *same sex* or the value girls place on same-sex popularity. Nor is pubertal development consistently related to girls' leadership behavior[19] or club participation.

On the other hand, pubertal development does significantly affect a girl's relationships with the *opposite sex*, as shown in Figure 5. In sixth and seventh grade, girls who have begun menstruating are significantly more likely to perceive themselves as popular with the opposite sex[20] and more likely to date than girls who have not attained menarche (Figures 5A,B).[21] In all cases, the girls who have begun menstruating indicate greater-than-average opposite-sex popularity and dating; while the less-developed girls show below-average perceived popularity with boys and lower levels of dating.[22] As we saw in Table 3, girls who have begun menstruating in sixth and seventh grade and early developers are more likely to have a developed figure than their later-maturing peers. It

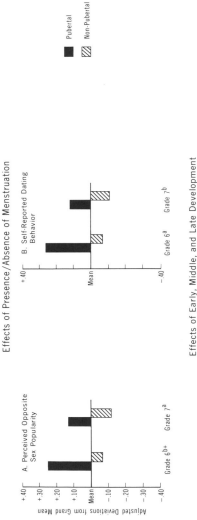

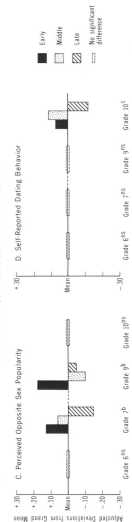

Figure 5. Pubertal development and opposite-sex relationships. A separate grand mean is used for each year and each variable. Actual height and weight are controlled. Significance of relationship between puberty and variable: (a) $p \leq 0.01$, (b) $p \leq 0.05$, (c) $p \leq 0.10$, (ns) not significant, (+) independent variable–covariate interaction significant, $p \leq 0.05$.

seems likely that the presence of a figure makes the girls who have attained menarche more attractive to boys. It is unclear whether, in addition, the heterosexual interests of the menstruating girls themselves are increased by their perception of their own figure or by internal endocrine activity.[23]

In Figures 5A,B, we contrasted girls who had and had not begun menstruating in terms of their relationship with the opposite sex. If we compare early, middle, and late developers for the same dependent variables, we find that, while the differences do not always reach significance, the results are in the same direction. Early developers are more likely than late developers to perceive themselves popular with boys and to date more. Figures 5C,D present the significant findings and show that this pattern of relationships continues into ninth and tenth grade (though not in a perfectly linear direction). Even though the late-developing girls now presumably have a visible figure, the early-developing girls still perceive themselves as more popular with boys than do late developers and they still date more.[24]

In sixth and seventh grade, there is evidence that early-developing girls care more about opposite-sex popularity than do late-developing girls. In answer to the question of how much they care about boys' opinions of them,[25] early-developing girls in sixth grade show an adjusted deviation of +0.10 above average, while late-developing girls have a below-average score of −0.18 ($p < 0.10$). On another similar measure[26] in Grade 7, early developers score 0.05 above the mean in caring about opposite-sex popularity and late developers show a below-average score of −0.07 ($p < 0.10$).[27] Similarly, according to the latter indicator in Grade 7, girls who have begun to menstruate place higher value on opposite-sex popularity than do nonmenstruating girls ($p < 0.10$).[28]

By ninth and tenth grade, earlier-developing girls no longer set higher value on relations with boys than do later-developing girls. (In fact, in ninth grade, a significant finding somewhat reversed in direction appears, with middle developers most likely and early developers least likely to value this type of popularity.)

In summary, early-developing girls and girls who have attained menarche indicate greater popularity and more active relationships with boys. This pattern begins in sixth grade and persists into tenth grade.[29] In addition, early developing girls care more about these opposite-sex relationships in early adolescence (sixth and seventh grade) but not in middle adolescence (ninth and tenth grade).

Thus, while early development appears to be a *disadvantage* for a girl's body-image, it is an *advantage* in terms of increased popularity with the opposite sex.

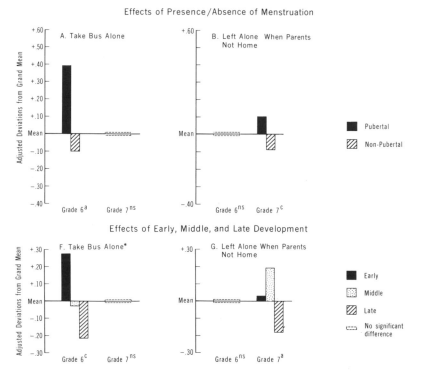

Figure 6. Pubertal development and independence from parents—sixth and seventh graders only. A separate grand mean is used for each year and each variable. Actual height and weight are controlled. Significance of relationship between puberty and variable: (a) $p \leq 0.01$, (b) $p \leq 0.05$, (c) $p \leq 0.10$, (ns) not significant, (+) independent variable–covariate interaction significant, $p \leq 0.05$. *, Asked in sixth and seventh grade only.

3.3. *Independence*

In addition to establishing a favorable body image and to learning how to relate to the opposite sex, another central task of adolescence is to develop greater independence from parents. Figures 6A–E show that on a variety of measures in sixth- and seventh-grade girls who have begun menstruating indicate significantly more independence than girls who have not yet menstruated. The girls who have begun menstruating indicate greater-than-average independence while their counterparts score below average. In specific, the girls who have attained menarche are significantly more likely to be able to take the bus alone in sixth grade,[30] more likely to be left alone in Grade 7 when parents are not home, more likely to babysit in sixth and seventh grade, more likely in

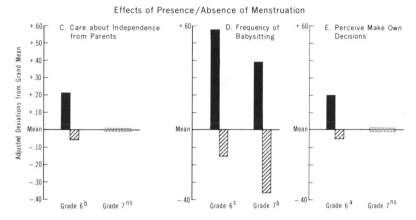

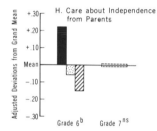

Figure 6 (cont.)

sixth grade to perceive that they make their own decisions, and more likely to care about independence from parents in sixth grade. Similarly, in Figures 6F–H we can contrast early, middle, and late developers. Significant findings show early developers more likely than late developers to take the bus alone in Grade 6, to be left alone home more in Grade 7, and to care about independence from parents in Grade 6.

These effects of pubertal development disappear in almost all instances by ninth and tenth grade, although ninth grade early developers are still the most likely to report they can go places without parents' permission ($p < 0.10$).

Thus, in sixth and seventh grade, girls who look older (i.e., those who have attained menarche) are also allowed to act older—that is, to be more independent. By tenth grade, when early developers no longer look older than their peers (since almost all girls have attained menarche), pubertal-development history no longer affects the level of independence allowed.

3.4. Academic Behavior

3.4.1. *School Performance*. The adolescent has to choose whether to conform or not to adult rules and emphases. One key area where such a decision has to be made involves schoolwork. The impact of early/middle/late development on schoolwork is depicted in Figure 7. Only Grades 6 and 7 are presented, since no significant findings occur later. Figures 7A–E indicate that in sixth and seventh grade early-developing girls are significantly less likely to show academic or intellectual success than late-developing girls, according to several indicators. All the bars representing the level of academic success for early-developing girls

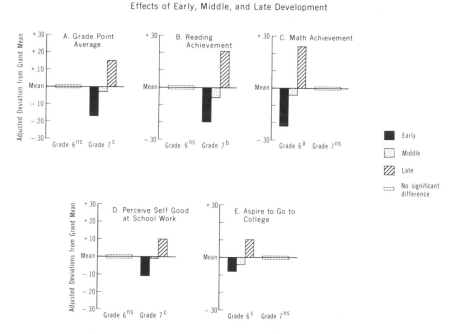

Figure 7. Pubertal development and achievement—sixth and seventh graders only. A separate grand mean is used for each year and each variable. Actual height and weight are controlled. Significance of relationship between puberty and variable: (a) $p \leq 0.01$, (b) $p \leq 0.05$, (c) $p \leq 0.10$, (ns) not significant, (+) independent variable–covariate interaction significant, $p \leq 0.05$.

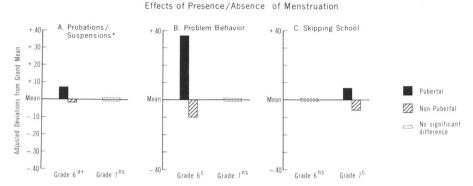

Figure 8. Pubertal development and school behavior problems. A separate grand mean is used for each year and each variable. Actual height and weight are controlled. Significance of relationship between puberty and variable: (a) $p \le 0.01$, (b) $p \le 0.05$, (c) $p \le 0.10$, (ns) not significant, (+) independent variable–covariate interaction significant, $p \le 0.05$. *This item is also contained in the Problem Behavior Scale.

descend below average while the bars for late developers rise above average. Early developers have significantly lower GPAs and score lower in reading and math achievement tests. It should be noted that the scores for GPA and achievement tests have been secured directly from school records.[31] In addition, early developers are less likely to rate themselves as good at school work[32] or to aspire to college.

Similarly, if we contrast girls who have begun menstruating to girls who have not, those who have begun menstruating show significantly lower reading and math achievement scores in Grade 7 ($p < 0.10$ in both cases).[33]

3.4.2. *School Problems.* Not only are girls who have begun menstruating in sixth or seventh grade less successful academically, but they also show more behavior problems at school,[34] as well. Figure 8 shows that, in sixth grade, girls who have begun menstruating are significantly more likely than average to have been put on probation or suspension, and to score high on a "problem behavior scale."[35] In Grade 7, these girls are more likely than average to report skipping school. The girls who have not attained menarche score below average in these school behavior problems.[36]

It is possible that girls who are more developed than their peers are distracted from their school work and are more likely to be tempted into deviant behavior because of their more intense relationships with boys.

An alternate hypothesis is that they find pubertal changes stressful, and this stress is reflected in their academic behavior. Or finally, it is conceivable that *nonpubertal* (nonmenstruating) girls are compensating for their lack of popularity with the opposite sex by investing themselves in their school work.

Whatever the explanation, the effects of patterns of pubertal development on school behavior problems have disappeared in our sample by ninth and tenth grades, just as the greater academic success of late-developing girls has disappeared by then. The difference between adolescents in Grades 6–7 and those in Grades 9–10 on these variables may be less substantial than first appears, however. As we noted above, this analysis utilized all cases measured each year. However, we also repeated the analyses in this paper, utilizing only those individuals who provided data for all 4 years; that is, individuals who did not drop out of the study in later years. Up until now the statistically significant differences reported for the total sample have not been substantially different from the results in the 4-year subsample, in terms of the direction of findings. However, when we look only at those students for whom we have data for 4 years in the academic realm, one difference among early-, middle-, and late-developing girls is altered: i.e., while in Grade 7 the late developers still have the highest GPA, the GPA of the early developers is no longer lower than the middle group nor are the differences nearly as large as before. (For the *full* sample early developers show an adjusted deviation of -0.17 and late developers a $+0.15$, $p < 0.10$; while for the 4-year sample the early developers show a -0.03 and the late developers a $+0.07$, $p > 0.10$.)

If we look more directly at differences in this realm of school behavior between students who remained in our sample for 4 years and students who dropped out, we find an interesting phenomenon. Table 5 presents this comparison by showing unadjusted means in GPA and school behavior problems for the two groups.[37] As can be seen in Table 5, the early developers in Grades 6 and 7 show significantly lower GPAs and more school behavior problems if they are in the group that will drop out of the sample than if they are in the group that remains for all 4 years. However, among middle and late developers, there are no significant differences along these variables between those who later drop out and those who remain.

Thus, these findings indicate that we have greater sample loss among these particular early-developing girls who are having school problems and not doing well academically in Grades 6 and 7. The question arises whether parents have deliberately removed these specific girls from the city public schools.

Table 5. Differences in Grade Point Average (GPA) and School Problem Behavior between Girls Who Remain in Sample and Those Who Drop Out

	White girls (unadjusted means)		Significance of difference between means (*t*-test)
	Girls who remain in sample	Girls who drop out	
GPA (Grade 6)			
Early developers	2.83	2.34	0.003
Middle developers	2.78	2.66	n.s.
Late developers	2.85	2.70	n.s.
GPA (Grade 7)			
Early developers	2.85	2.10	0.0001
Middle developers	2.67	2.63	n.s.
Late developers	2.85	2.88	n.s.
School problem behavior (Grade 6)			
Early developers	5.43	6.48	0.014
Middle developers	5.58	5.54	n.s.
Late developers	5.67	5.41	n.s.
School problem behavior (Grade 7)			
Early developers	5.40	5.77	n.s.
Middle developers	5.43	5.46	n.s.
Late developers	5.44	5.14	n.s.

4. SUMMARY AND CONCLUSION

In summary, a random sample of 924 school children from 18 public schools in Milwaukee was first interviewed in sixth grade, and then those children who remained in the public school system were reinterviewed in seventh, ninth and tenth grades. This report has focused on the impact of pubertal development on the 237 sixth-grade white girls with whom we started. We defined pubertal development in two separate but similar ways: (1) the attainment of menarche by the time of the interview in question; (2) early, middle, or late development compared to peers; that is, the relative early or late onset of menses. Not surprisingly, these two ways of looking at pubertal development yielded similar patterns of results in almost all cases.

4.1. *How Substantial Are the Effects of Pubertal Development?*

This paper set out to answer several questions: first, how substantial is the effect of pubertal development upon the adolescent girl? Our findings indicate that the effects are *specific* rather than global and extensive.

Despite theories of adolescent "storm and stress" (Hall, 1904) which imply that pubertal changes will negatively affect the self-image, overall adjustment, and relations with parents, we show little or no consistent impact of pubertal development in these areas. That is, pubertal development had no consistent effect on global self-esteem, overall levels of depression–happiness, degree of self-consciousness, perceived evaluation of parents, or on other indicators of affective parental relationships. Although Erikson (1968) has pointed to an adolescent identity crisis, pubertal development also shows no relationship in early or middle adolescence (Grades 6–10) to perceived stability of the self-picture, a measure of the extent to which the individual is confused or changes attitudes about her own identity. It is possible, however, that Erikson's identity crisis will occur later in adolescence; in fact, his theories seem more appropriate to a later stage than that measured here. All in all, in Grades 6–10, there are a great number of dependent variables uninfluenced by the level of timing of pubertal development.

The effects of pubertal development, as we have said, are specific rather than pervasive. The following areas are the ones affected in a consistent and significant way by pubertal development: the girl's body image, relationships with members of the opposite sex, level of independence, academic performance, and extent of problem behavior in school. It is interesting that these specific variable-clusters are all related to what have been identified as key developmental tasks or problems of adolescence: the need to incorporate physical changes into a new and favorable body image, the need to establish new relationships with the opposite sex, the task of developing independence from parents, and the problem of obedience to or rebellion against adult regulations, particularly in school (see Havighurst, 1953; Aldous, 1978).

4.2. *Is Pubertal Development Advantageous or Disadvantageous?*

Whether or not pubertal development has an effect and on what specific dimensions are only two of the questions to which the study was addressed. We also were interested in whether *pubertal change* and, in particular, early pubertal change *is an advantage or disadvantage for the girl.* Prior literature suggested that, in general, early development was a disadvantage for girls, at least initially. Our results indicate that the effect of early development depends on the particular dimension at issue; the findings are mixed. On the one hand, early development appears to be a *disadvantage* for the girls' body image, school performance, and school behavior. On the other hand, it appears to be an *advantage* in terms of popularity with the opposite sex and independence.

The *disadvantages* are particularly salient when we look at the girl's body image. The early-developing girl is generally more dissatisfied with her height and weight, and by ninth and tenth grade, she is also more dissatisfied with her figure. At the same time, she cares more than her later-developing peer about these very characteristics. Prior research indicates that caring a great deal about an area in which one evaluates oneself unfavorably can be particularly distressing (James, 1950; Rosenberg, 1967). Thus, it is likely that the early-developing girl experiences some distress because of her attitude toward her own appearance. This dissatisfaction of the early developers with their body image is probably due in great part to the fact that a higher proportion of them end up shorter and heavier than their later-developing peers.

We also have found that, in sixth and seventh grade, early developers are at a *disadvantage* academically. They are less likely to earn good grades and/or to score well on standardized achievement tests. They are also more likely to be behavior problems at school. We suggested that the early maturer's greater involvement with boys may have distracted them from school work and tempted them to deviate from school rules. Evidence has been presented in early publications (Simmons et al., 1979) that girls who date early are more likely to be the ones to score low in achievement tests, to have low GPAs, and to rate themselves as causing school behavior problems. However, an alternate hypothesis is that the *late maturers* compensate for their lack of popularity with the opposite sex by expending more energy on their school work.

Despite the above disadvantages of early development, the girl who matures more rapidly also experiences some *advantages*. She is more likely to perceive herself as popular with the opposite sex, and at least initially, she is likely to be allowed greater independence from her parents. It is unclear, however, whether the fact that she dates earlier is an advantage or a disadvantage. In a prior analysis, Simmons et al. (1979) indicated that dating in early adolescence has a negative impact on girls' self-esteem. Many early adolescent girls do not appear emotionally ready for this type of behavior. Findings from Douvan and Adelson (1966) also support this conclusion.

4.3. *Are Early Developing Girls More Adultlike?*

Aside from the issue of whether early development is an advantage or disadvantage, there is another question that is also relevant. That is, *do girls who reach puberty earlier* in adolescence and therefore resemble adult women more also *approximate adult attitudes and behavior earlier?* As we have seen, there are several ways in which girls who look older also act older. Girls who have attained menarche are more likely to date in Grades 6 and 7. They are also more likely to be allowed independence from parents. In addition, in sixth grade only, girls who have attained puberty are more likely than their counterparts to report that teachers expect occupational planning of them (adjusted deviations of +0.31 vs. −0.08, $p < 0.05$).

4.4. *A Possible Causal Sequence*

The findings summarized up to this point appear to fit the causal sequence diagrammed in Figure 9: that is, early pubertal development changes a girl's physical appearance in several ways. First, it makes her look older than her peers and probably leads adults to allow her more independent behaviors. Second, the early developer is likely to have a different body type than the later developer both in Grades 6 and 7 and in Grades 9 and 10. In sixth and seventh grade, the early developer is likely to be bigger and heavier than both her female and male classmates. In ninth and tenth grade, she is likely to be shorter than the late developer while still remaining heavier. This change means the early developer will be less apt to approximate the current American ideal of beauty than will the tall and slim late developer. These differences in height, weight, and body type are what appear to cause the early developer to have a more negative body image. Third, pubertal changes are associated with the development of a figure which is in all likelihood what renders her more attractive to boys. Fourth and finally, this development of a figure and the simultaneous endocrine changes may lead the early-developing girl to be more interested in boys as well as more attractive to them. These new relationships with boys may be responsible for her lower academic success and greater school behavior problems. Future analyses of these data will be needed to tease out the interrelationships among these variables in more detail.

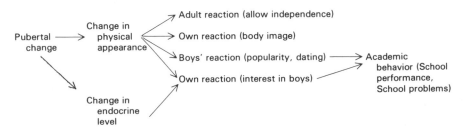

Figure 9. Proposed causal sequence of effects of pubertal development.

4.5. *How Long-Lasting Are the Effects of Pubertal Development?*

A final question addressed in this analysis involves the timing of the impact of pubertal development. Does the impact of pubertal development occur at the time of the change only or are there lasting effects of being an early, middle, or late developer? The California longitudinal studies (Jones, 1965; Peskin, 1973) suggest that there are both immediate and long-term effects of early and late development. Our data show many more consistent, significant effects of pubertal development in Grades 6–7 than in Grades 9–10. The differences between early developers and later developers in independence behavior are present almost exclusively in Grades 6–7—that is, only in those years when the early developers look more adult than other girls. Differences in academic behavior and school problems also seem to occur only in early adolescence.

The fact that there is a differential dropout from the sample, however, makes these last findings difficult to interpret. Early developers who are doing less well in school or who are showing problem behavior appear to be less likely than other girls to remain in the sample for 4 years. Had they remained in the sample, we might have continued to find greater deviance and lesser academic success among early developers in ninth and tenth grade, and we might have been less apt to conclude that many of the effects of pubertal development are short-lived.

While for some variables, the impact of pubertal development may be short-lived, there are certain effects that do continue into middle adolescence. An unfavorable body image among early developers persists into ninth and tenth grade in reflection of actual physical differences that also persist (primarily greater heaviness). In one area, the effects of pubertal development last even after the physical cues that triggered them have disappeared. Earlier-developing girls perceive themselves to be more popular with boys and/or to date more not only in sixth and seventh grade but also in ninth and tenth grade. Presumably, the early figure development attracted boys in sixth and seventh grade, but by ninth and tenth grade almost all girls have a figure. The early dating may have provided the early-developing girl with skills that persist into later years and help to maintain her popularity. Also, her early view of herself as attractive to boys itself may help to perpetuate this attractiveness.

As discussed in the Introduction, it has been proposed by some that early development would make adjustment to adolescence more difficult due to the premature termination of the latency period. There *is*, in fact, some evidence that adjustment at the time of menarche may be more difficult for early developers than for late developers. Early developers demonstrate a greater-than-average number of problems in school at the time of *their* menarche (Grades 6–7), while late developers do not exhibit a high level of school problems at a later time which is closer to their menarche (e.g., Grade 9). If, however, we look at the time of middle adolescence for all girls (Grades 9–10) in order to determine which group is experiencing more difficulty, there is no clear answer. Along most variables, there are no differences remaining between early and late developers. As noted above, where there are differences, some are favorable to early developers (popularity with the opposite sex), some are favorable to late developers (a positive body image).

In conclusion, our data give some support to the view that pubertal change can be stressful at least temporarily and in specific domains, especially when this change places one in the minority in relationship to peers. Early maturers who have changed and reached menarche when the majority of their peers have not are more likely than others to respond unfavorably to their body characteristics and, at least for the short-term, to show negative reactions in school. However, previous studies (Ames, 1957; Clausen, 1975; Jones and Bayley, 1950; Mussen and Jones, 1957) as well as our own prior analyses (Blyth et al., 1981; Simmons et al., 1979; Simmons et al., ms.) indicate that this same factor— early pubertal change—is an advantage, not a disadvantage, for the *boy* as opposed to the *girl*. The key difference appears to be whether the changes lead one to approximate the cultural ideal or not. For the *boy*, the physical changes of puberty render him more muscular and athletic and thus more in line with the American physical ideal for males (Dwyer and Mayer, 1968–1969). For the girl, the changes at first lead her to be bigger than all her male and female peers and then on average to be shorter and heavier than the later-developing girls. The result is that she is less likely to approximate the female ideal of beauty than the late-developing tall and slim girl.[38]

We therefore posit the following explanation of why pubertal change appears to have some immediate and short-term negative effects for early-developing girls, but not for either late-developing girls or early-developing boys. First, change itself has a potential for causing stress but only under certain conditions. Among those conditions are two affecting the *early*-developing girl: (1) the change places her in a minority relative to peers and (2) the changes are not clearly desirable ones. For the *late*-developing girl, pubertal change (when it finally occurs) places her in the majority; for the early developing *boy*, the changes are more clearly desirable.

According to the findings presented above, the girls who develop later than their peers show few negative reactions (other than a lower perceived popularity with boys) either in Grade 7, when most of their peers have attained or are about to attain menarche, or in Grade 9 or 10. In future analyses of these issues, we shall attempt to isolate the more extreme and deviant late developers to see if they react more negatively. We will analyze the more extreme early developers, as well, to discover if they exhibit negative reactions across a greater variety of psychological dimensions of adjustment.

Future research should also explore the impact of pubertal change under a greater variety of conditions. Are there factors that exacerbate, alleviate, or otherwise alter the effects of physical development in adolescence? For example, Clausen (1975) finds that there is a greater advantage to early development in the lower rather than the middle socioeconomic classes. A more rapid movement to physical adulthood may be of higher value in the lower classes because of the briefer period adolescence, as a social stage, occupies in the life cycle. Our own prior work on self-esteem in early adolescence suggests another set of conditions to investigate. We showed that *multiple simultaneous changes* may be especially stressful for the child (Simmons et al., 1979). In seventh grade, girls were particularly likely to exhibit lower self-esteem if they incurred three life changes simultaneously—change in school-type, early pubertal change, and early assumption of dating behavior. As noted above, we have a major interest in exploring the effects of pubertal change, as it occurs in school environments that are changing differentially.

Whatever the effects of pubertal development in early or middle adolescence, the long-range consequences for adult adjustment may be quite different (Erikson, 1968; Peskin, 1973). However, the theory that adolescent turmoil and distress have long-range positive effects and aid adult psychological well-being is one that clearly requires more extensive testing. In the interim, it is hoped that this research contributes to a better understanding of puberty in the adolescent life stage.

ACKNOWLEDGMENTS. This study has been funded by NIMH grant R01 MH-30739 and a grant from the William T. Grant Foundation. In addition, the work of the senior author has been supported by a Research Development Award from the National Institute of Mental Health, #2 K02 MH-41688 and the work of the second author by the Boys Town Center for the Study of Youth Development. Appreciation for criticisms and suggestions is expressed to Richard Bulcroft and Steve Carlton-Ford.

REFERENCES

Aldous, J. *Family careers: Developmental change in families.* New York: Wiley, 1978.

Ames, R. Physical maturing among boys as related to adult social behavior. *California Journal of Educational Research,* 1957, *8,* 69–75.

Bandura, A. The stormy decade: Fact or fiction. In D. Rogers (Ed.), *Issues in adolescent psychology.* 2d ed. New York: Appleton-Century Crofts, 1972.

Bealer, R. C., Willits, F., and Maida, P. R. The rebellious youth sub-culture—a myth. In D. Rogers (Ed.), *Issues in adolescent psychology.* 1st ed. New York: Appleton-Century Crofts, 1969.

Benedict, R. Continuities and discontinuities in cultural conditioning. In W. E. Martin and C. B. Stendler (Eds.), *Reading in child development.* New York: Harcourt, Brace and Jovanovich, 1954.

Blyth, D. A. Continuities and discontinuities during the transition into adolescence: A longitudinal comparison of two school structures. Doctoral dissertation, University of Minnesota, 1977. *Dissertation Abstracts International,* 1977, *38,* 1323A. (University Microfilms No. 77-18, 958).

Blyth, D. A., Simmons, R. G., and Bush, D. The transition into early adolescence: A longitudinal comparison of youth in two educational contexts. *Sociology of Education,* 1978, *51,* 149–162.

Blyth, D. A., Thiel, K. S., Bush, D. M., and Simmons, R. G. Another look at school crime: Student as victim. *Youth and Society,* 1980, *11,* 369–388.

Blyth, D. A., Simmons, R. G., Bulcroft, R., Felt, D., Van Cleave, E. F., and Bush, D. M. The effects of physical development on self-image and satisfaction with body-image for early adolescent males. In R. G. Simmons (Ed.), *Research in community and mental health.* Vol. 2. Greenwich, CT: JAI Press, 1981.

Bush, D. E., Simmons, R. G., Hutchinson, B., and Blyth, D. A. Adolescent perception of sex roles in 1968 and 1975. *Public Opinion Quarterly,* 1977–1978, *41,* 459–474.

Clausen, J. A. The social meaning of differential physical and sexual maturation. In S. E. Dragastin and G. H. Elder, Jr. (Eds.), *Adolescence in the life cycle: Psychological change and social context.* Washington, D.C.: Hemisphere, 1975.

Dornbusch, S., Carlsmith, J. M., Gross, R. T., Martin, J. A., Jennings, D., Rosenberg, A., and Duke, P. Sexual development, age and dating: A comparison of biological and social influences upon one set of behaviors. *Child Development,* 1981, *52,* 179–185.

Douglas, J. W. B., and Ross, J. M. Age of puberty related to educational ability, attainment and school leaving age. *Journal of Child Psychology and Psychiatry,* 1964, *5,* 185–196.

Douvan, E., and Adelson, J. *The adolescent experience.* New York: Wiley, 1966.

Douvan, E., and Gold, M. Modal patterns in American adolescence. In L. W. Hoffman and M. L. Hoffman (Eds.), *Review of child development research.* Vol. 2. New York: Russell Sage, 1966.

Dwyer, J., and Mayer, J. Psychological effects of variations in physical appearance during adolescence. *Adolescence,* 1968–1969, *3,* 353–380.

Eichorn, D. H. Biological correlates of behavior. In H. Stevenson (Ed.), *The Sixty-Second Yearbook of the National Society for the Study of Education, Child Psychology* Pt. 1, 1963, *62,* 4–61.

Erikson, E. H. *Identity: Youth and crisis.* New York: Norton, 1968.

Faust, M. S. Development maturity as a determinant in prestige of adolescent girls. *Child Development,* 1960, *31,* 173–184.

Faust, M. S. Somatic development of adolescent girls. *Monographs of the Society for Research in Child Development,* 1977, *42*(Serial No. 169).

Ford, R. N. A rapid scoring procedure for scaling attitude questions. *Public Opinion Quarterly*, 1950, *14*, 507–532.

Freeman, F. N. Intellectual growth of children as indicated by repeated tests. *Psychology Monograph*, 1936, *47*, 20–34.

Glass, G. V., Peckham, P. D., and Sanders, J. R. Consequences of failure to meet assumptions underlying the fixed effects of analyses of variance and covariance. *Review of Educational Research*, 1972, *43*, 237–288.

Gold, M., and Tomlin, P. Skeletal and chronological age in adolescent development. Mimeographed manuscript, 1975. Ann Arbor, MI: Institute for Social Research.

Hall, G. S. *Adolescence: Its psychology and its relations to physiology, anthropology, sociology, sex, crime, religion and education.* Vol. I and II. New York: D. Appleton, 1904.

Havighurst, R. J. *Human development and education.* New York: Longmans, Green, 1953.

James, W. *The principles of psychology.* New York: Dover, 1950. (Copyright 1890 by Henry Holt).

Jessor, R., and Jessor, S. *Problem behavior and psychosocial development: A longitudinal study.* New York: Academic Press, 1977.

Jones, M. C. Psychological correlates of somatic development. *Child Development*, 1965, *36*, 899–911.

Jones, M. C., and Bayley, N. Physical maturing among boys as related to behavior. *Journal of Educational Psychology*, 1950, *41*, 129–148.

Jones, M. C., and Mussen, P. H. Self-conceptions, motivations, and interpersonal attitudes of early and late-maturing girls. *Child Development*, 1958, *29*, 491–501.

Jones, M. C., Bayley, N., MacFarlane, J. W. and Honzik, M. P. (Eds.). *The course of human development.* Waltham, MA: Xerox College Publishing, 1971.

Livson, N., and Peskin, H. Perspectives on adolescence from longitudinal research. In J. Adelson (Ed.), *Handbook of adolescent psychology.* New York: Wiley, 1980.

MacFarlane, J. W. The impact of early and late maturation in boys and girls: Illustrations from life records of individuals. In M. C. Jones, N. Bayley, J. W. MacFarlane and M. Honzik (Eds.), *The course of human development.* Waltham, MA: Xerox College Publishing, 1971, pp. 426–433.

Mussen, P. H. and Jones, M. C. Self-conceptions, motivations and interpersonal attitudes of late and early-maturing boys. *Child Development*, 1957, *28*, 243–256.

Nisbet, J. D., Illsley, R., Sutherland, A. E. and Douse, M. J. Puberty and test performance: A further report. *British Journal of Educational Psychology*, 1964, *34*, 202–203.

Offer, D. *The psychological world of the teenager.* New York: Basic Books, 1969.

Peskin, H. Influence of the developmental schedule of puberty on learning and ego functioning. *Journal of Youth and Adolescence*, 1973, *2*, 273–290.

Peskin, H., and Livson, N. Pre- and post pubertal personality and adult psychological functioning. *Seminars in Psychiatry*, 1972, *4*, 343–353.

Petersen, A. C., and Taylor, B. Puberty: Biological change and psychological adaptation. In J. Adelson (Ed.), *Handbook of adolescent psychology.* New York: Wiley, 1980.

Poppleton, P. K. Puberty, family size and the educational progress of girls. *British Journal of Educational Psychology*, 1968, *38*, 286–292.

Rosenberg, F., and Simmons, R. G. Sex differences in the self-concept in adolescence. *Sex Roles: A Journal of Research*, 1975, *1*, 147–159.

Rosenberg, M. Psychological selectivity in self-esteem formation. In C. Sherif and M. Sherif (Eds.), *Attitudes, ego-involvement and change.* New York: Wiley, 1967.

Simmons, R. G., and Rosenberg, F. Sex, sex-roles and self-image. *Journal of Youth and Adolescence*, 1975, *4*, 229–258.

Simmons, R. G., Rosenberg, F., and Rosenberg, M. Disturbance in the self-image at adolescence. *American Sociological Review*, 1973, *38*, 553–568.

Simmons, R. G., Brown, L., Bush, D. M., and Blyth, D. A. Self-esteem and achievement of black and white early adolescents. *Social Problems*, 1978, *26*, 86–96.

Simmons, R. G., Blyth, D. A., Van Cleave, E. F., and Bush, D. M. Entry into early adolescence: The impact of school structure, puberty, and early dating on self-esteem. *American Sociological Review*, 1979, *44*, 948–967.

Simmons, R. G., Blyth, D., Bulcroft, R., and McKinney, K. L. The impact of puberty on adolescents: A longitudinal study. Paper presented at the 1981 Biennial Meeting of the Society for Research in Child Development, Boston, April 2–5, 1981.

Stolz, H. R., and Stolz, L. M. Adolescent problems related to somatic variation. In N. B. Henry (Ed.), *Adolescence: 43rd yearbook of the national committee for the study of education.* Pt. 1. Chicago: University of Chicago Press, 1944.

Stone, C. P., and Barker, R. G. Aspects of personality and intelligence in post menarcheal and premenarcheal girls of the same chronological ages. *Journal of Comparative Psychology*, 1937, *23*, 439–455.

Wilson, E. O. *On human nature.* Cambridge, MA: Harvard University Press, 1978.

FOOTNOTES

1. The term *disturbance* is used here to indicate any change in a direction presumed uncomfortable for the child. It is not meant to connote psychopathology.
2. According to Faust (1960), early developers rate low in prestige among other girls, but in Grades 7–9, they experience relatively high prestige.
3. Tasks of late adolescence (i.e., choice of an occupation and marital partner) are not discussed here.
4. In the evaluation of the sample design, an important criterion was whether the sample of schools reflected the population from which they were drawn. In fact, for each school type the sample schools are very similar to the population of schools on a variety of variables: median family income, achievement scores, teachers' background, mean percentage of children who move in or out of the school, mean percentage of teachers with only a B.A., and mean percentage of teachers with only 1 year experience. In addition, by weighting our sample to reflect the actual proportion of each type of school in the total population, we can estimate the extent to which a given characteristic would appear in the total population if the sample is representative. Such weighted estimates again turn out to be quite close to actual proportions (see Blyth, 1977).
5. It should be noted that relative onset of menarche refers to when a girl reached menarche relative to other girls in her grade level. It is not in any way adjusted for chronological age. That is, an early maturer is not *necessarily* maturing at an earlier chronological age than her peers. On the aggregate level, however, early maturers will have reached menarche at a lower mean chronological age than late maturers.
6. It should be noted that the analysis of covariance controls only for the linear element of height and weight, however. Future reports will present in more detail the linear and nonlinear effects of height and weight on these dependent variables. Also certain associated elements of body type probably are not being controlled—e.g., stockiness versus leanness, muscularity versus endomorphy, a mature versus a trim figure, a big versus a small frame. In addition, all analyses presented in Figures 1–8 test for interaction between height, weight, and the puberty variables in affecting the dependent variable. Only in a very few cases are such results significant ($p < 0.05$), and they are noted in the figures.

7. For any variable cluster we discuss, no statistically significant findings are omitted. They are included whether or not they fit the general pattern of results. In this report, however, we will not discuss variable-clusters in which there are isolated, unreplicated findings or in which consistent patterns across variables and/or ages are absent.

8. The self-esteem, self-consciousness, self-stability, and depression scales were evaluated using the Ford (1950) method of Guttman scale construction. Self-esteem was created using six items; the other three scales were constructed using four items each. All scales meet minimum criteria for the coefficient of reproducibility, scalability, and minimum marginal reproducibility (see Simmons et al., 1979).

9. The three body image variables (1) satisfaction with weight, (2) satisfaction with height, and (3) satisfaction with figure are based, respectively on the following three questions: (1) How happy are you with how much you WEIGH, (2) How happy are you with how TALL you are, and (3) How happy are you with your FIGURE. Each was measured using four response categories—"very happy, somewhat happy, not very happy, and not at all happy." All of these variables have been coded so that a high score indicates high satisfaction.

10. As noted above, almost all girls were menstruating by Grades 9 and 10 so that presence/absence of menstruation no longer is a relevant variable.

11. For all relationships reported in this paper, we have tested for homogeneity of variance. In this case, girls who have started their periods show significantly more variance, or variability, of response than girls who have not yet reached menarche.

    For dichotomous independent variables in analysis of variance and analysis of covariance, departure from homogeneity of variance does not seriously affect tests of significance for differences between means as long as the subgroup Ns are equal. In the seventh grade data for onset of menarche, the subgroup Ns are nearly equal (ratio $1:1.09$). As a result, we feel that the departures from homogeneity do not seriously affect any interpretation of mean differences between subgroups. For a more complete discussion of the assumptions underlying analysis of variance and analysis of covariance, see Glass, Peckham, and Sanders (1972).

12. The Pearson correlations between weight and satisfaction with weight range from -0.47 to -0.54 ($p < 0.001$) over the 4 years of the study; those between weight and satisfaction with figure range from -0.29 to -0.42 ($p < 0.001$). Heavier girls are less satisfied with both their weight and their figure.

13. There is one exception to the above pattern of significant findings disappearing when height and weight are controlled. In tenth grade, early developers still show significantly less satisfaction with their weight than average, and late developers still show greater satisfaction ($p < 0.05$).

14. In analysis of variance and covariance, if there are homogeneity problems and the independent variables are dichotomous and the cell sizes unequal, there may be problems in interpreting the significance of differences between means. The reported level of significance will provide a more liberal test than is sought if the group with the *smallest N* also has the *largest variance* (Glass, Peckham, and Sanders, 1972). The sixth grade results for onset of menarche, where there are departures from homogeneity, have this type of pattern. As a result, the statistical significance of these results should be considered tentative.

15. As noted above, in almost all cases when weight and height are controlled, the initial significant relationship between pubertal development and satisfaction with weight is reduced below the level of statistical significance, as is the ninth grade relationship between pubertal development and a girl's satisfaction with her figure.

16. It is unlikely that the totality of these differences in physical characteristics is being

captured when height and weight are controlled in the analysis of covariance (see Footnote 6). Neither interaction between height and weight nor the nonlinear elements of each are being controlled. This lack of total statistical control may explain why differences in adjusted deviations persist between early and late developers even after the linear elements of height and weight are held constant. For example, we might posit that it is the special combination of being *both* tall and slim but not extreme on either characteristic that places a girl at an advantage in terms of satisfaction with body image. In fact, in all instances (except that involving satisfaction with sixth grade figure) in which the significant relationship between pubertal development and satisfaction with body image does not disappear after controlling for height and weight, we find either: (1) a significant curvilinear relationship between height or weight and satisfaction with that body characteristic and/or (2) we find a significant interaction between height and weight in their effect upon that characteristic. Future reports will explicate these relationships.

17. The relevant items were, "How much do you care about how tall you are?," "How much do you care about how much you weigh?," and "How much do you care about your figure?." Four response categories were used: "care very much, pretty much, not much, or not at all." A high score indicates high concern about that body characteristic.

18. In tenth grade, early developers show significantly less variance than others in the degree to which they care about their weight. Not only do they care more about their weight then, but they show relatively little variability in the degree to which they care. The question arises, however, whether the level of significance of difference reported above is accurate given the fact that there is not homogeneity of variance on this variable in tenth grade.

    Although the interpretation of the effects of departures from homogeneity of variance on tests of significance is fairly clear for dichotomous independent variables, this is not the case for trichotomous independent variables. Based on the literature available to us at this time, we are unsure how various patterns of cell Ns and variances may affect tests of significance for differences when there are more than two categories. Thus, where there are departures from homogeneity for longitudinal puberty, the statistical results should be viewed as tentative.

19. However, Jones and Mussen (1958) found that early developers were less likely to be leaders or popular with the same sex (see Introduction).

20. The girls were asked, "How much do the BOYS at school like you? Do the boys like you very much, pretty much, not very much, or not at all?"

21. To measure the frequency and intensity of dating, we constructed a seven-item dating behavior scale from the following questions: (1) Do you ever go out with another girl and a couple of boys or meet a group of boys and girls at night? (2) About how often do you go out with a group of boys and girls at night? (3) Do you ever go to dances or parties where there are both boys and girls present? (4) Do you ever meet a boy somewhere and then do something or go someplace together? (5) Do you ever go out with a boy alone? (6) About how often do you go out with or meet a boy somewhere? (7) Do you have a special boyfriend? The scale was evaluated using the Ford (1950) method of Guttman scale construction. The average coefficient of reproducibility was 0.982, the average scalability was 0.917 and the average minimum marginal reproducibility was 0.797. While the measure of perceived popularity is subject to the distortion of all subjective measures, the fact that reports of actual dating behavior are consistent with perceived popularity suggests that those girls who see themselves as more popular are, in fact, more attractive to boys.

22. It should be noted that, in Grade 7, girls who have begun menstruating show signif-

icantly more variance (or variability) in dating behavior than girls who have not attained menarche. See Footnote 11 for a discussion of the use of homogeneity of variance relevant to this case.

23. The findings that menstruating girls have higher rankings on opposite sex popularity and dating than do nonmenstruating girls seem to be consistent with predictions from sociobiology (Wilson, 1978, pp. 121–128). Reproductively mature females can be expected to be more popular and date more than reproductively immature females since it is to the reproductive advantage of the species for attention to be focused on physically mature females.

24. The relationships between relative onset of pubertal development and perceived opposite sex popularity in seventh grade and dating behavior in tenth grade have problems with homogeneity of variance. See Footnote 18 for a discussion of the issue of homogeneity of variance relevant to this case.

25. Respondents were asked, "How much do you care about whether the BOYS at school like you? Do you care very much, pretty much, not much, or not at all?"

26. For this item, girls were asked, "Which would you most like to be, well liked by boys or good at the things you do?"

27. In this latter case there are homogeneity of variance problems. For further discussion of homogeneity of variance as it is relevant here, see Footnote 18.

28. There are homogeneity of variance problems in this case. For further discussion as it applies here, see Footnote 11.

29. Dornbusch, Carlsmith, Gross, Martin, Jennings, Rosenberg, and Duke (1981) report that they failed to find a significant relationship between dating and pubertal development. However, it is our opinion that their dating behavior measure is not as good as ours, since they used only a single-item indicator which asked whether or not the adolescent had ever been on a date (1981, p. 180). The reader should note that a similar measure was used in the Baltimore study (discussed above) and was found not to be valid. Basically, this is a phenomenological issue, i.e., adolescents engage in various forms of heterosexual interaction which adolescents do not label as dating, but which adults do.

30. The independence variables are all single-item indicators.

31. Student grades for individual courses were obtained from school records; we calculated a GPA score based on grades obtained in academic courses only. A 4-point scale was used.

   Sixth-grade achievement scores are taken from the subtests scores for reading and arithmetic of the Iowa Test of Basic Skills while seventh-grade scores are taken from the reading and math subtests of the Metropolitan achievement test. Scores are reported in standard score form.

32. Respondents were asked, "How good are you at SCHOOL WORK? Are you very good, pretty good, not very good, or not at all good at school work?" A high score indicates that the student rated herself highly. There are some problems here with homogeneity of variance. See Footnote 18 for further discussion relevant to this case.

33. For Reading Achievement, the menstruating girls show a below-average adjusted deviation of -0.12; the nonmenstruating girls score $+0.11$ above average. For Math Achievement the adjusted deviations are also -0.12 and $+0.11$ respectively. Several studies appear to contradict the findings in this section by showing higher IQ and/or achievement test scores among early, not late, developers. Of these, two are quite old (Freeman, 1936; Stone and Barker, 1937) and three were conducted in the United Kingdom (Douglas and Ross, 1964; Nisbet, Illsley, Sutherland, and Douse, 1964; Poppleton, 1968).

34. The Problem Behavior scale was created from 4 items: We asked about five types of

problem behavior. The items were asked as follows: (1) Do you get into a lot of trouble at school, a little trouble at school or do you never get into trouble at school? (2) How much trouble do your teachers feel you get into at school? Would your teachers say you get into a lot of trouble, a little trouble, or no trouble at school? (3) Since the end of school last year, how many times have you been sent to the principal's office because you had done something wrong? Have you never done this, done it only 1 or 2 times, done it 3 or 4 times, 5–10 times, or more than 10 times? (4) Since the end of school last year, how many times have you been placed on school probation or suspended from school? Have you never done this, done it only 1 or 2 times, done it 3 or 4 times, 5–10 times, or more than 10 times? (5) Since the end of school last year, how many times have you skipped school or played hookey? Have you never done this, done it only 1 or 2 times, done it 3 or 4 times, 5–10 times, or more than 10 times? Only the first four items were included in the problem behavior scale; the fifth item was used as a separate indicator ("skip school"). Prior to creating the scale, Items 3 and 4 were each recoded as a trichotomy by combining the three highest frequencies into one category.

35. However, menstruating girls show significantly more variance on these two variables than girls who have not attained menarche. See Footnote 14 for a discussion of homogeneity of variance as it is relevant to these cases.

36. While the relationship between problem behavior and *early, middle, and late development* was not found to be significant, the findings are in the same direction as those reported for *presence/absence of menstruation*. Early developing girls in sixth and seventh grade are more likely to exhibit problem behavior in school than are late developers.

37. Height and weight are not controlled.

38. Faust (1977) notes that the differences in height and weight between early- and late-developing girls disappear by adulthood.

Chapter 12

Sociosexual Development of Preadolescents

OUIDA E. WESTNEY, RENEE R. JENKINS, AND
CONSTANCE A. BENJAMIN

1. INTRODUCTION

Preadolescence is not a latent period but an active one, both biologically and socially. This span, from roughly 9 to 12 years of age, is characterized by progression in both sexual maturation and sociosexual interaction. Biologically, the early signs of the progression of sexual maturation toward the adult state occur in a somewhat predictable sequence (Tanner, 1978). However, the timing of these sequential events spans a broad normative range. Socially, it is a time span during which same- and opposite-sex peers enhance and solidify sex-role learning (Goldberg and Deutsch, 1977), and much clearer indications of sociosexual awareness begin to emerge (see Hill and Lynch, Chapter 10). The impact of the biological changes on the social changes has been the focus of considerable speculation and is being studied intensively by social and behavioral scientists.

 This chapter reviews theoretical considerations and research evidence regarding sociosexual behavior during the preadolescent period in general. An ongoing investigation of the sociosexual behavior of black preadolescents demonstrates the impact of individual and environmental (family and peer) factors on this study population. The emphasis is

OUIDA E. WESTNEY • Department of Human Development, School of Human Ecology, Howard University, Washington, D.C. 20059.   RENEE R. JENKINS AND CONSTANCE A. BENJAMIN • Department of Pediatrics and Child Health, College of Medicine, Howard University, Washington, D.C. 20060.

on social factors, but with relevant consideration of biologic and psychologic contributions. The behavior of these preadolescents is reviewed for females and males, with the sex differences in behavior noted.

2. THEORETICAL CONSIDERATIONS

The sociosexual behavior of preadolescents is influenced to the greatest degree by the antecedent stages of the sexual socialization process which begins at birth. In Broderick's review (1966) on sexual behavior among preadolescents, he acknowledges Freud's systematic theory of human development as pivotal in moving researchers toward modern reevaluation of sex in the development of children. He separated Freud's basic contentions into three main points:

1. Libidinal (sexual) energy is not a product but a basic life force that manifests itself from birth onwards.
2. The process of channeling this libidinal energy is essentially social rather than merely instinctual. That is, appropriate sexual aims (modes of sexual gratification) and sexual objects are learned.
3. The process of psychosexual development typically involves sequential progress through a series of more or less uniform states.

Although Freud's (1962) theory which emphasized instinctual sexual drives has fallen into disrepute among many scholars, its acknowledgement of biological maturation as being important in channeling the individual toward mature sexual behavior cannot be denied. The weight placed by Erikson (1963) on psychosocial development as crucial in heterosexual relationships complements Freud's conceptions.

Spanier (1977) later reformulated the concept of sexual socialization and identified five components of the developmental process: (1) the development of sex-object preference, (2) the development of gender roles, (3) the development of gender identity, (4) acquiring sexual skills, knowledge, and value information, and (5) the development of sexual attitudes. The purpose of this discussion is to shed light on the two latter components of this process as they relate to sexual behavior in preadolescents.

The fourth component of Spanier's concept of the sexual socialization process, the acquisition of sexual skills, knowledge, and values, refers to the process of acquiring sexual information, internalizing it, and attaching an adult rather than a childlike meaning to it. The socializing influences of family, school, peers, and other environmental factors determine how the sexual information is acquired and then formulated into a value. The fifth component concerns the motivational process behind translating sexual attitudes, along with sexual knowledge and values, into behavior.

As sexual skills, knowledge, and value information are obtained and sexual attitudes and behaviors are developed, they are acquired in interaction with biologic, psychologic, and social factors. It is the presence and quality of these interacting factors within the individual that determine the sexual behavior which results.

3. PREVIOUS RESEARCH

Given the assumptions concerning biologic and psychosocial influences on sexual development and behavior, what are some of the biopsychosocial factors which influence the sociosexual behaviors of preadolescents? Additionally, what are the progressive levels or activities in the development of these sociosexual behaviors?

3.1. *Biologic Factors*

The impact of biologic maturation, specifically sexual maturation, on sociosexual behavior less intimate than intercourse is not clearly understood. Newcomer, Udry, Bauman, Smith, and Gilbert (1979) noted in their study that biologic variables accounted for at least 34% of the variability for the sexual experience in adolescent females and 25% in adolescent males. Additionally, physical variables explained 11% of the variance in sexual intercourse in males and only 3% of the variance in female coital behavior. Included in this outcome (as a scale) were behaviors less intimate than intercourse, but the relationships for each of those behaviors (hugging, kissing) or the groups of behaviors, excluding intercourse, was not reported.

Age at maturation, however, does seem to have some effect on age of initiation of sexual activity. Kinsey, Pomeroy, and Martin (1948) and Chilman (1963) note that early-maturing males became sexually involved earlier than late-maturing ones. A similar but less strong tendency was found in girls. Zelnik, Kantner, and Ford (1980) in their study of black 15- to 19-year-old women found no clear relationships between age at menarche and the prevalence of premarital sexual activity. However, they reported that in whites, the earlier the age of menarche, the higher the prevalence of premarital sexual intercourse.

It has been assumed that pubertal hormones influence psychosocial behavior (Kestenberg, 1967a,b, 1968), but this remains to be demonstrated empirically. Endocrinologic studies (Gupta, Attanasio, and Raaf,

1975) suggest that increments in sex steroids during puberty correlated positively with Tanner's stages of genital development in boys and breast development in girls (see Warren, Chapter 1, and Daniel, Chapter 3). Since menarche tends to occur fairly predictably in the Tanner sequence at Stage 4, it would follow that there should be a correlation between the level of sex steroids and menarche. Based on his studies on pathologies of morphology which affect maturation, Money (1967) has inferred that pubertal hormones act as augmenting agents of human cognitional erotic arousal, though not as originators of such arousal. Hence the derivation of the relationship between sociosexual behavior and biologic maturation, either sexual maturation or hormonal change, has a logical and retrospectively reported basis, but it has not been clearly proven.

3.2. *Psychologic Factors*

An individual's sociosexual behavior is influenced by psychologic factors. The influence of psychologic factors on sexual behavior in preadolescents is not well understood. In adolescent samples, factors such as independence, self-esteem, achievement expectations, need for affection (Jessor and Jessor, 1975), academic achievement, low religiosity (Sorensen, 1973), passivity, and low ego strength (Cvetkovich and Grote, 1976) are related to premarital sexual behavior. Specific psychologic factors that have relevance to preadolescent sexual behavior are those that reflect the sexual learning process and the preadolescent's adaptation to pubertal changes.

During their development, young children learn information regarding the sexual differences between boys and girls in their homes and other early childhood environments. In the school-age period, the information which they learn begins taking on connotations which include male–female differences as well as complementary features. Based on Piaget's and Inhelder's (1969) theory of cognitive development, it is assumed that by preadolescence most children have attained concrete levels of operation, but few have achieved even early levels of formal reasoning. Despite limitations in their reasoning, they have some understanding of sex role expectations and are able to translate information to which they are exposed into concepts about sexuality that are meaningful (though not always accurate) to them.

One quantifiable means of assessing the sexual learning process is to determine the source and quality of the child's information regarding sexual issues. Thornburg (1970) reported that the peak age for first information about sex occurred during preadolescence, and that information on petting and intercourse was well known by late preadolescence.

However, much of the information was incorrect (Elias and Gebhard, 1969; Schwartz, 1969). In preadolescence as well as during adolescence, peers rank as the primary source of sexual information (Elias and Gebhard, 1969; Ramsey, 1943; Thornburg, 1970), particularly in the behavioral domain (Thornburg, 1972).

Sexual information is learned by preadolescents not only from peers but also from family interactions and media. This information about sexual development and behavior may be considered part of their sexual socialization. The information preadolescents obtain regarding sexual behavior is filtered through their own internalized value system and is modified constantly through communication with peers, parents, and media sources.

Psychologically, in addition to being influenced by sexual information, sexual socialization is affected by the preadolescents' feelings about their biological maturation. These feelings regarding biological maturation are important particularly with reference to changes in body image due to the development of secondary sex characteristics. (See Tobin-Richards, Boxer, and Petersen, Chapter 7.)

Growth of the breasts in girls, of the genitals in boys, of pubic hair in both sexes, and other physical changes are viewed as significant processes by developing preadolescents. The changes in their body image cause them to focus on themselves and to raise questions regarding the meaning of these modifications. For both sexes, there is some disequilibrium as the concept of themselves as individuals undergoes alteration in response to change in their body image. Beginning at about 11 years of age, a decline in self-esteem is reported for both boys and girls (Simmons, Rosenberg, and Rosenberg, 1973) with girls showing a greater decline than boys. Rosenbaum (1979) noted that breast development was an emotion-laden aspect of change for most girls.

3.3. Social Factors

Sexual socialization and sexual behavior in developing individuals take place within a social–psychological context and are influenced by parents (Maccoby and Jacklin, 1974; Margolin and Patterson, 1975), older siblings (Rosenberg and Sutton-Smith, 1964), peers (Finkel and Finkel, 1976; Mirande, 1968; Newcomer et al., 1979; Reiss, 1967; Teevan, 1972), and other environmental factors (Frueh and McGhee, 1975).

3.3.1. *Family.* Parents impact greatly on the development of sexual socialization in youngsters. They are of primary importance in infancy and childhood, influencing the development of sex-object preference, gender role, and gender identity of the growing child. Based on a review of research on sex-typing, Maccoby and Jacklin (1974) noted that parents who are highly available, nurturant, and powerful are most instrumental in influencing the sex-typing (and thus the sexual socialization) of their children.

Since preadolescence is an important stage for sexual learning, provision of sexual information is expected to be a key role of parents during this period. The fact is, however, that although parents are a source of sexual information, peers provide much more information at this time (Thornburg, 1970). Parents, nevertheless, continue to be primary in terms of influence (Thornburg, 1972). Despite the fact that peers are key sources of sexual information during the preadolescent and early adolescent periods, some upper-income parents (Elias and Gebhard, 1969) and low-income female parents (Fox, 1979) continue to be important providers of sexual information for their developing youngsters.

Although it seems reasonable to expect that socioeconomic factors, as mediated through parents, would clearly relate to the sexual socialization of developing children, findings regarding such relationships are mixed with regard to preadolescence and adolescence. The retrospective study by Elias and Gebhard (1969) that was cited earlier indicates no consistent correlation between sociosexual activity and parental occupational class for preadolescents. Kantner and Zelnik (1972), in their national probability study of 15- to 19-year-old women, found that the higher their socioeconomic status, the lower, generally, the proportion of coital experience. This relationship held true whether socioeconomic status was measured by family income, parental or guardian occupation, or poverty status. They noted, however, that this inverse relationship was more consistent for blacks than for whites. A similar pattern was reported in their 1976 survey (Zelnik, Kantner, and Ford, 1980).

Vener, Stewart, and Hager (1972) studied white adolescents in three Michigan communities and observed lower rates of advanced sexual behaviors in males and females whose parents resided in a professional-managerial community. On the other hand, Udry, Bauman, and Morris (1975) identified no difference in premarital coital rates for gradations of low income 10- to 14-year-old girls. This suggests that the relationship between socioeconomic status and sexual behaviors may be influenced by other variables.

Research regarding any other aspects of parental influence on the sexual socialization and behavior of preadolescents is sparse. Studies on teenage and older populations point to significant relationships between premarital intercourse and variables such as inconsistent home discipline (Ehrmann, 1959), one-parent family structures (Bowerman, Irish, and Pope, 1966; Kantner and Zelnik, 1972), and poor communication with parents (Kantner and Zelnik, 1972; Sorensen, 1973).

3.3.2. *Peers.* Peers have an increasing influence on the development of sexual socialization and sexual behavior after early childhood, and especially on preadolescents. Children become more aware of maleness and femaleness in the peer group of middle childhood (Goldberg and Deutsch, 1977). They learn the appropriate cultural behaviors which they will be expected to perform in later life. In the midschool age period youngsters tend to move away from the other sex. However, as they progress toward the end of the school age period, acceptance of other sex peers increases.

According to Sullivan (1953), as youngsters come to the end of the school age period and move into early adolescence, they develop a new kind of relationship with a peer of the same sex. This other child is thought of as a "chum" and is the individual's first real personal friend. Relationships with this close friend help the child in developing sensitivity toward another person. For most children, this relationship is not of a sexual quality, but Sullivan (1953) views it as being important in the child's personality development and in his/her movement toward heterosexual dyadic relationships.

As individuals progress through the adolescent period, the peer group plays an extremely important role in supporting or altering sex-role behaviors and expectations (Goldberg and Deutsch, 1977; Hill and Lynch, Chapter 10, this volume). During this time, there is a growing desire toward achieving some degree of intimacy with the opposite sex. Because of strong pressure to conform to peer opinions, expectations, and behaviors, many adolescents enter into intimate sexual experimentation as a result of peer influence. Among college students, the reference group influences sexual behavior to a substantial degree (Mirande, 1968; Teevan, 1972). Among the 12- through 15-year-old black and white adolescents who were studied by Newcomer and her associates (Newcomer, Udry, Bauman, Smith, and Gilbert, 1979), it was found that the best social predictors of sexual experience in both male and female were variables related to their reference group. The best predictor for the sexual behavior of girls was their perception of their opposite-sex friends' sexual experience, while the best predictor for boys was their perception of their same-sex friends' sexual experience.

3.4. *Preadolescent Sociosexual Activities*

Spanier's (1977) 4th stage of the sexual socialization process includes the learning of skills which will influence the individual's capability to behave in sexual contexts. This skill-learning process begins in early childhood, but is demonstrated more clearly in the school age period, first in the form of engagement in sex play (devoid of sexual connotation) with other children and then with increasing sexual overtones as the youngsters progress toward the end of the elementary school years. Several researchers (Broderick, 1965; Micklin, 1981; Ramsey, 1943; Sorensen, 1973; Vener, Stewart, and Hager, 1972) have studied pre- and early adolescent sociosexual activities taking into consideration the progressive aspects of these behaviors.

Ramsey (1943), in his study of sexual development in 12- to 16-year-old participants, classified heterosexual activities into preadolescent, early adolescent, and late adolescent behaviors. Under preadolescent behaviors, he included preadolescent sex play which encompassed manual exploration in association with direct observation of reproductive anatomy, exhibitionistic sex play, attempts at intercourse, oral contacts, and other forms of experimentation. For early adolescent heterosexual activity, he included a variety of petting techniques including kissing, manual exploration, and manipulation by the male of the female breasts and reproductive organs. Behaviors for late adolescence encompassed an increase in the variety, frequency, and complexity of petting as well as intercourse. Girls were not included in the study sample.

Broderick (1965) used an index of social heterosexuality to assess sociosexual development among urban black and white youngsters. He reported that between the ages of 10 to 13 years white children showed the traditional pattern of sociosexual development with girls being far more romantically oriented than boys although at about the same level of heterosexual interaction. Black boys were less reserved than white boys and at 12–13 years showed a higher level of heterosexual interaction than black girls.

In a later study, Broderick (1968) collected data from 10- to 12-year-old boys and girls regarding their attitudes toward marriage, kissing, and romantic movies as well as concerning their experience with kissing, dating, and being in "love." He developed a 5-step progression to heterosexual closeness as follows: (1) wanting to marry some day, (2) having a girl- or boyfriend now, (3) having ever been in love, (4) preferring the opposite sex as a companion for going to the movies and (5) having had a date. This progression, reportedly, held for all the children.

To measure heterosexual activity in their teenage white sample, Vener, Stewart, and Hager (1972) used a sexual activity scale which consisted of 8 progressive levels: (1) held hands, (2) held arm around or been held, (3) kissed or been kissed, (4) necked, (5) light petting, (6) heavy petting, (7) "gone all the way," and (8) coitus with two or more partners. The data indicated similarity in the progression of the sexual experience of boys and girls at the early levels of sexuality throughout all age categories from under 13 to over 17 years of age. For higher levels of sexual activities, Level 5–8, although the progressive nature of the involvements for both boys and girls was evident in every age category, girls reported less incidence of the activities. Additionally, boys reported involvement in heavy petting from the youngest age, while girls reported this at 15 years and older.

Sorensen (1973) categorized adolescent virgins into sexually inexperienced, sexual beginners, and unclassified virgins; and nonvirgins as serial monogamists, sexual adventurers, inactive nonvirgins, and unclassified nonvirgins. Early adolescents (13- to 15-year-olds) were more likely to be inexperienced virgins than older adolescents (16- to 19-year-olds) who were more apt to be sexual beginners, serial monogamists, and sexual adventurers. More females than males in the study were classified as virgins.

In his current study of pre- and early adolescent socialization and heterosexual behavior among a predominantly Caucasian sample, Micklin (1981) described heterosexual behavior according to 3 developmental levels: (1) social (having opposite-sex friends, dating in a group, and dating alone), (2) precoital (deep kissing, light petting, and "making out"), and (3) coital. Results indicated that in these 11- to 15-year-old subjects involvement in progressive levels of heterosexual behavior was age related. Social behaviors began at 12–13 years old, precoital behaviors at 13–14 years old, and coital behaviors at 14–15 years old. Boys were more advanced than girls in their behavior at each level.

In brief, it is clear that preadolescent sociosexual activities are primarily concerned with early levels of heterosexual interaction.

3.5. Summary

The sexual socialization process during preadolescence is concerned predominantly with Spanier's 4th component of the process: the acquiring of sexual skills, knowledge, and values which ultimately feed into the development of sexual attitudes or the predisposition to behave sexually. The sexual behavior which occurs during this last stage is influenced by parents, peers, and mass media as informational sources and sources of physical and verbal sexual cues.

The foregoing discussion has provided a theoretical and research frame of reference in which to view on-going investigation of sociosexual development in black preadolescents by the authors and June Dobbs Butts at Howard University. It is to this study and some of its findings that we shall now turn.

4. THE STUDY

The longitudinal study was designed to investigate sociosexual development and behavior in black preadolescents. Sexual socialization in these youngsters is the focus of the study because race has been identified as being a high-risk factor for sexual activity and pregnancy (Baldwin, 1980). A race-related factor which may be of significance for sexual activity is the earlier age of menarche in black girls (MacMahon, 1973).

The study is investigating the impact of biologic, psychologic, and social variables on the sociosexual development and behavior of the preadolescents. The 7 specific variables which are being investigated include biological maturation, psychological adjustment, sexual knowledge and attitudes, moral and ethical reasoning, family interaction, environmental factors (including peers), and socioeconomic status. At this stage of the study, the findings are largely descriptive. This chapter focuses on sociosexual development in relation to biological maturation, family interaction, environmental factor (peers), and psychological adjustment.

4.1. *Participants*

The 99 preadolescent participants in the study include 45 boys and 54 girls living within their family settings in Washington, D.C. and its suburbs. The volunteer sample was obtained through several sources including the Well-Child clinics of Howard University Hospital, independent schools, churches, health professionals, and other agencies. The ages of the boys ranged from 8.3 to 11.4 years, with a mean age of 10 years. The girls ranged in ages from 8.3 to 11.2 years, with a mean age of 10.1 years. Sixty-two of the participants were from middle-income and 37 from low-income families. Forty-five were from dual-parent families and 54 from single-parent families.

4.2. *Procedure*

A medical assessment was completed on all participants by two pediatricians with formal training in adolescent medicine. A standard age-appropriate history was obtained and physical examination was conducted. From this assessment, data on sociosexual events and behaviors and physical maturation characteristics were obtained. Most of the historical information was elicited through an open-ended interview rather than a questionnaire format. In almost all cases, each individual was examined by a pediatrician of the same sex as the participant.

Sexual maturation was assessed by staging the genital development in boys, breast development in girls, and pubic hair development in both sexes. It was scored according to Tanner's (1955) criteria on a scale of I–V, with I representing the prepubertal stage and V the adult stage. Reported heterosexual behaviors or *heterosexual physical activity* (HPA) ranging from game playing to intercourse were quantified by use of a weighted scale which utilized the following designations:

1. Game playing
2. Holding hands, hugging, or kissing
3. Light petting
4. Heavy petting
5. Coitus

The HPA score represents the composite sexual-behavior variable.

Prior to the medical history and assessment, the Wide Range Achievement Test (WRAT) was administered to each participant. At a later date, each youngster was interviewed by a trained researcher of the same sex using the Stimulus Instrument (developed by the Research Staff) to provide data on the participant's amount and level of sexual information and his/her attitude concerning adolescent sexuality, parent–child relationships, and peer- and media-participant interaction.

The Stimulus Instrument was designed to elicit information from preadolescents in a nonthreatening yet semistructured method, since open-ended questions yielded very little information in a pretest. The Stimulus Instrument consists of drawings, taped situations, and photographs from which study participants are asked to create stories or offer their views on the topic depicted by the stimulus materials. This allows a wide range of responses based on the creativity and informational level of the child. It requires very little reading skill and hence is not biased toward high academic achievers. Figures 1–5 depict a sample test situation from the Stimulus Instrument entitled the "Chase Scene." It was used to determine the participant's tendency to attach sexual connotation to heterosexual game playing. Figures 3–5 were used to detect any modification of the response based on the presence of opposite-sex and same-sex peers or adults. Responses ranged from rather benign tag games, hitting, and kicking to kissing or "humping" behavior.

Nine Stimulus items were given in two 1-hour interview sessions. The mean interrater reliability coefficient for the interview was 0.86.

4.3. Findings

We shall concentrate on the heterosexual behaviors as well as their relationship to maturation, family interaction, peer relationships, sexual reproductive information, and psychological adjustment.

Figure 1. Chase scene. Frame 1. Boy chasing girl. Frame 2. Boy overtaking girl. Frame 3. Boy catches girl.

Figure 2. Chase scene. Boy catches girl in presence of boys.

Figure 3. Chase scene. Boy catches girl in presence of girls.

Figure 4. Chase scene. Boy catches girl in presence of both boys and girls.

Figure 5. Chase scene. Boy catches girl in presence of adult.

4.3.1. *Heterosexual Behaviors.* In the study, the term sociosexual behavior is used synonymously with heterosexual behavior. The heterosexual behaviors ranged from having a boyfriend or girl friend to engaging in game playing with the opposite sex through hugging, kissing, fondling, and sexual intercourse. Table 1 lists the frequency of reported specific activities in which the boys and girls in the study participated. It is to be noted that the first item "Has boyfriend/girl friend" is not a part of the HPA scale, but it was included to provide a frame of reference in which to place the activities.

Table 1. Reported Heterosexual Activities According to Sex

	Boys (N = 45)		Girls (N = 54)	
Activity	Percentage	N	Percentage	N
Having boyfriend/girl friend	62	28	55	30
Playing games	17	8	27	15
Holding hands	11	5	6	3
Hugging	8	4	7	4
Kissing	13	6	16	9
Light petting	—	—	—	—
Heavy petting	4	2	—	—
Coitus	2	1	—	—

Table 2. Genital Development of Boys and Breast Development of Girls

	Boys (N = 34)			Girls (N = 49)		
	Mean age	Age range	N (percent)	Mean age	Age range	N (percent)
Tanner Stage I	9.9	9.1–11.0	22 (64)	9.7	8.1–11.2	19 (38)
Tanner Stage II	10.3	9.6–11.4	10 (29)	10.1	8.4–10.1	7 (14)
Tanner Stage III	10.8	10.4–11.1	2 (5)	10.5	9.1–11.0	19 (38)
Tanner Stage IV	—	—	—	10.9	10.3–11.5	4 (8)
Tanner Stage V	—	—	—	—	—	—

Some preadolescent boys, but not girls, had engaged in advanced levels of heterosexual physical activity. The girls had only been involved in activities up to Level 2 (holding hands) on the HPA Scale while the boys had engaged in the range of activities.

4.3.2. *Sexual Maturation.* Sexual maturation was assessed to provide information regarding the process of sexual development in the participants and to furnish a biologic frame of reference in which to examine their sociosexual behaviors.

In this sample of 9- to 11-year-old preadolescent boys and girls, 54% of the boys showed no signs of genital development (i.e., Stage I) and 33% of the girls had not progressed beyond Stage I of breast development. The remaining boys were at Stages II and III of genital development, and the remaining girls at Stages II–IV of breast development. Staging comparisons between breast development in girls and genital development in boys are listed in Table 2. Overlaps in the age ranges for Stages I–II in boys and Stages I–IV in girls are obvious.

Pubic hair development in girls was more advanced than in boys. The range of pubic hair development in the boys was from Stages I–III, while in the girls, it was from Stages I–IV. Data comparing pubic hair development stages for both sexes are listed in Table 3.

The correlations between the development of the genitals and pubic hair in the boys, and development of the breasts and pubic hair in girls were positive in direction for both sexes. The relationship was only significant for boys; $r = 0.74$, $p = 0.001$. Only one 10-year-old girl had reached menarche and one 10-year-old boy reported a first ejaculation.

4.3.3. *Family Interaction.* The primary caretakers for these adolescents were parents for 96% of the girls and 95% of the boys. The other caretakers were sisters and a grandmother. The mode of expressing affection

Table 3. Pubic Hair Development of Boys and Girls

	Boys (N = 34)			Girls (N = 49)		
	Mean age	Age range	N (percent)	Mean age	Age range	N (percent)
Tanner Stage I	9.9	9.1–11.1	27(77)	9.7	8.4–10.1	16 (33)
Tanner Stage II	10.7	9.6–11.3	6 (17)	10.3	9.1–11.5	18 (37)
Tanner Stage III	10.7	10.5–10.8	2 (5)	10.5	9.1–11.0	11 (22)
Tanner Stage IV	—	—	—	10.9	10.5–11.4	3 (6)
Tanner Stage V	—	—	—	—	—	—

was interpreted as physical (hugging and kissing), verbal (speaking kindly), and material (giving money and presents). The affection which fathers demonstrated toward their sons and daughters was perceived by 53.8% of the boys and 53.3% of the girls as being physical. On the other hand, a smaller number of the boys and girls (42.5% and 21% respectively) felt that their mother demonstrated affection by physical means.

Eighty-six percent of the girls and 68% of the boys felt closest to their parents as compared with siblings and other relatives. The girls who felt close to their parents engaged in less heterosexual physical activity as compared to girls who did not feel close to their parents; $x^2 = 65.52$, $p = 0.0002$. Concerning persons with whom the preadolescents discussed their problems, 78% of the girls and 86% of the boys reported that they discussed their problems with their parents. Eighty-two percent of the girls and 91% of the boys reported that their main source of information concerning reproduction was a family member, usually the mother.

Table 4 reflects the composition of the sample according to family size, i.e., small, medium, or large family, consisting of 2–4, 5–7, and over 8 persons respectively. For girls, family size did not affect the amount of physical affection (hugging and kissing) which they received from their parents. However, boys in small families had significantly more physical

Table 4. Family Size According to Sex

Family size	Males (percent) (N = 45)	Females (N = 52)
Small (2–4 members)	25 (55.5)	18 (34.5)
Medium (5–7 members)	15 (33.3)	22 (42.3)
Large (over 8 members)	5 (11.1)	12 (23)

contact with their fathers than boys from larger families; $x^2 = 26.26, p = 0.009$.

4.3.4. *Peer Interaction.* As noted earlier (Table 1), almost two-thirds of the boys and one-half of the girls reported boyfriend/girl friend relationships. The most common place for interaction to take place between the participant and the girl friend/boyfriend was at school as cited by 35% of the girls and by 24% of the boys. Thirty-seven percent of the girls and 2.2% of the boys interacted with their boyfriend or girl friend on the telephone, while 22.3% of the girls and 15.6% of the boys interacted in either the home of the girl or the boy. Using the "Chase Scene" as a stimulus for the preadolescents to express themselves, most of the boys and girls stated that they perceived play with the opposite sex as being positive. Eighty-two percent of the girls and 77% of the boys felt that preadolescent heterosexual behavior was influenced by peers. Eighty-four percent of the girls and 87% of the boys viewed play with the opposite sex as a positive activity.

The way in which adolescents perceive the sexual activities of their peers has been reported to be a strong influencing factor on their engaging in sexual intercourse (Jessor and Jessor, 1975; Newcomer et al., 1979). The influence of peers at an early age, when the dependency needs of the preadolescent are predominantly met by family, is less clear. Accounts of peer behavior are transmitted through conversation, hence the reported content of conversation with same-sex peers regarding the opposite sex was examined. At present their conversation is more oriented toward describing personal qualities of boys/girls in the school setting and on socially acceptable behaviors rather than about advanced sexual behaviors.

4.3.5. *Sexual Reproductive Information.* As noted earlier, most of the preadolescents reported that they received their information about reproduction from their mothers. Knowledge regarding reproduction was determined by the level of factual information possessed by the participant based on the following scale: (1) no information, (2) inaccurate information, (3) scant but accurate information, and (4) well informed.

For coding purposes, three content areas of the reproductive process were identified: (a) involvement of a man and a woman; (b) mention of the words sex, penis, or vagina; and (c) explanation of the union of sperm and the egg. Responses were coded as no information if neither a, b, nor c were included; inaccurate if any of these were mentioned but the information was wrong; scant if only one was included; and well informed if all were included.

Sample responses exemplifying level of knowledge are as follows:

1. "I don't know" (no information).
2. "A man's sperm and a woman's sperm come together" (inaccurate information).
3. "It [baby] came from the mother's vagina" (scant but accurate information).
4. "It involves sex between a man and a woman, and the sperm which is found in the penis fertilizes the egg" (well informed).

By dividing the sample according to age levels (10- and 11-year-olds) but not taking sex into account, we found that the older preadolescents displayed more knowledge about reproduction than the younger ones. Correlations of age in months with reproductive information yielded significant relationships for both sexes ($r = 0.738$, $p < 0.001$ and $r = 0.271$, $p < 0.01$ for girls and boys respectively). Comparing girls and boys at these age levels, the girls were more informed than the boys. Middle-income girls and boys were more "well informed" than their low-income counterparts (Table 5). Both for the females and the males, the preadolescents in single-parent families were more "well informed" regarding reproduction than were participants in dual-parent families (Table 6). The latter statement was more true for the girls than for the boys.

With regard to relationships between reproductive information and biologic maturation, girls showed a significant relationship between pubic hair development and reproductive information ($r = 0.25$, $p < 0.05$), but not between breast development and reproductive information. For boys, there was a significant inverse relationship between genital development and reproductive information, ($r = -0.30$; $p < 0.05$).

Table 5. Sexual Knowledge According to Income Status and Sex by Percentage

| | Income status | | | |
| | Male ($N = 42$) | | Female ($N = 49$) | |
	Middle ($N = 25$)	Low ($N = 17$)	Middle ($N = 33$)	Low ($N = 16$)
No information	24	47	18	6
Inaccurate information	8	—	—	—
Scant but accurate information	40	47	57	81
Well informed	28	5	24	12

Table 6. Sexual Knowledge According to Family Constellation and Sex by Percentage

	Family constellation			
	Male (N = 42)		Female (N = 49)	
	Dual (N = 22)	Single (N = 20)	Dual (N = 22)	Single (N = 27)
No information	31	35	14	14
Inaccurate information	4	4	—	—
Scant but accurate information	45	40	72	59
Well informed	18	20	13	25

These findings indicate that the more biologically mature the preadolescent boys were, the less accurately they reported information on reproduction. The reason for the latter finding is not clear. The more accurate the information which girls had about reproduction, the more information they also possessed regarding their own pubertal development as well as that of the opposite sex ($r = 0.41$, $p < 0.001$; and $r = 0.35$, $p < 0.01$, respectively). For boys, the relationships between these variables were inverse and not significant.

For girls as well as boys, there were positive significant relationships between level of reproductive information and the degree of sexual connotation which they attached to heterosexual play activity (see Table 7). This implies that preadolescents who have the most information about reproduction also are most likely to view heterosexual games as having sexual overtones. However, there was no significance in the occurrence of HPA based on level of reproductive information.

As was mentioned earlier, the WRAT was administered to all participants. For the girls, there were significant negative relationships between reproductive information and the WRAT reading and arithmetic percentiles: the higher the reading and arithmetic percentiles, the less their knowledge of reproduction. A negative but not significant relationship also existed between the girls' spelling percentiles and reproductive information. On the other hand, the relationships between the boys' WRAT reading, spelling, and arithmetic percentiles and reproductive information were all positive though not significant (Table 7).

4.3.6. *Psychological Factors.* The preadolescents were asked about their perception of their value in the family. All the girls reported that they felt positively valued, as did 94% of the boys. The participants were asked how they felt about their own maturation as well as how they thought their opposite-sex peers felt about their personal sexual maturation. Both the girls and the boys felt that their opposite-sex peers had more positive feelings about their personal sexual maturation than they had about their own maturation. Seventy-one percent of the girls felt that the boys viewed their personal sexual maturation positively, while 61% of the girls viewed their own maturation positively. The corresponding percentages for the boys were 58% and 53% respectively.

4.3.7. *Heterosexual Behavior and Relationships to Other Variables.* Heterosexual physical activity was assessed for girls and boys separately in relation to sexual maturation, feelings about their physical development, conversation with the opposite sex, and academic competence. These relationships are portrayed in Table 8. The associations between HPA and having a boyfriend or girl friend, and income level were assessed for girls and boys combined. Girls' pubertal staging was not related with the heterosexual physical activity score. For the boys, the relationships between genital development and HPA is approaching significance; $r = 0.247$, $p = 0.051$. However, within the sample, only 56% of the females and 33% of the males have secondary sex characteristics. Likewise, neither the girls nor the boys revealed significant relationships between their feelings about physical development and their heterosexual activities.

For girls and boys combined, the relationship between having opposite-sex friends and the HPA score was significant ($r = 0.27$, $p - 0.006$).

Table 7. Correlates of Reproductive Information and Other
Variables

	Boys		Girls	
	r	p	r	p
Age in months	0.271	0.006	0.738	0.001
WRAT				
Spelling	0.127	0.203	−0.187	0.085
Reading	0.219	0.074	−0.241	0.038
Arithmetic	0.231	0.063	−0.264	0.026
Pubic hair	0.238	0.058	0.247	0.034
Breast	—	—	0.146	0.143
Genital	−0.299	0.023	—	—
Degree of sexual connotation in heterosexual activity	0.250	0.049	0.768	0.001

Table 8. Correlates of Heterosexual Physical Activity Score

	Males (N = 45)		Females (N = 54)	
	r	p	r	p
Conversation about opposite sex	0.199	0.078	0.522	0.001
Feelings about physical development	0.200	0.094	0.099	0.471
Tanner Stages				
Pubic hair	0.020	0.447	0.027	0.421
Breast	—	—	0.035	0.400
Genitals	0.247	0.051	—	—
WRAT				
Spelling	−0.297	0.024	0.136	0.163
Reading	−0.271	0.036	0.168	0.112
Arithmetic	−0.363	0.007	−0.019	0.446

For girls, but not boys, there was a significant positive relationship between conversation about the opposite sex and heterosexual physical activity ($r = 0.522$, $p < 0.001$). Girls who discussed boys with same-sex friends had higher HPA scores than those who did not. For girls, there were positive but not significant relationships between the HPA score and the WRAT percentiles in spelling, reading, and arithmetic. For the boys, a significant inverse relationship existed between the HPA score and the WRAT percentiles in spelling, reading, and arithmetic. The boys with the higher HPA scores ranked in the lower percentiles in all achievement tests. No significant relationship between the HPA score and income levels of the participants was found.

4.4. *Discussion*

Findings on the progression of heterosexual behaviors in the preadolescents and the relationships between biological maturation, family interaction, peer relationships, sexual reproductive information, and psychological adjustment will be discussed.

4.4.1. Progression in Heterosexual Behaviors. In this sample of 9- to 11-year-old girls ($N = 54$), the modal reported heterosexual activity was "playing games," followed by "kissing," "hugging," and "holding hands." They reported no HPA beyond "kissing" and had not progressed beyond Level 2 on the HPA scale. The boys were more advanced than the girls in heterosexual activity, two of them reporting heavy petting, and one coital activity. However, although the boys engaged in Levels 1, 2, 4, and 5, involvement in the latter 2 levels was limited.

The characteristic levels of heterosexual involvement for girls as well as boys were early levels of heterosexual behaviors. Viewing these 3 years of preadolescent development as Spanier's 4th stage of sexual socialization, it appears reasonable to assume that youngsters would not be operating very much beyond these behaviors. Findings from subsequent assessments will chart later progression in heterosexual behaviors.

Recent studies reporting on the prevalence of this range of sexual behaviors (playing games through coitus) with comparable racial and age group characteristics could not be located in the available published literature. There are studies in which pre- and early adolescents were interviewed regarding a similar range of sexual behaviors. Broderick (1965) noted a lower level of heterosexual interaction in black girls as compared to boys at age 10–13 years. However, activity for behavior more intimate than kissing was not assessed. Two studies suggest that black teens report less midrange (petting, necking) behaviors preceding intercourse than do white teens (Sorensen, 1973; Udry, 1981). In these studies, also, females showed less involvement in sexual activity than males. Our study population reported less sexual activity at all levels when compared to larger studies of white children slightly older (Schoof-Tams, Schalaegel, and Walczak, 1976; Vener and Steward, 1974). Vener and Stewart's sample included some high-school students who were age 13 and younger. Schoof-Tams and colleagues queried children as young as age 11.

4.4.2. *Sexual Maturation and Heterosexual Behavior.* Our findings indicate that the sample is pre- and midpubertal, with girls somewhat ahead of boys based on Tanner's staging. Although the girls were more advanced than the boys maturationally, the boys, but not the girls, showed relationship between biological maturation and the HPA score approaching significance. This is important in view of findings regarding sexual activities in young black males in previous studies (Broderick, 1965; Udry, 1981). In this age group, it appears that for girls the progression of their biological maturation and that of their heterosexual interaction proceeds in a less synchronous manner than they do for the boys. Compared with the boys, the heterosexual interaction of girls progresses at a slower pace than their biological maturation. Hormonal and cognitive factors may be involved, as suggested by Money (1967), who stated that in addition to hormonal effects on sexual behavior beginning at the time of puberty and onward, males are more affected by cognitional erotic arousal than females.

Katchadourian (1980) indicated that, while male sexual interest level and behavior correlate well with testosterone levels in group studies, less evidence for a causal effect of increasing estrogen levels at puberty on sexual behavior in the female exists. A recent investigation of 12- to 17-year-olds by Gross and Duke (1980) revealed that age was a better predictor of dating than sexual development. Sexual behavior was observed to be weakly related to dating after age was taken into account.

Higher frequencies of reported sexual behavior and pregnancy in black early adolescents in comparison to white early adolescents may be affected by maturational (hormonal) influences. Since black American girls mature earlier than those of other races (Eveleth, 1979), it is assumed that pubertal hormones begin to rise at an earlier point in time. Based on endocrinologic assays and Tanner staging, black girls were found to be more advanced than white girls in their biologic maturation (Nankin, Sperling, Kenny, Drash, and Troen, 1974). They also noted higher blood levels of follicle-stimulating hormone in black girls than in white. The differential effects of this hormone on sexual behavior is not known.

4.4.3. *Family Interaction.* At this stage, most of these preadolescent girls continue to be closer to their parents affectionally, as compared with other relatives and with peers. They have not yet arrived at the stage of moving away from parents affectionally. The findings that girls who felt close to their parents were involved in less heterosexual physical activity than other girls in the sample is noteworthy. It suggests that close family relationships influence the preadolescent's interaction and heterosexual behavior. It could also be that after sexual activity, youngsters move away from parents. However, the degree of affection within the family seems to be a deterrent to certain types of sexual behaviors. Jessor and Jessor (1975) found that virgins were more apt to have mothers who demonstrated affectionate behavior toward them. It will be interesting to observe changes in sources of affection as these participants grow older.

Reportedly, these preadolescents discuss their problems mostly with their parents. This implies that they continue to feel comfortable in discussing their concerns with their parents and have not yet demonstrated any clear transition to the adolescent period.

4.4.4. *Peer Relationships and Sociosexual Behaviors.* The positive significant relationship which existed between the HPA score and having a girl friend or boyfriend is noteworthy. Although the behaviors in which these preadolescents were engaged were largely low levels of heterosexual physical activity, it is important to view this as a developmental frame of reference. Furstenberg (1976) noted that young adolescents who had opposite-sex friends and dated were more likely than others to be involved in advanced levels of sexual behavior as late adolescents.

Another interesting finding was the positive relationship between heterosexual physical activity and conversation with same-sex friends about the opposite sex, especially for girls. Preadolescent girls talk about their relationships more than the boys do. Same-sex friends are preferred above opposite-sex friends for discussing these relationships.

With the exception of early levels of boyfriend/girl friend relationships and conversation on benign topics, there did not appear to be consistent patterns of close heterosexual relationships. More advanced levels of peer relationships probably emerge at later levels of development.

4.4.5. *Reproductive Information.* With reference to reproductive information, parents reportedly remain the primary source of reproductive information for these preadolescents. As they grow older, it is anticipated that peers will become increasingly important in relation to their sociosexual development. It will be of interest to document transitions that may take place regarding their primary source of reproductive and other sexuality-related information.

Our data confirmed earlier findings (Elias and Gebhard, 1969) that middle-income boys and girls are more informed about factual reproductive information than low-income children. The finding that the preadolescent boys and girls in single-parent families had comparatively more factual information than those in dual-parent families may be explained by the middle-income status of many of the one-parent families as well as by the extra effort that is often expended by such parents to provide information for their children in an effort to prevent them from getting into sexuality-related difficulties. In these one-parent families, the girls had more factual information about reproduction than boys.

The relationship which emerged between reproductive information and heterosexual play activity indicated that the more accurate information that the youngsters had regarding reproduction, the more likely they were to attach sexual connotations to heterosexual play activity. Perhaps well-informed preadolescents, more than the others, are sensitive to matters related to the expression of sexuality.

4.4.6. *Psychologic Adjustment.* Both preadolescent boys and girls felt that they were highly valued by their parents. However, girls and boys alike seemed to view individuals of the opposite sex as feeling more positive about their own sexuality. The reason for this may be related to uncertainty about changes in their body images and to the feeling that one's own sex has problems which are greater than those of the opposite sex.

4.4.7. *Possible Sources of Bias in Interpreting the Data.* The caveat to interpretation of some of these variables is that they were elicited through semistructured format. Although an individual's reading level would not interfere, verbal expression might bias a few variables such as level of reproductive information or sexual connotation of play activities. Children who are closest to their families might be less likely to admit to early sexual behavior for fear of discovery and disapproval from their families. The interview from which sexual behavior was elicited and the interview in which family attitudes were explored were administered separately, constructed differently, and conducted by different interviewers, which decreased the possibility of response demand.

4.5. *Summary*

For this black low- and middle-income urban sample of preadolescents, boys and girls appear to advance sexually in differing realms at differing rates. Boys report more intimate sexual behaviors at an earlier age, while girls mature physically at an earlier age. Girls are more likely to give accurate information on the reproductive process, perceive sexual overtones in game-playing activities, and discuss boys with their friends. These observations may be affected by girls' greater mastery of verbal skills. Consequently, in this type of study where sexuality measures concentrate more heavily on verbal expression, girls appear more advanced than boys on several counts.

The pubertal development of girls in this study spans from Tanner I to IV. All of the girls were premenarcheal with the exception of one. Prior to menarche, these girls' pubertal development does not appear to relate to most of their sexual attitudes, social interaction with the opposite sex, or sexual awareness. The current analysis of this small sample does not lend itself to comparisons with existing literature on the timing of maturation, i.e., early versus late maturers. However, the lack of differences in this premenarcheal group of pre- and midpubertal girls leads one to consider menarche rather than breast development or physical size as the stronger of the biological modifiers in the sexual socialization process.

5. CONCLUSION

Findings of our study stress the acquisition of beginning levels of social skills, the obtaining of sexuality-related information primarily from parents, and the expanding of social relationships to include opposite-sex peers during preadolescence. This is in accordance with Spanier's concept of the sexual socialization process.

Further exploratory work concentrating on the period prior to sexual intercourse is critical to the continued unraveling of the multiple influences leading up to that event. When this work is linked to data gathered on the perceptions and experiences of sexually active individuals, the developmental framework for sociosexual behavior may be demonstrated more fully.

ACKNOWLEDGMENTS. Grateful acknowledgement is expressed to Irving C. Williams for his assistance in conducting the study, June Dobbs Butts for her editorial contributions, and Mrs. Althea G. Crawford for preparation of the manuscript. The research herein was supported by the Behavioral Science Branch, National Institute of Child Health and Human Development, through Contract NO1-HD-82840.

REFERENCES

Baldwin, W. H. Adolescent pregnancy and child bearing—Growing concerns for Americans. *Population Bulletin*, 1980, *31(2)*.

Bowerman, C., Irish, D., and Pope, E. *Unwed motherhood: Personal and social consequences.* Chapel Hill, N.C.: Institute for Research in Social Science, University of North Carolina, 1966.

Broderick, C. B. Social heterosexual development among urban negroes and whites. *Journal of Marriage and the Family*, 1965, *27*, 200–203.

Broderick, C. B. Sexual behavior among preadolescents. *Journal of Social Issues*, 1966, *22*, 6–21.

Broderick, C. B., and Rowe, G. P. A scale of preadolescent heterosexual development. *Journal of Marriage and the Family*, 1968, *30*, 97–101.

Chilman, C. The educational–vocational aspirations and behaviors of unmarried and married undergraduates at Syracuse University. Unpublished study, 1963.

Cvetkovich, G., and Grote, B. Psychological factors associated with adolescent premarital coitus. Paper presented at the National Institute of Child Health and Human Development, Bethesda, Maryland, May, 1976.

Elias, J., and Gebhard, P. Sexuality and sexual learning in childhood. *Phi Delta Kappan*, 1969, *50*, 401–406.

Erhmann, W. *Premarital Dating Behavior.* New York: Holt, Rinehart, and Winston, 1959.

Erikson, E. H. *Childhood and Society.* 2d ed. New York: W. W. Norton, 1963.

Eveleth, P. B. Population difference in growth: Environmental and genetic factors. In Falkner and J. M. Tanner (Eds.), *Human growth*, New York: Plenum, 1979.

Finkel, M. L., and Finkel, J. D. Influence of the peer group on sexual behavior: Implications for educators. *High School Behavioral Science*, 1976, *4*, 19–23.

Fox, G. L. The family's role in adolescent sexual behavior. Washington, D.C.: Family Impact Teenage Pregnancy Study, Paper C, 1979.

Fox, G. L. The family's role in adolescent sexual behavior. In Ooms (Ed.), *Teenage pregnancy in a family context: Implications for policy*. Philadelphia: Temple University Press, 1981.

Freud, S. *Three contributions to the theory of sex* (translated by A. A. Brill, originally published in 1905). New York: E. P. Dutton, 1962.

Freuh, T., and McGhee, P. E. Traditional sex role development and amount of time spent watching T.V. *Developmental Psychology*, 1975, *11*, 109.

Furstenberg, F. F. *Unplanned parenthood: The social consequences of teenage childbearing*. New York: Free Press, 1976.

Goldberg, S. R., and Deutsch, F. Peer/peer relationships: sibling and nonsibling interactions across the life span, *Life-span individual and family development*. California: Brooks/Cole, 1977.

Gross, T. G., and Duke, P. M. The effects of early versus late maturation on adolescent behavior. *Pediatric Clinics of North America*, 1980, *21(1)*, 71–77.

Gupta, D., Attanasio, A., and Raaf, S. Plasma estrogen and androgen concentrations in children during adolescence. *Journal of Clinical Endocrinology and Metabolism*, 1975, *40*, 636–643.

Jessor, S., and Jessor, R. Transition from virginity to nonvirginity among youth: A social–psychological study over time. *Developmental Psychology*, 1975, *11*, 473–484.

Kantner, J., and Zelnik, M. Sexual experiences of young unmarried women in the U.S. *Family Planning Perspectives*. 1972, *4*, 19–17.

Katchadourian, H. Adolescent sexuality. *Pediatric Clinics of North America*. 1980, *27*, 17–28.

Kestenberg, J. Phases of adolescence with suggestions for a correlation of psychic and hormonal organizations. Part I.

Kestenberg, J., Antecedents of adolescent organizations in childhood. *Journal of American Academy of Child Psychiatry*, 1967a, *6*, 426–463.

Kestenberg, J., Phases of adolescence with suggestions for a correlation of psychic and hormonal organizations Part II. Prepuberty, diffusion, and reintergration. *Journal of American Academy of Child Psychiatry*, 1967b, *6*: 577–614.

Kestenberg, J., Phases of adolescence with suggestions for a correlation of psychic and hormonal organizations, Part III. Puberty growth, differentiation, and consolidation. *Journal of American Academy of Child Psychiatry*, 1968, *7*, 108–151.

Kinsey, A. C., Pomeroy, W., and Martin, C. E. *Sexual behavior in the human male*. Philadelphia: W. B. Saunders, 1948.

Maccoby, E. E., and Jacklin, C. N. *The psychology of sex differences*. Stanford, California: Stanford University Press, 1974.

MacMahon B. *Age of menarche*. United States, Department of Health Education and Welfare, Publication No. (HRA) 74-1615. NHS Series 11, No. 133, National Center for Health Statistics, Rockville, Maryland, 1973.

Margolin, G., and Patterson, G. R. Differential consequences provided by mothers and fathers for their sons and daughters. *Developmental Psychology*, 1975, *11*, 537–538.

Micklin, M. Adolescent socialization and heterosexual behavior. Paper presented at the National Institute of Child Health and Human Development, Bethesda, Maryland, June, 30, 1981.

Mirande, A. M. Reference group theory and adolescent sexual behavior. *Journal of Marriage and the Family*, 1968, *30*, 572–577.

Money, J. Adolescent psychohormonal development. *Southwestern Medicine*, 1967, *48* 182–186.

Nankin, H. R., Sperling, M., Kenny, F. M., Drash, A. L., and Troen. Correlation between sexual maturation and serum gonadotropins: Comparison of black and white youngsters. *The American Journal of the Medical Sciences*. 1974, *268*, 139–147.

Newcomer, S., Udry, J. R., Bauman, K. E., Smith, M. L., and Gilbert, M. Determinants of adolescent sexual behavior: Biological, social and psychological factors. Presented at the Annual Meeting of the American Psychological Association, Montreal, September, 1979.

Piaget, J., and Inhelder, B. *The psychology of the child* (translated by H. Weaver). New York: Basic Books, 1969.

Ramsey, G. V. Sexual development of boys. *American Journal of Psychology*, 1943, *56*, 217–233.

Reiss, Ira L. *The social context of premarital sexual permissiveness*. New York: Holt, Rinehart, and Winston, 1967.

Rosenbaum, M. The changing body image of the adolescent girl. In M. Sugar (Ed.), *Female adolescent development*. New York: Brunner/Mazel, 1979.

Rosenberg, B. C., and Sutton-Smith, B. Ordinal position and sex role in identification. *Genetic Psychological Monographs*, 1964, *70*, 297–338.

Schoof-Tams, K., Schalaegel, J., and Walczak, L. Differentiation of sexual morality between 11 and 16 years. *Archives of Sexual Behavior*. 1976, *5*, 353–370.

Schwartz, M. S. A report of sex information knowledge of 87 lower class ninth grade boys. *Family Coordinator*, 1969, *18*, 361–371.

Simmons, R. G., Rosenberg, F., and Rosenberg, M. Disturbance of the self-image at adolescence. *American Sociological Review*, 1973, *38*, 553–568.

Sorensen, R. *Adolescent sexuality in contemporary society: Personal Values and sexual behavior*, 13 19. New York: World, 1973.

Spanier, G. B. Sexual socialization: A conceptual review. *International Journal of Sociology of the Family*, 1977, *7*, 87–106.

Sullivan, H. S. *The interpersonal theory of psychiatry*. New York: W. W. Norton, 1953.

Tanner, J. M. *Growth at adolescence*. Springfield: Charles C. Thomas, 1955.

Tanner, J. M. *Growth at adolescence*. Oxford: Blackwell Scientific, 1962.

Tanner, J. M. *Fetus to man: Physical growth from conception to maturity*. Massachusetts: Harvard University Press, 1978.

Teevan, J. Reference groups and premarital sexual behavior. *Journal of Marriage and the Family*, 1972, *34*, 283–291.

Thornburg, H. D. Ages of first sources of sex information as reported by 88 college women. *Journal of School Health*, 1970, *40*, 156–158.

Thornburg, H. D. A comparative study of sex information sources. *Journal of School Health*, 1972, *42*, 88–91.

Udry, J. R. A biosocial model of adolescent sexual behavior. Paper presented at the National Institute of Child Health and Human Development, Bethesda, Maryland, June, 1981.

Udry, J. R., Bauman, K. E., and Morris, N. M. Changes in premarital and coital experience of recent decade-of-birth cohorts of urban American women. *Journal of Marriage and the Family*, 1975, *37*, 783–787.

Vener, A., and Stewart, C. Adolescent sexual behavior in middle America revisited: 1970–1973. *Journal of Marriage and the Family*. 1974, *36*, 728–735.

Vener, A. M., Stewart, C. S., and Hager, D. L. The sexual behavior of adolescents in middle
    America: Generational and American-British comparisons. *Journal of Marriage and the
    Family*, 1972, *34*, 696–705.
Zelnik, M., Kanter, J. F., and Ford, K. *Determinants of fertility behavior among U.S. females
    aged 15–19, 1971 and 1976*. (Final Report, Contract No. 1-HD-82848). Washington,
    D.C.: National Institute of Child Health and Human Development, 1980.

Chapter 13

A Bargaining Theory of Menarcheal Responses in Preindustrial Cultures

KAREN ERICKSEN PAIGE

1. INTRODUCTION

The biological event of menarche is of immense social importance in all world societies. It is recognized everywhere as the best observable indication of a daughter's biological capacity to produce offspring. The most dramatic indicator of the social significance of menarche is that of the large and elaborate puberty ceremonies held in a large proportion of tribal societies in parts of sub-Saharan Africa, Polynesia, North America, and elsewhere. In these societies, preparation for the ceremony takes months with relatives and friends assisting the daughter's family in making costumes and masks for special dances, weaving new mats for guests to sit on, and promising to contribute enough food for a large public feast. Ethnographic accounts of these elaborate rituals make clear that tribal peoples are well aware that the appearance of budding breasts and pubic hair precedes the onset of menstruation by a few months, since the appearance of these physical characteristics in a young daughter frequently marks the beginning of preparations for the forthcoming menarcheal rite (see, for example, Powdermaker, 1971; Blackwood, 1935). When the daughter begins to menstruate, she may be kept in seclusion for the length of the flow. When she emerges, her family entertains relatives and neighbors for days and even weeks. During these community celebrations, marriage plans that have been negotiated during childhood

KAREN ERICKSEN PAIGE • Department of Psychology, University of California, Davis, California 95616.

may be finalized or new marriage proposals considered. Although pre-menarcheal betrothals are exceedingly common among tribal and peasant societies, the onset of menstruation is almost invariably a prerequisite to marriage.

This chapter sets forth a theory that menarcheal ceremonies are a form of political bargaining used by fathers to protect their rights to transfer control over a daughter's newly attained fertility in a legal marriage agreement in those societies in which more explicit forms of bargaining are unavailable. This theory, which has been tested on a large cross-cultural sample of societies, offers an alternative to the three classic interpretations of female puberty rites: transition rite theories, psycho-analytic theories, and structural–functional theories.

Transition rite theories consider menarcheal ceremonies as *rites de passage* which dramatize a girl's transition into adulthood. The best-known empirical study testing this theory was conducted by Brown (1963) on a sample of 75 preindustrial societies. She hypothesized that a dramatic public ritual at menarche is necessary only in societies in which a woman continues to live in her natal community after marriage; in societies in which she leaves her natal community to reside with her husband, the move itself provides a benchmark for status change. The results of Brown's analysis did show that ceremonies celebrating puberty, or menarche, were more likely to occur in societies in which postmarital residence tended to be either matrilocal or bilocal—that is, in societies in which a woman tended to remain in her natal community after marriage. Ceremonies were less likely to be held in societies with patrilocal or neolocal postmarital residence patterns, in which the woman tended to leave her natal community after marriage to reside in either her husband's natal community or a community in which neither of the spouses' parents resided. The statistical significance of the relationship between postmarital residence patterns and menarcheal ceremonies provided empirical support for Brown's hypothesis and thus supported the "transition rite" theory of societal responses to puberty.

Within the *psychoanalytic tradition*, theorists have attempted to extend and modify Freud's original thesis about the origins of men's fear of deflowering a virgin to account for men's fear of the onset of menstruation as well. Theorists following Freud's general argument have proposed that women perceive the onset of menstrual bleeding and bleeding at each subsequent menstrual period as a "narcissistic injury." The bleeding releases a woman's unconscious infantile aggressive impulses toward men, whom she fantasizes as having robbed her of her penis. To prevent women from directing these dangerous emotions against men in the community, societies have instituted ritual mechanisms such as menarcheal seclusion, social segregation, and taboos. These arguments are best articulated by Deutsch (1944), Abraham (1948), Chadwick (1952), and Bonaparte (1953), although only Chadwick and Bonaparte make a causal association between cultural rituals at menarche and women's psychodynamics.

The third classic approach, that of anthropological *structural–functional theory*, argues that menarcheal ceremonies, like most other significant public rituals held during critical events in the human life cycle, are symbolic expressions of structural tensions within a society or community, such as structurally induced conflicts over kin group control of a woman and her future offspring. The best-known application of this theoretical perspective to the analysis of menarcheal rituals is Richards's (1956) analysis of the connection between menarcheal ceremonies and anxiety about the future status of a daughter's potential offspring among the matrilineal Bemba in central Africa. Richards argues that the elaborate *chisungu* rite and the concern about attaching a kinswoman's potential offspring to her matrilineage are both consequences of the inevitable conflict that marriage of daughters produces in all matrilineal social systems. This conflict, which she describes as the "matrilineal puzzle" (1950), produces the tension between a woman's matrilineal kinsmen and her husband. In many matrilineal societies in Africa, a woman's marriage presents a problem for her kinsmen: how to persuade her husband to establish his household matrilocally under their authority while at the same time denying him full jural authority over his own children. Since the Bemba are too poor to offer much economic inducement to a husband to remain in his wife's matrilineal village, there is the real possibility that after marriage he will remove his wife and her offspring to his own natal community.

The theory described here is an elaboration and extension of Paige and Paige's (1981) social exchange theory about worldwide variability in ritual responses to each of the critical events in the human life cycle: marriage, childbirth, the sexual maturity of sons, and the onset of menstruation in daughters. Fundamental to this perspective is the assumption that in societies in which children are an important economic and political asset, a woman's reproductive capacity is a critical asset to the man or group of men who control it. Consequently, it is a source of much conflict among competing claimants.

Conflicts between men or groups of men over the control of a woman's reproductive capacity occur in all societies, including our own. These conflicts are particularly acute, however, in tribal societies, where the size and strength of a man's kin group is the major determinant of his wealth, status, and political power. In such societies, gaining a new member for one's kin group means gaining a contributor to the economy, a new supporter in a political faction, and an additional ally in a feud. A woman's biological capacity to bear children thus represents an important capital asset, and conflict over it is likely to be intense.

In most preindustrial societies, particularly those organized at the tribal level, there are no police or standing armies and there is no formal legal system outside the kinship structure. Disputes over rights to women must therefore be settled directly by bargains negotiated among the interested parties themselves. Since there is no binding authority, these bargains may always be overturned and new bargains made. This fundamental difficulty confronts any man attempting to assert or defend rights to women in the absence of centralized authority.

2. MENARCHE: A SOCIAL–PSYCHOLOGICAL DILEMMA

The appearance of the first menstrual flow is widely recognized as the first positive indication that a woman is physiologically ready to produce offspring. It is therefore the first point in the female reproductive cycle at which bargaining over rights to her childbearing potential begins. In any society in which a man's political and economic power is largely determined by the number of children he controls, it is essential that he acquire rights to a woman who can produce as many children as possible during his lifetime. If a woman's value is determined by the number of children she can produce, a critical factor in determining her potential reproductive output and thus her value as a wife is the time at which her reproductive span actually begins. In order to maximize the number of children produced who will actually survive to adulthood, a man should begin impregnating a woman as soon as she begins to ovulate. In theory, a woman should be able to produce a child every 9 or 10 months throughout a reproductive span lasting about 30 years at most. In practice, however, even if a woman were to survive through the duration of her reproductive life and conceive each time she ovulated, the actual number of viable offspring produced who would survive to adulthood would represent only a small proportion of actual ovulations and conceptions. Such factors as the length of a woman's reproductive span; maternal, fetal, and child mortality; and even the occurrence of ovulation can be neither predicted nor controlled by a husband. It is therefore important for a man to try to increase the probability of conception and birth by impregnating a woman as soon as she becomes fertile. Once a woman begins to ovulate, every ovulatory cylce during which she remains unimpregnated represents one less potential offspring that could be produced during her reproductive span.

The time at which a woman actually begins to ovulate cannot, of course, be directly ascertained, and ovulation may not begin to occur regularly for some time after menarche if at all. There are some data to suggest that the discrepancy between the onset of menstrual cycles and the onset of ovulatory cycles, sometimes referred to as "adolescent sterility," is recognized in a number of tribal societies. For example, Harner (1972) found that the Jivaro of Ecuador believe one should not expect a woman to bear her first child for at least 18 months after the onset of menstruation, and they estimate the date by how many times a certain tree blossoms after the first menses.

The discrepancy between the appearance of first menstruation and first ovulation, however, is actually not only highly variable but also impossible to predict for any single woman within a society. This means that menstruation can never be used as an indicator that any particular woman is ready to bear children. However, menarche is the only good external evidence men have that a woman is biologically capable of reproduction. To increase the probability of conception once ovulation does occur, a man should complete the process of acquiring rights to a woman as soon after her menarche as possible. Before menarche, of course, a woman is of no immediate reproductive value, and a man would be taking a considerable risk in settling a marriage bargain on a girl of premenarcheal age.

The bargaining theory of menarcheal ceremonies argues that menarche represents the point in a woman's life cycle at which her total childbearing potential is greatest and thus the time at which she is of maximum value in a marriage bargain. While marriage cross-culturally does not always coincide with the onset of menstruation, the appearance of this critical reproductive event is with few exceptions an essential prerequisite to any final settlement of the terms of a marriage bargain. The importance of menarche to a marriage settlement can create a difficult problem for a woman's father by limiting the pool of suitors with whom he can negotiate to those seeking wives after his daughter's menarche has occurred. Given the importance attached to a woman's reproductive capacity, a father's primary interest in a marriage bargain is to relinquish this resource according to the terms that are most financially and politically profitable. He would therefore like the widest possible choice of potential affines. Terms of a marriage bargain customarily require that a potential husband (and his family) compensate the father with resources of a value at least equal to the value considered by the father to represent his daughter's reproductive capacity. Marriage compensation may take the form of other capital, such as property or animals, or the direct exchange of women. It may also take the form of labor and special services from the husband or any future offspring, or the implicit promise of political and economic assistance from prestigious affines.

By depending on the biologically determined timing of a daughter's menarche to settle her marriage, however, a father can seriously jeopardize his ability to contract maximally favorable terms. There is always the possibility that the eligible males looking for wives at the time the daughter reaches menarche may not be the most prestigious potential sons-in-law or may be too poor or too unwilling to meet a father's demands for valuable compensation. Since a father can never exploit his daughter's fertility himself, nor even marry her to his own sons, he may be forced to settle an unprofitable marriage bargain with one of the suitors available at the time the daughter becomes fertile. Given the important implications of the timing of menarche in determining a father's bargaining position, it is not uncommon to find that a daughter's developmental progress is a major preoccupation of her family during her late childhood. While a suitor is most interested in marrying a woman with the greatest childbearing potential, a father is primarily interested in being in a position to take advantage of good marriage prospects as they become available. Ideally, he would like to settle her marriage at the time most suited to his own immediate interests during the years before her menarche. After all, he can use the compensation received in the marriage bargain to settle pressing blood debts, pay off loans from kinsmen, make tardy brideprice payments still outstanding from his own marriage, or invest in other reproductive capital by arranging good marriages for his sons or even himself. Instead of having to wait perhaps 13 years or even as long as 19 years until his daughter becomes marriageable, a father would like to be in a position to take advantage of current opportunities to form alliances with important affines, acquire the services of a son-in-law, or take advantage of an inflation in the customary rate of compensation received by other fathers in his community that year.

Thus if a father's ability to transact other important financial and political negotiations is dependent on the timing of his daughter's menarche, he can never be sure that she will actually become marriageable at the time when the compensation from her marriage will be most urgently needed for compensation to acquire other wives or for other important investments or obligations. His daughter may not begin to menstruate until years after his best chances for a good marriage have disappeared. In that case, he may have to settle for a less satisfactory marriage to avoid the risk of losing out on a bargain entirely. Once a daughter becomes fertile, in the absence of a marriage bargain, she represents a perishable commodity. If a father holds out too long for a profitable bargain, he risks losing out on a bargain entirely through the abduction of his daughter, or worse, being stuck with the cost of supporting a worthless spinster for the rest of his life.

3. Partial Solution to the Menarcheal Dilemma: Childhood Betrothal

It might appear that the widely practiced custom of betrothing daughters long before menarche would completely eliminate the dilemma of menarche. If marriage bargains could be negotiated at a time most advantageous to a father rather than subsequent to actual evidence that his daughter is fertile, the unpredictable timing of menarche would be completely eliminated as a factor in marital bargaining. Betrothal of daughters before menarche is practiced by 82% of sample societies. In most cases, however, it is an individual family option and not necessarily a mandatory or universal practice for the society as a whole. Betrothal investments usually take one of three different forms: the *"rearing,"* or *adoption, of the future wife* for varying lengths of time, either by the potential husband's family or in some cases by the potential husband himself; premarital *brideservice,* in which a suitor performs subsistence tasks and other services for his potential father-in-law; or the payment of gifts or portions of the brideprice (i.e., property or animals) which may later be counted as *installments of marriage compensation.*

The practice of rearing the potential wife involves to varying degrees the transfer of a young daughter from her family's household to that of either her potential in-laws or her potential husband. Among the Andamanese, for example, a young woman may go to live with her suitor's family for a few months so that they may publicize the betrothal, then return to her own family until the marriage terms are finally settled (Man, 1877). Among the Wogeo, a woman makes extended visits to her potential in-laws, during which they subject her to severe criticism and ridicule, perhaps as an attempt to reduce the amount of marriage compensation demanded by her father by publicizing her defects (Hogbin, 1944). Rarely, if ever, is the relationship established by "rearing" or adoption considered a legally binding marriage, even in cases where the suitor is allowed sexual access to the daughter during her residence. Usually the daughter must either return home during the final contract settlement or go through a menarcheal ceremony before the marriage becomes socially legitimate.

The practice of brideservice is the most frequent form of betrothal investment, even in those societies in which a future marriage contract involves the payment of capital assets. During the betrothal period, a young man may move into the household of his potential father-in-law, providing him with all or a share of the food he has gathered or hunted, working in his father-in-law's fields, or taking his father-in-law's side in feuds. Societies in which sexual access to a woman is permitted before marriage are, in a majority of instances, those which also practice brideservice. The young suitor lives in the household of his future wife during his years of service and may be allowed sexual access to her and in some cases rights to her domestic services throughout this period.

The third strategy involves the payment of sequential installments of property or gifts throughout the daughter's premenarcheal period, with settlement of a final marriage contract contingent either on the payment of a certain number of installments which cannot begin until after a daughter's sexual maturity, or on total payment. In some societies, the time at which the series of payments begins is a matter of ceremony, as among the Riffians of Morocco, who seal the payment by tattooing the daughter (Coon, 1931). Among the Azande of the Sudan, the suitor may take the young daughter to his own home before making payment, but the relationship is not considered a legal marriage until he has paid ten spears (Seligman and Seligman, 1932). While the payment of betrothal gifts allows the father ready resources to invest in other wives for his own family or to pay off pressing debts, frequently all or most of the gifts and property must be returned if a marriage contract is never finally settled. In some societies, if a fiancé does not eventually marry the daughter, the man who actually contracts the marriage may be obliged to pay compensation gifts to the original fiancé as well as to the woman's father.

4. ADVANTAGES AND DISADVANTAGES OF PREMENARCHEAL BETROTHAL

Clearly, premenarcheal betrothal would not be so widely practiced if it did not offer advantages to both the father and the suitor (or suitor's family). The advantages to a father are most obvious since such premarital investments allow him not only immediate access to some capital or labor, but also some choice as to the particular family or individual with whom he would most like to negotiate a long-term marriage bargain— for example, a preferred cousin or a family with an adjoining plot of land. When betrothal takes the form of "rearing the bride," some of the costs of raising a female of no immediate value shift from the father to a family who may eventually receive the benefits of her future reproductive capacity. While the father may run the risk of having his daughter deflowered while she is not directly under his supervision, the daughter does not yet have the capacity to produce offspring, so that allowing sexual access never jeopardizes the father's ability to negotiate the terms under which his rights to her offspring will be relinquished. Although a suitor's primary interest in a marriage bargain is access to a woman's childbearing capacity, investing in a premature woman offers at least three advantages to the suitor. First, just as a betrothal allows a father some flexibility in choice of suitor, it allows a suitor time to assess the feasibility of a future alliance with the young woman's family. Second, if a suitor is poor or subject to intense competition with other wife-seekers in his community, a betrothal allows him to begin paying off a future marriage debt over a period of years prior to a final settlement while gaining a competitive advantage that may be necessary once the daughter becomes marriageable. Finally, a betrothal period allows a suitor and his kinsmen certain powers of surveillance over the daughter and her family that would not otherwise be permissible, thereby minimizing the possibilities of a father's trickery and attempts to manipulate the conditions of a marriage contract. With greater accessibility to the daughter, the suitor and his kinsmen can more closely observe her gradual physical development, reducing the possibility that a marriage will be contracted before she is biologically fertile.

Despite the prevalence of premenarcheal betrothal, there is a considerable gap between a marriage promised and a marriage consummated. Betrothal is only a fragile guarantee of actual marriage. One of the principals to the future marriage bargain may die, particularly if the betrothal is between infants or young children. The chances that a young daughter will live to sexual maturity are by no means assured, given the high childhood death rates in preindustrial societies. For example, among the Ganda about 29% of the children are not expected to live to puberty; among the Navaho, this figure is about 30%; and among the Alorese, it is 48% (Nag, 1962).

If the father dies before the contract has been settled, other kinsmen who assume legal authority over the daughter's marriage may choose to negotiate with other suitors with whom an alliance would better suit their own interests. Similarly, if a suitor dies, the betrothal will of course become void and a new suitor will be considered. In addition to the obvious importance of mortality in minimizing the chances that a betrothal will ever become a marriage, numerous social and financial crises may arise to force either a father or potential suitor to break off marriage promises. A father may be forced to fulfill more pressing obligations by using his daughter either as compensation for blood debts or as a replacement for one of her married sisters who never produced children during her own marriage or who died in childbirth. In some societies, a father may not even be able to marry his daughter without the consent of his wife's family, who may have given him rights to his wife only on the condition that they have the final choice of his daughter's suitor and rights to her marriage compensation. Warfare or feuding may break out between parties to a betrothal agreement, thereby making further negotiations extremely difficult. A suitor may also have to break a betrothal agreement, particularly if he is unable to meet increasing demands for larger and better gifts or more years of service, if his father cannot fulfill his promise to provide the necessary wealth compensation for a final marriage, or if he must be called back to serve his own father in warfare or an economic crisis. And of course a suitor may tire of waiting for a late-maturing woman to reach menarche while other eligible women in the community are already married.

5. THE FATHER'S DILEMMA AT MENARCHE

Whether or not a betrothal promise has been made during a woman's childhood, her potential husband will still demand physical evidence of her reproductive capacity in the form of menarche before completing the marriage bargain. An equally important prerequisite to final settlement is usually the assurance that the potential husband will be recognized as the sole genitor of all his wife's future children. If another man can claim to have had prior sexual access to a sexually mature daughter, he can challenge the husband's rights to her future children. Thus once a daughter begins to menstruate, her father is faced with a serious dilemma. While he must wait until menarche to complete negotiations over his daughter's marriage in order to give evidence of her fertility, by waiting until she is sexually mature he may lose the ability to guarantee her future husband undisputed biological paternity to her future offspring.

Once a daughter attains sexual maturity, some other male not party to the marriage negotiations, or even the fiancé himself, may jeopardize her father's bargaining position by claiming prior sexual access to her, thus reducing her value as a wife and the size of compensation her father can demand. After menarche, all suitors, a fiancé, and any other interested claimants are obviously placed in a potentially commanding bargaining position since it is possible by seduction, elopement, or even gossip to question the virtue of the potential wife and thus make it difficult, if not impossible, for her father to demand maximum compensation for her. The major task of a father of a menarcheal woman is to defend his bargaining position by preventing all illicit attempts to claim her reproductive capacity. Once she is married, of course, this responsibility shifts from her father to her husband, but until then it is only the concern of the father and whatever kinsmen and friends in the community he can muster in his support. The father's task may be exceedingly difficult since, in almost all societies, young women reach sexual maturity surrounded by eligible males who live in the same community and sometimes even share the communal dwelling unit.

Young unmarried men, who are anxious to begin establishing themselves by building up the wealth and power that come with large numbers of children, must in most societies compete for wives with older polygynous males who could profit from acquiring an additional wife, or with older monogamous husbands who wish to replace a menopausal or barren wife with a younger and more productive one. Young men are therefore particularly likely to attempt to manipulate a marriage bargain illegally since they are least likely to have the necessary wealth for marriage payments. Even a fiancé can profit from forcing an early marriage by seducing his betrothed, since in this way he may prevent the father from holding out for larger and more expensive gifts or longer years of service indebtedness than he can afford, or prevent wealthier competing suitors from outbidding him in the final marriage contract.

Even when a father is able to prevent seduction and elopement of his daughter, he may not be able to protect her sexual reputation. As Mair (1971) points out, the importance of a woman's virtue in a marriage bargain has as much to do with her social reputation for chastity as with the more technical issue of the presence or absence of an intact hymen. If a young nubile daughter gains a reputation of having lost her physical virginity, or if she is flirtatious and attractive enough to create suspicion about her virtue, her father's ability to settle a good marriage bargain is as seriously jeopardized as it would be had she eloped. Her tarnished reputation not only suggests that her father is too weak to control her and thus also vulnerable to pressure to lower his compensation demands, but also raises the possibility that some unknown third party has had sexual access to her and may at some point challenge her future husband's biological paternity to her offspring. Any man in the community who is distantly enough related to the daughter to be a potential suitor and who has had frequent social contact with her can challenge her virtue, thereby damaging her marriage value to such an extent that no respectable male will want to marry her.

At menarche, then, a woman's father confronts a dilemma: he can marry off his daughter as soon as possible, thereby foregoing any advantages that may accrue from waiting for the best political and economic conditions for a marriage; or he can delay the marriage settlement long past his daughter's menarche to obtain the best possible marriage bargain, thereby running the risk of seriously jeopardizing his bargaining position by lowering his daughter's marriage value through her seduction, elopement, or loss of reputation.

6. RITUAL SOLUTIONS TO THE MENARCHEAL DILEMMA

Although menarche creates a social dilemma in all societies, the tactics a father uses to resolve it vary cross-culturally, depending on the economic and political resources he has at his disposal to reward his consanguineal kinsmen for aiding in the protection of his daughter's marriage value. Fathers who belong to powerful and solidary corporate kin groups, called strong fraternal interest groups, differ fundamentally in their menarcheal strategies from those in societies where fraternal interest groups are weak or absent. Paige and Paige's analysis of ritual politics demonstrates that fraternal interest group strength is the crucial determining variable that explains worldwide variation in the response to each reproductive dilemma. Societies with strong fraternal interest groups are those with stable, valuable resources such as herds or land cultivated by plow or hoe agriculture. In these societies, resources are valuable enough to require defense by a large military force and to be used in rewarding and reinforcing the loyalty of kinsmen. The strong fraternal interest group held together by defense needs and the reinforcement of wealth can engage in explicit bargains that involve the transfer of valuable resources from one group to another, and can defend these bargains against default through the use of force or force threat. Societies in which fraternal interest groups are weak or absent are those with an economic base that produces either "unstable" resources, such as fish or buffalo, that are highly perishable and that fluctuate unpredictably, or resources of no value in enforcing kin group loyalty, such as the resources of hunter–gatherers. Such resources need not be protected by a large military force, and their low value and perishability make them of little use in reinforcing the loyalty of kinsmen. These conditions inhibit the formation of stable, powerful kin groups and make explicit contractual agreements unnecessary, since such agreements could not be enforced.

6.1. *Menarcheal Strategies of Strong Fraternal Interest Groups*

In a society where a father has the economic resources to command the unconditional allegiance of large numbers of kinsmen to protect his interests, he is far more able to thwart illicit attempts to seduce his daughter, tarnish her reputation, or otherwise reduce her value prior to a final marriage agreement. Not only is he better able to protect her from the advances of secret lovers or abductors but, if an elopement or seduction does succeed, he is in a much better position to retrieve her by force if necessary, collect immediate and full compensation for damages, or demand an immediate legal marriage contract. If the seducer is too poor to pay wealth compensation, the father may demand that any children produced as a consequence of the seduction be turned over to him to be offered along with his daughter in a more suitable future marriage. He may even choose to kill or maim the seducer without fear of reprisal. The most significant consequence of greater military power to protect a daughter's marriage is that a father becomes much less dependent on the timing of the daughter's menarche for negotiating the marriage. Instead of having to succumb to pressure and prevent his daughter's seduction by settling for a less profitable marriage contract with one of the lazy, poor, or otherwise unsuitable potential husbands that may comprise the small pool of eligibles at the time of her sexual maturity, he can afford to hold out, perhaps for years past menarche, until he finds a bargain that best suits his political and financial interests.

Of course, if a father is powerful enough to base his marriage decisions more on financial and political considerations and less on the unpredictable timing of his daughter's sexual development, in all likelihood he will be negotiating bargains with suitors who are equally powerful and equally interested in maximizing their own opportunities in a marriage bargain. An important suitor with powerful kinsmen may be unwilling to relinquish a sizeable amount of property for a bride without guarantees that the daughter will be able to produce large numbers of children during his lifetime. Instead of basing terms of a marriage contract on such a fallible index of actual fertility as the appearance of first menstruation, he may insist on making compensation contingent on more precise indicators such as the regular appearance of subsequent menstruations, or he may insist that compensation be paid in installments with each installment contingent on the birth of a viable offspring. A powerful suitor is equally concerned with a father's willingness to use forceful measures to protect his daughter's virginity prior to marriage; this demonstration of protective ability not only minimizes the chance that competing males will claim rights to future offspring, but also provides a valuable indicator of a father's ability and willingness to use any means necessary to fulfill other terms of an explicit marriage bargain.

Among strong fraternal interest groups, ritual politics focuses on monitoring the terms of bargains already negotiated and bargains yet to be finalized. *Ritual surveillance strategies* used by fathers to solve the dilemma of menarche include virginity control rituals, such as clitoridectomy and infibulation of a daughter before she reaches sexual maturity, and public virginity tests at the time the marriage is consummated. Female genital mutilations do not prevent the loss of virginity, seduction, or even premarital pregnancy, just as virginity tests at marriage do not provide proof of biological virginity. What these surveillance rituals do demonstrate, however, is the seriousness of a father's intent to fulfill his part of a marriage agreement, even at the risk of physical injury to his daughter's valuable reproductive organs, or her barrenness or death. While it can rarely be proved that the blood on the bridal sheets is the product of a broken hymen and not a broken vaginal suppository of pigeon's blood or simply the blood of menstruation, the test does provide an opportunity for all parties to the marriage agreement to demonstrate public consensus that any future attempts by competing claimants to gain rights to the woman's fertility will be ignored.

Genital mutilations and public virginity tests are statistically rare in tribal societies. With rare exceptions, however, they are tactics used by strong fraternal interest groups. The most common surveillance tactic used by fathers in strong fraternal interest groups is the vigilant monitoring of a daughter's social behavior to protect her sexual reputation and make seduction difficult if not impossible. A father may surround his growing daughter with guards or chaperons who follow her everywhere, tattoo her with marks designating her as already spoken for, insist that she veil herself from head to foot whenever she leaves the family dwelling, or simply insist that she remain completely secluded inside the household.

6.2. *Menarcheal Strategies of the Weak: Puberty Rites*

In societies in which fathers lack the political resources of a strong fraternal interest group to protect a daughter's marriage value, the dilemma produced by menarche is far more serious and the ritual tactics used to resolve it considerably less potent. Without the military force of a large group of loyal kinsmen, a man's newly fertile daughter is especially vulnerable to seduction and elopement. Suitors and their families are also too weak to finance an expensive marriage contract or to enforce contract compliance if, for example, a wife fails to bear children or runs away. Therefore a suitor can gain little by postponing a marriage too long after an eligible woman reaches menarche. In fact, it is to his distinct advantage to acquire rights to her as soon as possible, before competing suitors, equally weak but equally anxious to gain rights to her reproductive capacity, claim her first. Under such circumstances, a father's ability to complete a successful marriage bargain can be seriously compromised.

Weak fathers are, of course, just as anxious as powerful ones to contract the best possible marriage, but without the backing of a strong fraternal interest group they must rely on alternate sources of political power by developing a temporary community-based coalition to protect a daughter's virginity and holding that coalition together at least until a suitable marriage can be successfully negotiated. For this strategy to be effective, the coalition must be developed by the time the daughter begins to menstruate. In societies where fraternal interest groups are weak or absent, menarche takes on immense social significance. It not only marks the time at which a father must begin mobilizing his temporary political faction, but also determines how much time he has before he must settle a marriage. The time he has available depends entirely on the strength of his temporary faction and his own ability to persuade that coalition to protect his interests.

The public ceremonies, feasting, and special gift exchanges associated with menarche thus can be interpreted as *mobilization rituals*. These public rituals are implicit bargaining tactics by which a father attempts to develop enough community support to protect his daughter's marriage value when more potent sources of influence are not available. As social mobilization rituals, menarcheal ceremonies are attempts to enlist supporters by showing them the power of the ceremony's sponsor, the girl's father, and persuading them of his generosity, his popularity, and the justice of his cause. By accepting his hospitality, community members implicitly renounce any illicit claims on his daughter. The extent of community participation and enthusiasm at the ritual also allows the father an opportunity to gauge the amount of political support available. Finally, giving the ceremony is a father's statement that he controls the rights to his daughter and a demonstration to potential seducers that he has many allies in the community who will support him if those rights need to be defended.

If a father is too poor to give a public ceremony, he can at least attempt to make his daughter as inaccessible as possible, for example, by barricading her in a seclusion hut and suggesting dire supernatural consequences awaiting any man who dares touch her. While such strategies are not as impressive as a public feast, they may succeed in discouraging some potential seducers long enough to settle a marriage. If all else fails, a third strategy is to arrange for a daughter's seduction to occur in public and to proclaim the seducer as her legal husband. This may be a convenient method for forcing a marriage of a daughter who is particularly promiscuous, unattractive, or otherwise difficult to marry.

There is abundant ethnographic support for this interpretation of menarcheal ceremonies in tribal societies with weak fraternal interest groups. Opler's (1941) lengthy interview with an informant from a North American foraging society, the Chiricahua Apache, shows clearly how a father can gauge the amount of community support he will receive once his daughter attains sexual maturity by the amount of assistance he receives from friends and relatives during the year-long preparation for the menarche ceremony. Enlisting support is no easy matter and usually requires a considerable amount of cajoling and bargaining. Among the Chiricahua, the menarcheal ceremony is the most important of all public rituals in the society, and numerous friends and relatives with special skills must provide assistance in order for the ceremony to succeed. First, the father must find an older woman who will guide the daughter through the ceremony proceedings. "This woman must be personally approached and asked to lend her help, and she may even refuse to participate. She must always be rewarded if she does perform this function" (Opler, 1941, p. 84). Next, a man must be found who will promise to supervise the entire dramatic sequence of the ritual, a man with the expertise to direct an elaborate stage play. In return for his assistance, the father promises a series of gift exchanges that may continue long after the ceremony has ended. Close relatives must also be persuaded to make elaborate dresses out of buckskin; this means that hunters must be enlisted to donate some of their skins from hunting expeditions. Dancers and mask makers must also be recruited. The Chiricahua informant, whose father was a mask maker, describes the constant pleading and urging required to convince all these crucial participants to commit themselves. All the relatives and friends who provide the father with the supplies, time, and energy necessary to prepare a menarcheal ceremony can be counted as members of a temporary political coalition supporting his claims to his daughter, his right to arrange a legitimate marriage bargain, and his rights to thwart the efforts of anyone who may dispute his claims at the time of menarche.

No amount of preparatory assistance enlisted by the father can counteract the political implications of poor attendance at the ceremony itself. Numerous problems can arise during the months of preparation, particularly if a father pushes too hard, makes false promises, or otherwise creates animosity. Turnbull (1962) observed a menarcheal ceremony among the Mbuti pygmies of Africa that was a dismal failure. The father sponsoring the ceremony was not very well liked in the community, so when the time came for the ritual to begin, few people attended and eventually even these began to show more interest in returning to their daily tasks than in participating in the festivities. No betrothals from eligible men were offered, and eventually the two menarcheal daughters for whom the ritual was being held were forced to wander from one community to the next begging for proposals. Word of the ceremony's failure had spread, however, and no young eligibles were willing to marry the daughters. As a last resort, one of the daughters was given in marriage as part of a sister exchange arrangement with a male relative.

7. Menarcheal Responses and Fraternal Interest Group Strength: Empirical Evidence

There is considerable empirical support for this social–psychological interpretation of menarcheal responses in tribal societies. The theory argues, first, that menarcheal ceremonies are mobilization rituals which should be most likely to be celebrated among societies in which fraternal interest groups are either weak or absent. These societies, in turn, should be characterized by subsistence economies that do not provide resources of enough political value to reinforce the allegiance of a large and loyal group of kinsmen, specifically societies with hunting–gathering, fishing, buffalo hunting, and shifting agriculture economies, all of which provide only unstable or low value resources. Second, the theory proposes that rituals such as genital mutilations and public virginity tests that mark the beginning and end of "social puberty" are surveillance rituals and should be most characteristic of strong fraternal interest groups. Among such groups, explicit contractual agreements over rights to a daughter's fertility can be made and defended because an economic base of stable, valuable resources, such as large herds of animals in pastoral economies and highly productive lands in hoe and plow agricultural economies, can reinforce the allegiance of a large and powerful group of kinsmen. In brief, the strategy of the weak is to engage in ritual bargaining at the onset of menstruation, while the strategy of the strong is to protect explicit bargains over rights to a daughter by demonstrating an ability to protect her sexual and social reputation prior to marriage.

The causal linkages between menarcheal ceremonies, fraternal interest group strength, and resource base were tested on a carefully selected sample of 108 tribal societies (see Paige and Paige, 1981, Chapters 2 and 3, for a detailed description of the empirical procedures). As predicted, menarcheal ceremonies were significantly more likely to occur in societies without strong fraternal interest groups ($r = 0.44$) and societies with unstable or low-value economic resources ($r = 0.46$). Since there was a very strong positive association between fraternal interest group strength and resource base ($r = 0.66$), the unique effect of each predictor variable was ascertained by calculating the standardized beta coefficients when the presence or absence of menarcheal ceremonies was regressed simultaneously onto resource base and fraternal interest group strength. The results showed that each variable had a substantial effect on menarcheal ceremonies independent of each other ($B_{resources} = 0.30$, $B_{strength} = 0.24$). Their additive effect was expressed by the large multiple correlation of 0.50, demonstrating that 25% of the variance in menarcheal ceremonies was accounted for by these two variables alone. Empirical tests of alternative theories of the cross-cultural distribution of female puberty rites showed clearly that the social exchange model outlined here has considerably greater predictive power than any other model in the social science literature.

The association between surveillance rituals during social puberty, strong fraternal interest groups, and a high-value resource base was tested by this author on a different cross-cultural sample of 151 tribal and peasant societies as part of a larger study of chastity control (see Paige, 1978, 1980). In this sample, 37 societies performed either genital mutilations ($n = 7$), public virginity tests ($n = 23$), or both ($n = 7$). These two rituals were combined into a single measure of virginity surveillance and correlated with the two predictor variables. As predicted, virginity surveillance rituals were significantly more likely to occur in strong fraternal interest groups ($r = 0.53$) and societies with a valuable resource base ($r = 0.43$). Since the two predictor variables are highly correlated ($r = 0.52$), the unique effect of each on surveillance rituals was calculated. Each variable had a strong independent effect on surveillance rituals ($B_{resources} = 0.21$; $B_{strength} = 0.43$), and the multiple correlation of 0.56 is sizeable. The theoretical model thus accounts for 31.6% of the worldwide variation in the practice of ritual surveillance when only two of such practices are considered.

8. IMPLICATIONS FOR THE STUDY OF MENARCHEAL RESPONSES IN AMERICA

The dearth of research on the pattern of social responses to female puberty in the United States is surprising given the immense body of sociological and psychological research on female psychosexual development, marriage, mate selection, and the family. The chapters on the social aspects of female puberty contained in this volume represent a new interest in the developmental process by which American women learn to conform to societal standards of premarital modesty, the process by which these standards become internalized in both sexes, and the relationship between biological puberty and social behavior. According to this research, it seems that social expectations about appropriate "nubile" behavior are clearly articulated prior to menarche, but the way in which these expectations become transformed into changed social behavior is not clear.

Neither is there a systematic attempt to explain intrasocietal variations in parental concern with a menarcheal daughter's sexual and social reputation in an urban technological society. An extension of the social exchange theory of menarcheal responses in preindustrial society would suggest that the success of explicit and implicit parental strategies to monitor daughters' behavior would depend on parents' relative socioeconomic status. In families with the greatest economic assets, as in the upper socioeconomic classes, the loyalty of children can be encouraged through promises of inheritance of wealth and social position. The wealthier the family, the greater the opportunity to engage in structural surveillance of nubile daughters through enrollment in class- and sex-segregated educational institutions throughout puberty and adolescence, residence in class-segregated communities, and even participation in class-segregated leisure activities, so that the daughter's choice of a future husband is limited to a pool of eligibles who are maximally homogeneous and similar in ascriptive status to the daughter's family. Among the wealthiest classes, where the preoccupation with mate selection is most intense, nubility ceremonies are celebrated which are closely analogous to the menarcheal ceremonies of preindustrial societies. It is possible to find similarities between American debutante balls and the tali-tying rites of the Nayar (Gough, 1955). In each case, the ceremonies publicly demonstrate the marriageability of a nubile daughter as well as her father's wealth and prestige in being able to sponsor such an expensive ritual. Debutante balls do not coincide with menarche, but they do coincide with the age at which daughters become legally adult and increasingly independent of the family, and thus more likely to exert individual control over mate selection despite a parent's wishes. As in tali-tying rites, during the debutante balls, each daughter is escorted by a family-approved male of the appropriate class who could in fact represent the pool of eligibles for marriage. Once the ball has occurred, the women who have taken part are recognized publicly as belonging to the appropriate social class and therefore recognized as desirable mates for males from the same class.

Families with fewer resources to devote to the surveillance of wives and children are just as anxious to ensure successful marriages and may resort to equally elaborate strategies to monitor nubile daughters. The issue of female premarital virginity is still an important one, as numerous opinion surveys indicate. A sizeable proportion of the population believes in the double standard—female virginity before marriage as an ideal, but not male virginity—although there is some indication that this attitude is changing. If families do not have the considerable resources to monitor daughters through class or sex segregation during puberty and adolescence, they can attempt to resort to the alternate strategy of placing daughters under the care of parent substitutes in the form of seg-regated living quarters in college, such as sororities. Such assistance by educational institutions is widespread, especially in those public insti-tutions where endogamous mate selection by women is most likely to be threatened. The development of the sorority in public land grant uni-versities as a mechanism for inhibiting hypogamy among middle- and upper-middle-class families has been investigated by Scott (1965). He shows how the growth of the sorority system in land grant universities coincided with the increase in enrollment of women, mostly middle class, in colleges where male students represented a much broader range of ascriptive statuses. To ensure that nubile daughters did not select hus-bands of lower status, sororities were instituted to maintain rigid sur-veillance over women's social activities and dating partners through physical segregation and a social life carefully organized by adults. Dat-ing was rigidly monitored through "exchanges" with fraternity and professional school males, and social commitments to these males in the form of "pinnings" and engagements were the focus of elaborate public ceremonies. Rules regarding behavior such as entering and leaving the sorority house were strict, with sign-in and sign-out procedures so that sorority "mothers" could keep careful records on the daily whereabouts of each woman.

Just as in preindustrial societies, families with no important eco-nomic resources or social prestige are considerably less successful in monitoring nubile daughters to ensure a successful marriage. National surveys have indicated a strong positive association between socioeco-nomic-status origins and premarital virginity and age of sexual initiation, with the lower-status women being initiated earlier and prior to marriage.

That surveillance mechanisms by the middle and upper classes may be successful in a society so heterogeneous with regard to class and eth-nic groups is suggested by studies of marriage mobility, which show that in the aggregate women are considerably more likely to marry men of the same ascriptive status—estimated by occupational prestige—as their fathers than men either below or above their fathers' status. While parents may aspire to hypergamous mating, these data suggest that such aspirations are not often realized. On the other hand, hypogamy is usually successfully inhibited.

Nubility has psychological consequences among American women, and ritual monitoring of reputation and virginity to maximize appropriate mate selection characterizes American society as well as other world societies. Public demonstrations of a daughter's ascriptive status through organized and elaborate debutante ceremonies or the structural segregation of women through the institution of sororities and sex-segregated education can certainly be interpreted as familial mechanisms for monitoring mate choice, just as menarcheal ceremonies, virginity tests, and female circumcision attempt to accomplish this aim in preindustrial societies.

References

Abraham, K. Manifestations of the female castration complex. In K. Abraham (Ed.), *Selected papers on psychoanalysis*. London: Hogarth Press, 1948.

Blackwood, B. *Both sides of Buka Passage*. Oxford: Clarendon Press, 1935.

Bonaparte, M. *Female sexuality*. New York: International Universities Press, 1953.

Brown, J. K. A cross-cultural study of female initiation rites. *American Anthropologist*, 1963, 65, 837–853.

Chadwick, H. The psychological effects of menstruation. *Nervous and Mental Diseases Monograph Series*, 1952, 56.

Coon, C. Tribes of the Rif. *Harvard African Studies*, 1931, 9.

Deutsch, H. *Psychology of women*. Vol. 1. New York: Grune and Stratton, 1944.

Gough, K. E. Female initiation rites on the Malabar Coast. *Journal of the Royal Anthropological Institute*, 1955, 85, 45–80.

Hogbin, H. I. Marriage in Wogeo, New Guinea. *Oceania*, 1944, 16, 324–352.

Harner, M. *The Jivaro*. Garden City, NY: Anchor Books, 1972.

Mair, L. *Marriage*. Harmondsworth, England: Penguin Books, 1971.

Man, E. H. On the aboriginal inhabitants of the Andaman Islands. *Journal of the Anthropological Institute of Great Britain and Ireland*, 1877, 12, 79.

Nag, M. Factors affecting human fertility in nonindustrial societies: A cross-cultural study. *Yale University Publications in Anthropology*, 1962, 66, 104.

Opler, M. *An Apache life-way*. Chicago: University of Chicago Press, 1941.

Paige, K. E. Codes of honor, shame, and virginity: A theoretical framework. Paper presented at the Ninth World Congress of Sociology, Uppsala, Sweden, August, 1978.

Paige, K. E. Female genital mutilations: World patterns and the case of Egypt. Paper presented at the American Anthropological Association Convention, Washington, D.C., November, 1980.

Paige, K. E., and Paige, J. M. *The politics of reproductive ritual*. Berkeley: University of California Press, 1981.

Powdermaker, H. *Life in Lesu.* New York: W. W. Norton, 1971.

Richards, A. Some types of family structure amongst the Central Bantu. In A. R. Radcliffe-Brown and C. D. Forde (Eds.), *African systems of kinship and marriage.* London: Oxford University Press, 1950.

Richards, A. *Chisungu.* New York: Grove Press, 1956.

Scott, J. F. The American college sorority. *American Sociological Review,* 1965, *30,* 514–527.

Seligman, C. G., and Seligman, B. Z. *Pagan tribes of the Nilotic Sudan.* London: George Routledge and Kegan Paul, 1932.

Turnbull, C. *The forest people.* New York: Simon and Schuster, 1962.

The Study of Puberty
Integrated Biopsychosocial Perspectives

Chapter 14

Future Directions in Research

Renee R. Jenkins

1. Introduction

The biosocial approach to the study of adolescent development offers a wealth of opportunities for collaboration between clinical specialists and social and behavioral scientists. This entire volume is based on that premise and represents a major step in that direction. The emergence of behavioral endocrinology as a discipline marks the conjoint interests of psychologists and endocrinologists in both the study of animals and humans (Beach, 1975). In pediatrics and adolescent medicine, the widespread use of Tanner (1962) staging of secondary sex characteristics sets the stage for the study of physiological and psychological correlates and the effects of pubertal growth on psychosocial functioning. In the clinical realm, psychiatrists are able to identify the interplay of maturational and behavioral events on a continuum from normative variation to psychopathologic responses.

In exploring the relationship between psychologic/adolescent and physiologic/pubertal development, a focus of interest for many disciplines, several issues must be considered. Although some issues are confounded by involving more than one discipline, most invite the cooperative efforts of various disciplines. Such issues concern the theory, methodology, population samples, and communication across disciplines. First, by setting forth theoretical constructs that have clear applicability to more than one discipline, a frame of reference is provided for input from each of these disciplines. Second, by looking across one's professional field and adapting useful methodologic tools from others,

Renee R. Jenkins • Department of Pediatrics and Child Health, College of Medicine, Howard University, Washington, D.C. 20060.

studies will become more comparable, thus reducing artifactual inconsistencies. Findings are strengthened when supportive evidence is provided in studies coming from more than one discipline. Third, comparability would be further enhanced if population samples were clearly identified by commonly used social indices. The temptation to generalize findings to socially dissimilar groups would be discouraged. This is particularly evident when one attempts to apply generalized findings to minority populations. The temptation is intensified in situations where data for that minority are sparse or where available data are unsatisfactory for methodological reasons.

Finally, interdisciplinary communication is most likely to be enhanced by research collaboration. Limited research dollars and directives from funding sources are strong encouragements for such unions. The bottom line is to answer research questions that are beneficial to any professional in pursuit of a clearer understanding of the developing individual.

This chapter explores some of the salient issues that provide an integrated biopsychosocial perspective to the study of puberty.

2. THEORETICAL ISSUES

The biosocial model for adolescent development is rooted in theories which attempt to identify the multiple influences on an individual's behavior and explore their interrelationships. One theory which is applicable to all stages of human development is the systemic approach (Shuster, 1980). This approach considers the individual from a holistic perspective which identifies the person as a system within a structure of systems (Figure 1). The hierarchy includes suprasystems such as the culture and communities to which the individual belongs, systems such as the family, and subsystems within each component system. Each system has as its boundaries the systems above and below it on the hierarchical scale (although overlap and interrelationships across systems exist). The biophysical, social, spiritual, cognitive, and affective (emotional) domains are subsystems, as shown in Figure 1. This theory does not propose to explain the interrelationships among systems or domains, but recognizes the dynamic quality of human functioning and describes the context in which the individual functions.

The biophysical, cognitive, and social subsystems are recognizable in theories which are specific to adolescent development. John Hill (1980) proposed a framework for conceptualizing adolescent development (Figure 2). The systems are identified as primary changes which are

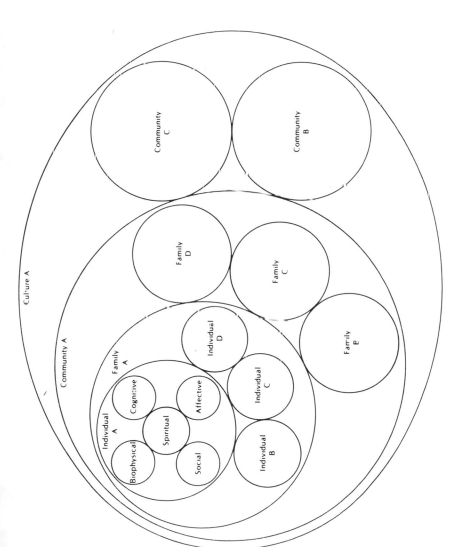

Figure 1. Hierarchy of social systems, suprasystems, and subsystems affecting the behavior of the individual as a system. (From C. S. Schuster and S. S. Ashburn. *The process of human development: A holistic approach.* Boston: Little, Brown, and Company, 1980. Used with permission.)

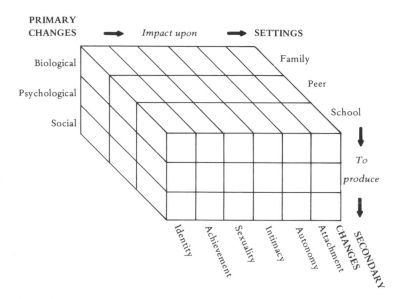

Figure 2. The framework of early adolescence. (From J. P. Hill. *Understanding early adolescence: A framework.* Carrboro, N.C.: Center for Early Adolescence, 1980. Used with permission.)

fundamental to all individuals moving through adolescence. Puberty is the biological change. Changes in reasoning and cognition represent psychological changes. The change in societal norms for behavior for this age group constitutes the social change. The psychosocial issues of adolescent development, identity, achievement, sexuality, intimacy, autonomy, and attachment are labeled secondary changes. The primary changes occur before the secondary changes and play a major role in their emergence. For example, puberty brings with it the need for one to alter self-concept and is a major determinant of the adolescent identity crisis according to Erikson (1968). The impact of all of these changes occur within specific settings and are modified by them. The major settings are family, school, and peers. Another system that influences adolescent development which has not been formally placed in Hill's theoretical schema involves the categories of gender, social class and ethnic background. These factors should not be considered afterthoughts as they are strong modifiers in the case of gender or potentially strong modifiers in the case of social class and ethnicity.

Hill's framework places adolescent issues in the context of the whole individual and is consequently rather general. Others have focused more specifically on the complexities of the specific hormonal–behavioral interactions. Petersen and Taylor (1980) propose two possible models for hormonal–behavioral interactions: (1) a direct effect model, using physiologic evidence to support psychologic changes or, (2) a mediated effect model, noting a complex chain of intervening variables which include social and cultural influences. Research evidence supports the mediated effect model according to these authors.

There are obviously other theoretical frameworks to consider. The organization and dynamics of these theories may vary but the components are almost always the same including biological, psychological, and social components. The expansion of the biological component to a continuum from normalcy to dysfunction and the importance of variability within normal samples is important. It is also a link connecting clinical research to theoretical social and behavioral research and to further applicability of research findings. What is still lacking however in these theoretical concepts is the specific effect of one component on another. The specific effect of biologic maturation on psychosocial development is of greatest concern when addressing the adolescent. Many chapters in this book addressed this issue. (See, for example, Petersen, Chapter 9; Simmons, Blyth, and McKinney, Chapter 11; Brooks-Gunn and Ruble, Chapter 8; and Tobin-Richards, Boxer, and Petersen, Chapter 7.)

3. METHODOLOGIC ISSUES

The research on the impact of puberty of psychosocial development in girls has produced conflicting and inconsistent findings. Differences in the populations sampled and methodologic differences appear to account for some of the inconsistencies. The methods of assessing pubertal status vary as does the timing of the data collection relative to pubertal status. Longitudinal studies have been tremendously helpful in pointing out the impact of some of these variations. The psychosocial variables most often used in pubertal status studies are personality traits, social status, cognitive differences, and sexual behavior (Chilman, 1963; Jones and Mussen, 1958; Kinsey, Pomeroy, and Martin, 1948; Petersen and Wittig, 1979; Simmons, Blyth, Van Cleave, and Bush, 1979; Stone and Barker, 1939).

3.1. Assessing Pubertal Maturation

The onset of puberty can be determined clinically by the appearance of secondary sex characteristics. Elevation of specific serum hormones as measured by radioimmunoassay techniques may precede clinical evidence of physical maturation. If one attempts to relate any psychologic change to the onset or timing of puberty, documentation of these changes may represent an immense methodologic problem. The selection of a suitable pubertal measure should be consistent with the hypothesis being tested. For example, Tanner (1962) staging may be an appropriate measure for looking at body image changes.

There is a great temptation to overgeneralize one's conclusions especially regarding hormonal changes and behavior. Even in the presence of significant correlations between endocrinologic and behavioral measures, the mediating mechanisms involved may not be identifiable. The assumption that serum changes in hormonal levels have immediate neurohormonal effects is not well substantiated. With rapidly improving technologic capability, more information on timing and specific mediating mechanisms may be available in the near future.

Given the current state of the art, more consistent criteria for pubertal status could be used for research purposes. Previous studies have used bone age, pre- or postmenarcheal status and menarcheal age (Faust, 1960; Jones and Mussen, 1958; Simmons et al., 1979; Stone and Barker, 1939). More recently Tanner's staging criteria have been used to examine psychosocial relationships (Frank and Cohen, 1979; Gross and Duke, 1980). Tanner's staging has also been used for testing covariation with hormonal measures (Apter, 1980; Gupta, 1975; Nankin, Sperling, Kenny, Drash, and Troen, 1974). Two investigative groups have reported correlations from 0.60 to 0.91 between self-rating of sexual maturity and physician examination of Tanner stages (Duke, Litt, and Gross, 1980; Morris and Udry, 1980). That self-reports are quite accurate reflections of physical maturity obviates the need to submit study participants to a physical examination. The necessity of an examination has been a major problem in studies conducted in school or home settings which the availability of a standardized self-report sexual maturation score eliminates.

The advantage of the self-report staging technique over menarcheal determination is that menarche occurs later in the pubertal process. Menarche most often occurs at breast Stage 4, and there is some evidence that hormonal levels rise most rapidly from Stage 2 to 4, then plateau at Stage 4 (Apter, 1980; Nankin et al., 1974). In addition, the psychologic correlates to breast development are much less frequently explored than menarche (Benedek, Pozanski, and Mason, 1979). The opportunity to include this physical change as a variable is enhanced with the use of Tanner's criteria. The possibility also exists that each of these pubertal changes may have different social meanings and psychological impact on girls as they mature. Hence, the choice to use menarche, sex maturation scoring, and other physical parameters in combination may be most profitable in sorting out separate effects.

3.2. *Assessing Psychosocial Maturation*

The biologic markers of pubertal status can be measured more objectively than measures of adolescent psychosocial maturation. In clinical assessment, early, middle, and late adolescence are determined by interviews which assess the patient's level of completion for specific developmental tasks (Zakus, Cooper, Leff, and Moore, 1980). A well-standardized research tool which incorporates these global tasks has not been developed for clinical use. A rating scale for this purpose has been proposed but not standardized (Magrab, Shearin, Bronheim, Jones, and Ahmen, 1981). In lieu of such a global assessment, standardized measures of anxiety, self-esteem, self-concept, and other personality traits have been used to assess relationships between pubertal maturation and psychologic development (Garwood and Allen, 1979; Jones and Mussen, 1958; Simmons et al., 1979).

One such measure is the Offer Self-Image Questionnaire (OSIQ) which assesses adolescent self-concept. Eleven separate scales representing an aspect of the adolescent's self-concept are organized under five dimensions: the psychological, social, sexual, family, and coping selves. The questionnaire was not constructed for the purpose of developmental rating and there are very few differences in age group ratings. Younger girls scored lower on coping and sexual self items, rating themselves as sicker and not in agreement that sex is a pleasurable experience (Offer, Ostrov, and Howard, 1981). Using the Offer Self-Image Questionnaire in a sample of eight twins, Frank and Cohen (1979) noted early pubertal children rated below all other pubertal levels on self- and body image as well as in the desire to take responsibility and plan ahead. There were no differences between pubertal level groupings for locus of control scores. Hence, in this very small study the OSIQ distinguished between early and advanced psychosocial development in some areas but not others.

3.3. *Longitudinal Studies*

Most of the research which captures the progressional quality of an individual's developmental process comes from longitudinal studies. The strength of a longitudinal design is primarily the ability to chronicle events as they occur for later analysis of patterns of developmental change and function. In a recent review, Livson and Peskin (1980) addressed the problems and strengths of longitudinal research on the adolescent. They identified over 70 studies which explored changes in identity formation, sex role identification, separation and autonomy, and environment and stress. These areas represent major psychosocial issues for the developing adolescent. One of the most interesting findings relative to the impact of pubertal timing to psychological correlates was the shift in advantages of late maturers compared to early maturers over time. The disadvantages that early-maturing girls suffered in teen years were not persistent and by age 30, early maturers were psychologically healthier than later maturers (Peskin, 1973). In the chapter by Tobin-Richards et al. (Chapter 7), the issues of what constitutes an earlier maturer and the relativity of maturation are raised, which speaks to the question of long-range effects. There is no alternative to a longitudinal design for separating permanent and transient effects from one developmental stage to the next.

4. LIMITATIONS OF POPULATION SAMPLES

Most available studies on puberty and psychosocial correlates are either composed of predominantly white populations, most often middle-class, or make no identification of the race or social class of the samples as though these were unimportant variables (Faust, 1960; Frank and Cohen, 1979; Jones and Mussen, 1958; Peskin, 1973; Stone and Barker, 1939). Referring back to the theoretical issues discussed earlier, whether one considers the family and community as suprasystems, as in Schuster's (1980) approach, or ethnicity and social class as additional categories within John Hill's (1980) early adolescent framework, these variables have a major impact on the interaction of the biology and psychology. There are advantages to study samples that include a more representative population as well as advantages to the in-depth study of very specific populations. The crux of the issue is the interpretation of findings and the tendency to overgeneralize conclusions.

The limited availability of data on pubertal or adolescent psychosocial development for blacks is in direct contrast to the number of publications on adolescent sexuality which include blacks in the sample population (Evans, Selstad, and Welcher, 1976; Finkel and Finkel, 1975; Goldfarb, Mumford, Schum, Smith, Flowers, and Schum, 1977; Russ-Eft, Sprenger, and Beever, 1979; Sorensen, 1973; Zelnik, 1979; Zelnik and Kantner, 1980). Data from the National Center for Health Statistics is almost always provided for whites and nonwhites (which have been predominantly black). With the increasing Hispanic population in the United States, estimated to be the largest minority by the mid-1980s

(Martinez, 1981), it will be interesting to observe the change in statistical reporting of U.S. data. (In the past, for example, Hispanics were included in the census and health statistics data base as whites; today, they are considered a separate group.) However, a look at the current information on blacks illustrates the following omissions.

4.1. Black Female Pubertal Development

Using the National Health Survey Data for 12- to 17-year-olds to examine sexual maturation in a nationwide representative sample, more advanced secondary sex characteristics were found for black girls as compared to white girls (Harlan, Harlan, and Grillo, 1980). Differences based on menarcheal and skeletal maturation comparisons were reported. However, it has been stated that different measures of pubertal development are, to a considerable degree, independent of each other. Unfortunately, consistent maturation staging was not conducted on girls less than age 12 in the health survey. Hence, data for onset of timing of puberty for American black girls are incomplete and comparisons between early physical developments could not be made.

In a biracial sample of children aged 5–14 years, black girls were observed to develop secondary sex characteristics at a younger age than white girls, with a mean age of 10.13 ± 0.25 for 50% transition between Tanner Stages 1 and 2 (Foster, Voors, Webber, Frerichs, and Berenson, 1977). In contrast to previously reported U.S. data on age of menarche (MacMahon, 1973), white girls menstruated earlier (mean age 12.69 years) than black girls (mean age 12.83 years). This sample resided in a semirural community and a significant proportion of the population was below the poverty level. There is some evidence that height and weight vary by income level (Schutte, 1980), although Harlan et al. (1980) did not find such a relationship for sexual maturation.

Hormonal studies for biracial American populations are limited and inconclusive. Nankin et al. (1974) found that pubertal black females had higher follicle-stimulating hormone (FSH) titers than pubertal white females. No consistent differences in luteinizing hormone (LH) levels were found. The authors acknowledged the limitations of their findings due to the relatively small sample and the overlap of gonadotropin levels at all stages of puberty.

4.2. Psychosocial Development of Black Adolescents

Black scholars have written detailed critiques noting the scarcity of literature on the development of normal black adolescents (Scott and

McKendry, 1977; Taylor, 1976). They decry the studies of the 1940s and 1950s in which black youth were portrayed as pathologically maladjusted as a result of prejudice and discrimination. Matriarchal family structures were linked to sex role conflict, low self-esteem, and poor academic performance for the young people in those families. Family strengths such as strong kinship bonds, strong work orientation, adaptability of family roles, and strong religious orientation (Hill, 1971) were rarely offered as molders of strong self-concepts. A great deal of the work on identity formation was concentrated on low-income blacks (Hauser, 1971), but often these findings were generalized by others to be true for all black youth.

In the early 1970s the concept of the disadvantaged, self-deprecating adolescent was challenged. Rosenberg and Simmons (1972) and Powell and Fuller (1973) demonstrated higher self-esteem in black children as compared to whites, using different self-esteem measures. Ladner's (1971) descriptive study of low-income girls in St. Louis found no evidence of young women with low self-esteem or severely damaged psyches, but rather an abundance of resourcefulness and hope for improving their lives. This study speaks to the psychosocial issues of adolescence, although it was not specifically designed to do so. Autonomy, sexuality, intimacy, and achievement were themes, as Ladner described patterns of declaring oneself an adult in the family home, of the importance of premarital intercourse, of close peer relationships, and of the vision of education as a path to upward mobility. In summary, although not an exhaustive review of adolescent psychosocial development in blacks, this discussion underscores the trends in the perspectives of researchers and suggests the need for a better balance of the examination and analysis of maturing experiences for young black people.

5. INTERDISCIPLINARY COLLABORATION AND COMMUNICATION

A wide range of interests and abilities exist between the varied disciplines, offering insight into the biologic, psychologic, and social interaction beginning at puberty and moving into adolescence. From the sociologist, one is reminded that basic demographic descriptions of the populations studied are crucial variables. Age, sex, socioeconomic status, and race are primary indices of social status. From the anthropologist, we are made more aware of the value of in-depth studies of single cultures as well as cross-cultural studies which observe variations in adaptations to the pubertal experience. The clinical specialties offer biological and hormonal measurements with increasing sensitivity and greater reliability. The psychologists often have taken the lead in placing many of these issues in a conceptual framework, looking at cognitive skills, sex roles, and group behavior. A professional may cross into another discipline in pursuit of knowledge, but a greater emphasis on collaboration between disciplinary fields is needed. Theoretical and methodologic issues that may serve as foci of cooperative efforts have been outlined in this chapter and in this volume. The potential advantages for project implementation and evaluation were not even touched upon. The practical application of research findings have relevance to many disciplines, particularly education, clinical psychology, social work, and clinical medicine.

The Institute of Medicine Conference on Adolescent Health and Behavior (1978) stressed the importance of recognizing variation in adolescent developmental rates for planning services and determining health policies for young people. Many of the "health-compromising" behaviors such as experimentation with cigarettes, alcohol, and sex serve important developmental functions. Appropriate responses to these behaviors may be to concentrate on avoiding associated adverse outcomes rather than to prevent their initiation. At the program level, being aware of the dysynchronous occurrence of physical and cognitive maturation, clinicians will not assume that a physically mature young woman is necessarily beyond the stage of concrete thinking. Hence, a counseling strategy that stresses futuristic rewards may not be effective (Blum and Goldhagen, 1980). Clinicians, particularly those in adolescent medicine, are distinctly aware of the usefulness of a developmental approach.

6. Conclusion

The barriers to communication and cross-fertilization of research ideas between clinicians and social/behavioral scientists may be conquered. The Conference on Female Puberty held at The Salk Institute and this publication stand as testimony to that statement. The appearance of new journals and greater familiarity with older journals with a multidisciplinary readership produce an ongoing method of exchange. A move toward more readable, less speciality-enshrined language is the key to this sharing process. As clearly lamented by a clinical colleague during a social science presentation, "Speak to me in English!" The possibilities for expanding on research collaboration between clinical medicine and social/behavioral scientists are worth all efforts to this end in pursuit of further definition of the biopsychosocial impact of puberty.

In the words of Katchadourian (1977),

> Ultimately, understanding the developmental events of the second decade, or for that matter any other decade of life, depends on our comprehension of the interactional patterns between biological and psychosocial variables. (p. vii)

ACKNOWLEDGMENTS. Sincere appreciation for organizational suggestions and editorial comments is expressed to June Dobbs Butts, Elizabeth McAnarney, Melvin E. Jenkins, and the talented women who edited this book. Special gratitude is given to my husband, Charles Woodard, for his unselfish support of my first publication of this magnitude.

REFERENCES

Apter, D. Serum steroids and pituitary hormones in female puberty: A partly longitudinal study. *Clinical Endocrinology*, 1980, *12*, 107–120.

Beach, F. A. Behavioral endocrinology: An emerging discipline. *American Scientist*, 1975, *63*, 178–187.

Benedek, E. P., Pozanski, E., and Mason, S. A note on the female adolescent's psychologic reactions to breast development. *Journal of the American Academy of Child Psychiatry*, 1979, *18*, 537–545.

Blum, R. W., and Goldhagen, J. Teenage pregnancy in perspective. *Clinical Pediatrics*, 1980, *20*, 335–340.

Chilman, C. The educational–vocational aspirations and behaviors of unmarried and married undergraduates at Syracuse University. Unpublished study, 1963.

Duke, P. M., Litt, I. F., and Gross, R. T. Adolescent's self-assessment of sexual maturation. *Pediatrics*, 1980, *66*, 918–920.

Erikson, E. H. *Identity: Youth and crisis*. New York: W. W. Norton, 1968.

Evans, J., Selstad, G., and Welcher, W. Teenagers: Fertility control behavior and attitudes before and after abortion, childbearing or negative pregnancy test. *Family Planning Perspectives*, 1976, *8*, 192–200.

Faust, M. S. Developmental maturity as a determinant of prestidge in adolescent girls. *Child Development*, 1960, *31*, 173–184.

Finkel, M., and Finkel, D. Sexual and contraceptive knowledge, attitudes, and behavior of male adolescents. *Family Planning Perspectives*, 1975, *7*, 256–260.

Foster, T. A., Voors, A. W., Webber, L. S., Frerichs, R. R., and Berenson, G. S. Anthropometric and maturational measurements of children, ages 5–14 years in a biracial community—the Bogalusa Heart Study. *The American Journal of Clinical Nutrition*, 1977, *30*, 582–591.

Frank, R. A., and Cohen, D. J. Psychosocial concomitants of biologic maturation in preadolescence. *American Journal of Psychiatry*, 1979, *136*, 1518–1524.

Garwood, S. G., and Allen, L. Self-concept and identified problem differences between pre- and post-menarcheal adolescents. *Journal of Clinical Psychology*, 1979, *35*, 528–537.

Goldfarb, J. L, Mumford, D. M., Schum, D. A., Smith, P. B., Flowers, C., and Schum, C. An attempt to detect pregnancy susceptibility in indigent adolescent girls. *The Journal of Youth and Adolescence*, 1977, *6*, 127–145.

Gross, R. T. and Duke, P. M. The effect of early versus late physical maturation on adolescent behavior. *The Pediatric Clinics of North America,* 1980, *27,* 71–77.

Gupta, D. Changes in the gonadal and adrenal steriod patterns during puberty. *Clinics in Endocrinology and Metabolism,* 1975, *4,* 27–56.

Harlan, W. R., Harlan, E. A., and Grillo, P. Secondary sex characteristics of girls 12 to 17 years of age: The U.S. Health Examination Survey. *The Journal of Pediatrics,* 1980, *96,* 1074–1078.

Hauser, S. T. *Black and white identity formation, Studies in the psychosocial development of lower socioeconomic class adolescent boys.* New York: Wiley-Interscience, 1971.

Hill, J. P. *Understanding early adolescence: A framework.* Carrboro, N.C.: Center for Early Adolescence, 1980.

Hill, R. *The strengths of black families.* New York: Emerson Hall, 1971.

Institute of Medicine. *A conference summary. Adolescent health and behavior.* Washington, D.C.: National Academy of Sciences, 1978.

Jones, M. C. and Mussen, P. H. Self-conceptions, motivations, and interpersonal attitudes of early- and late-maturing girls. *Child Development,* 1958, *29,* 491–501.

Katchadourian, H. *The biology of adolescence.* San Francisco: W. H. Freeman, 1977.

Kinsey, A. C., Pomeroy, W., and Martin, C. E. *Sexual behavior in the human male.* Philadelphia: W. B. Saunders, 1948.

Ladner, J. *Tomorrow's tomorrow, The black woman.* Garden City, New York: Anchor Books-Doubleday, 1971.

Livson, N. and Peskin, H. Perspectives on adolescence from longitudinal research. In J. Adelson (Ed.), *Handbook of adolescent psychology.* New York: Wiley and Sons, 1980.

MacMahon, B. *Age at menarche.* United States Department of Health, Education and Welfare Publication No. (HRA) 74-1615. NHS Series 11, No. 133, National Center for Health Statistics, Rockville, Maryland, 1973.

Magrab, P. R., Schearin, R. B., Bronheim, S. M., Jones, R. L., and Ahmed, S. W. The Georgetown adolescent psychosocial rating scale. *Journal of Adolescent Health Care,* in press.

Martinez, A. L. The impact of adolescent pregnancy on Hispanic adolescents and their families. In T. Ooms (Ed.), *Teenage pregnancy in a family context, Implications for policy.* Philadelphia: Temple University Press, 1981.

Morris, N. M. and Udry, J. R. Validation of a self-administered instrument to assess stage of adolescent development. *Journal of Youth and Adolescence,* 1980, *9,* 271–280.

Nankin, H. R., Sperling, M., Kenny, F. M., Drash, A. L., and Troen, P. Correlation between sexual maturation and serum gonadotropins: Comparison of black and white youngsters. *The American Journal of the Medical Sciences,* 1974, *268,* 139–147.

Offer, D., Ostrov, E., and Howard, K. I. *The adolescent, A psychological self-portrait.* New York: Basic Books, 1981.

Peskin, H. Influence of the developmental schedule of puberty on learning and ego functioning. *Journal of Youth and Adolescence,* 1973, *2,* 273–290.

Petersen, A. C., and Taylor, B. The biological approach to adolescence: Biological change and psychologic adaptation. In J. Adelson (Ed.), *Handbook of adolescent psychology.* New York: Wiley and Sons, 1980.

Petersen, A. C. and Wittig, M. A. Differential cognitive development in adolescent girls. In M. Sugar (Ed.), *Female adolescent development.* New York: Brunner/Mazel, 1979.

Powell, G. J. and Fuller, M. *Black Monday's children: A study of the effect of school desegregation on self-concepts of southern children.* New York: Appleton-Century-Crofts, 1973.

Rosenberg, M. and Simmons, R. G. *Black and white self-esteem: The urban school child.* Washington, D.C.: American Sociological Association, 1972.

Russ-Eft, D., Sprenger, M., and Beever, A. Antecedents of adolescent parenthood and consequences at age 30. *The Family Coordinator,* 1979, *28,* 173–179.

Schuster, C. S. The holistic approach. In C. S. Schuster and S. S. Ashburn (Eds.), *The process of human development, a holistic approach.* Boston: Little, Brown, 1980.

Schutte, J. E. Growth differences between lower and middle income black male adolescents. *Human Biology,* 1980, *52,* 193–204.

Scott, P. B. and McKendry. Some suggestions for teaching about black adolescence. *The Family Coordinator,* January, 1977, *26(1),* 47–51.

Simmons, R. G., Blyth, D. A., Van Cleave, E. F., and Bush, D. M. Entry into early adolescence: The impact of school structure, puberty, and early dating on self-esteem. *American Sociological Review,* 1979, *44,* 948–967.

Sorensen, R. *Adolescent sexuality in contemporary society: Personal values and sexual behavior, 13–19.* New York: World, 1973.

Stone, C. P. and Barker, R. G. The attitudes and interest of premenarcheal and postmenarcheal girls. *Journal of Genetic Pscyhology,* 1939, *54,* 27–71.

Tanner, J. M. *Growth at adolescence.* Oxford: Blackwell Scientific, 1962.

Taylor, R. Psychosocial development among black children and youth: A reexamination. *American Journal of Orthopsychiatry,* 1976, *46,* 4–19.

Zakus, G. E., Cooper, H. E., Leff, M. G., and Moore, V. M. Clinical assessment of the adolescent patient. *Journal of Current Adolescent Medicine,* 1980, *2,* 9–21.

Zelnik, M. Sex education and knowledge of pregnancy risk among U.S. teenage women. *Family Planning Perspectives,* 1979, *11,* 355–357.

Zelnik, M., and Kantner, J. F. Sexual activity, contraceptive use and pregnancy among metropolitan area teenagers: 1971–1979. *Family Planning Perspectives,* 1980, *12,* 230–237.

Index